NON-CYCLE PLAYS
AND FRAGMENTS

EARLY ENGLISH TEXT SOCIETY

Supplementary Text No. 1

1970

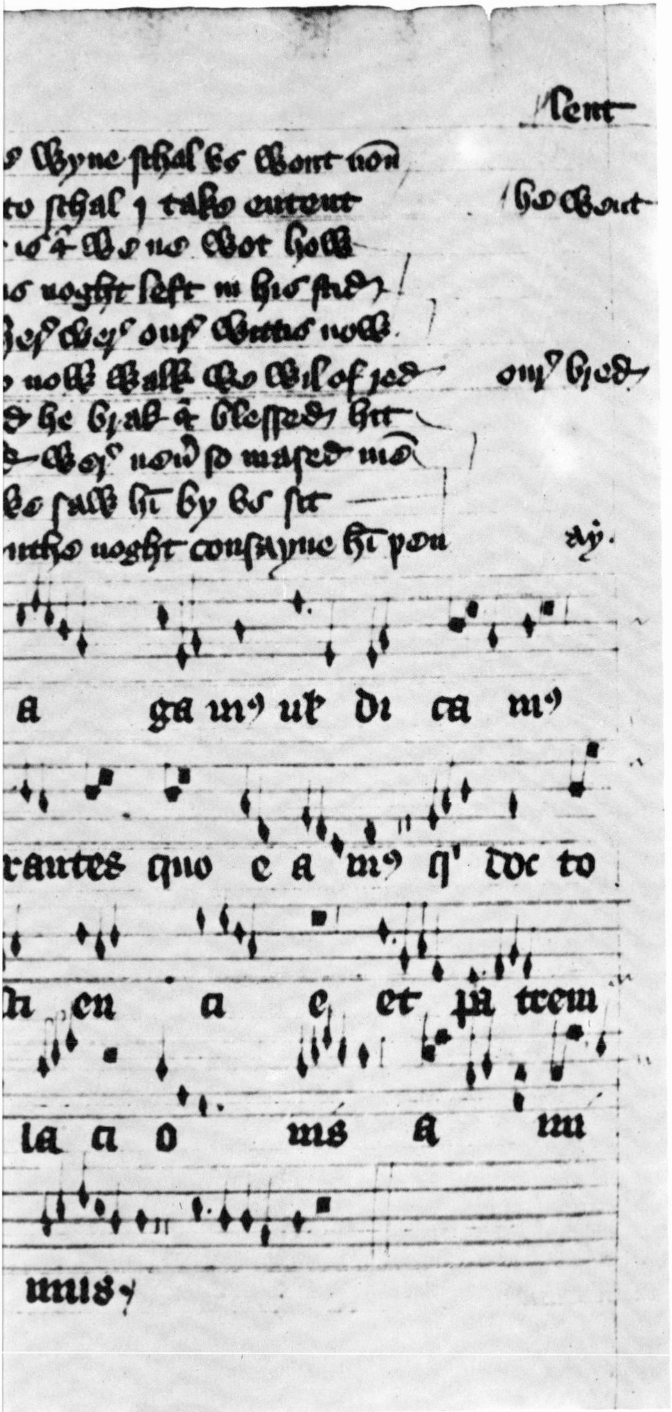

ry School MS. VI, f. 41v (Fragment C, lines 47–65)

NON-CYCLE PLAYS
AND FRAGMENTS

EDITED ON THE BASIS OF THE
EDITION BY OSBORN WATERHOUSE

BY

NORMAN DAVIS

WITH AN APPENDIX ON
THE SHREWSBURY MUSIC BY

F. Ll. HARRISON

Published for

THE EARLY ENGLISH TEXT SOCIETY

by the

OXFORD UNIVERSITY PRESS

LONDON NEW YORK TORONTO

1970

PRINTED IN GREAT BRITAIN
AT THE UNIVERSITY PRESS, OXFORD
BY VIVIAN RIDLER
PRINTER TO THE UNIVERSITY

PREFACE

THE Society's volume called *The Non-Cycle Mystery Plays*, edited by Osborn Waterhouse and published in 1909 as Extra Series 104, has long been out of print. When the Council decided some years ago that a reprint ought to be undertaken it resolved also to have the accuracy of the texts verified. This work had not gone far before it became clear that a simple corrected reprint could not accommodate the many changes that were called for, and that in addition the introduction and glossary required complete rewriting. An entirely new edition was therefore set on foot. The opportunity was taken to extend the range of the book by including a number of short dramatic pieces, most of which had come to light since Waterhouse's edition was made but were dispersed in various periodicals not always easy of access. In addition, Dr. F. Ll. Harrison kindly consented to prepare a transcript of the Shrewsbury music and write notes on its relations with that in other manuscripts. Otherwise it has seemed best to limit the aim of the book to providing texts of the plays as accurate as possible, with a sufficient glossary and some notes on verse technique and linguistic indications of date and place of composition, but without a running commentary. The texts are so various that unity of treatment is in any case unattainable. The plays which Waterhouse edited have been left in the order in which he printed them, to make reference from the old to the new slightly easier than it might have been; but otherwise there is not a great deal left of Waterhouse's book, and the title has been altered to suit the new contents. Since it would plainly be misleading to issue the new book under the old series number, and since the regular series is committed for some years to come, this volume has been chosen to initiate what is hoped to be an occasional series of 'Supplementary Texts'.

Though the responsibility for the book, with the exception of Dr. Harrison's contribution, is mine, I have had a great deal of generous help in preparing it. My heaviest debt is to the Revd. Professor T. P. Dunning, C.M., who made a very thorough first collation of the two manuscripts in the library of Trinity College, Dublin—the Northampton *Abraham* and *The Play of the*

Sacrament, the latter particularly exacting. Professor Bruce Dickins collated the Rickinghall Fragment and the Cambridge Prologue, and Dr. A. I. Doyle the Durham Prologue. Librarians, archivists, and keepers of manuscripts have contributed much. Special thanks and admiration are due to Mr. D. Charman, Archivist of the Ipswich and East Suffolk Record Office, who ran to earth the Book of Brome after it had been lost to scholarly view for a number of years—only to suffer the disappointment soon afterwards of seeing it removed, to widespread regret, from his office and from the country. Happily it has gone to a good home at Yale, and Dr. Herman W. Liebert, of the Beinecke Rare Book and Manuscript Library, has been very helpful in answering questions about it. Mr. William O'Sullivan, Keeper of Manuscripts in Trinity College, Dublin, gave important assistance to both Professor Dunning and me. Miss M. Grace, Archivist of the Norfolk and Norwich Record Office, answered many questions about the references to pageants preserved in the Norwich City records, and searched, alas unsuccessfully, for the eighteenth-century transcript of the Grocers' Play. Dr. R. W. Hunt, Keeper of Western Manuscripts in the Bodleian, kindly had the manuscript of *Dux Moraud* relieved of obscuring paper. Librarians of Shrewsbury School, the late J. B. Oldham and the present librarian Mr. J. B. Lawson, gave much help both when I visited the library and when I asked questions later. Mr. J. E. Fagg, Reader in Palaeography and Diplomatic in the University of Durham, provided a photostat of the Durham Prologue, and the Librarian of Cambridge University Library one of the Cambridge Prologue. Miss Margaret Weedon, Librarian of the Oxford English Faculty Library, kindly copied the newly assembled texts. Mr. N. R. Ker most generously allowed me to use his description of the Shrewsbury manuscript. Mr. M. B. Parkes gave his opinion on the date of the handwriting of *Dux Moraud*. Professor Angus McIntosh advised me on the language of the Shrewsbury Fragments. Mr. C. A. Robson assisted invaluably in the interpretation of the Anglo-Norman text of the Cambridge Prologue. Mr. R. W. Burchfield, in addition to the indispensable help that he has given to all the Society's editors in his capacity of Honorary Secretary, has in his other capacity of Editor of the *Oxford English Dictionary Supplement* done me the special service of lending me the Dictionary copy of Waterhouse, which contains important corrections in the hand of Henry Bradley.

For other friendly assistance I am grateful to Professor J. A. W. Bennett, Professor A. J. Bliss, Mrs. Margaret Blayney, Mr. John Robinson, Dr. Pamela Gradon, who succeeds Mr. Burchfield as the Society's Editorial Secretary, and Dr. Anne Hudson, the Executive Secretary.

For permission to publish new transcripts of some city archives I am grateful to the Norfolk and Norwich Records Committee. For permission to reproduce illustrations of manuscripts I am greatly obliged to the Governors of Shrewsbury School (the Frontispiece), the Board of Trinity College, Dublin (Plates I and II), and the Bodleian Library (Plate IV). The Royal Society of Antiquaries of Ireland has very handsomely allowed me to have Mills's facsimile of the now lost manuscript of *The Pride of Life* copied and reproduced as Plate III.

N. D.

CONTENTS

INTRODUCTION

THE plays and fragments in this volume differ greatly in age, in type, and in the completeness and trustworthiness of the text, and it is impossible to make useful generalizations about the way in which they may have been presented. The oldest manuscripts from which these pieces are taken are those containing the Cambridge Prologue (no. IX), which appears to have been written down hardly later than the end of the thirteenth century, and the Rickinghall or Bury Fragment (no. X), of the early fourteenth. Both of these give more or less parallel texts in French and English, the French preceding. At the other end of the scale, for the Norwich Grocers' Play (no. II) we depend upon nineteenth- and twentieth-century printed copies of a now lost eighteenth-century transcript of a text part of which gives its date as 1565; and for the Newcastle play (no. III) on an obviously degenerate eighteenth-century print of a lost manuscript of indeterminable age. In dramatic type, on the other hand, the earliest of these pieces are those in the Shrewsbury manuscript (no. I), the sole example in English of a set of plays in which liturgical drama in Latin is combined with vernacular passages—one of which is closely related to the corresponding play in the York cycle. Again, though most of the plays in this volume are on Biblical subjects which are also treated in the cycles, *The Play of the Sacrament* (no. VI) is unique in English as a 'miracle' play properly so called; *Dux Moraud* (no. VIII) is in some ways comparable in exploiting an old theme as a lesson on sin and repentance; and the Durham Prologue (no. XI) evidently introduced a 'miracle of the Virgin'. *The Pride of Life* (no. VII) differs again in being the earliest 'morality' in English and in forming a notable link between more fully developed plays such as *The Castle of Perseverance* and dramatic representations of the Dance of Death recorded on the Continent in the fifteenth century.

The place of these diverse works in the pattern of medieval drama has been extensively discussed, and will be considered here only incidentally. The purpose of this introduction is to outline the essential facts about the textual authority for each piece, and to bring together linguistic features which may help in determining the date and place of its origin.

I. THE SHREWSBURY FRAGMENTS

Manuscript. Shrewsbury School VI (formerly Mus. III. 42), ff. 38ʳ–42ᵛ. The manuscript comprises ii+44 paper leaves, so foliated; ff. i, ii, and 1 are medieval flyleaves, f. 44 is pasted to the back cover. Ff. 2–44 are in five quires of 8 leaves followed by one quire of 4, but the first leaf of quire 2 is missing. The medieval signatures begin with E 1 (f. 2), showing that four quires have been lost at the beginning. Size of page 8·2 × 5·7 inches, written space about 6 × 4 inches; ruled in ink for 27 or 28 lines of writing, but a fully written page occurs only on f. 38ʳ (the beginning of the dramatic fragments)—elsewhere the text is mostly in 7 lines, spaced for music, but varying greatly in the plays. Medieval binding of boards covered with leather. Written early in the fifteenth century, by one scribe throughout except for the lower part of f. 42ᵛ. The name *Arthur Gill* is carefully written (with a few disconnected words) in the left margin of f. 39ᵛ, and *William Bearsley* in three different styles at the foot of f. 40ʳ. These hands appear to be of about 1600. Ff. 2–37 contain extracts, written carefully and rubricated, with blue initials ornamented in red, from processional services with musical notes, beginning imperfectly with Holy Innocents and ending with Corpus Christi and the Dedication of a Church. F. 43ʳ, which follows the plays, contains a passage from the processional of Palm Sunday. Details of all the items are given by Young (*Drama of the Medieval Church*, ii. 520–3). He observes that the presence on ff. 23ᵛ–25ᵛ of a processional poem for the celebration of the translation of St. Chad connects this manuscript with a church in which he was especially honoured, which is most likely to have been in Lichfield or its diocese.

The plays begin on f. 38ʳ with two Latin sentences, written in red, taken from Luke 2: 8–9. The initial capital is decorated, two lines in depth, with trailing ornament nearly halfway down the page. Under this introduction, on the same line as its last two words, are the designation of the speaker 'iijᵘˢ pastor' and the cue 'We tib'. After this the text is written in verse lines, with most of the rhymes linked by brackets. The cue phrases are at the right margin, each opposite the end of the preceding speech, and the beginning of each speech is marked by a paragraph mark in the left margin. The English speeches are interspersed with the Latin passages and their music as they occur, except that on f. 38ᵛ, after a line across the page under line A 37 (and the cue line 38), an asterisk in the left margin shows that at this point should be inserted the Latin passage written in a different, cursive (but not necessarily appreciably later) hand, and set to music, on the lower part of f. 42^v. On f. 39^r, after the two lines A 47–8 which are at the top of the page, there is a space of about half an inch before 'Hic incipit officium Resurreccionis in die pasche' which introduces the second fragment. Under this the speaker is shown as 'iij^a m^a', for 'Tertia Maria'. On f. 40^r, after the last line of fragment B, there is a red line across the page and immediately under it 'Feria ij^a in ebdomada pasche discipuli insimul cantent' followed by the opening lines of C with their music. Other lines are drawn across the pages on f. 39^v, at the foot under B 33; f. 40^v, under C 4–5 and 13–14; f. 41^r, under C 40–1; f. 41^v, under C 54–5; f. 42^r, under C 70–1. The Latin texts without music are in red.

The manuscript was first brought to public notice by W. W. Skeat in *The Academy* of 4 January 1890, and he published the text of the dramatic fragments in the same journal on 11 January, under the heading 'Fragments of Yorkshire Mysteries'. Manly reprinted Skeat's text in *Specimens of the Pre-Shaksperean Drama* (1897), but with some new notes and different attributions of cues, and Waterhouse used both these editions in preparing his collection in 1909. In printing the fragments again (in a different order) in *Chief Pre-Shakespearean Dramas* (1924), Adams based his text on that of Waterhouse, which he said was 're-edited from the manuscripts'. But this is not so. Waterhouse made clear in his introduction (p. xv) that despite two attempts he had been unable to see the manuscript and was therefore compelled to base his text, and much of his introduction, on Skeat's articles. He said that he had collated the texts of Skeat and Manly; but Manly himself had relied on Skeat.[1] The first text after Skeat's of 1890 to be based on an examination of the manuscript was that published by Young in 1933, as Appendix B of his *Drama of the Medieval Church*. The present text, which rests on repeated new collations with the manuscript and photographs, agrees closely with Young's except for a few slight differences mainly in the expansion of abbreviations.[2]

---

[1] Waterhouse, however, introduced a few errors, which were reproduced by Adams: e.g. *hostis* for *hostio* B 24, *home* for *hom* C 67.

[2] The most important verbal correction made by Young was *quomodo* instead

It was Skeat who perceived that the manuscript contained three distinct dramatic fragments, each presenting one actor's part in a scene from a play, and that the words written separately to the right were his cues. The three plays he called 'The Angels and the Shepherds', 'The Three Maries at the Sepulchre', and 'The Two Disciples going to Emmaus'. That the actor of these parts played the Third Shepherd and the Third Mary appears from the headings of the first two fragments. The speaker is not named at the head of the third fragment, for 'Feria secunda in ebdomada Pasche' (Easter Monday). Skeat reasoned that the actor must have played Cleophas because he had to sing in the chorus of the apostles at the end, where 'the words suit him better than they do St. Luke, who, according to tradition and the Coventry Mysteries, was Cleophas's companion'. Because he believed the dialect to be of Yorkshire, and because of the similarity of one Shrewsbury stanza to a stanza in the York *Shepherds* play, Skeat conjectured that the fragments might belong to the lost Beverley cycle of plays; but Manly observed that the phraseology of the Latin introductions to the second and third fragments, and the provision of music for many of the Latin passages, show that they cannot belong to such a cycle but must be part of a series performed in church on the days and in the services celebrating the events of which they treat (*Specimens*, p. xxvii). Chambers, in *The Mediaeval Stage*, chs. xviii–xix, related these fragments to the many liturgical plays preserved on the Continent, commonly known as *Pastores*, *Visitatio Sepulchri*, and *Peregrini*, and Young, in providing a wealth of information on the development of these plays, used the terms *Officium Pastorum*, *Visitatio Sepulchri*, and *Peregrinus*. The titles used in this edition are those given by Manly. The second of them rests directly on the manuscript, and the others are acceptable parallels to it.

The liturgical character of these plays is apparent not only from the considerations put forward by Manly but from their preservation as an integral part of a manuscript of Latin anthems. The most closely connected with church services is the second, the *Officium Resurrectionis* or *Visitatio Sepulchri*, which takes us near to the origins of this kind of drama. Some of its Latin verses are identical, and others nearly so, with corresponding passages in

of *quoniam* (a wrong expansion by Skeat) in the prose after C 23. He also corrected the earlier editors' note, originating with Manly, that the opening Latin sentences of A are 'noted for voices'.

wholly Latin liturgical texts. The closest relation appears to be
with a processional from the church of St. John the Evangelist in
Dublin, in MS. Bodl. Rawlinson Liturg. d. iv, which contains a
Visitatio of which the following passages offer notable parallels to
our text:

> Deinde secunda Maria dicat:
>> Heu! consolacio nostra,
>> ut quid mortem sustinuit!
> Tunc tertia Maria:
>> Heu! redemcio nostra,
>> ut quid taliter agere uoluit!
> Tunc se coniungant et procedant ad gradum chori ante
> altare simul dicentes:
>> Iam iam, ecce, iam properemus ad tumulum,
>> unguentes dilecti corpus sanctissimum.

> > > (Young, i. 348; cf. Shrewsbury B 1–2, 21–2)

Towards the end the Third Mary is given the words, 'Surrexit
Christus, spes nostra; precedet uos in Galileam', which are the
same as our lines 35–6; but this implies no special relation because
these words, or slight variants of them (adapted from Matt. 28: 7),
occur in many other versions of the *Visitatio*.

No less remarkable than these liturgical associations is the
striking resemblance between parts of the first Shrewsbury fragment, the *Officium Pastorum*, and the York play (no. XV) on the
same subject. It is possibly significant that in this fragment the
Latin and the music are less prominent than in the other two, so
that it may have had a separate history; yet the difference may be
due only to the comparative simplicity of the Third Shepherd's
part. However this may be, Skeat pointed out in his first article
that the last stanza of the Shrewsbury piece (A 39–48) agrees
closely with lines 120–9 of the York text, which are also assigned
to the Third Shepherd:

> Nowe loke on me, my lorde dere,   120
>> þof all I putte me noght in pres,
> Ye are a prince withouten pere,
>> I haue no presentte þat you may plees.
> But loo, an horne-spone, þat haue I here,
>> And it will herbar fourty pese;
> þis will I giffe you with gud chere,
>> Slike noveltė may noght disease.

> Fare [wele], þou swete swayne,
> God graunte vs levyng lange;
> And go we hame agayne
> And make mirthe as we gange!

Line 44 of the Shrewsbury text is superior to the York equivalent in preserving the alliterating *hundrith* instead of *fourty*. The cue preceding this stanza in Shrewsbury, 'I mene', may very well be the end of the corresponding York line, 'Nowe watte ʒe what I mene'; and Skeat accordingly incorporated these words into his text. Less conspicuous but none the less convincing correspondences have been assembled by Frances M. Miller in 'Metrical Affinities of the Shrewsbury *Officium Pastorum* and its York Correspondent',[1] which emphasizes that similarities of thought and diction are strengthened by metrical agreements. There can be no doubt that the Shrewsbury and the York texts derive in some way from a common original, but it seems impossible to determine which of them represents its details better. Though the beginning of the fragment is marked by its decorated capital and formally written rubric, as if to introduce the dramatic section of the manuscript, these Latin sentences are on a different footing from the introductions to the second and third fragments. They are evidently to be sung by all the performers, not only by the Third Shepherd whose part follows.[2] (It is in fact very curious that a single actor's disconnected parts should have been so dignified by careful script and formal layout.) We do not know how many speeches may have come between the opening rubric and the first cue, 'We, Tib!' The York play has three twelve-line stanzas preceding this point in the story—the corresponding cue is 'We, Colle!' The first stanza recalls the prophecies of Hosea and Isaiah, the second tells how Balaam foretold the appearance of a star in the east, and the third voices the joy which must come from the fulfilment of this prophecy. At this point the star appears and the incident corresponding to the Shrewsbury fragment begins, in a different metre. It is therefore possible that one or two Latin sentences, perhaps set to music as at the beginning of the other fragments, and English speeches for at least some of the shepherds, came before what we now have. The order of the speakers is unknown. Skeat assigned all the cues of this fragment to the Second

---

[1] *M.L.N.* xxxiii (1918), 91–5.   [2] See Appendix.

Shepherd, which need not be right because in the York play the Third Shepherd does not always follow the Second.

There are no comparable similarities between the second and third Shrewsbury fragments and the corresponding York plays, or indeed any others.

Verse. The form of verse in which these plays were written can be seen only imperfectly from the fragments, and all three need not have been even predominantly in the same form. The last stanza of the *Officium Pastorum* is obviously incomplete, for it lacks rhymes for lines 47 and 48; comparison with the York stanza (pp. xvii–xviii) shows that it must have been a twelve-line stanza, of eight four-stress lines rhyming alternately followed by four three-stress lines with new alternate rhymes, *ababababcdcd*. Alliteration is prominent in both types of line, though not structural. This is the stanza of the opening and closing passages of the York *Shepherds*, but not of the middle section which corresponds to the opening of the Shrewsbury fragment; it appears also in eleven other of the York plays. No other part of the fragments offers this type of stanza so nearly complete; but, as Miss Miller observed, the other speeches of the Third Shepherd appear to be the *cauda* lines of it. The stanza cannot be identified in the other two fragments, which preserve no three-stress lines though they both diversify the English verse with metrical Latin passages. As they stand, the *Officium Resurrectionis* is written mostly in eight-line stanzas rhyming alternately, and the *Officium Peregrinorum* contains both these (at 6, 15, 24, 33) and quatrains of the same stress- and rhyme-pattern. There is no need to suppose that these are parts of twelve-line stanzas which would have been completed by other speakers; both eight- and four-line stanzas are used in the York plays and elsewhere; cf. e.g. VI below.

Language. Skeat emphasized the northern character of the language of the fragments, citing mostly vocabulary; Waterhouse added a few grammatical notes, not all correct. Skeat went so far as to say that 'the language is just that of the York plays', but this cannot be sustained: even the York stanza quoted above differs in some significant details from the corresponding Shrewsbury passage, most conspicuously in using *slike* instead of *suche*. Young was clearly right in saying that though the dialect is essentially northern, 'forms more appropriate to the north-west midlands . . .

are present'. Though he did not specify these, he probably had in mind the oblique form of the pronoun of the third person plural, which here is only *hom* (C 27, 36, 67) whereas the York plays nearly always have *þam(e)* or *þaim* and never *hom*. To this might be added *con* as the form of the auxiliary of the past tense sg. in C 13. Other features to be considered are the following:

Final unstressed *-e* in positions where it would be historically in place is often omitted in writing: e.g. *say* A 7, *bring* 29, *syng* 31, *put* 40. At the same time an *-e* is sometimes written unhistorically: *sene* A 9, *hase, bene* B 40, *gose* 43. Loss of the sound in the original is shown by rhyme in *saied* A 27, probably *bide, betyde, side* B 13–19 (rhyming on *wide*), *fang, gang, strang* C 6–12, *sit* 58, etc. Though some lines move slightly haltingly there are none in which metre demands the pronunciation of *-e*, and many which would be spoilt by it.

The reflex of OE. or ON. *ā, á* is regularly written *o* except before *w*: e.g. *so* A 7, *bothe* 14, *gon* B 34, *gose* 43, *on* C 13, *fro* 20; the rhyme sequences *gon: ston: wone: mon* and *mo: fro: so: wo* C 33–40 do not certify the sound. But the reflex of *āw* is written *aw* in *raw, knaw* C 24, 30, and the unrounded vowel is proved by the rhyming words *lawe, awe*. This is a feature not narrowly limited in area—it occurs even in the south-east[1]—but it is particularly well known in the north-west.

The reflex of OE. *a* before *ld* is written *o* in *bold* B 18, *hold* C 45; before *nd, ng* spelling varies: *fond* A 22, *fonde* C 44, *stondyng* C 35, but *hand* A 6 rhyming on *warand*; *song: among* B 30–2 but *lang* A 48 and *fang: gang: amang: strang* C 6–12. This last sequence probably indicates an unrounded vowel, for *gang* is overwhelmingly commoner than *gong*.

The reflex of OE. *a* before a nasal not in a lengthening group is written *o* in *mon* B 18, 32, *wont* C 48, but *a* in *man* A 5, *thank* 35, *same, name* 24–6. Its quality is not shown in rhyme.

The initial consonant of 'give' is written *g*, not *ȝ*, in *gift* and *gif* A 45; cf. *agayn* C 8. That of 'shall' and 'should' is always *sch*, not *s*; e.g. A 31, B 17. That of words earlier beginning with *hw* is always *wh*, not *qu* etc.; e.g. *whi* A 7, *where* C 18. Words containing earlier *ht* are written with *ght* or *ȝt*; e.g. *nyght* A 3, *liȝt* 14, *noght* B 42.

---

[1] See G. V. Smithers, *Kyng Alisaunder*, ii. E.E.T.S. 237 (1957), 47.

The vowel of unstressed inflexional syllables is usually written
e: e.g. *merueles* A 11, *raues* 15, *mynnes* 21, *fadres* 22, *tokenes*
B 38; *tacched* B 16, *tristed* C 13; *risen* C 16, *doluen* 19; but
i is about equally common before *s*: *Goddis* B 33, *wordis* C 15,
prestis 26, *caris* 31, *talis* 46, *wittis* 53, and a few endings are
represented by the abbreviation which usually means -*us*:
Jewus A 23, *angellus* B 31, C 35, *schewus* B 32. No forms
have -*us* written out.

Of inflexions, the only distinctive noun plural is *brether* A 4,
which is widespread in northerly areas.

In verbs, the present 3 sg. and the pl. without immediately
preceding pronoun both end in -*s*: *mynnes* A 21, *has(e)* B 26,
40, *schewus* 32; *raues* A 15, *makis* C 39. So does the imper.
pl.: *lettes*, *gose* B 42, 43. Pres. part. ends in -*yng*: *stondyng*
C 35.

Infin. is nearly always without ending, often confirmed by
rhyme: e.g. *be* A 19, *plese* 42, *bide* B 13, *see* 14; -*n* survives
only in *sayn* C 36, not in rhyme.

The strong past part. regularly keeps -*n*: *sen(e)* A 9 (in rhyme),
B 38, *gon* B 34, *bene* 40, *forlorn* 42 (in rhyme), *risen* C 16,
doluen 19, *farne* 36.

The following words are characteristic of the north or the north
midlands: *mun* A 12, *barn* 19, *mynnes* 21, *nemed* 26, *ȝone* 29,
thar 34, *presand* 42, *hundrith* 44, *at* B 29, *gang* C 8, *gaynest* 9,
bedene 29, *wil of red* 54, *samyn* 69.

The total effect of sounds, inflexions, and vocabulary is undoubtedly strongly north-west midland in character. The language
is not identical with that of the York plays, but it is not the language
of documents from Lichfield either, which are much less northerly
in type.[1] There is in fact little in it that cannot be found also in
MS. Cotton Nero A. x, the *Pearl–Gawain* manuscript, though of
course the converse is not true.

Writers on the Shrewsbury fragments have naturally been
impressed by the remarkable coincidence of their three subjects
with those of dramatic offices known to have been performed at

---

[1] I am indebted for confirmation of this opinion to Professor Angus McIntosh,
who has made a special study of manuscripts written in Lichfield. He selects as
particularly foreign to Lichfield the -*s* in pres. 3 sg., *g* in *gif*, *agayn*, *hom* instead
of *hem*, and *þai* rather than *þei*. Lichfield manuscripts were discussed by A. I.
Doyle in his Lyell lectures delivered at Oxford in 1967, not yet published.

Lichfield in the time of Hugh of Nonant, bishop 1188–98. His Cathedral Statutes contain these provisions:

Item, in nocte Natalis representacio pastorum fieri consueuit et in diluculo Paschae representacio Resurreccionis dominicae et representacio peregrinorum die lunae in septimana Paschae sicut in libris super hijs ac alijs compositis continetur.

Et prouidere debet [sc. the *Succentor*] quod representacio pastorum in nocte Natalis domini et miraculorum in nocte Paschae et die lunae in Pascha congrue et honorifice fiant.[1]

No comparable association of just these three performances at Christmas and Easter appears to be known elsewhere in England, though in view of the uneven survival of records this can hardly be very significant. Taken together with the celebration of St. Chad (see p. xiv above) it certainly suggests Lichfield as the home of the contents of the Shrewsbury manuscript; yet the language of the text in its present form cannot be that of Lichfield itself or the near neighbourhood. The diocese of Coventry and Lichfield at this date extended as far north as the Ribble, and no less than twenty-eight churches dedicated to St. Chad are known within it.[2] It is possible that the book belonged to one of those in Cheshire or north Staffordshire, or that it was written for the cathedral by a cleric trained in that region.

II. THE NORWICH GROCERS' PLAY

Text. No manuscript of the Norwich Grocers' Play, 'The Story of the Creation of Eve, with the Expelling of Adam and Eve out of Paradise', is now known; and no manuscript that could be called even approximately 'original' has apparently been seen for over two centuries. When Waterhouse edited the play in 1909 he was able to use an eighteenth-century transcript, but this too has now disappeared. Since it had not been mentioned for some time, when preparing the present edition I asked the City Librarian of Norwich if he could make special inquiries to see whether it might be among any of the collections in his charge. In consequence, a letter from the archivist of the Norfolk and Norwich Record Office

---

[1] Printed by Chambers, *Mediaeval Stage*, ii. 377, and Young, *Drama*, ii. 522, from *Statutes of Lincoln Cathedral*, ed. C. Wordsworth (Cambridge, 1892–7).

[2] F. Arnold-Forster, *Studies in Church Dedications* (London, 1899), i. 400.

dated 1 January 1962 reported that nothing was known of its present whereabouts:

The eighteenth-century transcript of the medieval Norwich Grocers' Play was never *officially* in the Muniment Room at the Castle Museum. In the early years of this century this Muniment Room was quite a rendezvous for Norfolk antiquarians, and no doubt they produced manuscripts to show each other. It is known that this transcript was in the possession of the antiquarian Robert Fitch who edited it in an early number of *Norfolk Archaeology*. The Castle Museum at present has possession of the 'Robert Fitch Collection' and I am satisfied that this transcript is not among the collection today. The 'Walter Rye Collection' is in the Norwich Public Library, it is fully listed and calendared and I can assure you that the transcript is not in this collection either.

Other inquiries and public advertisements produced no information. The latest person known to have worked on the transcript is Waterhouse, whose description of it therefore has special importance. Accordingly it is reproduced here with only minor rearrangements (pp. xxvi–xxix of his edition):

The Norwich *Grocers' Play* has been twice printed: in 1856, Robert Fitch, a local antiquary, contributed to *Norfolk Archaeology* an article containing a somewhat inaccurate transcript of an eighteenth-century manuscript; itself a copy of certain folios of the *Grocers' Book* which by that time was lost and has unfortunately not been recovered. In 1897 Manly reproduced, in his *Specimens of the Pre-Shaksperean Drama*, this version of Fitch. Since the *Grocers' Book* has been lost or destroyed, the earliest available version of the play is the eighteenth-century transcript made use of by Fitch in 1856, from which time it appears to have remained undisturbed until the summer of 1905, when I collated it with the two printed versions for the purposes of the present edition. For this opportunity to make use of the manuscript transcript I am greatly indebted to Mr. Walter Rye of Norwich; for he it was who searched for and found it, among the uncatalogued papers in the Record Room of the Castle.

This eighteenth-century copy is written clearly on quarto sheets of paper, and the lines of the verse portions are written undetached as if they were prose. The eighteenth-century copyist evidently strove to represent his original accurately, for the usual manuscript contractions are preserved: the letter *n* is often omitted and indicated by a stroke over the preceding vowel, *es* at the end of words is represented by a flourish, *er*, *ro*, etc. after *p* are represented by a stroke through the tail of the consonant, and a stroke over *c* serves to indicate a following *i*; *ll*, *h* and *d* are often crossed. In certain cases, the stroke appears over *n*, but that is only intended to prevent this letter from being mistaken for *u*. Mr. Walter Rye, who has an extensive acquaintance with the various handwritings of the Norwich Record-Room manuscripts, cannot say with certainty who wrote the transcript, but thinks that it may have been Sir John Fenn. The said gentleman was born at Norwich in 1739, was a man of strong antiquarian tastes, a member of the Society of Antiquaries, and procured and edited the manuscript of the *Paston Letters*: he also presented the manuscript of a great number of the Paston Letters, elegantly bound, to George III, and, in recognition of the gift and of his services to learning, was knighted by his sovereign: thus, Fenn is a not unlikely person to have made the transcript. On the other hand, Fitch, writing in 1856, refers to his original as 'a series of extracts, made early in the last century': a statement, however, which does not necessarily negative our supposition, since the epithet *early* is delightfully vague, and further, upon other grounds, one is not inclined to place great faith in Fitch's accuracy. The use of capitals and marks of punctuation in the manuscript is highly capricious, and has not therefore been reproduced in the present edition. Latin words and phrases are underlined.

The *Grocers' Book* from which some extracts are taken was begun on June 16, 1533, and opens on the first page with: 'In dei nomine Amen. The xvi. day of June in the xxv^th yere of þe reygne of ower Souereygne Lorde Kynge Henry the viij^th and in þe yere of ower Lorde God mccccccxxxiij this booke was made by the hands of John Howerson[1] & Robt. Reynbald, than beynge Wardens of þe crafte of Grocescraft[2] within þe Cyte of Norwiche, the whiche boke makyth mencion of þe Story of þe Creacion of Eve with þe expellyng of Adam & Eve oute of Paradyce, the whiche story apparteynythe to þe Pageant of þe Company of þe foresayd craft of Grocery, wherfor thys sayd Booke ys made for the sustentacion and mayntenans of þe same, declaryng & showyng þe name of þe Pageant, with all the Utensylles & necessaryes therto belongyng, all parcelles and charges yerely occupyed to þe same, and also all þe namys of suche men as be Inrollyd in þe sayd craft of Grocery within þe foresayd Cyte of Norwiche, &c.' ...

Immediately following the quotation given above is the version of the play in use in 1533; it is incomplete, being deficient from the call of Adam, after the Temptation, to the point where Adam and Eve are expelled from the Garden of Eden. The next extract is taken from the sixth and following folios of the *Grocers' Book*, and contains a second version of the play, the one in use in 1565, and which, with the

---

[1] This is evidently a misreading. Fitch read *Homerson*, and a John Homerston, grocer, was admitted freeman of Norwich in 10 Henry VII (1494–5) (J. L'Estrange, *Calendar of the Freemen of Norwich*, ed. W. Rye (London, 1888), p. 77).   [2] *Fitch* Grocers craft.

exception of one slightly mutilated stanza, is complete. Prefixed to this second version are a prologue or 'banns' and a second alternative prologue, the former to be used when the Grocers' pageant was the first one to be performed, and the latter when one or more pageants preceded the Grocers' play. The first stanza of this second, alternative prologue states that it is to be used when *The Creation of the World* and *The Fall of the Angels* have been performed. On some occasions evidently the first pageant or pageants were omitted; perhaps on account of insufficient funds in some of the guilds. The third extract is a copy of the thirty-fourth and following folios of the *Grocers' Book*, and consists of various entries, many of which give most important and detailed information respecting the manner of performing the play. (See pp. xxxii ff. below.)

Since Fitch provides the only other direct evidence for the transcript I have collated his text with that of Waterhouse. There are some differences of editorial policy, and many slight divergences in spelling. Fitch prints the text without division into stanzas, and without indentation of rhyming lines, except in the prologues to Text B. The remainder he divides simply into speeches, without saying whether or not he was following his exemplar in this. He imitates some of the manuscript abbreviations, especially that for -*es*, instead of expanding them, and prints *y* instead of Waterhouse's *þ* in words like *yᵉ*, in which it is common though sporadic. It was Manly who introduced stanza division, in which he was followed by Waterhouse; and he resolved Fitch's *y*- to *th*-, italicized. Manly reproduced Fitch's text for the most part faithfully. Adams based his text on Waterhouse, though he printed *th* instead of *þ* in accordance with his general practice. It is not clear why he said that Fitch's print had 'many inaccuracies' (p. 88), for he did not claim to have seen the transcript himself and even Waterhouse, who had, called Fitch only 'somewhat inaccurate'. In fact the differences of any substance between Waterhouse's text and Fitch's are fewer than these comments might suggest, nor does Fitch's reading appear invariably to be the inferior: at A 64 his *carnall* is apt as Waterhouse's *casuall* is not, and whatever the eighteenth-century transcript may have had the two words could be easily confused in many early hands; and at B³ 146 *Nowe* is better than *Howe*. Apart from such differences (which number eleven, recorded in the footnotes to this edition) there are some 68 places in which Fitch and Waterhouse differ in mere details of spelling. Most of the differences are extremely trivial: the largest category (22) concerns the presence or absence of a final *e*, which Fitch prints more freely than Waterhouse though the divergence is not always in the same direction; the next most numerous (14) concerns the doubling of letters in various positions, as *apere/appere*, *not/nott*, *dede/deede*; then (10) alternation between *i* and *y*, as *ribbe/rybbe*, *live/lyve*, and similarly (5) with *ou* and *ow*. Fitch either keeps the plural abbreviation or prints *s*, Waterhouse expands it to *es*. In a few forms Fitch seems more likely to be true to the early text, as *plese* instead of *please*, *gode* instead of *good* A 70–1. But in the present revised text I simply reproduce Waterhouse's spelling where the identity of the word is not in question, and I do not cumber the footnotes with Fitch's variants because in a text so uncertainly derived graphic minutiae of this kind have scarcely any interest. I depart from Waterhouse, however, in using *th* (not italicized because abbreviations in general are not so marked) instead of *þ*, because this form of the letter is not appropriate either to his eighteenth-century exemplar or to the sixteenth-century text which it purported to reproduce, and *y*, which is appropriate, is inconvenient to modern readers.

Norwich Pageants

The reference, in the second alternative prologue to Text B, to preceding pageants 'of God's mighty creation' and 'of pride and fall of angels that in Hell hath being' is illuminated by one of the sadly few records of pageants in Norwich. In 1852 Henry Harrod published documents he had discovered in the Record-room of Norwich Corporation.[1] One of them, which contains the earliest known reference to plays in Norwich, is part of the minute of the assembly of the Corporation on 21 September 1527. On this occasion a petition was presented by the Guild of St. Luke, an association of painters, braziers, plumbers, and other crafts, which had 'of long time past' been responsible for presenting pageants on the Monday and Tuesday of Pentecost Week. The cost had almost ruined the guild, which therefore asked the Corporation to order

---

[1] 'A few Particulars concerning early Norwich Pageants', *Norfolk Archaeology*, iii (1852), 3–18. Both the author and his work have suffered at the hands of later writers. Waterhouse persistently calls him 'Harrop', and corrupts his essentially correct transcription of the entry about the procession to the meaningless 'ad Capell in Campis Norwici modo sequi'; in both of which he is followed all too faithfully by Hardin Craig.

that each 'occupation' in the city should in future provide a pageant. This request was approved by the assembly and immediately enacted. Two copies of the record, apparently in the same hand, survive: one in the Assembly [Minute] Book, the other a fair copy, differing in a few words, in the Proceedings. Since Harrod printed the Minute Book version, and Chambers an extract from it,[1] I give below that of the Proceedings.[2]

[Assembly held on Saturday the feast of St. Matthew Apostle, 19 Henry VIII]

This daye the Alderman and Brethern of the Gilde of Saynt Luke in Norwiche did exhibite to the Mayer, Shireffes, and Comen Counsell of the Citie of Norwich wherof the tenour foloweth in thes wordes. To the right worshipffull Master Mayer of the Citie of Norwich humbly shewen and besechen your good maistershepps your dayly oratours and bedemen the Aldermen and Brethern of the Gilde of Saynt Luke the Euangelist within the Citie of Norwiche that wher of long tyme paste the sayd Gilde of Saynt Luke yerly till nowe haue ben vsed to be kept and holden withyn the Citie aforesaid the Mondaye in Pentecoste Weke, at which daye and the daye next folowyng many and diuers disgisinges and pageauntes as well of the liff and marterdams of diuers and many hooly sayntes as also many other lyght and feyned figures and pictures of other persones and bestes, the sight of which disgisinges and pageauntes, as well yerly on the said Monday in Pentecost Weke in tyme of procession than goyng aboute a grete circuitt of the said Citie, as yerly the Tuysday in the same weke seruyng of the lord named the Lord of Mysrule at Tomlond within the same Citie, have ben and yet is so covetid specially by the people of the countré, by force wherof yerly at that tyme more than any other tyme of the yere the people of the countré haue abundauntly vsed to resorte to the said Citie, by reason of which resorte of people as well many merchaundises as vitaille by the citezens and inhabitauntes withyn the said Citie yerly more at that tyme than eny othe⟨r⟩ tyme in the yere arn vttered and sold, to the grette releeff, socour, aide, and comfforte of the citezens and inhabitauns, and onlye the Brethern and Sister of the said Gilde yerly arn soore charged with reparacions, fyndyng, and settyng forth of the sayd pageauntes and disgisinges, which costes and charges causeth many persons beyng of substaunce and abilitie to withdrawe them selff and also ther goode myndes in suche maner that for lak of substancia⟨ll⟩ brethern and

[1] *Mediaeval Stage*, ii. 387.
[2] Norfolk and Norwich Record Office, Norwich Assembly Proceedings 1491–1553, ff. 129ᵛ–130ʳ. (Abbreviations are silently expanded.)

sistern, and ther myghty empty handes for sustentacion of the premysses, the said Gilde is almost decaye and not like in noon wise but to remayne in decaye, only⟨s⟩ your favorabill myndes and comfortabill aides and assistences be to the said Alderman and Brethern and to ther successours shewed in that behalff; wherffor maye it please your discrete wisdoms, the premysses tendirly considered, to enacte, ordeyn, and establisshe bye auctorities to you gyven that euery occupacion withyn the sayd Citie maye yerly at the said procession vppon the Mondaye in Pentecost Weke sette forth one pageaunt, by your discrete wysdoms to be assigned and appoynted of ther costes and charges, which shuld be to the wurship of the said Citie, profite of the citezens and inhabitauntes in the same, and also to the grette sustentacion, comfforte, and releeff as well of the said Gilde as brethern of the same; which fauorabill myndes and comfortabill aydes and assistences so shewed to your pore oratours shuld bynde them and ther successours dayly to pray to God for your prosperyties long to endure to the pleasure of God. Which herde and vnderstond by the hoole assemblé, it is therfor by auctorytie aforeseid agreed and enacted that certen occupacions within the said Citie shall yerly from hensforth fynde and sette forthe in the sayed procession one suche pageant, as shal be assigned and appoynted by Master Mayer and his brethern Aldermen, or the more parte of them. [*Instead of the last phrase the Minute Book has:* as more playnly appereth in a boke therof made.]

Harrod added that there was among the records a list of companies and pageants, written in the same hand as the minute he printed; so presumably consequent upon the decision taken. He gave no precise reference to it, and others have assumed that it was part of the same entry—Craig, for instance, quotes part of Harrod's text of the minute and adds, 'Then follows the list of subjects and crafts quoted below.' This is not so. The list is not in the Assembly Book at all, but in a volume of Norwich City records (now in the Norfolk and Norwich Record Office) called the 'Old Free Book', which contains mainly enrolments of freemen to 1549.[1] The situation is more complicated than Harrod made it appear, for this list of pageants is on the same page as the entry about the Corpus Christi procession which he quoted at the beginning of his article. The page is f. 162ʳ of the 'Old Free Book', the first of a gathering of four parchment leaves at the end; on the verso of the second leaf is an early index giving the folios on which each

---

[1] *The Records of the City of Norwich*, ed. W. Hudson and J. C. Tingey (Norwich and London, 1906–10), ii. 230. The texts are there transcribed, but without the second column; see p. xxx below.

craft and its freemen are listed. The hand of the list of pageants, as Harrod said, is the same as that of the minute of 1527, though the writing here is less regular; but the identity of hand need not imply a date immediately after the assembly in question, because the same hand appears to write the Proceedings until 1547. It is true that after about 1542 the style changes a good deal, and a date not far from 1530 is perhaps most likely. The following text of the list has been checked from the manuscript:

Pageantes

Primo	Mercers, Drapers, Haburdaissher[s] [*last inserted in a different hand*]	Creacion off the World
iij	Grocers, Raffeman [*i.e.* chandlers]	Paradyse
ij	Glasiers, Steyners, Screueners, Parchemyners, Carpenteres, Gravours, Caryers, Colermakers, with Whelewrites [*these last two words added later, after the title*]	Helle Carte
iiij	Shermen, Fullers, Thikwollenweuers, Couerlightmaker[s], Masons, Lymebrenneres	Abell and Cayme
v	Bakers, Bruers, Inkepers, Cokes, Millers, Vynteners, Coupers	Noyse Shipp
vj	Tailloures, Broderers, Reders and Tylers	Abraham and Isaak
vij	Tanners, Coryoures, Cordwaners	Moises and Aron with the Children off Israell and Pharo with his knyghtes
viij	Smythes	Conflicte off Dauid and Golias
ix	Dyers, Calaundrers, Goldsmythes, Goldbeters, and Sadelers, Pewtrers, Brasiers	The Birth of Crist with Sheperdes, and iij Kynges off Colen
x	Barboures, Wexchaundelers, Surgeons, Fisicians, Harde Waremen, Hatters, Cappers, Skynners, Glovers, Pynners, Poyntemakers, Girdelers, Pursers, Bagmakers, Sceppers, Wyerdrawers, Cardmakers	The Baptysme of Criste

| xj | Bochers, Fisshemongers, Watermen | The Resurreccion |
| xij | Wurstedweuers | The Holy Gost |

This list confirms the existence of the two plays which are mentioned in the second prologue to Text B as sometimes preceding the Grocers' Play—the Creation and 'Helle Carte', evidently a short title for the Fall of the Angels. Though the Grocers come second in the list they are numbered 'iij', and the Glaziers and their associates 'ij'. This was evidently the complete cycle of plays known in Norwich at the time of this record. As Waterhouse observes, it is abnormally simple, for it contains only half as many subjects as the Chester, the shortest of the four great cycles.

This list of pageants takes up roughly the right-hand half of the page (which is over eleven inches wide). To the left of it are two other columns of writing. The first is the list of crafts which Harrod described at the beginning of his article: 'The first entry I met with related to the Corpus Christi Procession, which, although the writing seems of an earlier character, may be of the same date as the entry in the Assembly Books quoted by Blomefield, 1489: "It was ordained in Common Assembly that all the Companies should go in procession on Corpus Christi Day before the procession." '[1] The writing is certainly distinctly earlier than that of the list of pageants; it is a good regular mid- to late fifteenth-century hand, which would be somewhat old-fashioned but not obsolete at the date suggested.[2] The column is headed: 'Processio in festo Corporis Christi ad Capellam in Campis Norwici [sc. St. Mary-in-the-Fields] modo sequenti.' The second line is 'In primis luminare circa Corpus Christi ante processionem et quelibet Ars cum vexillo'; and below this in single file are the names of thirty-one crafts, beginning 'Reders, Smethes, Coryoures, Barkeres' and ending 'Grocers, Mercers', followed by 'The procession; The Shreves clethyng; Maistere Shreves; The Maires clethyng; Maister Mayere; Maistere Aldermen with bokes or bedes in ther handes'. The names of all the crafts, from *Reders* to *Mercers*, are embraced by a long bracket in the left margin, beside which is written, in the hand of the list of pageants, 'new orderd'; and the second column, which is again in the pageant hand, gives the new order—but of only twenty-four crafts, beginning 'Smythes,

---

[1] F. Blomefield, *History of Norfolk*, iii (London, 1806), 176. This entry is not now in the Assembly Books.   [2] Tingey (p. xxviii, n.) dates the list '*c.* 1449'.

Masons, Carpenters, Reders', numbered j to iiij, and ending 'Groceres and Mercers'. The most interesting change, in view of the 1527 minute, is that before 'Groceres and Mercers' appears 'Saynt Lukes Gild', which did not figure at all in the original list. It may be that this revised order is to be connected with another decision of the Corporation mentioned by Blomefield under the date 1533—no original record appears to survive: 'This year was settled the order of the procession of the occupations, crafts, or companies, to be made on Corpus Christi day, from the common-hall, by Cutler-row, and so round the market, to the hall again, which order the said companies are to go in, at the riding of the mayor and at all times when summoned, to attend the court, for the worship and honour of the city.'[1] This date would accord well with the writing of the revised order by the clerk who compiled the Assembly minutes at this period.

It is a curious feature of these lists of the processional order and of the pageants that, though they are on the same page and two of them are in the same hand, there is no simple correlation between procession and pageants. In particular, the revised procession contains twenty-four crafts and St. Luke's Guild, but the list of pageants mentions no less than sixty-three crafts and omits the guild; and even the leading crafts in each group are not always prominent in the processional order—neither Glaziers nor Dyers appear in the revised procession, though Dyers were in the earlier list. The procession is stated to be on Corpus Christi Day; the pageants are known from the 1527 minute to have been at Whitsun. The participants overlapped, but were evidently not identical.[2]

Returning now to the *Grocers' Book*, we find a series of accounts which give many particulars relevant to the play as well as to the Corpus Christi procession. Waterhouse digests most of the information in them, but they are more illuminating in the original order and I therefore reproduce Fitch's text below (expanding abbreviations and modifying punctuation). In particular, Waterhouse remarks that 'the accounts for 1535 and 1536 distinctly refer to the performance taking place on Corpus Christi Day'; but it will be seen that this is not in fact so. Though the costs of the

---

[1] Blomefield, iii. 206–7.

[2] For particulars of a procession held by a single guild in Norwich on its patron saint's day see *Records of the Gild of St. George in Norwich, 1389–1547*, ed. M. Grace (Norfolk Record Soc. ix, 1937), pp. 16–18. This embodied a representation of St. George and the Dragon.

Pageant and of Corpus Christi Day are usually mentioned together, this certainly does not mean that the play was performed on that day—rather the reverse. The accounts follow:

Folio 34 ff.

Assembly of the Company of Grocers, holden at the Black Fryers, 8 May 1534. Chosen for Alderman of the Company, Mr. Robert Greene, and 2 Wardens, 2 Assisters, 4 Surveyors of the Pageant, 1 Bedell. An assessment of 22s. 10d. made on the Company, whereof paid for nayles, 9½d.; for forlockys, wyer, whypcord, and marham, 14½d.; sope to grese the wheles, 1d.; aples and fyggs, 4d.; oryngys, 10d.; 3 lb. datys, 1s.; 1 st. almonds, 3d; fumygacions, 6d.

Item, a new heer, with a crown for the Serpent, 6d. Item, to Sir Stephyn Prowet for makyng of a newe ballet, 12d.[1]

Item, 3 payer of glovys for Adam, Eve, and the Angelle, 3d.
Item, for mendyng of the Gryffyn and off the Father's glovys, 10d.
Item, for a present govyn for the borowyng of the organs, 4d.
Item, to Jeffrey Tybnam playeng the Father, 16d.
Item, to Mr. Leman's servant playing Adam, 6d.
Item, to Frances Fygot playing Eve, 4d.
Item, to Thomas Wolffe playeng the Angelle, 4d.
Item, to Edmund Thurston playeng the Serpent, 4d.
Item, to John Bakyn playeng at the organs, 6d.
Other repairs of the Pageant, 8d.
Item, to 4 men for ther labowrs, wayghtyng upon the Pageant with lewers, 16d.
Item, for a horse, 12d.
Item, for ½ a barell of bere, 10d.
Item, for brede, beffe, vele, motton, and othyr vytalls, with the dressyng, 4s. 6d.

---

[1] Fitch notes: 'Sir Stephen Prewett was seventh Prebend of the College of St. Mary in the Fields in 1536, and one of the Stipendiary Priests of St. Peter Mancroft Church.' For St. Mary's, see Blomefield, iv (1806), 173. Blomefield also has the following entry on p. 187 of the same volume, under 1556, 7 Sept.: 'Sir Stephen Prewet or Prowet, then parish chaplain, was instituted to the rectory of St. Peter in Mancroft . . . and was inducted and held it for life . . .; at his death . . . the impropriator made a donation of it in 1562 to Sir Robert Dixon.' The will of Stephen Prout or Prowet of Norwich, clerk, was proved in 1559 (*Index of Wills proved in the Consistory Court of Norwich, 1550–1603*, ed. M. A. Farrow (Norfolk Record Soc. xxi (1950), p. 136)).
    Waterhouse notes that the churchwardens' accounts of St. Mary's at Bungay in Suffolk likewise show payments in 1526 for copying the game-book, and to Stephen Prewett for his labour in the matter. He adds that if this entry refers to our play at all it must refer to the A version, since the other was begun in 1565.

House ferme for the Pageant, 2s.
Item, for beryng of the stremers on Corpus Christi day, 2d.
Item, for the offryng, 5d.

Assembly at the Yeldhalle, 7 May 1535, elected officers; 20s. assessed, etc. The account of the Surveyors for all charges that yere, viz. for settyng forthe of the Pageant, house ferme for the same, Corpus Christi day, and the Bedell his fee, amounts to 17s. 5d.

Assembly held at St. Peter's Churche, 18 May 1536, elected officers. The charges of the Pageant allonly, with Corpus Christi day, did amownte to 21s. Mem., Bedell's fee, 2d. House ferme for the Pageant, 2s.

Assembly holden at Yeldhalle, 27 Aprelle 1537, elected officers; assessed 28s., wherof was levyed 26s., and the rest cowd not be gathyrd bycause the Pageant went not forth that yere.
Item, thys yere the Pageant went not at Wytsontyde, howbeyt ther went oute in costs in makyng therof redy, and also yt went that yere in Octobyr in the processyon for the byrthe of Prynce Edward. So that the charges both tymes dyd amownte to 14s. 4d.

Assembly at Black Fryers, 19 May 1538, elected officers; asesmant 14s; charges 19s. 2d.

Assembly at Guyldhalle, 9 May 1539, elected officers. Assessment 16s. 6d., arrerages 2 last yeres 8s. 6d.; item of both, 25s. of which was levyed by the Surveyors 19s. 4d. Charges this yere 27s. 9d. the more bycause they bought that yere newe cokelys and many other thyngs that war in dekaye.

Assembly at Guyldhalle, 16 Aprell 1540, elected officers. Mr. Nycholas Sotherton, Alderman. At thys assembly the Surveyors toke upon them to set forth the Pageant, and to bere all charges of the same, to pay the charges on Corpus Christi day, the house ferme of the Pageant, and the Bedell hys fee, and they to have for these foresayd charges and for ther labours 20s. 28s. 6d. assessed.

Assembly at the Yeldhalle, 27 Aprell 1541; officers elected; assessed 24s. Mr. Wylliam Rogers, Alderman.

Assembly in St. Andrewes Churche, 1542; officers elected; assessed 20s. 2d.

Assembly at Common Halle, 5 May 1543; officers elected. Charges of Pageant and Corpus Christi daye last yere 23s. 8d.; assessed now 24s. Charges of Pageant, etc., undertoke for 20s.
Agreed that every man beyng a Grocer inrollyd within the Cyty of Norwiche shall, the Sondaye next aftyr Corpus Christi day, come to the

Common Halle chappell at 9 of the clocke in the forenoone, and there here masse.

[No assembly for three years]

Assembly at Common Halle, 6 June 1546; officers elected. Bedell to have yerely 3s. 4d. For charges of Corpus Christi daye, etc., for 3 yeres, etc., assessd 51s. 6d.

[Remainder of this year's accounts do not concern the pageant, except the following:]

Payments 38 Hen. 8 on Corpus Christi daye for the offryng at the Common Halle, 4d.; and to the 4 Waights, 1d.

Item, to the Surveyor for datys, almondys, and perfumes for the Gry-ffyn, 5d.

1546. The 3rd Assembly holden at the Common Halle on Pentecost Sondaye [made ordinances for elections]. Accordyngly were chosen 4 aldermen and 8 comyners, who chose Mr. Wylliam Rogers for ther Alderman, 2 Wardeyns and 2 Surveyors for settyng forth the processyon on Corpus Christi day, and for the Pageant yf it go forth the next yere; and 1 Bedell.

Dyner at the Common Halle, 12 June 1547.

Payd on Corpus Christi day, for the offryng at the Common Halle at the Meyer's guyld, 4d.; to the 4 Waights, 1d.; and perfumes for the Gryffyn, 3d. Payd Sonday next after Corpus Christi day to Sir Kemp, prest of the Common Halle, for certen this yere, 5s. Payd howse ferme for the Pageant, 2s.

1556. Payd for a yard and ½ of yellow buckram to make a cote for the Pendon Bearer — 16d.
for makynge and payntynge the sayde cote — 12d.
for payntynge and gyldynge the Gryffon — 3s. 4d.
for the hyer of a hear and crowne for the Angell, and for caryeng of the Gryffon — 4d.
for perfumys for the procession — 20d.
payd him that bare the Pendon — 2d.
payd for collerd thryde to bynde the flowers — 2d.
for a splytter that shadowed the Gryffon — 3d.
for the dynners of the Angell and Pendon Berer — 12d.

total 9s. 3d.

1557. Payde upon Corpus Christi daye for settyng forth the procession:
payd for the hyer of an Angells cote, and for 2 crownys and hearis to bear[er]is to beare the Arms — 8d.
payd for a crowne and heare to him that bare the Gryffon — 2d.
payd to 3 ladys that bare the Gryffon, Arms, and Grocery — 4d.

payd for beryng the Pendon 2d.
payd for 6 oz. of perfume 2s.
for orengys, fygys, allmondys, datys, reysens, preumes, and aples to
garnish the tre with 10d.
for collerd thryd to bynd the flowers 2d.
for theyr brekfastys that daye 8d.

1558. Payd on Corpus Christi day at the offryng, 4d.; and to the
Wayghts 2d. 6d.
for hier of 1 angells cote, 2 crowns, and 1 heare 8d.
to 3 ladys ut supra 4d.
for apples, etc., ut supra 12d.; and Pendon Berer 2d. 14d.
perfumes 2s. 4d. Item, for notmyggys, clows, macys, and gylden of
sertayne poses, and for colerd thryd 14d.

summa 6s. 2d.

1559. No Solemnité

1563. Assembly, 13 May 1563. It was enquyryd by Mr. Aldriche for the
provysyon of the Pageant to be preparyd ageynst the daye of Mr. Davy
his takyng of his charge of the Mayralltye. And yt ys agreyd by the consent of the Companye then present that the Surveyors shall furnysh the
same and prepare a devyce ageynst the day. Charge was 6s. 8d.

Inventory of the particulars appartaynyng to the Company of the
Grocers. A.D. 1565
A Pageant, that is to saye, a howse of waynskott paynted and buylded
on a carte with fowre whelys
A square topp to sett over the sayde howse
A Gryffon, gylte, with a fane to sett on the sayde toppe
A bygger iron fane to sett on the ende of the Pageante
iiijˣˣ iij small fanes belongyng to the same Pageante
A Rybbe colleryd red
A cote and hosen with a bagg and capp for Dolor, steyned
2 cotes and a payre hosen for Eve, stayned
A cote and hosen for Adam, steyned
A cote with hosen and tayle for the Serpente, steyned, with a with
[= white] heare
A cote of yellow buckram with the Grocers' arms for the Pendon Bearer
An Angells cote and over hoses of apis skynns
3 paynted clothes to hang abowte the Pageant
A face and heare for the Father
2 hearys for Adam and Eve
4 head stallis of brode inkle with knopps and tassells
6 horse clothes, stayned, with knopps and tassells
Item, weights, etc.

Folio 66:

Item, yt is to be noted that for asmuch as for the space of 8 yeris ther was neyther semblye nor metynge, in the meane season the Pageante remaynynge 6 yeris in the gate howse of Mr. John Sotherton, of London, untyll the ferme came to 20s.; and bycaus the Surveiors in Mr. Sothertons tyme would not dysburs ani moni therfor, the Pageante was sett oute in the strete and so remayned at the Black Fryers brydge in open strete, when bothe yt was so weather beaten that the cheife parte was rotton; wherupon Mr. John Aldrich, then Maior the yer 1570, together with Mr. Thomas Whall, Alderman, offred yt to the Company to sell for the some of 20s., and when no person wold buy yt for that price and that yt styll remayned, and nowe one pece therof rent of and now another as was lyke all to come to nothinge, Nicholas Sotherton, then offycer to Mr. Maior, was requested to take yt in peces for the dept dewe to hym for the seyd howse ferm therof for 6 yeris aforesayde, at 3s. 4d. a yer, who accordinglye dyd take downe the same and howsed yt accordinglye.

Text B of the play, therefore, 'newly renewed and according unto the Scripture' in 1565, came at the very end of the Pageant's career.

Verse. The two texts differ in the metrical structure of their lines. Text A is written in lines of the 'fifteenth-century heroic' type, sometimes susceptible of being scanned as iambic pentameters—

> 14 Bothe flesche and bone I do thys creatur blysse
> 18 Ys thy hyghe excellent magnyficens—

but more often containing four strong stresses with a variable distribution of weaker syllables, and a marked caesura—

> 2 In the hévenly émpery Í am résydent
> 55 O gémme of felícyte and fémynyne lóve.

Text B in its first prologue apparently begins in the same metre; but from the second stanza the lines become longer and move as rough alexandrines, some of them quite regular—

> 18 Wherín of frútes pleasánt no kýnde theróf shulde wánte
> 20 To drésse and képe the gróunde and éate what frúte hym lýste.

This metre continues in the second prologue and throughout the play except for the song at the end.

Despite this difference in length of line the two texts show a

comparable variety in grouping the lines into stanzas—though
Fitch largely ignored this (and his exemplar treated the text as
prose) Manly and later editors were clearly right to distinguish
stanzas according to rhymes. Nevertheless the boundaries of
stanzas, mainly in B, are not always clear. Even when a well-
established pattern such as that of 'rhyme royal' can be observed,
a stanza often uses a rhyming sound which occurs also in the preceding or following stanza, sometimes in both; and with less-well-
marked types it may be impossible to say whether a long stanza is
intended or rather a concatenation of shorter ones.

In Text A there are probably twelve complete stanzas. Seven of
them have seven lines with the rhymes arranged as in 'rhyme royal',
ababbcc. One (55–8) is a simple quatrain with alternate rhyme; one
(59–64) has six lines, a quatrain followed by a couplet on the first
rhyme, *ababaa*. The remaining three are complex. Lines 81–90
are best regarded as a single ten-line stanza, a double quatrain
followed by a couplet, *ababbcbcaa*. A different ten-line structure
occurs in 24–33, *ababbcccdd*, and a somewhat similar nine-line
form in the second stanza, 8–16, *ababbcdcd*. Though these last are
linked by rhyme to neighbouring lines, this appears to be the
grouping intended because it embodies the pattern *ababb* characteristic of rhyme royal and related stanza forms.

In Text B both the prologues are in seven-line stanzas of the
usual rhyme pattern, but of the remainder only six stanzas in this
form can be identified—lines B3 1–7, 83–9, 104–10, 123–9, 130–6,
137–43. The rest of the text is divided in a large number of
different ways, sometimes of uncertain intention: in particular,
111–18 are likely to have been designed to form the pattern
ababbaba, and are best regarded as an eight-line stanza; but the
following lines 119–22 continue the *a* rhyme though they stand
well as a separate quatrain. Another quatrain occurs at 100–3,
linked by rhyme to both the preceding and the following stanzas.
Another eight-line stanza, though with a different rhyme arrangement at the end, occurs at 17–24 (the sixth line incompletely
preserved); this also continues the last rhyme of the preceding
stanza. Three stanzas have nine lines, with varying rhymes: 8–16
abbacccdd, 65–73 *ababbbcbc*, 74–82 *aaabbbcbc*. Three have ten: 36–45
ababbcccbb, 144–53 *ababbcccdd*, and 90–9 *ababbcbcdd*—a pattern
similar to A 81–90. One has six: 59–64 *ababab*; one has eleven:
25–35 *ababbcccddd*; and one thirteen: 46–58 *ababbcbccdcdd*.

Language. There is no reason to suppose that the text of the Norwich plays represents a language substantially different from that
which John Homerson and Robert Reynbald, grocers of Norwich,
and their successors in the Company, were accustomed to hear and
to write—no doubt the anonymous eighteenth-century transcriber
made mistakes, but he would not wilfully misrepresent his original
and probably reproduced most of it faithfully enough.

Not much in the language is distinctive. One characteristically
East Anglian spelling survives in two occurrences of *xall* 'shall'
A 87 and 88 s.d. Of pronunciations indicated by rhyme, the most
noteworthy is that of *lyke* B³ 27 paired with *eke*. Spellings of 'like',
both verb and adjective, as *leke* are especially common in the
eastern counties (though not exclusively there) in the fifteenth
century—e.g. V. 261; rhymes of this kind are rather more widespread in the sixteenth.[1] The pronunciation of the rhyming words
spelt *gyve, lyve, meve* B³ 30–2 is not entirely certain: *meve* is found
elsewhere spelt *myve*, presumably implying a pronunciation with a
short /i/;[2] but, on the other hand, both *geve* and *leve* are common
forms in East Anglia as well as in the north in the fifteenth century[3]
and *geve* is widespread and very frequent in the sixteenth, so that
this, with the vowel /i:/, appears to be the more likely basis of the
present rhyme.

The rhyme *love*: *behofe* A 55–7 depends on the lengthening of
the vowel of *love* to /o:/, and subsequent raising; that of *fylde*:
wylde: *dystylde* B³ 84–7 on shortening of the /e:/ in ME. *feld* to /i/
(cf. the spelling *shylde* B³ 140, and also *wyll* 'well' A 37); that of
feare: *care* B³ 104–6 on the falling together of ME. /ɛ:/ and /a:/
before *r*, which Dobson says is 'not common before 1650', though
he has found rhymes from 1590. (*Feare* also rhymes with *apere*
B³ 71–3, *care* with *ar* B³ 65–7.)[4] The rhyme *spright*: *lyght*: *wight*
B³ 145–8 shows the predominantly eastern loss of the fricative
before -*t* well known in the fifteenth century, and indicated also by
the spellings *abought* A 72, *dowght* B³ 36. The rhyme *blysse*: *ys*:

[1] See E. J. Dobson, *English Pronunciation 1500–1700* (Oxford, 2nd edn.,
1968), § 138; A. Kihlbom, *A Contribution to the Study of Fifteenth-Century
English* (Uppsala, 1926), pp. 36–8; H. Kökeritz, 'Dialectal Traits in Sir Thomas
Wyatt's Poetry', *Medieval and Linguistic Studies in Honour of Francis Peabody
Magoun, Jr.* (New York and London, 1965), p. 299.

[2] Dobson, § 132 n.

[3] Cf. the spelling *geffe* A 76 (but *gyve* again B³ 5), in which the *ff* may well
represent /v/; see for example Kökeritz's article cited in note 1 above, p. 296).

[4] On all these see Dobson, §§ 11, 18, 204 n. 4.

mysse A 14–17, *blyste: myste* B¹ 22–4 depends on the early association of *bless* with *bliss* which affected the form of the verb commonly up to the seventeenth century.

In inflexions the main point of interest is that the 3rd person sg. pres. indic. of verbs normally ends in *-th*, never in *-s*: *hathe* A 56, *sheweth* B¹ 15, *begyneth* B² 8, *hath* B³ 48, *doth* 51, etc. But a number of forms in Text B³, in rhyme, have no inflexion: *meve* 32, *have* 44, *make* 50, *conceyve* 55, *requyre* 130. Strong past participles are usually without *-n*, whether in rhyme as *gyve* B³ 30, *abode* 144, *unlode* 146, or within the line as *broke* 67, *eat* 76, *stroke* 104; but *fal[l]en* B¹ 5, *gyven* B³ 75. The weak participle is without ending in *plant* B³ 3 (cf. *plantyd* A 5). The plural of the pres. indic. of 'to be' is mostly *ar(e)*, A 83, B³ 110, 137, etc., but also *be* B¹ 5, B³ 146. The pronoun of the second person plural sometimes has *you* in the nominative, as A 65, 73, B³ 51, though *ye* also occurs.

Two syntactical points are worth notice. The verb *do* is very frequent in auxiliary function: A 13, 14, 68, B¹ 16, B² 17, B³ 12, etc., negative in A 66, B³ 71, interrogative in B³ 79. It is never used as a full verb in the sense 'put', or as a causative. The regularity of this even in Text A suggests that the surviving text is not much older than the date at which it was copied into the *Grocers' Book*. The use of *his* to form genitives is well established in Text B: *God his creacion* B¹ 9, *mankynde hys creacion* B² 6, *man his sustentacion* B³ 2.

In vocabulary the outstanding feature is the flourish of 'aureate terms' at the beginning of Text A, which in this way is perhaps most like the opening of *Mankind*. In Text B, though there are some words of this kind they are less concentrated. Most of the words are of fairly long standing—even one now so unfamiliar as *plasmacion* A 8 is substantially recorded from the fourteenth to the seventeenth century; but *honoracion* B³ 24 is known elsewhere only in *Dives and Pauper* (written early in the fifteenth century), and *soporacion* A 12 and *forepredestinacion* B³ 149 appear nowhere else. In contrast with these learned words, at least two are distinctly limited in regional distribution: *haight* 'command' B³ 42, which *O.E.D.* errs in describing as 'after 15th c. only Sc.', and *sythys* 'sighs' A 90, which is widespread in dialects though not recorded by *O.E.D.* until 1609.

It is remarkable that, though the two texts must be at least thirty years apart in composition, no significant grammatical differences between them are apparent.

III. THE NEWCASTLE PLAY

Text. The Newcastle Play of Noah's Ark resembles the Norwich Grocers' Play in having no surviving manuscript on which the text can be based. But it is in far worse case than the Norwich Play because the existing copy has obviously been not only modernized in language but gravely corrupted so that parts of it yield neither metre nor sense. The only text, from which all editions have perforce been constructed, was printed in a book by Henry Bourne, a curate of All Hallows in Newcastle, entitled *The History of Newcastle upon Tyne; or, the Ancient and Present State of that Town*, which was published in Newcastle in 1736, four years after the author's death. The play was inserted as an afterthought, while the book was in the press; for it begins at the very foot of p. 139, which is not at all concerned with guilds or town ceremonies but begins the description 'Of Fishergate and Wall-Knowl'. There is a headnote in small type, beginning in the right margin but extending into a line across the page: 'The following Play coming too late to my Hands to be inserted in its proper place, I am obliged to mention it here. It is intituled, NOAH'S ARK; or, The Shipwrights ancient PLAY, or DIRGE.' Immediately under this heading come the first stage direction and five lines of text disposed in two columns of small italic type. The rest of the play occupies the whole of p. 140 and over half of p. 141, and after the end of it the text of the book runs on from its catchword near the bottom of p. 139, with no further comment on the play. This text of Bourne's was reprinted in 1789 by John Brand in his *History of Newcastle upon Tyne*. He made no detailed comments, and printed the text as Bourne had done, divided into speeches but not into stanzas; but he silently made a few slight 'improvements' such as altering 'thou shall' to 'thou shalt' (41, 129) and 'be' to 'lie' (105). In 1825 Thomas Sharp added as an appendix to his *Dissertation on the Pageants . . . at Coventry* the Newcastle text taken from Brand: 'Mr. Brand's account of the Corpus Christi Plays at Newcastle upon Tyne, having been accidentally omitted in its proper place, is here printed from his History of that Town' (p. 221). He gave simply a faithful reprint adding nothing of his own. The first attempt to construct a text both fully intelligible and formally satisfactory was made by Holthausen in 1897 in *Göteborgs Högskolas Årsskrift*, iii. He emended extensively, marked stanza divisions, and added a commentary on language and background which remains valuable. In 1899 Brotanek, in *Anglia*, xxi, printed opposite the text as given by Sharp a complete reconstruction of the conjectural original in the northern dialect of the second quarter of the fifteenth century. His emendations and stanza divisions often differed from Holthausen's. When Waterhouse constructed his text ten years later he based it on Bourne, 'with a minimum amount of correction and emendation; all the other versions have been consulted and all variants of real importance in any of these have been given in the footnotes'. This use of 'variants' is not very apt, for they are of course no more than conjectures.

Waterhouse says of Bourne's text (p. xxxvi):

Bourne, in his transcript, with the best of intentions no doubt, modernised the spelling throughout; but apparently he did not understand his original very well, since, in very many instances, he has put down verses which are incapable of bearing any meaning at all, and has left them in such a state that it is extremely difficult to conjecture what his original gave him. Three lines he has omitted, and states the fact, but other places in the play seem to have suffered from the same process, although he has not acknowledged it.

There is some misunderstanding in the last sentence; Bourne nowhere says anything about omitting lines, nor does anyone else until Brotanek. He conjectured from the failure of rhyme after line 51 that three lines had been lost. This is possible, but not much necessary narrative material is lacking here —all the dimensions of the ark need not have been given—and the loss of one line may suffice to account for the irregularity. Whether it was Bourne himself or the manuscript he copied that modernized the spelling there is no means of knowing.

In the present edition I have considered Bourne's text again, and have taken a slightly different view of some passages in which it is unsatisfactory in sense or form. I have not attempted to make a complete reconstruction, but only to suggest approximately how the corrupt passages might be supposed to have been planned. The sum of these is so great that the usual method of footnotes is too clumsy a way of displaying the changes. I have therefore judged it best to reproduce Bourne's text in addition to the edited version.

In the latter all departures from Bourne are italicized to draw attention to them, but they are not otherwise annotated unless the emendation is due (as it often is) to one of the editors before Waterhouse, or in two important cases to Henry Bradley. I have gone further than Waterhouse in indicating northern dialectal forms which restore rhymes. If it is right, for instance, to alter Bourne's *loath* (116) to *laith* to rhyme with *skaith* it is equally so to alter *die* (32) to *dee* to rhyme with *fee*, especially since the analogous spelling *ee* for 'eye' appears in Bourne's text in 143; and once this is admitted other changes such as *sae* and *strae* for *so* and *straw* (31–3) follow naturally. But I have done this only for the sake of rhyme: if the southern forms rhyme correctly, as *foe: go* 183–5, I have not disturbed them; nor when they are within the line. This procedure, of course, leaves great inconsistencies of language; but Bourne's text is too uncertain a foundation on which to build a thoroughgoing reconstruction such as Brotanek undertook. Such a venture requires more knowledge of the date and conditions of composition than we possess. It cannot be assumed that the play would ever have been perfectly homogeneous in every one of its linguistic forms—the surviving fifteenth- and sixteenth-century records of the city companies certainly are not—and it is very probable that the more conspicuous dialectal features would be gradually modified over the years by the pressure of the literary language; so that a theoretical reconstruction is unlikely to recapture the true state of the text at any time.

Though a good deal is known about the Newcastle guilds and their plays and Corpus Christi processions, no records of the Shipwrights comparable to those of the Norwich Grocers appear to have survived. Many documents belonging to other guilds contain references to plays, and some of them give the subject assigned to the company.[1] The earliest mention is in the Coopers' 'ordinary' dated January 1427 (by modern reckoning), and after that they appear at various dates in the books of the Tailors, Saddlers, Tanners, Fullers and Dyers, Weavers, Barber-Chirurgeons

---

[1] For abstracts see Brand, ii. 315 ff.; E. Mackenzie, *A Descriptive Historical Account of the Town and County of Newcastle upon Tyne* (Newcastle, 1827), ii. 661 ff.; for accounts *Extracts from the Records of the Merchant Adventurers of Newcastle-upon-Tyne*, ed. F. W. Dendy (Surtees Soc., 1894, 1899), ii. 164 ff. There are summaries in Holthausen's edition and Chambers, *Mediaeval Stage*, ii. 385, 424. According to Mackenzie (p. 691) the Shipwrights' ordinary dates only from 1636.

with Chandlers, House-Carpenters anciently called Wrights, Masons, Glovers, Milners or Millers, Curriers Feltmakers and Armourers, Slaters, Glaziers with Plumbers Pewterers and Painters, and Cooks. In the Merchant Adventurers' accounts for 1552 an item records the payment of £31. 1s. 11d. 'for the fyve playes, whereof the towne must paye for the ostmen playe iiij li'. In the Millers' ordinary under 1578 it is provided that they shall play 'the ancient playe of their fellowship', called 'the Deliverance of the Children of Isrell out of the Thraldome, Bondage, and Servitude of King Pharo' 'whensoever the generall plaies of the towne shall be commanded by the mayor'. This suggests that the performances were no longer annual; and there are similar provisions in the Carpenters', Masons', and Joiners' ordinaries, the last dated 1589. While they did flourish they are all stated to have been held on the feast of Corpus Christi.

From these records, together with our play of Noah's Ark, the following elements of the Newcastle cycle can be worked out:

Bricklayers and Plasterers	The Creation of Adam
Shipwrights	Noah's Ark
Slaters	The Offering of Isaac by Abraham
Millers	The Deliverance of the Children of Israel
Glaziers, Plumbers, etc.	The Three Kings of Cologne
Bricklayers and Plasterers	The Flying of Our Lady into Egypt
Barber-Chirurgeons, etc.	The Baptizing of Christ
Fullers and Dyers	The Last Supper[1]
Weavers	The Bearing of the Cross
House Carpenters	The Burial of Christ
Tailors	The Descent into Hell
Masons	The Burial of Our Lady St. Mary the Virgin

There are six companies whose plays are mentioned but not named, as well as the Merchant Adventurers who were responsible for five. Since others may have given more than one, the full cycle may have been about twenty-five plays; but only Noah's Ark, sadly battered, has survived.

Verse. The text has been so badly transmitted that the original verse-form is sometimes hard to perceive. Yet some attempt must be made to understand it because emendation often depends on

[1] Deduced from the list of stage properties.

the editor's view of rhyme and rhythm. Clearly the lines are mostly arranged in pairs, sometimes both of four stresses (as in the passage 39–94), more often both of three (as 5–38, 168–99), often also a line of four stresses followed by one of three (as 1–4, 131–9). Lines of different lengths may be variously combined within a single speech: God begins with four lines of alternately four and three stresses, but continues with a long sequence of three-stress lines. The rhymes are in all these cases alternate, and often mark out quatrains though there are a few groups of six lines with the same pair of rhyming sounds, as 9–14, 75–80, 81–6, 186–91. It may be that this is a sufficient analysis of the metre of most of the play, and that no longer units were intended; but some quatrains are linked to others by rhyme so that a number of eight-line stanzas can be distinguished: some consisting simply of two quatrains with the same rhymes throughout, as 87–94 and 39–46 when emended, others with a change of one rhyme in the second half: *ababbcbc* 1–8, 31–8, *ababacac* 59–66, *ababcbcb* 67–74. Yet there are rhyme-links also between some quatrains and preceding groups of different form, as 15–18, 101–4, 128–31; and three quatrains share a rhyme in 101–12.

Apart from these forms depending on simple alternation of rhyme and sometimes of line-length there are a few deviations at important points in the play. The entry of the Devil is marked by his opening tail-rhyme stanza of six lines (95–100), the long lines with four stresses and the tail-lines with three, rhyming *aaabba*. His speeches to Noah's wife, and her replies, begin with two tail-rhyme stanzas of nine and six lines (113–21, 122–7), and there is another on Noah's return (148–55) of abnormal shape because there is only one four-stress line in the middle—*aababaab*. The jerky, two-stress lines of Noah's speech after his drink (156–9) are presumably intentionally distinctive; and the last stanza of all, the only one of five lines, is another special case. Alliteration is common throughout, but not regular enough to be of use in textual reconstruction except in a few passages, notably 48.

Language. Though Bourne's spelling and grammar are predominantly those of the eighteenth-century literary language, he has allowed a few strikingly northern dialectal forms to survive and others can be detected behind the modernized version. There are also some typically northern words.

In *wayns, baynes* 150–2 the spelling *ay* represents the reflex of OE. or ON. *ā, á* (ON. *ván*, OE. *bān*). This, with *ai*, is familiar in the north from the fourteenth century onwards. The unrounded pronunciation of the vowel which it implies—no doubt by the date of the play raised to a mid-front vowel—is confirmed by the spelling of *skaith* 117 (ON. *skaði*), in which the long vowel develops from short *a* in the open syllable. Consequently also Bourne's *loath* 116 must be an alteration of original *laith* (OE. *lāþ*). The corrupt rhyme at 173–5 implies the same vowel in the reflex of OE. *māra*, to rhyme with *fayre* 'fare'. The rhyme spelt *so, straw* at 31–3 can also be corrected by assuming the same sound again in both words: OE. *swā*, ON. *svá* could give either *swae* or *sae*, ON. *strá* would give *strae*; and in the opening eight lines (which may be regarded as one stanza, in spite of differences of line-length which may not be original) the printed *show, foe, do*, and *go* can be brought into line by assuming the shortened northern form *tae* instead of *do* (since *take* is in any case the usual verb with *vengeance*), and replacing the other forms by *sae, fae, gae*. These last spellings are a compromise. According to the convention used in *wayns*, etc., the vowel should be spelt *ay* or *ai*, but such spellings as *say* for 'so' are so misleading to a modern reader as to be unsatisfactory as emendations—even though *say* 122 is likely, if not certain, to be an instance in Bourne's text itself. The Scottish convention *ae* is therefore adopted, in preference to the older *a* which does not indicate that the vowel is of mid-front quality. The spelling *sair* in Bourne 48 must stand for *sere*, sometimes spelt *seir* 'various' (ON. *sér*); it implies that the reflexes of OE. *ā* and ON. *é* before *r* had fallen together.

In *ee* 143, *slee* 112 the spelling *ee* represents the reflex of OE. *ē* and ON. *æ* formerly followed by /j/ (OE. *ēge*, ON. *slœg-r*). Like the spellings in the previous paragraph this is established early in northern texts. Pronunciation as a monophthong is confirmed in these two words by the rhyme with *me*, and also in *dee*, printed *die* 32, by the rhyme with *fee*.

The rhymes of *wives* with *life* and *stiff* which appear to lie behind the printed text at 10–14 and 169–71 evidently rest on a pronunciation with voiceless consonant implied by common northern spellings such as *wyffis, wifis*. (Rhymes in which one of the words concerned has an ending and the other has not can be found widely in ME.)

Distinctively northern or north midland, though not confirmed by rhyme, is *wark* 'work' 47.

In inflexion, the most important form is [*thou*] *wends* 161, rhyming *friends*. Though Bourne prints the subject pronoun *you* this must rest on a misunderstanding at some stage of *y* in the function of *þ*, because Noah's wife addresses him as 'thou', not 'you'; *wends* is thus 2 sg. present indic., and the same ending appears within the line in *thou has* 195 (but *hast* 152). The ending of the 3 sg. is also mostly -*s*:*rewes* 1, *wakens* 44, *has* 69, *trickles* 143, *thinks* 197. There are a few exceptions: *hath* 60, 134, 146; but none of these are in rhyme.

The demonstrative plural 'these' is *their* 3.

In vocabulary, the following words are characteristic of northern or north midland texts: *hoope* 8 (especially north-eastern), *seam and rowe* 26, *tent* 39, *ever(y)ilk* 47 and *ilk a* 69, *seir* 48, *worklooms* 80, *spyer* 84, *gare* 110, *whunt* 112 (a northern variant of *quaint*, elsewhere *wheint*, etc.), *bewschere* 114, *lain* 135, 164, *slike* 141, *atour* (especially Scottish) 143, *wayns* 150, *thrae* 181, *rake* 182, *clink* 187.

In contrast to so many northern or northerly features, the rhyme *boat*, *sprot* 82–4, if the latter word is correctly reported, depends on a more southerly pronunciation: *sprot* descends from OE. *sprota* so that its *o* is assured. It appears therefore that the author knew both the rounded and the unrounded variants of the reflex of OE. *ā*, and forms such as *go* 31, *bone* 61, *both* 68 need not necessarily be later alterations. The use of both types can easily be paralleled, for instance in the Towneley Plays. It is worth notice that in the earliest surviving ordinances of the Newcastle Merchant Adventurers, dated 1479–80,[1] several of the linguistic features of this play recur: the spelling *ay* in *mayd* 'made', *playce*, *saym*, etc.; the forms *wark* and *everylk*; but the reflex of OE. *ā* is nearly always spelt *o*—*most*, *no*, *hold*, etc., though there are some cases of *hald* beside *hold* and *a* is kept before *w*, as would be expected, in forms like *awne*, *knawen*. An apparent minor difference is the use of *sike*, *syk(e)* for 'such', which in our text is likely to have been *slike*, Bourne's *like* 141.

The difference in the treatment of OE. *ā* is perhaps enough to permit the cautious conclusion that *Noah's Ark* was written earlier than the Merchant Adventurers' ordinances. There is no

[1] Ed. Dendy, vol. i.

doubt that the unrounded vowel is indigenous to the region, and the forms with *o* are due to the spread of the more southerly pronunciation. It seems reasonable to date the play a generation or so before the ordinances—say about the middle of the fifteenth century, perhaps a little earlier. This is precisely the period from which we have the first records of the Newcastle cycle; and there is good reason to think that in spite of modernization and manifold corruption this text preserves some genuine relics of the Shipwrights' Play as it was then performed.

IV. THE NORTHAMPTON *ABRAHAM*

Manuscript. Trinity College, Dublin, D. 4. 18, Catalogue no. 432, ff. 74ᵛ–81ʳ. The book is a composite volume, formerly in the library of Archbishop Ussher, containing a collection of unrelated manuscripts. For essential help with the following description I am indebted to Mr. William O'Sullivan, Keeper of Manuscripts in the College.

The manuscripts in the book were probably bound together in Ussher's time. The present binding dates from about 1820, but the spine was renewed in 1907 and 1938; it bears the title *Tractatus Varii*. The leaves are foliated throughout the volume from 1 to 155, in a hand of the eighteenth or early nineteenth century, and there is no earlier foliation. The first two manuscripts, ff. 1–22 and ff. 23–58, are parchment, and contain French and Latin works in hands of the thirteenth and fourteenth centuries. The succeeding manuscripts, from f. 59 to the end of the book, are paper. It is uncertain how many distinct manuscripts are bound together, but there are at least three, and probably four, one with longer leaves which are doubled up to fit the binding.

The part of the book with which we are concerned is the first of the paper manuscripts, all the main text of which is written in a single hand of the mid fifteenth century from f. 59 to f. 85. F. 86 is blank on both sides, and f. 87 is a severely mutilated sheet of a calendar which is likely to have been used as a wrapper when this manuscript was unbound. F. 88, in a hand of different type, is the first leaf of the next manuscript. The leaves of ff. 59–86 measure, apart from occasional mutilations, about 7·6×5·2 inches. They have been separated, and there are no signatures or catchwords, so that the quiring cannot be determined. From obvious dislocations of some of the texts it is clear that certain leaves after f. 70 have been bound out of their correct order and wrongly foliated; the correct order is 70, 72, 71, 75, 73, 74, 76. Most of the pages are written fairly fully except for a half-inch margin at the left and at the foot. The number of lines of writing on the page varies a good deal: in the play it is from 29 to 34, with a varying number of ruled lines across the page to separate the speeches.

Ff. 59–72 and 75 contain miscellaneous English poems, beginning with a copy of Chaucer's *Steadfastness* without its opening stanza and ending with a group of strongly Yorkist political poems. The first of these (ff. 67^r–69^v) celebrates the battle of Northampton; the most important is a 75-line carol (ff. 70^v, 72^{rv}, 71^r) on the battle of Towton, which ends with rejoicing at the coronation of Edward IV. The following are the reference numbers in the *Index of Middle English Verse* and its *Supplement* of all the poems in the order in which they occur: 3190, 2742, 3636, 3638.3, 3784.6, 1585.5, 2446.5, 4120.6, 1924.5, 158.4 (followed by a six-word nonsense charm 'for the crampe'), 2609, 455, 508, 3856.5, 1380, 700. The whole series was edited by Brotanek in *Mittelenglische Dichtungen aus der Handschrift 432 des Trinity College in Dublin* (Halle, 1940); the political poems were first published by Madden in *Archaeologia*, xxix (1842), 330–47, and most recently by Robbins in *Historical Poems of the XIVth and XVth Centuries* (1959), nos. 87, 89, 90, 91. F. 73^{rv} and the top of f. 74^r contain a list, still in the main hand, of Christian kings of the world and of the kings of England from Alfred onwards, giving the duration of each reign except the last, which is that of Henry VI. The remainder of f. 74^r continues the list of kings in a sixteenth-century hand which Mr. O'Sullivan believes to be that of Bartholomew Butler, who was York Herald in Henry VIII's reign and was created first Ulster King of Arms in 1552.[1] The last name in the list is Henry VIII, and since the last words of this entry, 'Rayned xxxviij yeres', are in a different ink from the rest and were evidently added after Henry's death, Butler must have possessed the manuscript before 1547. (Another hand has written 'God saue King H the viijth, Amen' in the space between the earlier and the later lists.)

On f. 74^v the play begins, without title, in the main hand again. F. 75, as noted above, is out of order and does not belong to the

---

[1] *Cal. Pat. Rolls Edward VI*, iv. 304.

play, which continues without a break on f. 76ʳ; but f. 76ᵛ and f. 77ʳ, having presumably been accidentally left blank when two leaves were turned over instead of one, are occupied by skilful pen drawings of coats of arms headed 'Duodecim pares francie'— these words and the names above the shields apparently in Butler's hand. F. 77ᵛ takes up the play again with no break in the text, and it then continues to its end at the foot of f. 81ʳ.

Ff. 81ᵛ and 82ʳ are blank. F. 82ᵛ begins a list of mayors and bailiffs of Northampton, with the heading: 'Hic sunt maiores et balliui de North' a primo anno regni regis Ricardi usque in hunc diem'. It is neatly set out in columns, the mayor's name to the left, the two bailiffs bracketed together in the middle, and the year to the right. Though three leaves have been cut out after f. 82 the foliation takes no account of them and the list continues with no break on the leaf numbered 83, and goes on to 85ʳ quite regularly. The first years of new reigns (Henry IV, Henry V, Henry VI) are preceded by centred headings, and eight of the entries are followed by brief annalistic notes in Latin, all but one of a single line, written slightly smaller and underlined. They are as follows:

4 Richard II	In predicto anno fuit parliamentum apud Norhampton
5 Richard II	Terremotus fuit die Veneris proximo ante festum Pentecoste dicto anno vᵗᵒ. Et in dicto anno fuit surreccio in Kent per Jak Strawe qui interfectus fuit per Walleworthe tunc maiorem London'
11 Richard II	In dicto anno xj fuit bellum apud Ratcote brigge
22 Richard II	Rex Ricardus depositus fuit anno xxijᵒ supradicto
3 Henry IV	In predicto anno iijᵒ fuit bellum apud Shrouesbury
14 Henry IV	In anno xiiijᵒ supradicto fuit surreccio de lollelardys
3 Henry V	In anno tercio supradicto fuit bellum de Agyncourte
28 Henry VI	[In anno xxviijᵒ supr]adicto fuit surreccio in Kent per xxx m¹ virorum.

This last entry is at the foot of f. 84ᵛ. On f. 85ʳ about halfway down the page there is a slight space between the entries for 36 and 37 Henry VI, and after the entry for 'Anno xxxviijᵒ' a Latin note twelve lines long, and filling the rest of the page, records the battles of Ludlow and Northampton and gives the names of some of those killed there. This note is still in the main hand, but the writing is smaller and only a few words are underlined, not the whole passage as in the earlier notes. (A few words are lost in the last three lines where the edge of the paper is torn, affecting also ff. 83 and 84.) F. 85ᵛ contains the Northampton entry for 'Anno xxxix', and after it another Latin note fifteen lines long, in exactly the same style as the preceding one, records the battles of Wakefield, St. Albans, and Ferrybridge (the description shows that Towton is meant—Ferrybridge was a preliminary skirmish). The last sentence, in the same hand but in a more formal style, is: 'Et dictus Rex Edwardus coronatus fuit apud Westm' die dominica in vigilia apostolorum Petri et Pauli [sc. 28 June] in dicto anno et in anno primo regni sui'. Under this, in the same style, is the record of Northampton officers for 'Anno primo', then the centred heading 'Anno regni regis Edwardi quarti primo', and finally 'In isto anno primo fuit parliamentum apud Westm' quod incipit in crastino animarum' [sc. the morrow of All Souls' Day, 3 November]. The rest of the page (nearly half) is blank.

The last entries date the end of the scribe's work to a year not earlier than 1461. If the tense of *incipit* (inconsistent with *fuit*) in the final sentence could be taken at its face value it would narrow the date to the period between Edward IV's coronation on 28 June and the opening of his first parliament on 4 November of that year. On the whole this seems likely to be right: the exact day of the opening of parliament is of more interest if it is to come than if it is over, and this part of the sentence could have been added after the anticipatory *fuit* had been written; moreover, the day given is one day out—the 1461 parliament met on 4 November, not 3. (It had been summoned on 23 May for 6 July, but because of disturbances in the north was prorogued on 13 June until 4 November.[1]) But the date of the copying of the play, as distinct from the historical entries, needs closer examination. When Brotanek edited the play in *Anglia* (1898) he wrote, concerning the list of mayors and bailiffs:

Dieses verzeichnis, mit welchem eine kurze lateinische chronik von England verbunden ist, wurde in einem zuge geschrieben bis zum 36 regierungsjahre Heinrich VI. Da das spiel von Abraham in ganz demselben schriftzügen und mit derselben tinte niedergeschrieben wurde, dürfen wir wohl dessen aufzeichnung in das jahr 1458 (36 H.VI) und nach Northampton verlegen. (p. 22)

---

[1] F. M. Powicke and E. B. Fryde, *Handbook of British Chronology* (2nd edn., London, 1961), p. 533; C. L. Scofield, *The Life and Reign of Edward IV* (London, 1923), i. 178; *Rot. Parl.* v. 487.

Waterhouse accepted 1458 as 'a very probable date for the com-
pilation of this Dublin version of the play'. Waterhouse had evidently not examined this part of the manuscript himself, for his
description is a sadly garbled adaptation of Brotanek's, both confused in its order and inconsistent with itself: he writes of 'the
short Latin Chronicle extending as far as the thirty-sixth year of
Henry the Sixth's reign, immediately *preceding* . . . our play; which
latter is then followed . . . by a bailiff's register, extending as far as
the first year of Edward the Fourth's reign'. The notion of the
short Latin chronicle, an absurdly grandiose description of the
few scattered notes, he took from Brotanek without understanding
its relation to the list of mayors and bailiffs (not the same thing as
a 'bailiff's register'); and he placed it before instead of after the
play. But neither he nor Brotanek noticed that the slight change in
the Northampton entries after 36 Henry VI, though it evidently
marks some interruption in the writing, cannot mean that everything in the manuscript up to that point was written in 1458, and
the rest in 1461 or partly in the intervening years. It cannot mean
this because the poem celebrating the battle of Towton is, as
Brotanek saw, in the same hand as the play, and this poem comes
before the play (despite the dislocation of some leaves). The battle
of Towton was fought on Palm Sunday, 29 March 1461; but the
poem celebrates also the coronation of Edward IV, which places
it after 28 June—evidently soon after:

> Almighti Jhesu save þe Rose and geue hym his blessyng,
> And al the reme of Englond ioy of his crownyng,
> þat we may blesse þe tyme þat euer God sprad þe floure.

Support for a date in 1461 comes also from the last of the political
poems, 'Twelve Letters save England', which speaks of 'Edward,
kyng most ryall' (l. 67); but this need not necessarily be later than
the coronation, for Edward was enthroned on 4 March and accepted
as king from that date. It appears, therefore, that the part of the
manuscript immediately before the play and also that following it
were written in the latter half of 1461, so that the play itself must
have been written down at the same time. Though the text does
not seem to be seriously corrupt it has enough errors to show that
—as would be expected in such a manuscript—it is not an author's
copy. How much earlier it may have been composed can be only
approximately estimated from some features of the language.

The play is carefully set out, each speech being marked off by a red line across the page under the last line, with the name of the next speaker generally above this line to the right; but for the first four speeches the names *Deus* and *Abraham* are each centred on a separate line above the speech, and underlined. The few stage directions, in Latin, are written in the same way as the speakers' lines but marked off by lines above and below. The initial letter of each line is touched with red. Rhymes are bracketed in red; the short rhyming lines are usually written to the right of each group of longer lines, and again bracketed. Punctuation, by points and virgules, is fairly full on the first two pages, but after that is rare.

Nothing in the play, or in the rest of the manuscript except Butler's notes, connects these texts with Ireland, and the presence of the manuscript in Dublin is not evidence of its origin. Seven pages of particulars of the officials of Northampton could surely be of interest only to a Northampton man, and Brotanek was right in assigning the manuscript to the town. It does not, of course, follow that the play was either composed or acted there, though the character of the language would not exclude this—this manu-script is a commonplace book into which the compiler wrote an assortment of things that interested him, no doubt drawn from various sources. Chambers observed that there is no record of medieval dramatic performances in Northampton (*Mediaeval Stage*, ii. 386). Nevertheless, since the manuscript must have been written there, whereas its preservation in Dublin is accidental, it is better to identify the play as 'the Northampton play', as this edition (following Brotanek) does, than to continue to call it 'the Dublin play' with Waterhouse and others.

Five other English plays on the theme of Abraham and Isaac survive—the separately written Brome text and those in the Chester, *Ludus Coventriae*, Towneley, and York cycles. The Northampton play is independent of all these; but Brotanek showed that there are grounds for thinking that its structure may have been influenced by an earlier text of a French play on the subject in *Le Mystére du Viel Testament*, especially a version of it printed in Paris in 1539.[1] The resemblance is not close in detail— the French text is almost four times as long as the English—but the sequence of speeches in both is similar, and though this may at

[1] Ed. J. de Rothschild, S.A.T.F., ii (1879), 13–79.

least in part be due to coincidence in treating the inherited story, it is remarkable that Sara (who is not even mentioned in Genesis 22) appears as a speaking character in two corresponding places in both these plays but in no other of the English versions.

In preparing his text, Waterhouse said, he used the only two previous editions, that by J. P. Collier in *Five Miracle Plays* (1836, an edition privately printed and limited to 25 copies) and Brotanek's in *Anglia*, xxi (1898), 21–55. From one or two of his notes it appears that he saw the manuscript, but his transcript is not nearly so accurate in detail as Brotanek's. His main departure from Brotanek was to set out the text in stanzas instead of in speeches, and since this makes the metrical structure much clearer I have followed him in this. This text rests on repeated new collations by Professor T. P. Dunning and me; but Brotanek left little to correct.

Verse. There are two distinct types of stanza, and some variations. Most of the play, from 48 to 247 and from 286 to 365, is written in tail-rhyme stanzas of the common eight-line pattern, the long lines having four stresses and the short lines three, rhyming usually *aaabcccb* but twice, 72–9 and 192–9, *aaabaaab*. Another stanza, 248–59—at the climax of the play when Abraham prepares for the sacrifice—is of similar structure but extended to twelve lines, rhyming *aaabcccbdddb*. The last four lines, which are an epilogue addressed to the audience, have the form of a half-stanza of the same type, rhyming *aaab* with the *b* sound taking up the third rhyme of the preceding stanza.

The remaining five stanzas are alike in concluding with five-line *caudas* of which the first and fifth lines rhyme together, and the other three. In other respects, notably in length of line, they vary. At the crisis of the action, when the Angel brings God's countermand (260–85), the two stanzas giving the Angel's speech and Abraham's reply are parallel, with eight lines before the *cauda* rhyming *ababbcbc*. The intended movement of these eight lines is not quite clear: some of them, especially the opening lines of each stanza, could be read with five stresses—

> Hábrahám, leue óf and dó not smýte;
> Withdráwe þyn hónd, ít is Góddes wílle!

But most could not be so read without strain, and it is most likely that they were designed on the same model as the four-stress lines of the tail-rhyme stanzas, with liberal allowance for slurring unstressed syllables—

> Hábraham, leue óf and dó not smýte;
>> Withdráwe þyn hónd, it ís Goddes wílle!
> Take vp Isáac, þi són so whýte,
>> For Gód wol nót þat þóu hym spílle.
> He séeþe þat þou art rédy fór to fulfílle
> His cómaundemént, in wéle and wó.

In the *cauda* the first and fifth lines have three stresses, the others four, though the latter have fewer unstressed syllables than the first eight lines of each stanza. The other stanzas of similar pattern are the first three of the play; but in these the long lines cannot comfortably be read with only four stresses. The structure of many of them is loose, but by the use of such devices as rests at the caesura and hovering stress on inflexional endings and other normally light syllables they can be made to fit reasonably well into a seven-stress rhythm, doubtless meant to introduce the play, with God's declaration, impressively—

1–4   Of áll þíng þer éuer wás Í am þé begýnnere,
>> Boþe hévenlý and érthly, ánd of hém þat bén in héll;
> At mý biddíng was wróught bóþe góode mán and sýnnere,
>> Áll in íoy tó haue dwéllid, tyl Ádam tó syn féll.

The first and second stanzas of the play have twelve such long lines, the third eight. All begin with the rhyme-scheme *ababbcbc*, and this with the *cauda* accounts for the whole of the third. The four additional lines in the first and second stanzas are differently treated: stanza 1 introduces a new rhyme, *cdcd*, but stanza 2 repeats the second, *cbcb*. The rhymes of the *cauda* are not linked in any way to those of the long lines, so that the seventeen lines of stanza 1 rhyme *ababbcbccdcdefffe*, but the others have one rhyme fewer.

Language. The spelling in general shows little that is distinctive at its date. For the most part it does not conflict with the evidence of the rhymes, and so evidently does not seriously misrepresent the sounds of the original text.

Final unstressed *-e* is shown to have been lost in the scribe's usage by the many words which historically had no vocalic ending but are spelt with *-e*: e.g. *haþe* 11, *childe* 15, *moste* 19, *wele* 22, *shope* 51. It is shown by rhyme to have been lost already in the original: e.g. the nouns *name* 50, *wrake* 342, *place*, *grace* 177–8, the pl. adj. *hye* 56, the adv. *hye* 281, the infins. *tell* 5, *fele* 21, *say* 45, *fulfille* 70, *acorde* 93, *dye* 173, and many others.

The reflex of OE. *ā* is normally written *o*; *more* 217 rhymes on *store*, *wherefore*; *sore* 147 on *afore*; *sore*, *hore* 244–5 on *store*; *wote* 258 on *þrote*, and also on *rote* (ON. *rót*). Similar to this last in rhyming on the reflex of OE. *ō* are *go* 66, 73, *wo* 74, *mo* 76, and many others. The rhyme of *anon* 131 with *son* is presumably on /u/, with shortening of the vowel after raising before *n*.[1] In contrast to all these the exclamation *gawe* has *a* every time it appears, 148, 283, 306.

The reflex of OE. *a* before a nasal not in a lengthening group is regularly written *a*: *man* 3, *þank* 39; in a lengthening group it is *o* in *hond* 261. In an open syllable it rhymes with short /a/ in the sequence *Abraham*: *am*: *name* 48–50.

The reflex of OE. *ǣ²* when shortened is written *a*: *lat* 110, 112, 173, *last* 'lest' 91, 226; *last* 'endure' 293 rhymes on *haste* 'hast'.

The reflex of OE. *ēo* is written *e*, and *forbede* 188 rhymes on *nede*, *dede* 'deed'; but *de(e)de* 140, 142 rhymes on *stede* 'place'. This suggests that historically tense and slack *ē* rhymed together, at any rate before *d*; but in the stanza 184–91 the three rhyming words just noticed are evidently distinguished in sound from the other rhyming pair *dede* 'dead': *brede* 'bread' (OE. *ēa*). Presumably the vowel in these words had already been shortened.

The reflex of OE. *ȳ* is written *i* or *y*: *fyre* 130, 145; *defilde* 122 rhymes on *childe*, *wilde*. But *by þe* 'redeem thee' 210 rhymes on *by þe* 'concerning thee' and on *sle the*. This could be accepted as an adequate rhyme only if the preposition had its alternative form *be*, which is usually unstressed but here must be stressed.

[1] See Dobson, § 148 n.

The reflex of OE. *y* is usually written *i* or *y*: *synnere* 3 rhymes on *begynnere*; *fulfille* 70 on *peretylle*, *wille* and 264 on *wille*, *spille*, *tylle*; *lyst*, *kyst* 212–14 on *myst*. But *mystrest* (from a possible OE. **trystan*) 20 rhymes on *best* (adv.); *wist* 333 rhyming on *best* 'beast' might be comparable, but is rather to be related to the lowering of earlier *i* shown by spellings such as *leving* 36, *prevely* 83, and the rhymes of the second stanza in which *skylle* 19 rhymes on *fele*, *wele*, *mele*, *helle*, *telle*. (These could be explained by raising of the vowel in *fele*, etc., as in the Brome play (see p. lxvi); but this seems to be precluded by the rhyme with *helle* and *telle*, since the etymologically short *e* is not normally so raised. *Well* rhymes on *hell* and *tell* in stanza 1 also.) Outside rhyme spellings with *u* appear in *furst* 24, *trust* 64.

The reflex of OE. *u* in open syllable is written *o* and rhymes with that of OE. *ō*: *wode* 145: *goode*: *hode*.

The initial consonant of 'give' is written *y* in *yeue* 225, 339, but *g* in *geue* 146. Both *y* and *g* also occur in *ayeyn(e)* 10, 291, *ageyne* 351, *-agayne* 360. Words containing earlier *-ht* are written with *ght* or *ȝt*, as *wrought* 3, *riȝt* 22, but the spellings *doughtles* 65, 82 (beside *doute* 90, 318) suggest that the fricative before *t* had been lost; *howȝ* 89 implies the loss of the sound finally also.

An individual form of interest confirmed by rhyme is *ȝynge* 'young' 25: *þinge*: *bidding*.

In unstressed inflexional syllables the vowel is usually written *e*, but in nearly a third of the total it is *i*, or occasionally *y*, often recurring in the same word: e.g. *dwellid* 4, *displesid* 5, 9, 80, 184, *plesid* 101, 115, *blessid* 316, 356, 358, *nedis* 73, *lendist* 36, *sparedist* 288, 294, *lepiþ* 131; *hertys* 37, *nedys* 182, *levyr* 80. None of these occurs in rhyme. There are two cases of *-us* in *clopus*, *othus* 205–6, rhyming on *you þus* in which the stress is doubtless to be placed on *you*, giving the same rhythm as *by þe*, *sle the* in the following stanza and in similar phrases in Chaucer, Gower, and elsewhere.

The following are the main points of verbal inflexion:

Pres. indic. 2 sg. (and past 2 sg. of weak verbs) ends in *-st*: *lendist* 36, *gladest* 37, etc., *haste* 289 rhyming on *last*. 3 sg. ends in *-þ* (variously spelt): *haþ(e)*, *hathe* 5, 9, 13, 76, etc., *doþe* 20, 298, *loueþ* 18, *sitteth* 334. Pl. usually has no ending, but occasionally *-n*: *ben* 2, 306, *owen* 28, *done* 93. Imper. pl. is usually uninflected but has *-þ* in *makeþ* 97, *lepiþ* 131, *takeþ* 137.

Infin. never ends in *-n*: *se* 313 rhymes on *degré*, *telle* 29 on *helle*, etc. Past participles of strong and anomalous verbs often have *-n*: *ben* 44, 319, 349, *done* 287, *sene* 366, *slayne 343, *riden* 194, 195 (none of these in rhyme); but often do not: (*i*)*do* 78, 104, 131, 176, *fare* 89, *forsake* 344 (rhyming on *Isaac*), *wonne* 363. Several past parts. have the prefix *i-*: *ido* 78, 131, 233, 310, *i-esid* 119, *ithanked* 302.

Of the personal pronouns, in 2 pl. *ye* and *you* are usually distinguished as nom. and oblique, but *you* is used as nom. in 327; in 3 pl. the nom. is *þei* 306, oblique *hem* 2, 201.

The vocabulary is commonplace, with no words conspicuously regional. *Frende* 239 is used in the ON. sense 'kinsman', but this appears even in Chaucer so is insignificant.

The general effect of spellings, sounds, and inflexions is of a midland dialect with no strongly marked character. The rhyming together of originally different qualities of $\bar{e}$, and the tendency to lower *i*, point to the east. The Norse-derived form *þusunde* (so expanded from MS. *m^l* because of the rhyme) suggests the same at this late date (though earlier it appears even in Laȝamon (C)); *ȝynge* has northerly associations but is widespread. Against these indications is the isolated pair of *-us* endings; but Brotanek notes that such forms, including *clothus* itself, appear in Northampton records.[1] It is likely enough that the play was composed in or near Northampton itself.

As for date, the apparently complete loss of final unstressed *-e* suggests that the original text was written in the fifteenth century rather than the fourteenth. Other indications are too vague to improve on the obvious conclusion that it must have been somewhat earlier than 1461, the date of the manuscript, since this is clearly a copy. The almost regular observation of the distinction between *ye* and *you* suggests a rather early date; it might be supposed that the retention of *-th* in the 3 sg. pres. of verbs pointed in the same direction, were it not that the Norwich play preserves it equally well in 1565. If the rhyme between *name* and *am* is accurate (as the rhymes in general are) it implies that the vowel of *name* had not yet

---

[1] *Dichtungen*, p. 196.

been raised so far as to be apprehended as a mid rather than a low front vowel; but though the raising of this sound must have been largely a fifteenth-century process the details of its stages are obscure. A date in the first half of the fifteenth century is as close as the evidence allows.

V. THE BROME *ABRAHAM*

Manuscript. 'The Book of Brome' now in Yale University Library, ff. 15^r–22^r. This is a commonplace book of the late fifteenth century which first became known when it was in the possession of Sir Edward Kerrison of Brome Hall in Suffolk (east of Brome village, about two miles north of Eye). Miss Lucy Toulmin Smith described the manuscript, and printed the play, in *Anglia*, vii (1884), 316–37. The whole book she soon afterwards printed for private circulation, with the title *A Common-place Book of the Fifteenth Century* (on the spine and half-title *The Boke of Brome*), and this edition was published by Trübner in 1886. In 1887 her text of the play was printed again in *The Norfolk Antiquarian Miscellany*, edited by Walter Rye, vol. iii. Miss Toulmin Smith recorded the discovery of the book in the muniment-room of the manor of Brome, which had been bought by Sir Edward Kerrison's grandfather from the Cornwallis family, owners of it since early in the fifteenth century. She observed that the many accounts which are written in the book relate mainly to Stuston, a manor about a mile north of Brome village on the road to Diss in Norfolk, which is the nearest town; and she pointed out that the Cornwallis family had owned Stuston and the neighbouring Oakley and Thrandeston manors as well as Brome. It appears therefore that the book had remained in or very near the place where it was compiled; for though the accounts are doubtless later than the other entries there is nothing to suggest that these were written elsewhere. After the death of Sir Edward Kerrison it became the property of one of his nieces, the Hon. Mrs. Rosamund Douglas-Hamilton, of Oakley House[1]—less than a mile from Brome Hall. When she died in 1947 it passed to her nephew Major E. M. Hovell, of Eye, and at his death in 1959 to his cousin Mr. Denis Hill-Wood, who deposited it

---

[1] R. L. Greene, reported in J. E. Wells, *Sixth Supplement to a Manual of the Writings in Middle English* (New Haven, 1935), p. 1468; also *Early English Carols* (Oxford, 1935), pp. 347–8.

on loan in the Ipswich and East Suffolk Record Office, in Ipswich, still in its native county about 25 miles from its place of origin. There it remained until December 1965.[1] In 1966 Mr. Hill-Wood sold it and it crossed the Atlantic to Yale.

The book is of paper, comprising 81 leaves so foliated in a modern hand, about $8 \times 5\frac{1}{2}$ inches (the edges variously frayed), bound in a medieval rough parchment wrapper with a flap, reinforced at the back with leather. Mr. Thomas E. Marston attributes the paper, from its watermarks, to France or the Low Countries about 1465–75.[2] The collation is as follows:

2 flyleaves, the first cut out; first quire of 22 leaves, one cut out after f. 7; second quire of 24 leaves, one cut out after f. 41; third and fourth quires of 16, each having five cut out—five after f. 46, one after f. 62, three after f. 65, one after f. 66; fifth quire of 12; 2 flyleaves, conjugate with those at the front.[3] The book thus originally contained 94 leaves, including the four flies. None of the excisions affects the text of the play or the poems, or indeed of the accounts as far as can be judged.

There are no signatures or catchwords. The contents are very miscellaneous and the written space irregular. The writing is in two main hands: the first copied all the verse and some legal documents, the second other similar documents and private accounts. The first hand is regular though rather coarse, and looks professional. It is typical of the late fifteenth century, and an inscription on the wrapper (see p. lxi) shows the writer to have been

[1] This account of the history of the manuscript since 1947, and the opportunity to consult it, I owe to Mr. D. Charman, East Suffolk County archivist. When preparation of this edition began the book had been lost to public view; Mr. Charman, at my request, undertook to try to trace it, and succeeded to admiration. See his letter in *T.L.S.*, 25 December 1959, p. 755.

[2] See his description of the book in *Yale University Library Gazette*, xli (1967), 141–5. His account is less than fair to earlier scholars. He says: 'All modern versions of this play derive from the inadequate 1886 edition; its origin and its relationship with other mystery plays await examination in a scholarly edition.' As will appear below, some modern texts derive from Miss Toulmin Smith's first edition of 1884, which though limited in aim was remarkably accurate and quite sufficient to permit examination of the origin and relationships of the play; and this examination, far from being 'awaited', has been conducted vigorously. Mr. Marston also errs in writing of 'Sturton' instead of Stuston.

[3] For particulars of the collation I am indebted to Dr. Herman W. Liebert, librarian of the Beinecke Rare Book and Manuscript Library at Yale.

alive as late as 1492. His work in the book itself cannot be earlier than 1454, because among the copies of legal documents is one dated January 32 Henry VI, which was that year. The second hand is loose in style and usually hasty, though by no means unskilled. Its general qualities make it look later than the first hand, but the differences are of style rather than date and there cannot be a long interval between the two. This second hand is that of Robert Melton of Stuston, who was one of the executors of John Cornwallis who died in 1506; Melton seems to have acted as steward of some of the Cornwallis manors. His accounts are of various dates from 15 to 23 Henry VII, that is, 1499 to 1508. Two pages are written in a third hand of a distinctly later type, but probably still of the first half of the sixteenth century. The different kinds of material, and the hands, are distributed irregularly through the book:

Ff. 1^r–26^v in the first hand, with trivial exceptions: f. 1^r, 'Man in merthe hath meser in mynd', 26 lines, *Index* 2064, and 'The hart lovyt þe wood', 4 lines, *Supplement* 3372.6; f. 1^v, eight lines of 'proper terms' partly in a rudimentary cipher (e.g. 'F (*for* B) hert hfrbprpxkth' = 'A hert herborowith'), below which are two columns, the first giving a set of five antifeminist puzzles in the same cipher, the second the precepts beginning 'Fyrst arysse erly', *Index* 799; ff. 2^r–3^r, a poem on fortune-telling by dice, beginning at the second line, illustrated on f. 2^v by marginal sketches of various throws, *Supplement* 3694.3 (also some Latin words and glosses in another hand written vertically in the left margin of f. 2^r); ff. 3^v–4^v blank except for three names in different hands, and 'At Stuston', on f. 4^r; ff. 5^r–14^v, the legend of *Epotys*, *Index* 220; ff. 15^r–22^r, the play, *Index* 786; f. 22^v blank; ff. 23^r–26^v, a poem on the fifteen signs of Doomsday, incomplete, *Index* 1823.

F. 27^{rv}, Robert Melton's account, in his hand, for corn sold in 23 Henry VII.

Ff. 28^r–44^r in the first hand: ff. 28^r–38^r, a version of 'Owain Miles', *Index* 1767; f. 38^v blank; ff. 39^r–44^r, a life of St. Margaret, incomplete, *Index* 2673; f. 44^v blank.

Ff. 45^r–46^v, Melton's accounts of corn bought in 18 and 19 Henry VII; f. 47^r, brief receipt, undated, in a later hand.

Ff. 47^v–60^r in Melton's hand: ff. 47^v–50^r, 'the felson book' of

Stuston, recording payments of rent (see *M.E.D.* under *filsting*); f. 50ᵛ blank; ff. 51ʳ–59ʳ, instructions for the conduct of a court baron and a court leet; f. 59ᵛ–60ʳ, an agreement for the sale of barley to Melton in 19 Henry VII.

Ff. 60ᵛ–61ʳ, in a third and later hand, 'the boke for the holle taske of Sturston' (a record of payments); f. 61ᵛ–62ʳ blank.

Ff. 62ᵛ–67ᵛ in Melton's hand: f. 62ᵛ, accounts for 15 Henry VII; f. 63ʳ, accounts for 19 Henry VII; f. 63ᵛ, recipe for a medicine for jaundice; ff. 64ʳ–65ʳ, note of church dues at Stuston; ff. 65ᵛ–67ᵛ, accounts for 17 and 16 Henry VII.

Ff. 68ʳ–77ʳ in the first hand: legal forms of private deeds, mainly conveyances of property, concerning various places in Suffolk, Norfolk, Lincolnshire, and Cambridge, of dates from Edward III to 32 Henry VI. These were evidently meant as models to be imitated: the Latin text of each is given, then a close English translation.

Ff. 77ᵛ–78ᵛ in Melton's hand: f. 77ᵛ–78ʳ, accounts for 17 Henry VII; f. 78ᵛ, a list of prayers to be said; f. 79ʳ blank.

F. 79ᵛ in the first hand: a carol of the Annunciation, *Index* 3736.

F. 80ʳ in Melton's hand: directions for a trental.

F. 80ᵛ–81ʳ in the first hand: f. 80ᵛ, part of Lydgate's 'Pageant of Knowledge', *Index* 576, 3651, three stanzas, and two lines adapted from the envoy of Chaucer's *Steadfastness*; f. 81ʳ, a quatrain beginning 'I stond as styll as ony ston', *Supplement* 1367.9, followed by another beginning 'Lux ys leyd a downe' —an error for 'Lex . . .', *Index* and *Supplement* 1870; f. 81ᵛ, disconnected notes, mainly in Melton's hand, crudely written.

There is also, on the inside of the front parchment cover, a draft or copy of a Latin receipt dated 1 May 7 Henry VII, i.e. 1492. The hand appears to be that of the first scribe.[1]

It appears that the compiler began with the intention of collecting short moral pieces and trivial sayings as well as the edifying longer poems which are more appropriate company for the play; but even in the part of the book which is predominantly in the first hand he left many blank pages, and yet wrote other short pieces at the end of the book. The legal documents on ff. 68–77, though in the first hand, are strangely out of keeping with the poetical part of the manuscript, evidently meant for practical use

[1] See S. J. Kahrl, in *Theatre Notebook*, xxii (1968), 157–61; N. Davis, ibid., xxiii, no. 2 (1970).

in a way that 'commonplace-book' material usually is not. By the time they were written the original purpose of the collection would seem to have been abandoned, and an example set for Robert Melton's still more workaday exploitation of the empty pages. The documents are surely later than the poems, but the hand is not appreciably different and the interval cannot have been very long. The documents must have been written later than January 1454, but how much later cannot be judged because they are not a systematic series but a random collection going back to Edward III. It is likely that the first scribe had finished with the book before Melton began to use it for his accounts, the earliest of which is dated 15 Henry VII, 1499; and indeed the first scribe's spelling and other linguistic features are characteristic of the third rather than the fourth quarter of the century.

The play, like some of the other poems in the book, is written with some elaboration. It begins at the top of f. 15^r with a large decorated capital whose flourishes extend across the page and down it to the third line of writing from the foot. The whole of the first line is written in red, in large formal letters, with the ascenders of *d*, *h*, and the two *t*s extended upwards in braided flourishes. The word *Fyrst* beginning line 6 also has a large initial, though much less conspicuous than the opening one; and the first letter of each line is touched with red. On each page throughout the play ascenders in the top line are thickened and flourished. Speakers' names are written in the left margin opposite the beginning of each speech, and the first word or two of the speech is underlined in red. So are a large number of words within the line throughout the play, but the principle on which these are chosen is not apparent: some of them are obviously important, especially names and designations of relationship such as *wyffe* 7, *chyld* 12, *Fader* 14, *son* 15, all of which are underlined almost every time they occur; but also marked are *lyvelod* 4, *erth* 6, *creaturys* 8, *sacryfyce* 39, 42, *offryng* 49, *best* 52, *hyll* 56, *lyffe* 81, *blood* 97, *fagot* 116, *handys* 120, *harte* 121, *backe* 130, and many others equally miscellaneous. Some of them are perhaps important enough to merit special emphasis, but it is not clear that they are more so than other words that are not underlined. Rhymes are bracketed on the first page only, at the foot of which line 30 is written outside the brackets to the right. Subsequent stanzas are not distinguished in any way. Some of the short lines (55, 113, 146, 177, 232, 268, 352, 363, 438) are extended by space-fillers. At the end *Finis* is written to the right, opposite the last line. There is no punctuation.

Though the play has been reprinted (sometimes with modifications) at least fourteen times, the text appears never to have been collated with the manuscript since Miss Toulmin Smith's editions, so that all the succeeding copies depend ultimately on hers. Her first edition, in *Anglia*, vii, was remarkably accurate though not quite flawless; her second, in *A Common-place Book*, suffered from a sprinkling of printer's errors. Manly, in printing the play in *Specimens*, i. 41–57, based his text on both these editions and when they differed he preferred the former. He also set out the text more regularly in stanzas, and made several important emendations mainly to restore rhyme. Waterhouse similarly took his text from Miss Toulmin Smith, but with unfortunate precision reproduced a number of the errors of her later edition. He adopted some of Manly's emendations, but his version is on the whole distinctly less accurate and obscures the form of a number of stanzas. His edition was followed in most of the later reprints, for example by Adams in *Chief Pre-Shakespearean Dramas*, pp. 117–24; Adams took over some corrections from Manly which he described as emendations though several of them are true readings derived from Miss Toulmin Smith's first edition. The text in this volume rests on a collation with the manuscript while it was at Ipswich, later checked from microfilm. Many emendations have been adopted, mainly from Manly and Holthausen, for the sake of rhyme, but some obviously defective passages have resisted correction.

A remarkable feature of this play, often discussed since Miss Toulmin Smith pointed it out, is that for over two hundred of its 465 lines, and those in the central dialogue between Abraham and Isaac, it is closely similar to the Chester play on the same subject (ed. H. Deimling, E.E.T.S., E.S. lxii (1892), no. IV). The similarity is partly in the development of the dialogue in a way for which the Biblical narrative provides no model, but largely also in widespread identity of expression and of rhyme-words. The passages concerned are Brome 105–315 and Chester 229–420; most of the Chester text Waterhouse printed below his Brome text, but this has been omitted in the present edition because the Chester edition is readily available. The nature of the relation between the two has been much debated and agreement cannot be said to have been reached. For instance, Hardin Craig in 1955 still held that 'the Brome Abraham and Isaac is obviously a skilfully developed version of the Chester Abraham and Isaac',[1] though the contrary arguments of J. Burke Severs ten years earlier appear to be decisive.[2] Severs showed that the Brome text is the more coherently developed, and concluded that the Chester version must descend from a corrupt form of the original that lies behind it. More detailed work on the language of the two plays might contribute to understanding of their relation. For instance, corresponding to Brome 149–50,

> Wy bere ȝe ȝowre sword drawyn soo?
> Off ȝowre contenaunce I have mych wonder,

Chester 277–80 has

> Father, tell me of this case,
> why you your sword drawen hase,
> and beare yt naked in this place;
> thereof I have great wonder.

The word-order of line 278 is awkward, evidently dictated by the rhyme; and the rhyme-form *has(e)*, common elsewhere in Chester, is foreign to the dialect of Brome.

Verse. There is some uncertainty about the verse-form of parts of the Brome play. It begins regularly with five-line stanzas, and there are also many immediately apparent quatrains with alternate rhyme; but after these have been counted there remain many lines which can be grouped into stanzas only by assuming an unusually wide variety of pattern. Rhyme is obviously an essential feature of any stanza scheme, yet there are many places in which an expected rhyme does not occur: e.g. *glad* 29 is in rhyming position with *rest* and *best*; *dysmasyd* and *plesyd* 93–4 with *seyd*; *bere* 130 with *schuld*; *on too* 152 with *wonder*; *me* 166 with *don*; *goo* 402 with *ȝynd*. (Occasionally a bad rhyme may be regarded as a possible assonance, as *grace*: *wysse*: *arysse* 333–5.) In such places one or other of the original words must have been altered at some stage of transmission, and though it is sometimes easy enough to see which it is and to restore the pattern by a simple emendation, in other passages no such plain substitution will suffice and the alteration seems to have gone beyond the single rhyme-word (e.g. 443–6). The scribe of the present manuscript was evidently insufficiently interested in preserving correct rhymes; or perhaps he lost heart

[1] *English Religious Drama*, pp. 309–10.
[2] *M.P.* xlii (1944–5), 137–51.

when confronted by so many irregularities—he marked the rhymes correctly in the first five stanzas, but in the sixth, which is of different form, he bracketed *rest* with *glad*; after this, which is at the foot of the first page, he marked no rhymes at all.

The matter is important beyond the technique of the play itself; it concerns the relation of the Brome to the Chester play, which is almost regularly written in eight-line tail-rhyme stanzas. In particular, Miss M. D. Fort held that the occasional triple rhymes in Brome were taken over from the tail-rhyme of Chester.[1] But this view ignores the occurrence of triple rhyme in other stanza-forms, notably the nine-line and thirteen-line forms rhyming (*abab*)-*ababcdddc* which are used, for example, in 280 stanzas of *The Castle of Perseverance*.[2] Though the range of stanza-forms to be found in the Brome play is unusual, considerable variety within a single play is common enough; many examples occur in all the Macro plays and in the *Ludus Coventriae*, and it may be significant that these texts are placed by their language in east midland areas from which the Brome compiler might well have acquired his exemplar.

When allowances have been made for defective transmission, it appears that the Brome author used stanzas of four, five, six, seven, eight, nine, and twelve lines, most of the lines having four stresses but some tail lines in the longer stanzas three. The most frequent form has four lines, rhyming *abab*; there are 25 such quatrains well preserved: 33–40, 59–62, 72–5, 101–8, 133–40, 153–64, 169–72, 181–4, 194–7, 208–11, 235–54, 293–6, 316–27, 456–9, and with emendation four others: 129–32, 149–52, 165–8, 443–6 (emendation uncertain); and another which as it stands rhymes *abba*, 273–6. Next in importance is the five-line stanza with which the play opens, rhyming *abaab*; there are 13 such stanzas: 1–25, 76–90, 198–207, 306–15, 353–7, and with emendation four others: 91–100, 348–52, 398–402; and one other group of five lines which does not fit the rhyme pattern and is presumably defective, 337–41, *ababc*. Six-line stanzas are few and not well preserved; yet they seem to be a genuine form. There are five in all: four apparently intended to rhyme *ababba*: 41–6, 116–21, 383–8, 460–5, though all need emendation and two of them elude it; one rhymes *aabccb*, 342–7. Seven-line stanzas are more regular, six in all: three rhyming

[1] *P.M.L.A.* xli (1926), 832–9.
[2] See *The Macro Plays*, ed. M. Eccles, E.E.T.S. 262 (1969), p. xv.

ababcbc, 109–15, 122–8, 212–18, and with emendation two others, 26–32, 228–34; one might be intended to rhyme *aabbccc*, 428–34, though as it stands two of the rhymes are only assonances and the other depends on the transposition of a manuscript line. Eight-line stanzas mostly rhyme *ababcddc*, the *c*-line usually having three stresses. Of a total of nine there are five such: 173–80, 277–84, 367–74, 403–18, and with emendation two others, 285–92, 435–42; one, with simple emendation, rhymes *abaabcbc*, 375–82, and another, with transposition of a line, in the same way; 141–8. Nine-line stanzas are the most difficult to identify. There appear to be eleven in all, but only four of them are reasonably well preserved: three rhyme *ababcdddc* in the familiar way: 63–71, 219–27, 447–55, and the same pattern seems to have been corrupted in 185–93 (emendation uncertain), 255–63, 264–72, 297–305, 328–36, 419–27; one rhymes *abaabcddc*, 389–97, which seems to lie behind 358–66 also. The single twelve-line stanza must rhyme *ababab-abcddc*, 47–58, but here again the last rhyme has been spoilt.

Some of the more complex stanzas can be seen to mark a particular stage in the action—the unique twelve-line one gives Abraham's speech promising an offering to God; the first of those with nine lines gives the conclusion of the Angel's command and Abraham's acknowledgement of it; the Doctor begins his epilogue with an eight-line stanza; the first of those with seven lines concludes the opening scene between Abraham and Isaac. On the other hand, it cannot fairly be claimed that every change of versification is designed to draw attention to an outstanding passage, and much of the variety must have been introduced for its own sake.

Language. In this play rhymes are often less serviceable as a guide to pronunciation than they should be. As the previous section shows, a number of expected rhymes fail because of the substitution of another word for one of the original pair or group. In addition there are many rhymes which, though not destroyed altogether, are defective because an alternative form of one of the words has been substituted. It is sometimes impossible to know which of the forms as they stand correctly represents the original, since either could be justified. For instance, the scribe's usual spelling of 'well' is *wyll*, which suggests raising of the vowel (see p. lvi above), but it rhymes on 'feel' spelt *fell* at 17, 38, 86 (also on *knell* 'kneel'), and on 'deal' spelt *dell* at 258, 409, in which the spelling seems to

indicate shortening of the vowel but not raising; either /i/ or /e/,
in all these words, may have been the sound intended. Similarly
'speed' is spelt *spyd* 376 rhyming on *dred*, but *sped* 389 rhyming on
dede, sede. The verb 'give' is *ȝyffe* 368 rhyming on *leve* 'live'; an
acceptable rhyme could depend on either *ȝeve* or *live*. Again, *hand*
213 rhymes on *lond, stond*, 296 on *wythstond*; such words are more
often spelt with *o*—e.g. *sond, wythstond, lond* 68–70, *sond, hond*
146–8—but there are no rhymes which certify the original forms.
In some places the original is determinable from a rhyming word:
erthe 76 rhyming on *steryd, aferd*, 220 and 286 rhyming on *sword*,
which has an alternative *swerd*, must have been substituted for
erd(e); the rhyme of *can* 100 on *son* indicates that the original was
con with the vowel /u/ of the older plural; that of *schowyd* 435 on
lewyd implies the alternative *schewyd*. Such blemishes, and the
many completely spoilt rhymes, show that the scribe, or a prede-
cessor, did not greatly concern himself to copy his original precisely or to represent sounds accurately or consistently; and it is
therefore impossible to place much confidence in the phonetic
significance of spellings which cannot be checked by any rhyme.
A number of spellings are nevertheless of interest in themselves.

> Final unstressed -*e* is shown to have been lost in the scribe's
> pronunciation by his frequent failure to write it where it is
> historically in place, and also by occasional words—not very
> many for this date—in which he wrote *e* unhistorically: e.g.
> *wyffe* 7, 84, *wysse* 106, *queke* 140, *eyne* 221, *fleysse* 223,
> *nedysse* 228, *pesse* 339. It is shown by rhyme to have been lost
> in the original: e.g. the nouns *gren* 67, *sted* 144, the adj.
> *myld* 373, the adv. *longe* 232, the infins. *won* 12, *fell* 20, 40,
> 89, *asay* 35, *wythstond* 69, *kyll* 77, *dey* 251, and many others.
> The reflex of OE. *ā* is written *o*: *sore, more* 224–5 rhyme on
> *werefore, woo* 309 on *doo, lore* 412 on *before, euermo* 433 on *to*.
> The reflex of OE. *a* before a nasal not in a lengthening group is
> written *a* in *thanke* 318; *rame* 328 rhymes on *Abraham*. In a
> lengthening group the spelling varies between *o* and *a* as noted
> above, and rhyme is never decisive.
> The reflex of OE. *ē*, as noted above, is sometimes written *y*,
> especially in *wyll* 'well' but also in *spyd* 376 and (a special
> case) *byn* 71; but these rhyme on words written with *e*. Out-
> side rhyme is *swyt* 350. Such spellings with *y* are conspicuous

in the scribe's other work in this manuscript; e.g. in *Epotys* 13 he writes *knys* 'knees' and in *Owain* 261 *tryn* 'trees'.

The reflex of OE. *ēo* is written *e*, and *forbede* 196 rhymes on *dede*, which in turn rhymes on *sped*, *sede* 389–92, but on *stede* (v.) 278. The reflex of OE. *ēg* is written *ey*, but *eyne* 221 rhymes on *fyn*, *dey* 251 on *hardly* and 279 on *lye* 'jacere'.

The reflex of OE. *y̆* is normally written *y*: *hyll(e)* 41, 56, 237, 415 rhymes on *wyll* (n.), 175 on *spyll*; *mynd* 287 rhymes on *wynd* (v.). But 'did' is written *ded* 194.

Spellings not confirmed by rhyme include the following:

ar appears for earlier *er* in *hart* 2, 83, 93, etc., *ȝard* 170, *ward* 'world' 238, *warke* (n.) 278, 404, (v.) 302. This type of spelling is characteristic of the scribe; e.g. in *Epotys* he writes *warke* 155 and 218 though it rhymes on *kyrke* and *chyrch*.

e appears sporadically for earlier *i* in *medyll-* 34, *heder* 105, 359 (both rhyming on *togeder*), *hethyr(e)* 352, 355, *queke*, *qweke* 140, 386 (beside *qwyke* 141, 373).

The initial consonant of 'give' is written *ȝ* in *ȝeve* 50, 215, *ȝeffe* 254, 402, 433, *ȝyffe* 115, 368, *ȝoffe* 3; 'again', 'against' are *aȝeyn* 48, *aȝens* 80, 418. Some words which etymologically begin with a front vowel have *ȝ* or *y* prefixed: **ȝevyn* 'even' 110, *ȝynd* 'end' 399, *yeþed* 334.

The initial sound of 'cheer' and 'change' is written *sch* in *schereys* 18, *schonge* 179. This is also the regular way of writing the initial sound of 'shall' and 'should' (e.g. 43, 54), never *x*, though the scribe often writes *xall* and *xuld(e)* in the other poems and the legal documents in the manuscript.

The initial sound of words earlier beginning with *hw-* is usually written *w*: *wych(e)* 17, 199, *wer* 19, 42, etc., *wethere* 36 (beside *whether* 44), *wat* 52, 168, *wy* 136, 149, *wan* 204, *wyll(e)* 227, 377; but *qw* is used in *qwyll* 462.

Words containing earlier *-ht* are written usually with *gth*, sometimes with *t*: *mygth* 192, *nygth* 23, *rygth* 110, 182, etc.; *nogth* 171, *nowgth* 143, *wrogth* 404 (rhyming on *nott*); *allmyty* 51, 384; *browt* 367, *nowt* 337, *owt* 169, *thowt* 339. In addition, *-gth* is a spelling for *t* in *smygth* 300, 337, 338, and also in *hydygth* 165, *fyndygth* 300, 304—as *th* also is in *smyth* 288, *senth* 317. (On the other hand, *-g-* is merely superfluous in *lygth* 303, *degth* 310.) Taken together these spellings show that the fricative before *t* had been lost in the scribe's pronunciation.

In unstressed inflexional syllables the vowel is usually written *y*: e.g. *madyst* 6, *schereys* 18, *comandyth* 60, *grantyd* 11, *drawyn* 149; *preyrys* 104, *monys* 269, *sorys* 435, *chyldryn* 16, 32, 198; *nedysse* 228, *onys* 201, 371; rarely *i*, as *mayist* 316. So also in other unstressed syllables: *exampyll* 45, *owyn* 97, *heuyn* 120, etc., *sythyn* 178. But when the final consonant is *r* the vowel is often written *e*: *eyther* 446, *fayer(e)* 18, 103, 218, etc., *moder* 423, *offere* 281, *other* 198, 210, *suffere* 284, *wethere* 36, *wyther* 162; though *y* also appears in *fadyr* 21, 210, *ʒowyre* 180, *hethyre* 355, *slendyr* 126, *togedyr* 227, *watyr* 455. The only case of *u* is *dystempurst* 263. The quality of the vowel of *brerys* 324 (where the ending is written with the usual abbreviation) is shown by the rhyme with *her ys*. The rhyme of *kneys* 176 with the infin. *chese* shows that in this word the ending was not pronounced as a separate syllable.

The following are the main features of verbal inflexion:

Pres. indic. 2 sg. (and past sg. of weak verbs) normally ends in -*st*: *hast* 3, etc., *lovyst* 61, *makyst* 262, *madyst* 6; but *breke* 156, *grevyd* 270. In 3 sg. the ending -*th* is frequent: *comandyth* 50, *brekyth* 127, *begynnyth* 147, *reysyth* 299, *standyth* 324, *hath* 340; but -*t* appears in *lovyt* 258, *knowyt* 320, *schoyt* 440, *weryt* 464, and no ending in *love* 38, *make* 283. There is a single case of -*s* in *schereys* 18. In three places the ending is written *d*: *lovyd* 44, *brekyd* 152 (where *d* is written over another letter), *begynnyd* 208. This is evidently an alternative spelling for *th*, as Manly recognized (except in *brekyd*, which Miss Toulmin Smith had read, defensibly, *brekys*); it is the reverse of the repeated *erthe* where rhyme requires *erd(e)* (76, 220, 286). Since these spellings are eccentric, and mislead a reader by suggesting a past tense, they are here emended to -*th*. The pres. pl. is without ending.

Infin. is usually without ending (often verified by rhyme, e.g. *won* 12, *fell* 20, *be* 42, *doo* 111), but monosyllables occasionally have -*n*: *don* 56, 85, 293, *go(o)n* 420, 422, 429, 431; none of these is certified by a good rhyme, but 420 and 429 require the *n* in assonance. Consequently Holthausen's emendation of 444, supplying *slayn*, is formally acceptable. The unstressed form of 'have' is *a* in 73, 74, 192, 193.

Past participles of strong and anomalous verbs sometimes have -*n*: *byn* 71 and *slayn* 187 in rhyme, also *byn* 415, *don(ne)* 54,

112, 168, 265 7, *drawyn* 149; but more often not: *doo* 308 and *goo* 201 in rhyme, also *be* 72, 74, *draw* 154, *forbore* 73, *ʒoffe* 3, etc. The prefix *i-* never appears.

Of the personal pronouns, in 2 pl. *ʒe* and *ʒow* are regularly used; in 3 pl. the nom. is *they* 46, oblique *them* 8, 450, possessive *hyr* 450.

The vocabulary contains a few words of predominantly northern or north-east midland currency: *barn* 106, *ʒon* 123, 328, *bon* 131, probably *dede* 280, *gayn* 331; *kerche* 285 and *ʒyn* 351, 353, 415 seem to be especially East Anglian.

The scribe's orthography, in such matters as the use of *y* in *wyll* 'well', *e* in *queke*, *w* in *wer*, etc., *gth* in *rygth*, etc., and of *y* in unstressed syllables, is fully in keeping with the association of the manuscript with northern Suffolk; but one or two forms, notably *ward* 'world' and *warke* 'work', are characteristic rather of more northerly areas. These are the scribe's forms, not (or not necessarily) the author's, for they appear in other poems in the manuscript which have no claim to the same authorship. The features shown by rhyme to have been in the original text do not depart from the ordinary forms of the east midlands. The complete loss of unstressed *-e* in this region probably indicates the fifteenth century, but to allow for the extensive corruption which the text has clearly undergone the date of composition should probably be placed early in the century.

VI. THE PLAY OF THE SACRAMENT

Manuscript. Trinity College, Dublin, F. 4. 20, Catalogue no. 652, ff. 338ʳ–356ʳ. The manuscript is a composite volume containing a number of miscellaneous texts of the sixteenth and seventeenth centuries entirely unrelated to the play, which is the sixth item in it. The book belonged to John Madden, President of the Royal College of Physicians of Ireland, who died in 1703. His manuscripts were bought after his death by John Stearne, Bishop of Clogher, who presented them to Trinity College in 1741. The Madden manuscripts are catalogued in Edward Bernard's *Catalogi Librorum Manuscriptorum Angliæ et Hiberniæ* (1697), vol. ii, part 2, pp. 57–60, in which the present manuscript is no. 1666. (Among its contents the play is not mentioned.) This manuscript remained without foliation until the present numbering was added by Mr. William O'Sullivan in 1958.

Folios 338 to 357 (the last blank, unnumbered), which contain only the play, have now been removed from the volume and are kept separately, unbound, in a paper folder. They are of paper, in two quires of 8 leaves followed by one quire of 4. There is a water-mark of a hand with a star-shaped flower above the middle finger, and with the figure 3 and a pattern of lines on the wrist. It is not identical with any of Briquet's numerous illustrations of this type of mark, but the pattern on the wrist brings it nearest to his no. 11388. This example is dated 1546; most of his others are from the middle two decades of the sixteenth century. Briquet observed that the type became commonplace in the north-west of France; the earliest specimen he knew was of 1526, though simpler forms of the hand-and-star mark appear in Italian and French papers of the fifteenth century (e.g. nos. 10706 ff., 11088 ff., 11134 ff.) and also in the manuscripts of the *Ludus Coventriae* (the interpolated folios) and of *Mankind*.[1] The size of the page is about 8.4×6 inches, written space about 7.5×5 inches except for the speakers' names. These quires were evidently a separate entity earlier in their history, for the recto of f. 338 is so soiled and rubbed that it must have been for some time the unprotected outer leaf.

The play begins without heading at the top of f. 338ʳ. The pages are not ruled and the number of lines varies greatly, from 24 to 34 with a preference for 28 to 30, excluding speech-prefixes. These prefixes are mostly in the left margin approximately opposite the beginning of the speech, but if one happens to come at the top of a page it is centred. Stage directions are written across the page, inset slightly further than the speeches; and they and the speech-prefixes are usually lightly covered with yellow crayon. After each speech and stage direction a line is ruled across the page. Rhymes are carefully bracketed up to f. 343ʳ, but after that only irregularly. In tail-rhyme stanzas the short lines are written to the right.

Three hands can be distinguished in the play (not two, as Water-house said). The first scribe, A, wrote from the beginning to the first half of the eleventh line of writing on f. 338ᵛ, line 39 of the pro-logue. The second, B, began with the word *many* in that line and

---

[1] C. M. Briquet, *Les Filigranes*, iii (1907), p. 573; 'Main généralement lacée au poignet, aux quatre doigts serrés, le pouce très écarté'; *Ludus Coventriae*, ed. Block, p. xii; *Macro Plays*, ed. Eccles, p. xxxvii.

continued until two-thirds of the way down f. 341ʳ (end of l. 188).
A then resumed and continued to the fourth line on f. 343ᵛ (end of
l. 326), when the third scribe, C, took over, writing the short line
327 to the right opposite A's last rhyme-bracket (see Pl. II).
C continued to the foot of f. 346ʳ (l. 484). A then resumed and went
on to the seventh line on f. 349ʳ (end of l. 644), after which C took
over again and wrote to the end of the play, including the final notes.
At the end of these the initials *R C* are written as a monogram at
the foot of the page, below a blank scroll. The division of labour
was thus: A, 1–39, 189–326, 485–644 (a total of 336½ lines); B, 39–
188 (149½ lines); C, 327–484, 645–1007 (521 lines), and the notes.
In addition, C wrote all the speech-prefixes in A's last section
except *Malcus* 493. A's hand is small, of essentially secretary type,
with the lines well spaced. He began the play neatly and carefully,
but after the first page rapidly lost regularity of form and layout;
his later sections are hasty and untidy. B's hand is not very different
in general character, but has more variety of letter-formation and
is more upright and lighter in weight. C's is older-fashioned, a
fluent rounded cursive with prominent bows and descenders,
larger than the other two hands but with the lines closer together;
it makes a more professional impression than the others. Hands A
and B seem to be of the early sixteenth century, and if Briquet's
dating is to be trusted the watermark suggests that they were
writing well on in the century. C must obviously be contemporary
in spite of its somewhat earlier air.

The play was first edited by Whitley Stokes in *Transactions of the
Philological Society*, 1860–1 (Appendix, pp. 101–52). His text,
which was divided into speeches with lines indented to follow
the rhymes, was accurate in all but a few details. Manly used it,
collated with the manuscript, in *Specimens* (1897), i. 239–76, but
introduced division into stanzas. Waterhouse, in turn, based his
edition on Manly's text, 'collated with the manuscript, and with
Whitley Stokes's version', but he made many mistakes and broke
up the eight-line stanzas into quatrains and the nine-line ones into
groups of four and five lines. The play was printed again by Adams
in *Chief Pre-Shakespearean Dramas* (1924), the text based on
Waterhouse collated with Manly and Stokes, the stanzaic divisions
following Manly. The present text rests on several new collations
by Professor Dunning and me, and some new readings are offered.[1]

[1] The most important is *Conuiuium* 840, previously read, unintelligibly,

The stanza divisions are generally the same as Manly's, but a few differ slightly. To simplify reference in the glossary the lines are numbered consecutively, as in Stokes's edition, from the beginning of the prologue to the end of the play. In the play itself the numbers are therefore higher by exactly 80 lines than Manly's or Waterhouse's.

The Legend. *The Play of the Sacrament* is the only thing of its kind in medieval English. It is concerned neither with Biblical narrative nor with the lives of saints, but with an extraordinary legend of the desecration of the host by Jews and their ultimate conversion by the miracles that follow. Stories of Jewish outrages upon consecrated wafers are known on the Continent from the fourteenth century onwards. The commonest version sets the events in Paris in the year 1290: a poor Christian woman anxious to recover a gown pledged to a Jewish moneylender promises to bring him the wafer she receives at communion; when he receives it he stabs it and submits it to many tortures; it bleeds, but is not destroyed; the Jew's family, appalled at his frenzied conduct, reveal what he is doing and he is arrested and burnt; his wife and children are baptized. The essentials of this story appear in Italy as early as Villani's *Cronaca*, written before 1348,[1] and are still repeated in *L'Histoire de l'Hostie Miraculeuze*, by a Carmelite named Fr. Leon, printed in Paris in 1664—a translation of which William Hone published in London in 1822 under the title *The Miraculous Host Tortured by the Jew, under the reign of Philip the Fair in 1290*. The *Journal d'un bourgeois de Paris* records that on 15 May 1444 a solemn procession was held in Paris to commemorate the miracle of the host.[2]

Dramatic treatments of this theme are recorded in Italy, the Netherlands, and France. For example, in 1473, as part of a festival held in Rome in honour of Leonore of Aragon, Florentine actors performed a play of the miracle of the host; about 1500 a Dutch play, 1,325 lines long, was written by one Smeken and

---

Dominum. Professor Dunning observes that the reference is to the well-known hymn to the Blessed Sacrament, 'O Sacrum Convivium', which was originally the antiphon of the Magnificat for the Vespers of the Feast of Corpus Christi.

[1] Stokes gave this and other references in the introduction to his edition of the play, p. 103 n. An early manuscript of the *Cronaca* contains an illustration of the poor woman handing over the wafer in exchange for her gown; see L. Magnani, *La Cronaca Figurata di Giovanni Villani* (Rome, 1936), pl. xl.

[2] L. Petit de Julleville, *Les Mystères*, ii (Paris, 1880), 193–4.

acted at Breda—but it differs in that the persecutor is not a Jew but a doubting Christian;[1] an Italian play embodying essentially the early version of the story was printed several times in the sixteenth century;[2] and a French play is preserved in two sixteenth-century editions. Since neither of the French texts is dated it is uncertain which is the earlier; the longer title is *Le jeu et mystere de la sainte hostie par personnages*, printed for Jehan Bonfons. Under the title are the lines

> Lysez ce fait grans et petis
> Comment ung faulx et mauldit juifz
> Lapida moult cruellement
> De l'autel le sainct sacrement.

This play, 1,590 lines long, extends the number of characters to twenty-six.[3]

Though the central device of attempted destruction of the host is the same in the English play as in the surviving Continental versions, the setting, most of the characters, and the whole tone of the conclusion are different—the action is placed in 'the forest of Aragon, in the famous cité Eraclea' in 1461, instead of Paris in 1290; the betrayer of the host is a rich merchant eager for further gain, not a poor woman in debt; the Jew's wife and children play no part, but he has four accomplices; in the end the Jews are baptized, not burnt; even the merchant is forgiven, under penance —in the Italian play the poor woman also repents and is pardoned, but in the French version she too comes to a bad end. The English playwright evidently had sources which cannot now be identified, and how much is his own we cannot tell. Miss F. E. Barns traces the use of *Jonathas* as the name of the Jew to a legend known in Belgium in 1370, and suggests that the change of scene from Paris to Aragon was made in the text played in Rome before Leonore of Aragon in 1473, which the English writer may have seen or heard about. She suggests also that this version 'may have included conversion of the Jew at the end'.[4] No copy of a text of this form appears to have survived. The introduction to the printed *Rap-*

[1] W. Creizenach, *Geschichte des neueren Dramas*, i (Halle, 1893), 332, 340–1.

[2] *La Rappresentatione d'uno Miracolo del Corpo di Christo.* I have used the Florence edition (*nuouamente ristampata*) of 1555.

[3] Petit de Julleville, ii. 574–6; see further Craig, *Religious Drama*, pp. 325–6.

[4] 'The Background and Sources of *The Croxton Play of the Sacrament*', Chicago dissertation, 1926. For discussion of the special motive of the English play see Cecilia Cutts in *M.L.Q.* v (1944), 45–60.

presentatione sets the scene in Paris as usual; the treatment of the outrages on the host is much simpler than in the English play—the Jew fries the host in a pan and stabs it, but the sequel is neither so fearsome nor so dramatic: the Jew does not go mad, and the reproachful Christ does not appear. The English play also stands alone in incorporating a scene of comic buffoonery between a quack doctor and his boy (525–652) which is clearly influenced by folk-play conventions, and has indeed been thought, with good reason, to be an interpolation into a text originally wholly serious.[1] No close analogue to this episode has been discovered.

Verse. Most of the play is written in four-stress lines arranged in quatrains with alternate rhyme, many of which are linked by rhyme to form eight-line stanzas, *ababbcbc*, though a considerable number remain detached. Thus in the prologue there are five eight-line stanzas (1–16, 29–36, 45–52, 61–8), and seven separate quatrains (17–28, 37–44, 53–60). The last twelve lines (69–80) are best taken as a single stanza, *ababbcbccdcd*. In the play itself eight-line stanzas and single quatrains appear in 81–248, 258–73, 283–322, 332–67, 377–488, 653–716, 742–813, 826–1003. Latin lines sometimes form part of the stanza scheme (e.g. 749, 753), but sometimes stand outside it (e.g. 717–18, 741). In a few places it is possible that linking of a different kind was intended: both the quatrains in 37–44 and in 968–75 have the same *a*-rhyme and could be regarded as eight-line stanzas *ababacac*; in the quatrain 270–3 the *b*-rhyme repeats the *a*-rhyme of the previous quatrain, and also of the following nine-line stanza; the *a*-rhyme of the quatrain 653–6 and the *b*-rhyme of 657–60 repeat the *c*-rhyme of the seven-line stanza 646–52. But some or all of these may occur by accident rather than design. The sequence of three quatrains 719–30 is surely intended to form a twelve-line stanza; after the Latin introduction it presents the passionate appeal of Jesus to the Jews which is the turning-point of the play. This speech continues with the only ten-line stanza, 731–40, *ababbccccb*. Another twelve-line stanza is used in 814–25.

In the main action of the play there are in addition four nine-line stanzas of the form *ababcdddc*, the fifth and ninth lines having three stresses: 249–57 (emended), 274–82, 323–31, 368–76. All these occur at significant points in the drama: the first marks the

---

[1] Craig, *Religious Drama*, pp. 326–7. For the Doctor in folk plays see Chambers, *Mediaeval Stage*, i. 213, etc.; *The English Folk-Play* (Oxford, 1933).

introduction of Aristorius to the Jews; the second opens Jonathas's bargaining; the third depicts Aristorius's acceptance of the plan; the fourth comes just as he has stolen the host. There is another group of distinctive stanzas in the scene with the cauldron, in which Jonathas finally goes mad: three are eight-line tail-rhyme stanzas of the usual form, *aaabcccb*, 489–96 and 504–19; the intervening one as it stands has seven lines with only two rhymes, *aaabaab*, and it may be that a sixth line with the *a*-rhyme has been lost—there are no other stanzas of this form in the play. There is a single five-line stanza just before the arrival of the Doctor and his boy at 520–4, *ababb*. The closing quatrain, 1004–7, stands apart in having only one rhyme throughout.

The episode of the Doctor introduces greater metrical variety. It is mainly in the tail-rhyme stanza which had appeared for the first time in the previous scene (525–96 and 622–45). In 597–600 there is a single four-line stanza of unusual shape, with a three-stress last line and rhyming *abba*, then a unique group of seven lines, *aaaaaab* (601–7), then fourteen lines in rhyming couplets, still with four stresses but with an excess of weak syllables (608–21). The scene is closed, with the dismissal of the pair, in a seven-line stanza *ababbcc*, 646–52.

Most of the variation, therefore, is clearly associated with stages in the development of the action. The author's interest in form is further shown by the frequent use of alliteration to give weight to particular passages, such as Jonathas's description of his jewels in 161–72, or the plotting of his accomplices in 209–22, and especially in the *tour de force* of his speech in 95 ff., where four lines alliterate in alphabetical order and the next fifteen do so in part. It seems likely that there has been some scribal dislocation here, for the order of the string of names is immaterial and it ought not to have been beyond the writer's powers to maintain the alphabetical sequence.

Language. Though the three hands differ in style, their systems of spelling are in general similar. All the scribes use most of the common abbreviations, C rather more freely than the others. Three problems call for comment: (1) A and C often add to final minim letters an elaborately curved superscript finial (several examples in Pl. II). This frequently serves as an abbreviation for -*m* or -*n*, as, for example, in *meu'* 404 for Latin *meum*, or *passyou'* 38, 933, rhyming on *doune*, *down*. But in the last example the -*n* of *down* has the same finial, and so have many other occurrences of indubitable *m* or *n*. In this position it is evidently a meaningless flourish. The mark is therefore treated in this edition as rhyme or word-structure demand; if it is inessential it is ignored. C used two other superscript marks in some respects similar: one a stroke, generally almost straight, which has the usual function of replacing *m* or *n*: so clearly, for example, in *myn* 368, *commandementys* 729— this is seen in *commyth* in Pl. II, line 12; the other often with a rising curve and always with a hook below to the left, as in the last word in Pl. II, line 9. The latter is often used above a group of minims, and might be supposed to indicate an additional *m* or *n*; but often this cannot be so, either because the letter is written double already, as *gonne* 353, or because it would not be doubled in the position in question, as *judgement* 434. The mark is evidently therefore not an abbreviation, but a means, sporadically used, of distinguishing *n* from *u*. (2) After the digraph *ou*, in C *ow*, a superior *r* is often written where either *-er* or *-r* might be intended. When the possessive adjectives of the first and second persons plural are written in full they are occasionally spelt *(y)ouer*, *(y)ower*, as 10, 66, 133, 228, but oftener with *-our* or *-owr* only, as 37, 65, 66 (2nd), 134, 143, 229; and the latter form is more appropriate to words such as *langow*^r and *socow*^r 819, 821. It therefore seems best to treat the superior *r* in this position as representing simple *r*, but to expand it to *wr* in the small number of places in C where it follows *o* alone: e.g. *yo*^r expanded to *yowr* 858, 860, 861. (3) All three scribes, but B proportionately more than the others, indicate the inflexion of the possessive and the plural of nouns by the usual loop attached to the final letter of the word. The scribes differ in spelling the vowel of unstressed inflexional syllables, including possessives and plurals when they are written in full. (There are no important variations according to the following consonant.) A uses *e*, *y*, and occasionally *i*, the others *e* and *y* only. In A, *y* and *i* together are approximately as numerous as *e* or very slightly preferred to it, and in B the same is true of *y*; the number of forms concerned in each section is just under fifty. But in C, where the total is over 150, more than 130 have *y*; and this quality of vowel is confirmed by the rhymes of *Jewys* 719 with *blysse* and 844 with *thys*, and of *lawys* 763 with Latin *meis*. In expanding the abbreviation in all three sections, therefore, *-ys* is generalized. Some of the effect of differences among the scribes can readily be seen by comparing lines 932–47 (C) with the slightly altered version of them given in the prologue, 37–52 (A and B).

All the scribes use *sh* for /ʃ/ (medially occasionally *ssh*), and all use *y* in the function of *þ* though only sporadically and in short words such as *þe*, *þat*, *þer*, especially when abbreviated; *ʒ* is used only by C, and very rarely—perhaps three times in all. All spell the reflex of OE. *a* before a lengthening group predominantly *o*: A, *hond*, *lond*, *-stond* 500, 503, 625, *strong*, *hong*, *long* 489–91; B, *-stond* 86, *wond* 88, *among* 105; C, *hond* 430, (-)*stond* 662, 918, *among* 878, *long* 468, *strong* 466, 876. A and C occasionally write *a*: A, *handys* 219, *hange* 264; C, *hand* 770, *hangyd* 447; the number of opportunities in B is too small to be significant. No rhymes exist which would indicate the form of the original. For earlier /e:/ the spelling *y* is occasional in A, *kype* 221, *hyre* 'here' 631; B, *appyred* 47 (but *appere* 63), *pryst* 133; C, *pryst* 841 s.d.; cf. *swymfull* 809. But C writes *fere* 'fire' 684, which is also implied by rhyme in 694. All occasionally have *e* for earlier short /i/, or sometimes perhaps /y/: A, *mekyll* 13, *sekyrly* 262, *wet* 268, *sleppe* 526, rhyming on *-shyppe*; B, *ded* 42, 44, *mekyll* 62, *wette* 147 (but *wytte* 139), *well* 122, *delygently* 126; C, *preuely* 390, *ded* 735, *velanye* 735, *thether* 847, *besy* 870, *knett* 985; cf. also the rhyme *onkynd* 720 : *frende*. All three write *g* in 'give' and 'again': A, *geve* 282, *gyff* 539, *gyven* 585, *gouen* 39, *agen* 235; B, *govyn* 54, *agen* 155; C, *gyf(f)* 897, 652, *forgyfe* 756, 822, *gyuyn* 981, *gaue* 405, *agayn* 421, 434, 869, *agaynst* 786. The rare exceptions are in C, *aʒens* 789, 913, 978. All three sometimes write *ar* for earlier *er*: A, *hart* 5; B, *clark* 137; C, *harkyn* 393, *harte* 748, though *er* forms also occur. All three write *th* for earlier *d* in words like *father*: A, 1; B, 66; C, 430. There are minor differences in the representation of earlier *-ht*: all use *-ght* mainly (e.g. *bowght* 4, *myght* 54, *almyghty* 332), but A has numerous variants—*rycht* 192, *myt* 207, *my⌈g⌉the* 496, *mytheti* 285, *owyht* 567, *-leyt* 538 (rhyming with *-yght*), as well as the unhistorical *dowght* 296. B also has *dowghtys* 68, 69. C has *drawte* 340, *strayt* 351, *bowt* 721. The most important difference is that A very often writes *w* for earlier (and later) *wh*, which is the usual spelling in both B and C: so A, *wan(e)* 22, 305, *wat* 241, 272, 308, 514, *wer(-)* 195, 238, 597, *wyche* 20, beside *whan* 320, *what* 610, *whych* 11, *whyll* 510; B, *whyll* 136, *who* 124, *whose* 150, but *woso* 86; C, *-whatt* 680, *when* 427, 688, *wher-* 894, *why* 720 ff., *whyche* 742, 802, *whyle* 735, 855. B alone spells 'please' *place* 73, and 'sail' *sale* 116, rhyming on *tale*.

Of the manuscript spellings Waterhouse remarked: 'That the former scribe was an Irishman seems highly probable from the frequency with which he confuses *u, w* and *v*, and *t* and *th*, a peculiarity which appears very rarely in the rest of the play' (p. lvi). As examples he quoted *hat* 2, 556, 612, *spekyt* 571, *waytheth* 120, *amatystys* 161, *awoyd* 500, *sawe* for *save* 77, *walew* 290 (numbers here adjusted to this edition). By 'the former scribe' he evidently meant A and B together, for he said that the banns with verses 1 to 246, i.e. lines 1–326 in the present numbering, were written by one scribe. Of his examples, *waytheth* and *amatystys* were written by B, and neither is significant because *-th-* in *waytheth* is an easy antici-pation (cf. A, *sytthyt* 531) and *amatyst* is the normal medieval form of the word. The others are indeed in A's hand (and *hat* occurs again in 517), but the use of *t* in 3 sg. pres. of verbs, and of *w* for *v*, is common in late Middle English, especially of the east and north; cf., for example, VIII, pp. cviii, cix below. C confuses *w* and *v* equally, as *awance* 737, *vyse* 758. Such spellings need not be due to an Irish scribe. Professors Angus McIntosh and M. L. Samuels, in 'Prolegomena to a Study of Mediæval Anglo-Irish', *Medium Ævum*, xxxvii (1968), 1–11, remark that in this play 'the forms can be sorted into two layers, one Irish and the other probably Norfolk' (p. 7). They regard as typical of the Irish layer *wonneth* 'dwells' [13, 19], *solle* 'soul' [860], *sawe* 'save' [77], *dyrknes* 'darkness' [752], *bryne* 'bring' [4]. Thus all three scribes are concerned—*wonneth* and *bryne* are by A, *sawe* by B, *solle* and *dyrknes* by C. Of these, *dyrknes* cannot be accepted as typically Irish, for *dirk-, dyrk-* appears in the work of authors so positively eastern as Bokenham, Capgrave, and Margery Kempe as well as the *Ludus Coventriae* and *Wisdom*. Nor is the doubling of consonant letters as in *wonneth* and *solle* confined to Ireland; and the significance of *bryne* is very doubtful: it is written *brye* with a stroke above, and A makes many mistakes. Such forms as these are not convincing evidence of Irish influence.

In a number of places all the scribes write forms which the rhyme —for the most part reasonably careful—shows to be unoriginal. Thus at 154–6 *honer* and *reporte* cannot possibly rhyme in any form (and *honer* seems to be unparalleled), but B not only writes them but thoughtlessly brackets them as if they did; at 352 C writes *rest* in rhyme with *almyght*, apparently by attraction to *taste* and *cast* in the preceding stanza (he does not bracket rhymes in this passage); at 595 A writes *wyse* in rhyme with *lyfe*, etc. Such manifest errors ought clearly to be emended if an acceptable correction can be devised (as it has not yet been in 154–6), and this has been done in this edition; but some other cases are not so simple.

It is apparent from consonant assonances such as *jentle* 105, 385:*temple*, *gete* 210:*wreke*, *streme* 782:*meane*, *wepe* 980:*meke*, which do not seem to be corrupt, that rhymes less than perfect were found acceptable. In view of this, emendation of the assonance *ry[c]h* 245:*lyke* is probably not called for. Yet how far imperfect rhyme between vowels may have been tolerated is uncertain. In 73 *here ys* rhymes on *dystresse* and *processe*, but in 518 *is* rhymes on *thys*, *iwyse*. In 140 *Shelysdown* rhymes on *wonde*, but in 148 on *down*; both cannot be exact. In 103 *sold* rhymes on *world*, and this text is much too late for such a form as *werold*. No emendation suggests itself to improve the rhymes *hall* 270:*sell*; *bleyke* 477:*stryke*; *sothe* 705:*-with*; *thus* 731:*crosse*. On the other hand, where well-known alternative forms exist which would restore a rhyme quite simply it is likely that an originally good rhyme has been spoilt because a scribe has substituted a form more familiar to him. It happens that C can be seen in the act of doing this: in 383 he first wrote *cure*, meaning 'cover', in rhyme with *treasure*—that the by-form *cure* was the author's can be seen from 659 where it rhymes on *sure*, supported by *recuer* 522; but C struck it out and wrote *couere* instead. (Conversely, in 879 he first wrote *payne*, against the rhyme, and corrected it to *tene*.) In such cases it is evidently right to restore the rhyme, and this has been done as follows: *bey* (so spelt 225 and 252) for MS. *bye* 30:*ley*; *lasse* for *lesse* 315:*passe*; *com* for *came* 427:*wysdom*; *brynne* for *brenne* 670:*thynne* (cf. *brynny[n]g* 613); *rin* for *run* 675:*herein*; *fere* for *fyre* 694:*were*, 907:*autere* (cf. *fere* 684:*nere*); *pytt* for *putt* 860:*wytt*; *knaw* for *know* 960:*lawe*; *mare* for *more* 968:*welfare*. Two types of imperfect rhyme have been left unaltered because it is uncertain how, or whether, they should be corrected. First, in 222 *wyst* rhymes on *caste*, *prest*, and *agast*. It would be possible to substitute the eastern form *west* and the variants *kest* and *agest*; but the last is rare, and in 350 *cast* rhymes on *taste*, in 688 and 692 *agast* rhymes on *fast* and *hast*, and in 511 *fast* on *poste*. It seems that the normal form was *-ast*, and that before *-st* variation of the vowel in rhyme was accepted. Second, in 722 *frende* rhymes on *onkynd*, *pynde*, *mynde*. Since rhymes between such words are common in the east, and could be on either sound, the manuscript forms are retained. For similar reasons *hyre* 631, rhyming on *inquere*, *nere*, is kept.

The rhymes already discussed cover a number of the most important features of pronunciation. The principal remaining points are the following:

Final unstressed -*e* of ME. is written erratically by all three scribes, and at the late date of the manuscript the sound was no doubt lost altogether. Many rhymes confirm its loss in the original also: e.g. the nouns *synne* 66, *mold* 82, *tale* 114, the plural adjs. *moste* 3, *all* 221, the infins. *saye*, *sey* 11, 33, *hold* 84, *abyde* 124, *fulfyll* 150 (and many more), the past pl. *stode* 69.

The reflex of OE. *ā* is normally written *o*: *hold*, *told* 84, 85 rhyme on *mold*, *gold*; *gon*, *euerychoon* 521, 523 on *doon*; *clothe*, *loth* 702, 704 on *sothe*; *more* 908 on *restore*; *Gost*, *most* 963, 966 on *cost*. But outside the rhyme the past tense of 'rive', written *rofe* 48, is *rave* 943; and in 968, in contrast to 908, *mare* is required by rhyme though *more* is written. The reflex of OE. *āw* is written *ow* in *know* 960, but the rhyme (as noted above) is on *lawe*.

The reflex of OE. *a* before a nasal not in a lengthening group is regularly written *a*, and *man* 534, 881 rhymes on *Braban*, *Leuyathan*. Lengthened in an open syllable it rhymes on the reflex of OF. *a*: e.g. *nam* 254:*fame*, *blame*; *lame* 770:*blame*.

The reflex of OE. *ǣ²* is usually written *e* (sometimes *ea* as *teache* 975). It rhymes on the reflex of OE. *ē* and *ēo*: e.g. *mene* 197:*wene*, 79:*sen*, *bene*, *tene*, similarly 284, 877; *led* 572:*med*; *sprede* 823:*hed* 'heed'. The reflex of OE. *ēa* also rhymes on ME. tense /e:/ in *beleue* 206:*preue*, *meue*, *cheue* (cf. *prefe*:*thefe* 443–7); yet in 782–5 the assonance *streme*:*meane* contrasts in the stanza structure with the rhyme *tene*:*bene*.

The reflex of OE. *ǣ²* when shortened is usually *e*: *lesse* 70 rhymes on *dystresse*, 167 and 180 on *dresse*; but the rhyme at 315 requires *lasse*.

The reflex of OE. *ȳ* is written *y* in *fyre* 485, 670, 697, etc., not in rhyme; but *e* in *fere* 494, 684, rhyming on *clere*, *nere*, *appere*, *chere*, and this form is required by the rhymes at 694: *were*, *clere*, and 907:*autere*.

The reflex of OE. *y* is usually written *y*: e.g. *synne* 66, rhyming on *in*, *hylle* 193 on *tyll*, etc., *fyll* 235 on *wyll*. But it is *e* in *stere*

f

263, 699, rhyming on *pere*, *clere*, and within the line in *besy* 870, *knett* 985; see also p. lxxviii above. Before lengthening groups *y* is written in *mynde*, *onkynd* 198, 200, rhyming on *bynd*, *blynd*, and similarly in 386–91: but the same words in 720, 725 rhyme on *frende* as well as *pynde*. It is possible that this rhyme depends on the common variant *frind* and a shortened vowel in the other words; but it could also depend on the variants *mende*, *-kende*, *pende*; cf. especially the conditions in VIII, p. cvii below. In 30 the rhyme on *ley* requires *bey* for MS. *bye*.

Some rhymes imply developments in earlier diphthongs: *sale* 'sail' 116 rhymes on *tale*; *eyn* 'eyes' 540 on *vryne* (but *hey* 'high' 509 on *praye*); *bowght*, *nowght*, *thowght* 724–9 on *tawght*.

The following are the main points of verbal inflexion:

Pres. indic. 2 sg. (and past 2 sg. of weak verbs) ends in *-st* in the work of all three scribes: A, *janglest* 573; B, *hast* 157; C, *kepyst* 378, *woldyst* 773. 3 sg. usually ends in *-th*: A, *wonneth* 13, *owyth* 260, *longeth* 265, *me thynketh* 318; B, *spryngyth* 91, *renneth* 94, *doth* 124; C, *sayeth* 343, *hath* 363, *commytht* 375, *me thynkyth* 376, *dwellth* 591. For occasional forms in *-t* see p. lxxix above. There are also a few without ending: the common *me thynk(e)* 200 (A), 847, 980 (C), *make* 388 (C). The only form in *-s* is *hase* 463 (C), rhyming on *space*. Pl. usually has no ending, but sometimes *-n*: A, *waytyn* 190, *doon* 209, *ben* 305; C, *arn* 386, *goon* 392 s.d., *carpyn* 394, *desyryn* 762, *bene* 839. A once has *-th* in *breweth* 515. Imper. pl. is usually uninflected but occasionally has *-th*: *beth* 67, *voydoth* 640. Past pl. is nearly always without ending but has *-n* in *gouen* 39.

Infin. is usually without ending, confirmed by rhyme as noticed above, p. lxxxi; but a number of verbs, nearly all monosyllabic, sometimes have *-n*. Examples confirmed by rhyme are: *bene* 76 : *sen* pp., 287 : *mene*, etc., 464 : *kene*, etc., 785 : *tene*; *doon* 236 : *doune*, *doun* 335 : *sone*; *gon(e)* 353 : *fone*, 521 : *euerychoon*, 987 : *on*; *hanne* 634 : *physycyan*; *sene* 183 : *grene*, *seen* 286 : *mene*, etc. : *seyn* 136 : *atteyn*, etc., 244 : *frayne*. Outside rhyme are *doon* 294 (A), *gon(e)* 350, 836 (C), *castyn* 220, *walkyn* 304 (A), 358 (C).

Past parts. of strong verbs are not treated significantly differently by the three scribes. A few are without *-n*, both within the line as *gett* 388, *smytte* 463, and in rhyme or assonance as *take* 305, *wreke* 212. The majority have -*n*. Examples other than monosyllables are not numerous, and none are in rhyme: *knowen* 56, 92, 108, 642, *gyven*, *gyuyn*, *govyn* 585, 981, 54, *smytyn* 465, *soden* 706. Monosyllables are *do*(*o*)*n*(*e*), *donne*, 11, 494, 688, 696, 802, and in rhyme 524, 564, 912 (the last rhyming on *done* infin.); *gon*(*e*) in rhyme 652, 655; *se*(*e*)*n*(*e*) 575, and in rhyme 74, 465, 480; *borne* 'carried' 848; *sworn* 281. The prefix *i*- appears once, in the weak pp. *imett* 237.

Of the personal pronouns, though the distinction between *ye* nom. and *yow* oblique is generally observed (e.g. lines 270–7), *yow* is sometimes used as the nominative by all three scribes, e.g. 76, 183, 286, 317, 609, 731, 734, 981. In 3 pl. the regular forms are *they* (for which A writes *þe* 31, 200, 203); *ther*(*e*), e.g. 29, 52, 213, 397 (*thyr* once 51 (B)); *them*, e.g. 84, 400, 401, 425, 651–2, 997; *hem* appears once 127 (B).

In syntax, the verb *do* as an auxiliary is prominent: 42, 44, 147, 201, 209, 242, 421, 490, 734, 737, 855, 937, 939, 980. Though in some of these passages, notably 42 and 44, it would be possible to regard the use as causative, the contexts are against it and so is the action of the play.

Two aspects of the vocabulary are of interest. First, a number of 'learned' words are first recorded here, and some uniquely: *attrueaunce* 128, evidently derived from OF. *estruiance* 'instruction', is recorded by *M.E.D.* only in this place; *condescent* 123 is only here in *M.E.D.*, but *O.E.D.* has later quotations as well, in different senses; *condolent* 748 is one of only three occurrences, all of about the same date, in *M.E.D.* (*O.E.D.* cites also *condolaunt* from Caxton), and the only one meaning, apparently, 'contrite'; *largyfluent* 826 is the only occurrence in *O.E.D.*; *medycament* 582 is earlier than *O.E.D.*'s first quotation in 1541, and its sense 'treatment' is not recorded at all; *necesse* 774, as a noun, is only here; *negacyon* 602 anticipates *O.E.D.*'s first quotation of 1530, which is even then in a purely technical sense. Secondly, some words are regionally limited—some very generally, as the predominantly northern and north-midland *bydene* 882, 986 (both in rhyme), *byggly* 218, *boun* 269, *carpe*, -*yn* 392, 394, *grue* 155 (unless it is an error for *greue*), *heyle* 619, *hope* meaning 'believe' 843, 849, *mekyll*, *mykyll* 13, 62, 750, etc. (beside *moch*(*e*) 97, 104, etc.), *yon* 853, and at this date *sekyrly* 262; perhaps two more narrowly localizable—the form *cure*, a variant of 'cover', which is used at 81 and 659 and required by rhyme at 383 is found elsewhere in the works of Lydgate, Capgrave, and Margery Kempe, the *Ludus Coventriae*, and the *Promptorium Parvulorum*; *swemful, swymful* 800, 805, 809 (recorded only in the fifteenth century—see *O.E.D.* under *sweam* n.; but probably the same as *swinful* 'sorrowful' recorded by *E.D.D.* from Suffolk) is also in Lydgate, Margery Kempe, Margaret Paston, the *Ludus Coventriae*, and the *Promptorium*. These are all characteristically East Anglian texts.

The extent of scribal interference with the rhymes suggests that a considerable time separated the original text from the surviving copy. There are other inconsistencies which point in the same direction; notably, the almost complete establishment of *their* and *them* in the pronoun of the third person plural is characteristic of a late date, but the preservation of *-n* in a number of verb forms, infinitive and present plural, is distinctly older-fashioned. There may be local as well as chronological layers in the present text which would account for the coexistence of variants such as *rave* beside *rofe, fere* beside *fyre*. Some of the vocabulary suggests a northerly area, but the rarity of the *-s* ending in the third person singular, the prevalence of *o* for OE. *ā*, and the common lowering of *i/y* to *e*, indicate rather the east midlands. The language as a whole has much in common with that of *The Castle of Perseverance*; see M. Eccles's edition of *The Macro Plays*, E.E.T.S. 262 (1969), pp. xi–xv.

The two English place-names in the play obviously have some bearing on its origin and currency. The banns announce a performance 'at Croxston on Monday' (74), and the Doctor is said to live at 'þe colkote, a lytyll besyde Babwell Myll' (621). The former need not define the provenance of the play closely, for the very nature of the proclamation implies a travelling company. The second is probably more significant—at any rate of the origin of the episode of the Doctor, if not of the play as a whole, because such a reference would be pointless unless the audience knew of Babwell. Babwell Priory was a Franciscan house a mile or so from Bury St. Edmunds on the road to Thetford in Norfolk,[1] and one of the

---

[1] D. Knowles and R. N. Hadcock, *Medieval Religious Houses, England and Wales* (London, 1953), p. 190.

numerous Croxtons is less than three miles from Thetford (there
is another in Norfolk, near Fakenham, and others in Lincolnshire
and Cambridgeshire), and so about twelve from Babwell. The regioe
of Thetford is a possible one for the origin of the play. It may have
been composed not long after 1461, the date the manuscript gives
for the events; but this copy must be half a century or so later.

VII. *THE PRIDE OF LIFE*

Manuscript. The manuscript of *The Pride of Life* no longer exists.
It was part of a collection of deeds and other documents preserved
by the canons of Christ Church, Dublin. After the disestablish-
ment of the Church of Ireland in 1869 the collection was deposited
in the Public Record Office in the Four Courts building in Dublin.
During the political disturbances of June 1922 the building was
destroyed by explosion and fire, and the records were totally lost.[1]

In 1891 the Royal Society of Antiquaries of Ireland had published, under the title *Account Roll of the Priory of the Holy Trinity,
Dublin, 1337–1346, with the Middle English Moral Play 'The Pride
of Life'*, a description and edition of the manuscript by James Mills,
deputy-keeper of the Public Records. It was Mills who devised the
title of the play by which it has since been known. The play was
written, very untidily and evidently hastily, in vacant spaces of the
verso of a parchment roll of accounts of the Priory. The skins
containing the accounts, originally four distinct documents, had
been stitched together—Mills believed much later, probably not
less than a hundred years after they were made—to form a roll
11 feet $8\frac{1}{2}$ inches long and from $8\frac{1}{4}$ to $11\frac{1}{4}$ inches wide. The play was
on the back of the second account in the series, which referred to
the period from 30 June 1343 to 5 January following. It appears to
have been written in the first half of the fifteenth century. It was in
four columns, described by Mills as 'rather crowded'; the first of
them, being near the edge of the skin, had been a good deal discoloured so that in some places all trace of the writing had disappeared. Besides being divided into columns the surviving part of
the play was separated into two sections by the writing already on
the roll when it was added. It is also obviously incomplete evidently

---

[1] This has escaped recent bibliographers, including Stratman (no. 2236) and
Robbins-Cutler, *Supplement* (no. 2741); but it was noted by Seymour in 1929
(*Anglo-Irish Literature*, p. 121).

because when it was copied there had been another skin stitched to the roll which had later become detached and lost. There are two lacunae in the course of the surviving text, and from the prologue it is clear that a large section is missing at the end. The places at which the breaks occur can be partly understood from the distribution of the lines in the four columns and two divisions:

1–38	127–60	161–96	197–234
39–126	235–326	327–416	415–502
(lacuna)	(lacuna)		(rest lost)

Lines 415 and 416 were written twice.

Mills described the handwriting of the play as follows: 'The copy has been made by the hands of two distinct scribes. One is a clerkly set hand, rather infirm or out of practice, perhaps. The other is a very irregular current hand. This latter copyist was evidently quite unaccustomed to writing English; hence there is constant confusion between þ and y, and ȝ is used in the most uncertain manner; indeed the spelling generally is often very puzzling' (pp. 185–6). The lines written in the 'current' hand were: 1–4, 33–80 (82 in Mills's edition, corrected by Brandl), 127–54, 327–438; those in the 'set' hand were: 5–32, 81–126, 155–326, 439–502. As frontispiece to his edition Mills provided a facsimile, made by photozincography, of part of the roll showing sections of the play and their relation to some of the accounts. The four columns shown begin at lines 39, 235, 327, 415. The reproduction is not very clear, but since the photograph from which it was made has not survived it is the best evidence we now have for the layout of the text and the appearance of the hands. It is therefore reproduced here, as well as a copy of such a copy could be made, with the permission of the Royal Society of Antiquaries of Ireland and by the technical skill of the photographer to the University Press, Oxford. From the facsimile it may well seem that Mills did more than justice to the 'clerkly' scribe, whose work is not always much easier to read than that of his incompetent colleague. It is worth notice also that, in the 'set-hand' part of the facsimile (column 2), the end of each speech is marked by a line across the column, with the next speaker's name to the right.

Text. The present edition is necessarily based on earlier printed editions, except for the very small part that can be checked from the facsimile. Fortunately there is good reason to think that the printed texts present as faithful a transcript as could fairly be expected from so ill-written a manuscript. Mills was obviously a skilled and careful scholar. His first edition was soon followed by a second by Alois Brandl, in his *Quellen des weltlichen Dramas vor Shakespeare* (Strassburg, 1898). Brandl acknowledged the help of W. W. Skeat, who had handed over to him a collation of the manuscript which he had made with the object of a new edition, and of Mills, who had undertaken another collation on his behalf. Brandl's text is therefore likely to give a substantially accurate account of what could be read. Then in 1902 Holthausen, in *Archiv*, cviii, attempted a reconstruction of the text in more readable form, based on Brandl's but with new emendations partly drawn from reviews by Kaluza and Manly, and with the more eccentric spellings normalized. He had not seen the manuscript. For his edition in 1909 Waterhouse 'collated Mr. Mills' text with the manuscript and compared it with that of Prof. Brandl'. His footnotes show that he also used Holthausen's edition. He made only a small number of substantive changes, mostly slight; he regularized word-division, punctuation, and the use of capitals, but preserved the spelling except that, as Holthausen had done, he printed *þ* instead of *y* where *þ* was the letter intended. For this edition I have reviewed the earlier work and have in some places reverted to readings altered by Waterhouse, mainly in the conjectural supply of words that were illegible in the manuscript.

There is one reading of some interest, derived from the facsimile; in view of the extensive speculation the word has attracted it may be noticed here as a conspicuous example of the difficulty of reading this text. In line 333 the first word was read by Mills as *gocyl*, with a note that *o* and *c* were very uncertain. Miss Toulmin Smith conjectured that the word intended was *gentyl*, the scribe having omitted the abbreviation mark for *n*; this was accepted by Brandl in his translation, and by Waterhouse; but it makes poor sense in a passage deploring corruption—Meed made a judge, Force overcoming law, Love turned to lechery, and so on. Manly wished to keep *gocyl*, which he took to be 'guzzle';[1] Holthausen understood it to be a spelling of *jogyl* 'juggle'; *M.E.D.* (1963) places it under *goki* 'fool', with a query whether it should be read *gentyl*. But Carleton Brown long ago showed that the immediate source of the

---

[1] *J.E.G.P.* ii (1898), 420.

lament of the Bishop in this play is a treatment of the ancient theme of 'The Twelve Abuses of the Age', in Latin elegiacs accompanied by an English rhyming paraphrase.[1] Versions of the lines occur in some twenty manuscripts: see *Index* and *Supplement*, no. 906. Some are printed in Brown's *Religious Lyrics of the XVth Century*, pp. 268, 345–6, others in Robbins's *Historical Poems*, pp. 143–5, 326–7. In a number of texts the first line of the English has some such form as '3yfte hys mad domesman, *gyle* is mad chapman' (so MS. Worcester Cathedral F. 154, f. 110ᵇ). This is patently the clue to line 333 of our play. Brown wrote: 'After referring to the facsimile page of the manuscript, printed by Mills as the frontispiece in his edition, . . . I am inclined to believe that the actual reading of the manuscript is *goyl*; and I am supported in this opinion by Mr. Flower of the Department of Manuscripts in the British Museum'; adding that '*goyl* as a spelling of *gyle* need not surprise us'. He certainly identified the word correctly, but the right reading is surely *geyl*. Brandl said that this scribe tended to change *e* into *o*. Rather, he scarcely distinguished the two letters in some positions —compare, for instance, in the facsimile (Pl. III) the *e* of *cepman* in column 3, line 7, of the verse text with the *o* of *of* immediately below it. In *geyl* the lower curve of the *e* is touched by the on-stroke of the *y* in a confusing way, but there is no need to doubt that the scribe intended to write *ey* here, representing the reflex of ME. *i*, as he did more clearly in *bleynd* 'blind' ten lines below. The same paraphrase helps the identification of *slet* in line 343. Some manuscripts show the corresponding word as *sly* or *sley*, but Ashmole has *sleght*, which certifies *slet* in our text—not *slot* which Waterhouse read and emended to *sot* 'true'.

Theme. Despite the defective state of the text it is possible to make out, by comparison of the prologue with later passages, how the action developed. Brandl and Hardin Craig give useful brief accounts,[2] the emphasis of which might be modified somewhat as follows. The King of Life boasts of his invincible power, and is encouraged in his arrogance by his knights Strength and Health. His Queen reminds him that he cannot escape death, and that he should fear God. He abuses her and scorns her advice, and is

[1] 'The "Pride of Life" and the "Twelve Abuses"', *Archiv*, cxxvii (1912), 72–8.

[2] *Quellen*, pp. xiii–xv; *Religious Drama*, pp. 343, 347–8; Chambers mentions the play inadequately in *Mediaeval Stage*, ii. 155.

again supported by the two knights and by his messenger Mirth or Solace. But the Queen sends the messenger to bring the Bishop, who delivers a homily on the degeneracy of the world and men's need of the grace of God, and then directly warns the King to think of death. The King angrily dismisses the Bishop, and sends a challenge to Death. With the ensuing speech of the messenger the text breaks off, but the prologue shows that Death accepted the challenge, came and fought against the King of Life and conquered him. The penultimate four stanzas of the prologue change from narrative to homily of general application, taking up the theme of the seizure of the soul by fiends and the power of Our Lady to intercede for its salvation. They do not say that this was what happened to the King of Life, who is not mentioned after line 92. The implication is doubtless that it was, for the final stanza embraces all that goes before as 'þis oure game schal gin and ende'; but there is nothing to show that the fiends, Our Lady, the soul, and the body were represented on the stage.[1]

The play is thus, as Craig says, 'essentially a play on the certainty of death', and has obvious affinities with the Dance of Death. It is much cruder, and apparently much earlier, than the play closest to it in English, *Everyman*; and no particular sources for it have been found.

Verse. The surviving parts of the play are all written in quatrains, rhyming *abab* (the second half of the quatrain beginning at 125 is lost). A few pairs of quatrains have one rhyming sound in common: the second and third quatrains of the prologue, and the fourth and fifth, have the same *a*-rhyme; so have those in 343–50 and 383–90; the quatrains in 247–54 have the same *b*-rhyme; the quatrain 105–8 has for its *a*-rhyme the *b*-rhyme of the preceding quatrain, so that the two could be held to form an eight-line stanza of the common pattern *ababbcbc*; so, in spite of the change of spelling (by the same scribe), could the two quatrains in lines 69–76. In view of the far greater number of unconnected quatrains it is unlikely that these were designed in the eight-line form. The pattern in 335–42, as they stood in the manuscript, is peculiar. If the consonants beginning the final syllables are included in the rhyme, as

---

[1] A. Williams, in *Annuale Mediaevale*, iv. 13–14, goes beyond the text in saying, 'Certainly, *Pride of Life* follows *The Castle* in having the King of Life saved through supernatural intervention'.

they normally are, *trecri* 335 rhymes on *lecuri* 339 and *uileni* 337 on *glotuni* 341, crossing the quatrain boundaries to form a stanza *abcbadcd*. This would be unique in the play. But Brown, in the article quoted above (p. lxxxviii), noted that the order of rhymes in the source texts showed that those of the play were misplaced; and the present text has been emended accordingly.

Though this simple rhyme-pattern is common in some of the cycles—it is important, for example, in the Towneley *Conspiracy* —it is not elsewhere used throughout a whole play. And even here the stanzas are not uniform in structure and vary greatly in movement and weight: the predominant form has lines of alternately four and three stresses ('ballad metre'), but six of the surviving stanzas have four stresses in all four lines (the imperfect stanza at 125–6 was of this type also), and a number of others, difficult to determine, have three stresses throughout. The clearest cases of this last type are probably lines 235–8, 303–6, 343–50, 399–406, 459–62. Many others could be so read, for their odd lines are conspicuously shorter than the usual four-stress lines; but possible variations in the treatment of weak syllables, or opportunities for secondary stress in compound words—not to mention the possibility, strong in this text, of defective transmission—make the writer's intention uncertain. Such are 33–6, 45–8, 53–6, 127–30, 171–4, 203–6, 211–14. Some of these more concise stanzas seem to have been placed for particular effects: 235–8 sums up the Queen's warning; 303–6 marks the complacent withdrawal of the King; 399–406 sum up the Bishop's injunction. There is no doubt that the stanzas at the other extreme, those with four stresses in all four lines, were chosen for their greater appropriateness to situations requiring weight and dignity. The prologue opens with two stanzas of this form. Another at 29–32 introduces the Queen. The play itself opens with three and an unknown number following, exhibiting the King in his boastful pride; these stanzas are additionally weighted with alliteration, usually on all four stresses— presumably this was originally regular but has been corrupted, as by the substitution of *lestenith* in 118 for *herknith*, or of *likinge* in 31 for some such word as *speding*. Alliterative phrases are frequent also in the lighter stanzas, but they are not systematically sought.

Language. This play presents an unusually strong contrast between the usages of the two scribes. Brandl denoted the writer of what

Mills called the 'set' hand by A, his colleague of the 'current' hand by B, and this is adopted here. As Mills remarked, B's spelling is eccentric in various ways. His most conspicuous irregularity concerns initial ȝ. This, in addition to its normal function as the equivalent of *y*, which B also uses (e.g. *yif* and *ȝour* in successive lines, 387–8), appears instead of *þ* and also of *h*. Thus *ȝe* can represent *þe*, whether the definite article, as in 58, 59, 67, 71, or the pronoun, as 145; and also *he*, as 33, 40, 68, 69. The former substitution is familiar enough in earlier Middle English manuscripts, for instance in the third hand of MS. Auchinleck (cf. the use of *z* in IX below, and in MS. Bodleian Laud 108), but the latter is distinctive. In a few places also (139, 420, 431) *þ* is written instead of ȝ. Since these spellings are uncommonly confusing to a modern reader, they have been normalized in the present text and the manuscript form relegated to the footnotes. This scribe's *þ* is often identical with his *y*, but as this is commonplace in late Middle English it is normalized without notice; he used a true *þ* as well, especially from 391 onwards. A similar multiple use of a single letter concerns *c*, which in addition to its normal function as in *cumli* 46, *coupe* 69, easily extended to cover final /k/ as in *mac* 47, 400, serves for the affricate /tʃ/, as *cumlic* 33, *suc* 35, 148, 328, *mucil* 38, *spec* 62, *lec* 64, *precit* 69, *cepman* 333, *trecri* 335, *lecuri* 337, *cildrin* 340, *ric*(-) 351, 355, 363, *prec* 417. This is not regular: the same sound initially is written *ch* in *chong* 130, *churg, churc* 423, 425. On the other hand, *ch* represents /k/ in *charp* 53, *char* 53, 432 (but *car* 427), *chout* 68, *cham* 69. In a few places *c* further appears to represent medial /ʃ/, as *bicop* 67, 73, *ficis* 361; though in view of *bissop* 407, *bisop* 424, it might be argued that the sound intended was /s/. The usual spelling of initial /ʃ/ is *sch*, as *schend* (MS.) 140, *schalt* 392, etc., and also in *schir* 'sir' 391, 424, 435, but *screu* 421. Similar to the use of *c* for /tʃ/ is that of *g* for the corresponding voiced sound in *chong* 130, *sig* 358, 360. The extension of this to *churg* 'church' 423 is evidently not a mere error; *M.E.D.* quotes *cherge* from a Manning manuscript and a Norfolk Gild return, and *chyrge* from *Torrent*. The use of *g* in *þing* 'think' 365, 391, 399, may be a reverse spelling dependent on the unvoicing of /g/ in this position; and *chagler* 409 is likely to represent 'cackler' (so in effect Brandl) rather than 'jangler' (*M.E.D.*). A third use of a single letter corresponding to various spellings in other systems concerns *t*. In addition to its normal function this may appear (1) instead of final *d*, mostly in weak past tenses and participles and derived adjectives, as *lerit* 4, *lettrit* 45, *precit* 69, *warnit* 70, *saurit* 71, *onlerit* 340, *irerit* 342, *deit* 386, sometimes elsewhere as *leut* 4, *touart* 369; (2) instead of *þ* or *th* in verbal endings, as *bet* 3, *hat* 33, *becomit* 46, *louit* 51, *dot* 55, *chout* (=*couth*) 68, *kyt* 80, *farit* 361, *got* 374, and finally in other words as *leint* 34, *strynt* 36 (*streyint* 332), *fort* 43, *det* 55, 438, *mout* (rhyming on *coupe*) 71, *wyt* 133, *reut* 346, *sot* 358, 360, *treut, truyt* 330, 334; (3) instead of *-ght* (etc.) as in *mit* 37, 143, 431, *sit* 39, *brit* 139, *rit* 438, *þout* 397. B oddly transposes *n* and *y* in *kyntis* for *knytis* 33, 56, 135—cf. *knitis* 154; but *herkynt* 1 is like *herkint* IX. 1—cf. p. cxiii below. For earlier *hw-* B regularly writes *w*, as *wat* 37, *wyc* 'which' 58, *wan* 73, *wosa* 'whoso' 358, *war* 417, *wyle* 433. For *w* he often writes *u*, in all positions in the word: *uey* 393, *uer* 414, *uil* 402, *ouin* 79, *iuis* 346, *lau* 332, *dau* 334. He often writes *h* superfluously before an initial vowel: *hal* 1, *hold* 2, *hend* 52, 374, *hind* 70. In much the same way as he writes simple final *-g* in *sig*, B omits the customary *-e* after *u* in words like *leu* 57, *liu* 145, *hau* 151, 354, *lou* 337, 385. He seldom writes a final *-e* at all in any of the places where it would be historically appropriate—e.g. in the plural adjectives in 1 and 2, the infinitives in 42, 43, 48, and a great many others. There are rare exceptions, as *toke* 61 (where it is unhistorical), *coupe* 69, *kete* 135, *truþe* 143.

Beside these idiosyncrasies A's spelling is comparatively orthodox. He uses *ʒ* in the normal way, as *ʒe* 11, *ʒou* 15, *ʒelþe* 218, *ʒiue* 258 (cf. B *yif* 415), *oʒein* 124, 286, etc. Once, it is true, it replaces *þ*, in *þede* 250, but it is never used instead of *h*. The sounds /tʃ/ and /ʃ/ are spelt *ch* and (*s*)*sch* respectively—*louelich* 29, *chirche* 187, *wirch* 189; *sched* 8, *schal* 103, *schullin* 13, *bisschop* 449, *flessch* 19. For the dental fricatives *þ* is used initially in small words like *þe, þat*; *th* is commoner elsewhere, as *beth* 5, 9, *herkenith* 6, *mirth* 14, *deth* 28, but *þ* is occasional as *deþis* 91, *boþe* 194. For the present tense of verbs, both 3 sg. and pl., the ending is sometimes abbreviated by raised *t*, which Mills and Brandl expand to *-it*; but as Brandl remarks, the numerous forms written in full nearly all have *-ith*. This is evidently the correct expansion (comparable to *with* for *wᵗ*, though at the same time *hit* 236 is written *hᵗ*), and it has been adopted in this edition. Final *-d* is so spelt, as *auaunsyd* 298, *bileuyd* 326. Earlier *ht* is usually written *ʒt*: *kniʒt-* 90, 114, 158, *miʒt*(-) 92, 196, *riʒte* 156, *aʒte* 82, *ikaʒte* 106, *noʒt* 110, 192, *doʒtely* 283, but *doghti* 260; it is never rendered by simple *t*. Scribe A prefixes *h* superfluously only in *heme* 83. He writes final unstressed -*e* freely, sometimes where it is historically correct, as *hende* 5, *mylde* 6, *ende* 7, *spede* 8; often where it is not, as *blode* 8, *dreme* 81, *stone* 102, *worlde* 122. The only distinctive feature of his spelling, a striking one beside its general commonplaceness, is his regular use of *qwh-* for *hw-*: *qwhen* 93, 172, 184, *qwher* 162, 171, 263, *qwho* 166, *qwhat* 239, *qwhile* 250, and many others.

The vowels of unstressed inflexional syllables ending in a consonant are spelt by both scribes overwhelmingly with *i*, whatever the consonant. A occasionally uses *y*, as in the past participles *auaunsyd*, *bileuyd* noticed above. There are only a few examples of *e*, as *itaken* 86, *grauen* 443 (A), *lernen* 404 (B). It happens that no rhymes confirm the quality of the vowel.

The state of final unstressed -*e* in the original is difficult to determine. The rhythm of many lines seems to require it—e.g. 6, 162, 191, 230, 256—but many others are complete without it— e.g. 8, 32, 91, 120, 258. One rhyme demands it—*þe sope:to þe* 235–7, though the form *sope* is not in fact grammatically correct here; perhaps it is an alteration of *to sope*, or analogically patterned on it. But other rhymes exclude it: the infins. *led* 42, *dit* 78, *trist* 143, *bode* 169, *tene* 453, and the adj. pl. *gret* 336, rhyme on words which certainly had no final -*e*, and several others on words that probably had none, such as *fiʒt* 241, *riche* 289. The ending of *maistrye* 463 had evidently been reduced. The sound seems to have been lost in general, but to have been available as an alternative if convenient for the metre.

Rhymes are mostly accurate. Assonance between words ending in different consonants appears in *ikaʒte* 106:*lafte*, *bronde* 247: *wronge*. A few rhymes show discrepancies between the copy and the original, none of them very important. In 403 *charite*, rhyming on *lit*, must be a substitution. In 35 *suc* does not fit the rhyme on *cumlic*. (It is B's form also in 148 and 328; A writes *siche* 317, *suche* 490.) In 57 *likynd* (vbl. n.) does not fit the rhyme on *kyng*; in 395 *man* does not fit *opon*. All four of these are in B's hand. In 86 A writes (according to Brandl) *itaken* in rhyme with *wrake*.

The most significant remaining features of spelling and sounds are the following:

The reflex of OE. *ā* is written *o* by both scribes: A, *sore* 215, *more* 217, *ro* 268, *go* 270; B, *lor* 45, -*mor* 47, *wo* 327, *ago* 329; and where it arises from *a* before lengthening groups, A, *londe* 275, *bronde* 277, *honde* 480; B, *hold* 2, *bold* 4, *stond* 144, *fond* 146. B's *baldli* 127 presumably keeps the short vowel before the consonant cluster; *halt* 359 keeps it in the syncopated form, which is proper to the 3 sg. only but is used here as a pl. (cf. *þai* 361). The only rhyme certifying pronunciation is *wost* 279: *bost*.

The reflex of OE. *a* before a nasal not in a lengthening group is nearly always written *a*; *name* 456 rhymes on *blame*, but *man* 395 on *opon*. In *stont* 318 the vowel may be influenced by other parts of the verb.

The reflex of OE. $\bar{æ}^1$ is written *e*: *strete* 257 rhymes on *mete* 'meet'. When shortened it is written *a* in *dradd* 24; so is the shortening of $\bar{æ}^2$ in *lafte* 108, rhyming on *ikaʒte*.

The reflex of OE. *o* lengthened in open syllable in *bode* 169 rhymes on OE. *ō* in *gode*.

The reflex of OE. *ēo* is written *e*: *lede* 254 rhymes on *blede*.

The reflex of OE. *y* before a lengthening group is written *i* or *y*: *kinde* 208 (A) rhymes on *finde*, *onkynd* 345 and *mind* 349 (B) on *bleynd* and *find*. In other positions it is written *i*: *hil* 301 rhymes on *wil*. Outside rhyme A writes *mirth* 279, *mery* 280.

Earlier *e* before *nd* is written *i* by B in *hind* 70, and *y* in the rhymeword *wynd*, but kept in *wend* and *send* 73, 75.

The reflex of OE. *ēg*, and its ON. equivalent, is written *ey*: *deye* 190, 211, 316 (A) rhymes on *eye* 'fear' (OE. *ege*), *dey* 392 (B) on *bisey* (OE. *besegen*); *eye* 'eyes' 242 (A) on *maistrye*.

Earlier *i* in *hider* 12 rhymes on *e* in *weder*.

The earlier group *engþ* appears in A as *einth*: *streinth* 243, *streynth* 303, *leynth* 305; B writes *streyint* 332, *strenyt* 153, *leint* 34, but also *strynt* 36, *strent* 135, 147.

The descendant of OE. *feala* 'many' appears as *fale* 207 (A) rhyming on *tale*; but *fel* 378 (B) rhymes on *wel*.

The form of 'say' is *sig(ge)* 220 (A), 358, 360 (B).

The following are the main features of inflexion:

Noun plurals and genitives nearly all end in *-is*. Exceptions, apart from the commonplace ones such as *men*, are pls. *eye* 242, *dau* 334 (OE. *dagum*), *daus* 370 (rhyming on *lauis*); *barons* 115; gen. sg. *soule* 94.

In verbs, the pres. indic. 2 sg. (and past sg. of weak verbs) usually ends in *-(i)st* in both scribes: A, *liuist* 180, *haddist* 183, *hast* 207, *saist* 179, *seistou* 191, *wost* 279 rhyming on *bost*;

B, *ureist* 416, *lisst* 421, *haddist* 396. A has also *-is* in *spekis* 192, and *sitt*is 276 (ending abbreviated); and beside *schalt* 204 he uses *pou schal* 165, 190, 297, 299. 3 sg., as noted above, p. xcii, normally ends in -(*i*)*th* in A, *ledith* 25, *dredith* 27, 28, syncopated in *kith* 92, etc., and in -(*i*)*t* in B, *helpit* 37, *becomit* 46, *begynit* 53, *dot* 55, syncopated in *bid* 49. A has also *rennis* 266 (*metis* 444 is conjectural). The pres. pl. usually has the same form as the 3 sg.: A, *beth* 5, 86, *takith* 96, rhyming on *awakith* sg.; B, *bet* 3, 340, *lokit* 344, *eteit* 362, *louit* 367. A has a few forms without ending, *be* 259, *have* 227, 284. B once uses the syncopated form of 3 sg. in plural function: *halt* 359. Plural imperatives also end in -(*i*)*th* or -(*i*)*t*: A, *herkenith* 6, 15, *listenith* 471, also *stondit* 117; B, *bringit* 139, but *herkynt* 1.

Infin. is normally written without *-n* by both scribes, often certified by rhyme: A, *misse* 30, *spille* 124, *wirch* 189, *deye* 190, *fiȝt* 241, *ryde* 290; with *-n* are *done* in rhyme 284 and within the line 283, *ben* 473; B, *miss* 40, *led* 42, *stond* 43, 144, *spar* 55, 402, *be* 66, and many others, but *lernen* 404 within the line. The suffix *-ye* is kept in *carye*, *sparye* 82, 84 (A), but *spar* 402 rhymes on *yar* (B); cf. also *sauy* 406.

In the pres. pl. of preterite-present verbs *-n* survives in *schullin* 13 (elsewhere *schal* 120 etc.), *wittin* 483.

Past participles of strong verbs are more commonly written without *-n*: *ikorre* 121, *ibor(r)e* 123, 184, 491, *forlore* 186, *ilore* 493, *icom* 157, *henge* 481; all these in A. Where rhyme is decisive such forms are confirmed: *aslawe* 473, *todraw* 481, and two forms in B, *ibound* 328, *ifound* 354. A sometimes writes *-n* also: *bycomin* 22, *ikorne* 114, *i*[*s*]*worne* 116, *grauen* 443, and even *itaken* 86 though it rhymes on *wrake*. Monosyllabic verbs are sometimes without *-n*, as *ago* 329 in rhyme, *go* 330 (B), but more often have it: *sene* 451 and *gone* 470 in rhyme, *ben* 291 (A), *isen* 142 in rhyme, *sen* 357, *don* 334 (B).

Past participles mostly have the prefix *i-* if there is no other prefix. Examples of strong verbs are in the preceding paragraph; weak verbs are the following: A, *ibroȝt* 93, *ikaȝte* 106, *isente* 475; B, *imad* 150.

Of the personal pronouns, in 2 sg. the enclitic pronoun is weakened in *wolte* 218; cf. *woltou* 417, *artou* 455, etc. In 3 sg. fem. A has *scho* 99, 100; B *ho* 49, 59, *a* 48. In the neut. both scribes usually write *hit*: 61–3, 156, 390, 426; but *it* 134 (A).

In 2 pl. *ʒe*, *ʒ(o)u*, *ʒour* are usual in both hands and are kept apart normally; B has *ou* and *or* 387. In 3 pl. the nom. does not occur in A; B has *þai* 361, 365, 367, *þe* 374, *he* 345. The poss. is *har* 370 (B), and obj. *ham* 104 (A), 372 (B).

This manuscript has the advantage over most of its contemporaries that its approximate place of writing is certainly known. There is no doubt that the play must have been copied on to the roll in Dublin, and it is a notable example of the different spelling systems that could be used by two men working side by side. Mills plausibly suggested that two monks might have copied it hastily, on the first convenient parchment, from a text brought by a passing visitor. Brandl, followed by Waterhouse, argued that the scribes must have followed a written original, not worked from dictation or from memory, because of errors such as confusion of *s* and *f* in 42 and 360 and the supposed omission of an abbreviation mark in *gentil* 333. The last of these cannot be sustained (see p. lxxxviii above), and in view of the general coarseness of B's letter-forms the others cannot be either. The differences between the two men's treatment of the text are such that they can hardly have been copying from the same manuscript; one of them may have been copying, the other working from dictation. If this is so the copyist was surely A, who despite some lapses maintained a fairly regular and traditional orthography. The simplest (though not the only) explanation of B's wholesale omission of final *-e*, and of *ʒ* in words like 'right', would be that he was working from dictation in the fifteenth century after both these sounds had been lost. Dictation would not in itself account for his other peculiarities, but it would leave him freer to indulge them than copying an exemplar would.

There is a striking resemblance between many of the linguistic features of this play and those of the 'Kildare poems', as Heuser convincingly showed in his edition of them.[1] The links he noted are partly in scribal practice which cannot be confirmed by rhyme: e.g. the strong predominance of *i* in unstressed endings in both hands, which contrasts unusually with southerly features such as syncopated forms in 3 sg.; predominant *i-* in past participles; occasional infins. in *-y(e)*; particular forms such as *lib*, *sig(ge)*, *chong*, *streinth*, *throgh*; or the pronouns *þai*, *har*, *ham*, and in part

---

[1] W. Heuser, *Die Kildare-Gedichte* (Bonn, 1904), pp. 66–71. Though this book was published five years before Waterhouse's he took no account of it, and most later writers on the play have, perhaps in consequence, ignored it.

ho in the play (B) corresponding to *ȝho* in the poems. He might have added that B's *bis(s)op* and perhaps *ficis* recall numerous spellings in the Kildare texts with *ss*, such as *fissis*, *fleis(se)*, *waiïssing*, and that even the confusion of *þ* and *ȝ* appears once in *fleeȝ* for *fleeþ* (*Cokaygne* 103). But in rhyme also there are important agreements: OE. *ā* is always *o*; *a* before a single nasal is *a*, and it is particularly noteworthy that 'upon' occurs repeatedly spelt *apan*, and rhymes on *man* (also on *can*, *þan*, etc.) as it does in the play; OE. *ēo* and *y* are similarly unrounded; final -*e* has largely been dropped; final -*n* is lost in infins. and past participles except monosyllables; the pres. pl. in -*þ* rhymes with the 3 sg. There are in addition some significant individual rhymes in both manuscripts; e.g. as the play has the assonances *ikaȝte*:*lafte* and *bronde*:*wronge* the poems have *betauȝt*:-*craft*, *hond*:*strang*; the by-form *fale* 'many', otherwise restricted in currency, rhymes in the play 207 on *tale*, in *Cokaygne* 95 on *niȝtingale*. Despite the occasional northerly features of A's work (*qwh*-, *scho*, -*is* in pres., *schal* in 2 sg., -*en* in past parts.) and the eccentricities of B's spelling, there is so much common ground between the play and the poems that Heuser was surely right in claiming that the exemplar of the play was Anglo-Irish. This conclusion is strengthened by comparisons he made between the poems and other Irish manuscripts, notably the fifteenth-century Dublin manuscript of *The English Conquest of Ireland*,[1] which Brandl had already briefly compared with *The Pride of Life*. Some significant similarities in that text are occasional spellings such as *bissoppes*, *fleysly*; the pronouns *sho*, *thay*, *har(e)*, *ham*; infins. such as *defouly*, *tholy*; regular *i*- and frequent -*t* in past parts., as *ichaunget*; characteristic forms such as *fale*, *sigge*, *streynth*, *throgh* (Heuser, pp. 61–6). All these and many other manuscripts in the English of Ireland are now authoritatively discussed by A. McIntosh and M. L. Samuels in the important article in *Medium Ævum* (1968) referred to on p. lxxix above.[2]

Heuser observed further that there is a more general resemblance between the metrical technique of the play—which as noted above is unusually simple—and that of the homiletic poems in the Kildare manuscript. These are written in similar cross-rhyming quatrains varying in the number of stresses to the line, though with far fewer

[1] Ed. F. J. Furnivall, E.E.T.S., o.s. 107 (1896).
[2] See also *The Virtues of Herbs in the Loscombe Manuscript*, ed. A. Zettersten (Acta Universitatis Lundensis, Sect. 1. 5, 1967).

three-stress lines than the play. It might perhaps be added that one of the poems, called by its author 'þis sarmun', is in part remarkably like the Bishop's sermon in the play:

> þei3 man be rich of lond and lede
> And holdiþ festis ofte and lome,
> Hit is no doute he sal be ded,
> To 3eld recning at þe dome.

Admittedly nothing could be more commonplace. Heuser took the view that though the immediate exemplar of the play must have been Anglo-Irish, whether the original was equally so was 'more than doubtful' because of the references to Berwick-on-Tweed and 'Gailispire on þe Hil' (285, 301). Mills had written:

... that the work is an English not a Dublin composition seems certain from the three place-names which occur. Berwick-on-Tweed is mentioned in a way in which only one writing in England would be likely to refer to it. The earldom of Kent is conferred as a reward on the messenger, and it has been pointed out that this earldom was vacant from soon after the beginning of the fifteenth century. The third name is the Castle of Galispire on the hill. Of this place I have not yet obtained any satisfactory identification; but it is certainly an English, not an Irish name.

The castle has still not been identified. Brandl guessed Galleyhill in Berkshire, on what grounds he did not say; a better guess on linguistic grounds would be Gasper in Wiltshire (formerly in Somerset), which was written *Gayespore* and *Gayspore* in the thirteenth and fourteenth centuries.[1] This remains a puzzle. The other two names need not exclude an Irish origin. The reference to the earldom implies no special territorial interest. And though 'Hen to Berewik opon Twede' at first sight suggests a starting-point in the south of England, the town could also be regarded as the north-eastern, rather than simply northern, extremity of the country and so a proper enough opposite to a place in southern Ireland.

The vocabulary includes a small number of more or less unusual words, which do not form a coherent group. *Boun* 32 and *charp* 53 (i.e. *carp* in the sense 'speak') are predominantly northerly, the latter especially in alliterative verse, but are too common and widespread to be particularly indicative. *Munit* 47 (if this is indeed the right reading) is more limited to the north, and the form is western.

---

[1] J. E. B. Gover, A. Mawer, and F. M. Stenton, *The Place-Names of Wiltshire* (E.P.N.S. xvi, 1939), p. 181.

Grou 132 is still more northern in the records; but the reading is not certain—the scribe is B, and, as *M.E.D.* suggests, perhaps *greu* might be read, giving a more easily explicable rhyme (on the variant *beheue*). Yet the sense of *grou* is distinctly apter, and the unusual rhyme can be defended. *Alyng* 134 seems to be predominantly western; *stotey* 36 is recorded elsewhere only in *William of Palerne* (similarly linked with *strengþe*), and to that extent has western associations. One word does appear to be distinctly western— *lake* 269 must mean 'stream', not 'lake', over which not even this messenger would 'leap lightly'. That is, it is *O.E.D.*'s *lake* sb.³, OE. *lacu*. Though this is common in place-names in the midlands as well as the south, in ME. use it appears to be characteristically western and south-west midland, and mainly south-western in modern dialects.¹ Its distribution is therefore comparable to that of *fale*, which occurs mainly in texts of south-western origin, though also in Thomas Chestre and in *Otuel and Roland*.² This is one of a number of southern and south-western features in Anglo-Irish, as Heuser shows (pp. 54–5) and McIntosh and Samuels confirm; *lake* could well be another.

None of the objections to an Irish origin of the play appear to be decisive. Its linguistic affinities with the Kildare poems are not only in scribal usage but in a distinctive cluster of criteria certified by rhyme, and it is reasonable to conclude that it was composed as well as written down in Ireland.

The same linguistic affinities are relevant to date of composition. Some of the rhymes would in any case suggest a date somewhat earlier than that of the manuscript: the rhyme *soþe*:*to þe* is of a type unlikely to be later than the early fifteenth century (it is still found in Hoccleve); the assonance *ikaȝte*:*lafte* confirms, against scribe B's simplified spellings, the preservation of the fricative before *t*. But the general similarity of sounds and forms indicates that the composition of the play cannot have been very much later than that of the poems—certainly not a century later. There is good reason to date the writing of the Kildare manuscript in the first quarter of the fourteenth century; some of the poems in it were

---

¹ See A. H. Smith, *English Place-Name Elements*, ii (E.P.N.S. xxvi, 1956), 8; *D.O.S.T.*, under *lake* n.², 3; *E.D.D.* under *lake* sb.².
² For its south-westerly associations see Jordan, *Me. Grammatik*, § 73 Anm. 2. For the others, *Lybeaus Descomus*, ed. M. Mills, E.E.T.S. 261 (1969), pp. 34, 37; *Firumbras and Otuel and Roland*, ed. M. L. O'Sullivan, E.E.T.S. 198 (1935), O. l. 2098.

composed before 1300, but at least one was not—the poem on the death of Peter of Bermingham, who died in 1308. *The Pride of Life* is therefore likely to have been composed as early as the middle of the fourteenth century. This would make it much earlier than any other substantially surviving moral play; but its simple structure, spare treatment of dialogue, and unsubtle presentation of character are in keeping with this.

VIII. *DUX MORAUD*

Manuscript. Bodleian MS. Eng. Poet. f. 2 (R). The description in the *Summary Catalogue* under no. 30519, by F. Madan, is as follows:

> In English, on parchment: written in the 14th cent.: a roll 4ft. 2 in. × 3¾–4 in., in two pieces, in a cloth box 5⅜ × 1½ squ. in.: in parts almost illegible.
>
> A roll of English poems, apparently songs: those on the recto are secular, those on the verso religious. The first on the recto is headed 'Dux Moraud' (Duke Vagabond) and is thirty-six lines, beginning 'Emperoures & kynges bekende'. This interesting roll is written on a margin (cut off) of an Assize Roll for Norfolk and Suffolk of the second half of the 13th century, a small part of which is left.
>
> Referenced in 1892 or 1893.

In addition to its major misunderstanding of the contents, this account needs modification in some particulars. The parchment roll itself is 2 ft. 11¾ in. long; the other 14 in. in Madan's description includes a strip of coated buckram, the same width as the parchment, stitched to the top to protect it. This was apparently added (together with the box) when the roll was 'referenced' in 1892 or 1893. The two pieces of parchment, the first of which is about 1 ft. 8½ in. long, are now joined by a strip of the same buckram, about ⅞ in. wide, pasted on; but surviving holes show that they were originally stitched together. They were already joined when the text was written, for the scribe allowed for the stitching and there is no break in the stanza structure or the sense. The date of the original roll is probably rather later than 'the second half of the thirteenth century'. Fragments of some of the entries survive on the verso, most of them below the last part of the play. A column of names, partly cut away, with sums of money written opposite them, is preceded by the remains of a heading:

Fugitiuo*rum et* amerciamento*rum* Coram W de Ormesby
Transgre*ssibus* in com̄ Norff' et Suff' aud*iendis et* term[i]nandis.

The first editor of the text, Wilhelm Heuser (see below), noted
with respect to the first line that 'Ormesby liegt bekanntlich in
Norfolk'. But this in itself means little. The reference is not to the
place, but to a judge; and this can hardly be other than William de
Ormesby, an eminent judge in the reigns of Edward I and Edward
II, whose name appears a great many times in the Patent and Close
Rolls from April 1292 until shortly before his death in 1317. He is
first mentioned as a justice in eyre and of oyer and terminer in
Lancashire and other northern counties, and he was in Scotland
on the King's service in 1296. It is true that he took his name from
Ormesby in Norfolk, and was probably born there; certainly he
lived close by, for the Patent Roll records his complaint in 1297
that while he had been in Scotland his goods at Caister had been
stolen—Caister, a mile or two from Ormesby, was later the site of
Sir John Fastolf's castle. But, though his work was occasionally in
East Anglia in the last years of the thirteenth century, it was for the
ten years from about 1305 that, as Tout puts it, he was 'very active
as justice of assize' in Norfolk and Suffolk; the last date when he
was so occupied seems to be February 1316.[1] It is therefore rather
more likely that the present roll dates from the early years of the
fourteenth century than from the thirteenth; the handwriting of
course cannot be dated closely enough to determine this. On the
other hand, the record cannot be later than Ormesby's death in
1317.

The handwriting of the play is very much later, of the fifteenth
rather than the fourteenth century and probably of the second
quarter[2]—it resembles that of some Paston documents of about
1440–50. The hand is coarse and often irregular in form and
spacing, but considering the awkwardness of writing on a long
narrow strip of this kind it is reasonably competent. The text is
easily legible except where there has been physical damage, but in
some places this is severe. At the foot of the recto the surface of the
parchment has cracked and partly flaked away, taking some of the
writing with it. Doubtless in order to prevent further deterioration
this part of the roll had long ago been covered with adhesive paper,

[1] See *D.N.B.*
[2] Mr. M. B. Parkes, who examined the manuscript at my request but without
knowing my opinion of its date, reached the same conclusion.

presumably once transparent but so obscuring several lines that they could not be read at all, and ultra-violet light would not penetrate. At my request the Keeper of Western Manuscripts—who took the view that the paper was in any case doing no good—very kindly had it removed in the summer of 1967. Though some of what had been written under it turned out to be too far gone, several words not previously made out could be read. At the head of the verso the damage is more extensive, though of a different kind; it is the result of rubbing and soiling of the exposed part of the roll, before the nineteenth-century buckram was added. Much of the first stanza on the verso (lines 151–63) is simply worn away, and ultra-violet light brings up only a little.

The text of the play is written in verse lines, with the rhymes linked by brackets of various shapes (as the facsimile shows), and the tail-lines often though not always set to the right. There are 150 verse lines on the recto, of the total of 268. A line across the roll marks the end of each speech, but there are no indications of speaker except the heading, and no stage directions. The disjointed nature of the content shows that the entire text is a single actor's part in a morality play—in some ways comparable to the Shrews-bury fragments, but without the cues so prominent there. This fact remained long unrecognized. Madan's entry in the *Summary Catalogue*, quoted above, failed to perceive that a coherent plot could be traced throughout the disconnected parts. Chambers remarked in 1945, 'I shall always regret that I once came upon the manuscript and failed to recognize its nature'.[1] Credit for under-standing it belongs to Heuser, who in *Anglia*, xxx (1907), published the text with a valuable commentary and extracts from analogues. His text where the manuscript is legible was mostly very accurate. In the almost obliterated lines at the top of the verso he printed a number of words that cannot now be read at all; I record them in the footnotes—though not all appear to fit the context—because it is likely enough that more could be seen in his day. I have followed Heuser also in numbering the speeches, so that an attempt can be made below to outline their relation to the other parts of the play; but I depart from his numbering after X—his X (b) I number XI, since it is separated from the preceding stanza by the usual line and is evidently a distinct speech, his XI, XII, and XIII become XII, XIII, and XIV, and XIV includes also Heuser's XIV be-

[1] *English Literature at the Close of the Middle Ages*, p. 65.

cause lines 151–63 must form a single speech—the dividing line he mentions in his footnote to 160 does not exist, only a crease in the parchment. From XV the numbers coincide again. The only other edition of the play has been that by Adams, in *Chief Pre-Shakespearean Dramas*, pp. 207–11. He reprinted Heuser's text without checking it against the manuscript, but altered the speaker's name at the head from '[D]ux' to '[D]uk' (in fact *Dux* can be read), and emended lines 20 and 47. He provided conjectural speakers' names for the missing speeches, explanatory passages filling the most important gaps in the plot, scene divisions, and some stage directions.

Plot. The name *Dux Moraud*, or *Duk Morawd* as it appears in line 27, is obviously that of the character whose part this is; it need not have been the name by which the play was known. It occurs nowhere else, and its significance is unknown; Craig[1] rightly observes that there is no satisfactory ground for associating it with *maraude* 'vagabond' as Madan was apparently the first to do. But the story of an incestuous daughter who kills her mother and her child, and finally her father as well, is known in a number of versions in both Latin and English. The closest to the present play is a poem extant in three manuscripts, differing somewhat in content, printed by Heuser and earlier by Horstmann.[2] The parallels make it possible to reconstruct the action of the play with some confidence, as follows. Conjectural events are in parentheses; numbers refer to the speeches in the text:

I. Dux Moraud addresses the audience, with the request for silence usually made in prologues, and continues with a boastful speech about his own power similar to those of Aristorius in *The Play of the Sacrament* and the King of Life in *The Pride of Life*.
(His wife tells him that she is about to go on a journey.)
II. He expresses approval and urges her to come home soon.
(She hopes he will behave well in her absence.)
III. He promises to resist temptation and sin, and prays for Christ's help.
(She takes leave of him.)
IV. He gives her an affectionate farewell.

---

[1] *Religious Drama*, p. 327.
[2] By Heuser in *Anglia*, xxx, 201–5, by Horstmann in *Altenglische Legenden, Neue Folge* (Heilbronn, 1881), pp. 334–8. See *Index*, nos. 1107, 1762.

V. He approaches his daughter and declares his love for her.
(She accepts his advances.)

VI. He expresses his delight and suggests that they should go to her room.
(Apparently his wife returns and discovers their illicit relationship.)

VII. He tells his daughter of his fear that the 'traitor' will reveal their secret unless she is killed.
(The daughter kills her mother.)

VIII. Dux Moraud asks his daughter if she has killed their enemy.
(She assures him that she has.)

IX. He expresses relief and delight.
(The daughter gives birth to a child.)

X. He is horrified at the thought of the scandal that will follow, and asks to see the child.
(She brings it.)

XI. He tells her to kill the child.
(She does so, and returns to tell him.)

XII. He is again in excellent spirits now that the risk of exposure has been removed.

XIII. He proposes to go into the country, apparently to cultivate good relations with neighbours. [Some readings are uncertain.]

XIV. This is the stanza that is largely illegible. As far as it can be made out, Dux Moraud takes affectionate leave of his daughter. [Heuser—who read less of the preceding stanza—understood it differently, taking the first part to contain instructions to the daughter to dispose of the child's body, and the second part to give Moraud's joyful greeting to her when she has returned from doing so. Adams separated the two parts by his scene division, 'The danger of discovery being over, Duk Moraud returns, to greet his daughter with joy'. But this cannot be right: there is no line marking the end of a speech, and 'Have good day' (which is one of the phrases that can faintly but clearly be seen) was much more often a formula of parting than of greeting—cf. VII. 447 and speech XX below.]

XV. Dux Moraud is again in good heart and boasts of his person and position.

XVI. He hears a church bell and decides to go to church.

XVII. He comes out of church repenting of his sin and anxious to confess.
(A priest comes to him.)

XVIII. He welcomes the priest and makes his confession.
(The priest requires him to abandon his sinful life and imposes penance.)

XIX. Moraud accepts the penance to save his soul.
(He goes home.)

XX. He greets his daughter [saying 'Hail', not 'Have good day'].
(She returns his greeting, expecting to resume their cohabitation.)
XXI. He tells her to say no more of this, for he has renounced his sin
and undertaken to do penance.
(She reproaches him for having led her into such wickedness and then
forsaken her; and she wounds him mortally—according to the poem in
MS. Rawl. 118,

> And whane hire fader on slepe was
> She went here þeder a wole gode pas
> And cutte his þrote a-too.)

XXII. He feels death approaching, and prays Jesus to forgive his
daughter and have mercy on his soul.

This need not have been the end of the play. These events
occupy only the first half of the poem printed by Horstmann; in
the latter part the woman goes to another country and lives for a
time as a prostitute, but eventually repents, dies, and is forgiven.

Verse. There is considerable variety in both length of line and
structure of stanza. Some lines obviously form part of stanzas that
are incomplete here because the remainder of them was spoken by
another actor; and some which could form a complete stanza may
also be part of a larger unit. Most lines have three stresses, but
some, usually but not always in sequence, have four—especially in
the stanzas beginning at 59 and 164. In the longer stanzas there are
some two-stress lines and many 'bob' lines of a single stress. The
most frequent pattern is the common six-line *aabccb*, which appears
in at least thirteen stanzas: 40–5, 119–36, 145–50, 177–94, 206–29,
263–8. The three lines 230–2, the last lacking a rhyme, are evidently
the second half of a stanza of this kind. The related type of eight
lines, *aaabcccb*, occurs only in two stanzas, 237–52. The metrical
structure of 151–63, now almost illegible, cannot be determined
with confidence. If it were not for Heuser's readings the existence
of some of the conjectured lines, especially 153 and 156, might be
doubted, for the parchment is now so discoloured that nothing,
not even rhyme-brackets, can be identified at these points; but in
view of his substantial accuracy elsewhere the pattern he presents is
probably to be trusted. If it is right, 151–6 form another six-line
stanza of the favoured kind (the same as the preceding one), but
157–63 make an exceptional combination of the six- and eight-line

structures, having three lines in the first part of the stanza and four in the second. In view of the unusual arrangements in some other stanzas of which the text is not in doubt, as noticed below, it seems most likely that 151–63 formed a single stanza.

Most of the rest of this actor's part is written in the thirteen-line stanza with which it opens. The rhymes in all but one of these stanzas are arranged *ababababcdddc*—a pattern especially favoured in *The Castle of Perseverance* (which has over 220 stanzas of this shape), prominent also in the *Ludus Coventriae*, and occasional in the Towneley cycle. There are seven stanzas of this form: 1–39, 72–97, 100–12, 164–76. All but the last have a single-stress bob as the ninth line, but line 172 has two stresses—this stanza is throughout weightier than the others, having four instead of three stresses in the long lines, and heavy alliteration. One other stanza, 59–71, is similar in structure to the majority of this pattern (though again with longer main lines) except that the *a* rhyme is repeated instead of a *d—ababababcaaac*.[1] The nine lines 46–54, rhyming *ababcdddc*, are likely to be the latter part of a thirteen-line stanza. The eleven lines 195–205 are exceptional: they begin like a six-line stanza but the seventh line is a bob and the remainder has the same form as the end of a thirteen-line stanza—*aabccbdeeed*. The ten lines of the penultimate stanza 253–62 are also arranged in a way unique in the play—*ababaacddc*. There remain four groups of lines with alternate rhyme, two of four lines, 55–8 and 233–6, one of six, 113–18, and one of eight, 137–44. These could stand alone, but might also be parts of longer stanzas. Lines 98–9 do not rhyme, and must be part of a stanza.

Language. The rhymes show no important discrepancy between the language of the scribe and that of the original, though in a few places he uses discordant variants of a commonplace kind. The most unusual rhyme is *drywe:rywe* 128–9, in which *drywe* is the verb 'drive' (used in the sense 'suffer', *M.E.D.* under *driven* 10 (a)), and *rywe* must be an adjective descended from OE. *hrēow*, though *O.E.D.* records *rue* only as a noun. If the rhyme is true it means that the *w* in *drywe* is not merely a spelling for /v/ but a phonetic

---

[1] Heuser's text obscures the form of this stanza by printing the bob as the tenth instead of the ninth line. It is, as usual, to the right of the long lines in the manuscript, but was certainly written before 68 because the last word of that line is crowded in below it. Adams corrected the order silently, no doubt on the basis of the stanza structure.

variant. The quality of the rhyme *kyrk*: *work* 179–82 is uncertain: either /i/ or /e/ could be justified.

Final unstressed -*e* is freely written, sometimes where it is not historically in place, as *tylle* 20, *fone* 32, *gone* 34, *tythe* 61, *none* 189. In many words no -*e* is written where it would have been appropriate, as *fas*, *plas*, *falas* 10–12, *mak* 24, *hot* 27, *pray* 43, *slaw* 95, *blam*, *nam* 198–9, *begyn* 211, *blyn* 244. It is shown by rhyme to have been lost in the original: e.g. the nouns *wylle*, *hille*, *sille* 14, 16, 18, *gras*, *fas* 72, 74, *blam* 184; the pl. adj. *gay* 250; the adv. *hend* 231; the infins. *mynt* 26, *led* 107; the 1 sg. *say* 205.

The reflex of OE. *ā*, including words in which it developed from *a* before a lengthening consonant group, is usually written *o*: *none*, *one*, *fone*, *gone* rhyme together at 28 ff., *none* and *bone* 189–90, *lond* and *hond* 56–8, 133–6, *fonde* and *honde* 81–3; *bolde*, *holde*, *solde* 2 ff. rhyme on *folde*, *fro* 264 on *to*. It is exceptionally written *a* in *lare* 167, 217 and *sare* 171, rhyming on *fare*, *care*.

The reflex of OE. *a* before a nasal not in a lengthening group is written *a*: *thanc* 73, *scham* 144; *name*, *game*, *tame* 27 ff. rhyme on *fame*, *nam*(e) 67, 199 on *blam*(e).

The reflex of OE. *ǣ*¹ in *red* 105 rhymes on that of *ǣ*² in *led* and probably *ēa* in *qued*. The reflex of OE. *ēo* in *dere*, *lere* 238–9 rhymes on that of *ē* in *here*. Earlier *ē* is written *y* in *kyppe* 39, rhyming on *scheppe* 'ship' (but *kepyn* 48 not in rhyme), and in *fylde* 150, not in rhyme.

The reflex of OE. *ȳ* is usually written *i* or *y*: *pride* 21 rhymes on *wyde*, etc., 172 on *ryde*; *mynd*, *kynd* 164, 168 on *fynd*, *lynd*. But before *nd* it is written *e* in *kende*, *mende* 1, 3, rhyming on *sende*, *hende*, and *mend* 148 rhyming on *wend*, etc. The short sound in *syn* 240, 261 rhymes on *blyn*, 208 on *begyn*; *hille* 16 and *fulfylle* 41 rhyme on *wylle*, etc. But it is written *e* in *wenne* 47, though the rhyme is *synne*. Outside rhyme *e* appears in *dede* 99, *mery* 100, 107, 110, 164, *merth*(*is*) 68, 136.

Words containing earlier *iht* are written with either *yt* or *yth*, as *bryt* 119, *knytys* 3, *lyt* 170, *myt* 221, *mytty* 235, *ryt* 175; *bryth* 63, 75, *brythest* 65, *lythe* 84, *myth* 68, 118, *nyth* 69. Earlier -*th* is sometimes written *t*, as *wyt* 22, *fryt* 165, and numerous endings in 3 sg. of verbs; and -*t* is written *th* in *tyth*(*e*) 61, 200. (Initial *t* is spelt *th* also, in *thowr* 138.) Most of the -*iht* words rhyme between themselves, but *syte, bryth*, and others in the stanza beginning at 59, and *myth* 197, rhyme on *tyth(e)*.

Words containing earlier *oht* are written with *owt*, never *owth*, as *bowt(ys)* 52, 186, *browt* 101, *dowty* 36, *nowt* 125, *thowt(ys)* 53, 66, 121, etc.; but *out* in *douter* 217, 233, 237. This group rhymes only within itself.

The use of *w* for *v* noticed above in *drywe* 128 in rhyme appears also, outside rhyme, in *schrywe* 210 as well as initially and medially in *weleny* 39, *wyage* 41, *ewyl* 105.

Spellings not concerned in rhyme include the following:

e appears occasionally for earlier *i*: *scheppe* 35, *weleny* 39, *peper* 180, *leuende* 234, *smetyn* 255; *dede* and *mery* (noticed above) could also be so explained, and perhaps *bleli* 230 (reduced from *blethely* as *worly(ch)* 37, 55, 79 from *worthly*).

The initial consonant of 'give' is always *g*: *geue* 31, 87, 142, 204, *forgeue* 187; similarly *gyftys* 31; also *ageyne* 45, *ageynus* 197.

ȝ is used initially in *ȝe* 8, *ȝow* 7, *ȝoure* 13, *ȝemen* 4, *ȝendyr* 179, *ȝon* 89, etc.; *y* is used in this function only in *yangelyngys* 8, *yon* 95. The letter-form *y*, in addition to its very common use for the vowel, serves for *þ*, and is so printed in the present edition. It is used initially in short words, commonly abbreviated, such as *þat* 6, *þer* 18, *þan* 29, etc., but also medially as *neyþer* 24, *worþiest* 70, *soþe* 71, and in some words which earlier had *-der*: *queþire* 34, *peþer* 180. *Th* is an alternative both initially as *thorow* 46, *thowtys* 53, and medially as *welthys* 14, *merthis* 68.

A striking peculiarity of this scribe's spelling is his omission of *h-* in most forms of 'have': *aue* 16, 64, 91, etc., *auen* 73, *auyn* 136, *ast* 186, *auyt* 191, *ad* 126, 127, in addition to the fairly common weak form *a* 102, 104. This is not quite universal—*h-* survives in *ha* 161, *haue* 267, *had* 222. In other words it is written normally—*holde* 4, *hende* 7, etc.—except in *allys* 'halls' 142.

The initial sound of words earlier beginning with *hw-* is regularly written *qu-*: *quan* 173, *quat* 88, *sumquat* 188, *queþire* 34, *quy(l)k* 219, 262, *quylys* 209. Almost the converse appears in *sueyerys* 'squires' 4.

The initial sound now spelt *sh* is usually written *sch-*: *schewe* 13, 62, *schrewed* 103, etc. But parts of 'shall' have *x-*: *xal* 12, 21, 48, etc., *xalt* 73, 77, *xul* 91, *xuld* 104, 128, etc., except *suld* 102;

and 'she' is regularly *che*, as 101, 102, 104, 106. On the other hand, 'child' is spelt *schyld* 114, beside *chyld* 218. A parasitic *c* appears in *sclawe* 121, 222, *sclow* 225, beside *slo* 133.

In a few words an earlier final -*d* in an unstressed syllable is spelt *t*: *korownyt* (past part.) 30, *formyt* (past t.) 47, *wykyt* 53, 252 (beside *wykkyd* 243). In *ryngant* 178 the ending may have been influenced by the corresponding French inflexion.

In unstressed inflexional syllables the vowel, when not abbreviated, is usually written *y*: e.g. *kepyn* 48, *aryn* 6, *bowyn* 33, *smetyn* 255; *moryst* 68, *pottyst* 144; *auyt* 191, *rengnyt* 29, *korownyt* 30; *erlys, barunnys, bachelerys* 2–3, *ellys* 21, *cursydnessys* 214; *chambyr* 84, *ʒendyr* 179. There are a few cases of *i*: *quepire* 34, *merthis* 68, *rayis* 176, *opir* 265; and some of *e*: *auen* 73, *schrewed* 103, *neyper* 24, *korteyser* 28, *worpiest, wytthest* 70, *fayrest* 166. Once *u* is written, in *syttun* (-*n* represented by a stroke above) 171. The abbreviation customary for -*us* is used in *resoun*us 13, *ageyn*us 197, *synn*us 216, 229. Since this has slight support from *syttun* it is so expanded here (as by Heuser), though without much confidence. It is noticeable that all the examples are after *n*, and it may have been only a scribal trick to use it in that position, without regard to the precise quality of the vowel—there are no rhymes to indicate this.

The following are the main features of inflexion:

Noun plurals and genitives nearly all end in -*ys* or -*is*; exceptions are *fone* 32, *dawe* 124 (OE. *dagum*).

In verbs, the pres. indic. 2 sg. (and past sg. of weak verbs) ends in -*st*: *ast* 259, 262, *moryst* 68, *pottyst* 144; but also in -*ys* (abbreviated) in *wrowty*s, *bowty*s 51, 52, rhyming on *thowty*s. In 3 sg. the ending is written -*t*: *rengnyt* 29, *comyt* 148, 263, *auyt* 191. Pres. pl. ends in -*n* in *aryn* 6, *bowyn* 33, *rydyn, gone* 34, but without it in *are* 10, 173, 209, *scheppe* 35; *xul* 91 keeps the old vowel of the pl., but *xal* 92 has taken the form of the sg. Imper. is without ending: *mak* 8, *set* 11.

Infin. is usually without ending (often verified by rhyme, e.g. *mende* 3, *holde* 4, *sende* 5, *mynt* 26), but occasional forms, none in rhyme, have -*n*: *ben* 134 and *don* 249 before words beginning with a vowel, and *auen* 73, *auyn* 136, 205, *kepyn* 48, *leykyn* 65, 170, *makyn* 76, *syttu*n 171, *wendyn* 83. Pres. parts are *ryngant* 178 and, with extension of function, *berende* 75, *leuende* 234.

Past participles of strong and anomalous verbs sometimes end in -*n*: *knowyn* 15, *castyn* 63, 169, *wo(u)ndyn* 70, 85, *slayne* 98, *ben* 105, *begotyn* 113, *woxyn* 175, *forsakyn* 239, *smetyn* 255, *don* 259, 262. But none of these is in rhyme, whereas numerous forms without -*n* are fixed by rhyme: *bownde* 86, *fownde*, *found* 92, 104, *wownd* 106, 115, 117, *slaw, sclawe* 95, 121, 222, *forsake* 241, *take* 242. The prefix *i*- never appears.

Of the personal pronouns, in 2 pl. *ʒe, ʒow, ʒoure* or *ʒowre* are regularly used; in 3 pl. the nom. is *þei* 34, obl. *hem* 174. The relative pronoun is *quyk* 219, *quylk* 262, beside usual *þat*.

The vocabulary contains a number of words, and variant forms, which are predominantly northern or north-east midland in currency: *beyne* 42, *boun* 147, *ded* 'death' 101, *duere* 25, 174, perhaps *egment* 226 (though it occurs once in Chaucer), *ʒendyr* 179, *ʒon* 89, *kyrk* 179, *leykyn* 65, 170, *quy(l)k* 219, 262, *syttys* 'sorrows' (*O.E.D., site* sb.¹) 171, *slo* 133, *tent* 87, *werd, word* 'world' 15, 189.

Many particulars of the language are distinctive: spellings with *x*- and *qu*-; loss of the fricative before *t* in *ryt(h), browt*, etc.; spellings such as *kende*, and their rhyming with *sende*, etc.; *e* for *i* in words like *smetyn*; -*yt* in 3 sg. pres.; *che* for 'she'; predominance of *y* in unstressed syllables; some characteristic words. These, in association with more widespread features such as the relation of the vowels in *honde* and *name*, the general loss of -*e*, and the distribution of -*n* in verbal inflexions, are well known in texts from East Anglia in the fifteenth century. Many of them appear in the Macro plays, the *Ludus Coventriae*, and the more provincially coloured writers of the Paston letters; some in one text if not in another— notably, the present participle endings -*ende* and -*and* (here -*ant*) are not used in the letters but occur, as minority forms presumably obsolescent, in *The Castle of Perseverance*. The closest resemblance to the particular blend of constituents in *Dux Moraud* is to be found in B.M. MS. Sloane 2593, the famous collection of poems, largely carols, printed by Thomas Wright over a century ago and often drawn upon since in anthologies.¹ This manuscript is clearly

¹ *Songs and Carols*, ed. T. Wright (Warton Club, 1856); B. Fehr, 'Die Lieder der Hs. Sloane 2593', *Archiv*, cix (1902), 33–70; extracts in R. L. Greene, *The Early English Carols* (Oxford, 1935) and *A Selection of English Carols* (Oxford,

from Bury St. Edmunds, probably, as Greene says, from the monastery; it is dated by Greene in the first half of the fifteenth century, by Fehr, Robbins, and *M.E.D.* about the middle of the century. Heuser remarked (*Anglia*, xxx, p. 198) that the pronoun form *che* was known to him only in *Dux Moraud* and in this manuscript. In fact it is not quite so rare: for example, it is regularly used by one of Agnes Paston's clerks writing in her name from Norwich from about 1450 to 1458. (It is found occasionally also in *William of Palerne*, much earlier and of mixed scribal character.) All the other features mentioned above appear conspicuously, though not entirely consistently, in the Sloane manuscript, which agrees with *Dux Moraud* in having frequent *qu-* instead of the more widely used *qw-*. The two most important details in which the play differs are its regular *geue* (instead of *ʒeue*) and its use of *quy(l)k* (twice, as relative). The former is not remarkable in East Anglia in the fifteenth century: it appears in the Macro plays as an alternative, and is regularly used by several of the Pastons and their clerks (including the one who writes *che*). The latter, however, is very rare, not to be found in the letters at all; *qwilk* does occur in a Norwich guild return.[1] It must surely have been old-fashioned; on the other hand *peper*, with *p* for earlier *-d-*, is advanced.

The strongly East Anglian character of the language of the play is consonant with the Norfolk–Suffolk origin of the parchment roll on which it is written. The apparent date of the handwriting, perhaps the second quarter of the fifteenth century, also fits most of the language very well. The forms of the present participle, and of *quy(l)k*, are archaic at this date, but obviously the present text is a copy of an earlier one. This, together with the similarity of some of the versification to that of *The Castle of Perseverance*, may suggest an original early in the fifteenth century.

IX. THE CAMBRIDGE PROLOGUE

Manuscript. Cambridge University Library Mm. I. 18, f. 62ʳ. The manuscript is a composite volume containing seven miscellaneous Latin tracts of various dates from the twelfth to the

1962); R. H. Robbins, *Secular Lyrics of the XIVth and XVth Centuries* (Oxford, 2nd edn., 1955) and *Historical Poems of the XIVth and XVth Centuries* (New York, 1959). The most recent description of the manuscript is by Greene, *Selection*, pp. 173–4.

[1] *English Gilds*, ed. Toulmin Smith, E.E.T.S., o.s. 40 (1870), p. 37.

fifteenth century. The second item comprises thirty leaves of parchment, of which twenty-nine are occupied by the *Summa Magistri Guidonis* [*Fabe*], a list of saints' days, and odd notes. The last, which measures about $8\frac{3}{4} \times 5\frac{3}{4}$ inches, is a palimpsest, and its lower right-hand corner has been cut away without affecting the text. The French and English texts here printed are written, in the same new hand throughout, close to the left margin. The English follows the French immediately, with no space or other indication that a change has occurred.

The Library Catalogue describes the final leaves thus: 'The last two leaves contain a list of Saints' Days that have vigils, &c., and a hymn, partly in French and partly in English, beginning "Oez, oez, seygnur, oez, oez." ' R. H. Robbins recognized that the 'hymn' was in fact the prologue to a play, and published the text for the first time in *Modern Language Notes*, lxv (1950), 30–5; at that time the leaf was numbered 58. He dated the handwriting, apparently correctly, 'not later than about 1300, and possibly the last quarter of the thirteenth century'. This is earlier than any other surviving dramatic text in English. The present text has been collated with the manuscript by Professor Dickins and me, and differs slightly from Robbins's in both French and English.

The French and the English fragments do not correspond in detail, so that neither can be a simple translation of the other; but the general content is the same—an audience is enjoined to listen quietly, and not disturb 'our game' (cf. VII. 111, XI. 3) on pain of punishment at the command of an emperor.

Verse and Language. Both the French and the English texts have 22 lines of essentially octosyllabic or four-stress type, rhyming in couplets. In the English version most of the rhymes are accurate, but not all: *atwe* 3 does not fit *go*, which must be right; *binde* 17 rhymes imperfectly with *swenge* (MS. *sowenge*). These spoilt rhymes show that the text has suffered in transmission.

There are several exceptional spellings:

z, which has the same shape as in the French *oez* etc., often replaces *þ*, e.g. *zat* 2, 4, 5, 12, *z'* 13, *zing* 2, but evidently serves as *ȝ* in *zet* 17. The intention of *zu* 17 is not clear. It is an unlikely spelling, even here, for the prefix *to-*, and 'you' does not fit the sense; it is evidently corrupt and has been emended. *þ* is also used eccentrically, replacing *ȝ* initially in *þet* 21 and before *t* in *moþt* 4, *naþt* 6; the fricative is not expressed in *uyt* 14.

The sound /ʃ/ is written *sc* in *scame* 7, but the same spelling replaces *s*, probably indicating an intrusive /k/, in *scuerie* 'swear' 9; 'shall' is written *sal* 17, 20. There is uncertainty in the use of *u, v,* and *w*: *uer* 'were' 7, *scuerie*; *ev* 'you' 2, 4, 7, *vitles* 15 'witless'; *awonge* 'seize' 13. Initial *h* is written superfluously in *hure* 8, *his* 11, *heuer* 19; historical *h-* is kept in *hit* 7, 15, but lost in *it* 20.

The spellings *oe* in *soe* 'see' 19, *u* in *bu* rhyming with it (also in 15), and *eu* in *beut* 'are' 5 presumably represent a front rounded vowel. The use of *u* in *hur* 'here' 2 is extremely rare; *M.E.D.* records it from the Vespasian Homilies but considers it an error, which is likely enough.

The only pronunciation certified by the rhymes which is significant for localization is *fale* 5 rhyming on *tale*. Other sounds are shown in spelling: the reflex of OE. *ā*, and *a* before lengthening groups, is written *o* as *no* 2, *go* 4, *awonge*; that of *a* before a single nasal is written *a* as *scame* 7, *man* 11; that of *y* is written *u* in *muchel* 7 (the sound /u:/ is still spelt *u* in *nu* 1, *rume* 3, *lude* 6).

In unstressed inflexional syllables the vowel is written *e* except in *herkint* 1. An earlier final *-þ* is always written *t*: *sittet* 1, 3, 22, *herkint* 1, *beut* 5, *makiet* 6, as also in *bot* 'both' 7; so is earlier *-d* in the weak past part. *igadert* 5. The state of final *-e* cannot be determined from rhymes, but from the metre it appears to be well preserved except in eliding position: it is required in 6, in 8 even before (*h*)*ure*, in 12, 18, and in 22 in *mine* though not in *stille*.

In inflexions the main points of interest are in verbs, in the forms of the pres. pl. indic. and imper. ending in *-t* noticed above. 1 sg. pres. ends in *-ie* in *scuerie* 9, and *-i-* is also kept in imper. pl. *makiet* 6; 3 sg. is syncopated in *hat* 13, 17; past part. has the prefix *i-* in *igadert* 5. Of pronouns, 1 sg. is *I* 9 but *ich* 21; 3 pl. nom. is *þey* 5.

At the early date indicated by the handwriting most of the more irregular spellings can be paralleled in other manuscripts: comparable uses of *ʒ* and *þ*, for instance, in Bodl. MS. Ashmole 360 and B.M. MS. Royal 2 F. viii (see e.g. Carleton Brown, *English Lyrics of the XIIIth Century* (Oxford, 1932), nos. 37, 63). The spellings indicating rounded front vowels, the retention of *-i-* in *scuerie, makiet*, the past part. prefix *i-*, and especially the form *fale* (see p. xcix above) suggest the south-west of England. Yet the apparently unrounded vowel in *man* is out of keeping with this, and so, strikingly, are the pronoun *þey* (cf. *he* even in the easterly X) and *sal* 'shall'. In its mixture of features otherwise known mainly in the south-west and in the north midlands the language of this fragment resembles that of *The Pride of Life*. A remarkable coincidence of detail appears in *herkint* 1 (in which the order of the letters is made clear by an accent on the first of the three minims) and *herkynt* in *Pride of Life* 1; on the other hand, the fragment has *sege* 'say', not *sig*(*ge*). From so small a sample no firm conclusion can be drawn. It would not be surprising if this also came from Ireland, but there is no indication in the manuscript of any Irish association.

X. THE RICKINGHALL (BURY ST. EDMUNDS) FRAGMENT

Manuscript. British Museum, Additional Roll 63481 B. This is a scrap of parchment measuring about $6\frac{5}{8} \times 4\frac{5}{8}$ inches, which came to the Museum with the papers from Redgrave Hall, Suffolk, in 1921. The handwriting of the recto is of the early fourteenth century. On the back of the roll are accounts in Latin of the year 1370 relating to the manor of Rickinghall in Suffolk, which formerly belonged to the Abbey of Bury St. Edmunds. The dramatic fragment was published by J. P. Gilson in *The Times Literary Supplement* for 26 May 1921, pp. 340–1; there were further comments in the two succeeding weeks by W. W. Greg (p. 356) and Paul Studer (p. 373), and Kenneth Sisam, referrring to it at p. xxvi of his *Fourteenth Century Verse and Prose* (Oxford, 1921), noted that the dialect of the English was East Midland. A. Brandl reprinted Gilson's text in *Archiv*, cxliv (1923), 255–6. The manuscript has been collated twice again for the present edition by Professor Bruce Dickins and by me. The spelling has been brought nearer to that of the original by printing *þ* instead of *th* which Gilson substituted; the scribe in fact used *y* except in *þat* in line 5.

Verse. The following description is by Professor Dickins. The text begins with two verses in Latin, a pentameter and a hexameter, written in a single line. Thereafter follow two six-line tail-rhyme stanzas in Anglo-Norman, rhyming *aabccb*, spoken by a somewhat assertive king, conceivably Herod. Then come nine lines in English loosely rendering part of the French, probably not a condensation as Gilson suggested. These are also in tail-rhyme, and Greg conjectured that, since there ought to be a rhyme to *lond*, the scribe had omitted by mistake most of lines 1–3 and on noticing this discarded the parchment, which was to be used for baser purposes a couple of generations later. The missing passage might possibly be reconstructed thus:

<blockquote>
listeþ to me
Erles and barouns and chivalré
And al þat in court stond;
Lordinges . . .
</blockquote>

There are three further lines of French, with the Latin stage direction 'Tunc dicet nuncio' written in the margin.

Language. Rhymes reveal nothing of significance for localization. The reflex of OE. *i* in open syllable is written *e* in *weten* 5 but *i* in *witen* 11. The reflex of OE. *ēo* is written *e* in *ben* 8. Vowels of inflexional syllables are written *e* except in *comin* 9. In verbal inflexions, all occurrences of pres. pl. indic. and subj. end in -*n*: *weten* 5, *ben* 8, *comin* 9, *arn* 10, *witen* 11. The pronoun of 3 pl. is *he* 9, 11. As far as they go, these features are consistent with the east midland origin which the provenance of the manuscript suggests.

XI. THE DURHAM PROLOGUE

Manuscript. Durham Dean and Chapter MS. 1. 2. Archidiac. Dunelm. 60, dorse. This is a piece of parchment measuring about $10\frac{1}{2} \times 5\frac{1}{4}$ inches, containing, in the words of the summary on the dorse, 'Notificac*io* fact*a* domi*no* Tho*me* ep*iscop*o Dunelm' p*er* prior*em et* ca*pitulu*m Dunelm' sup*er* ap*ro*priac*i*o*ne* ecclesie de Bolum facta Abb*ati* et Co*n*uentui de Alba landa x^mo die mens*is* Apr*ilis* a*n*no d*omini* mill*esi*mo ccc. lix°.' Above this inscription the text of the prologue is written in a neat hand of the early fifteenth century—presumably that of a monk or associate of the monastery. It is carefully laid out, with the first three rhyming lines of each stanza bracketed in the usual way and the tail-rhyme line to the right; the fifth and sixth lines of each stanza are written in one long line, which is bracketed to the tail-line above. At the top of the sheet before the verses begin is an inscription which seems to read 'W W Willm', and to the right of the fourth stanza, written vertically downwards, is 'Fuit homo'. These are apparently in the same hand and ink as the prologue, and look like pen-trials. Two words, illegible, have been erased after the prologue. The text is for the most part clear enough, but somewhat rubbed at the foot to the right.

This prologue was first published by Miss J. Cooling in *The Review of English Studies*, N.S. x (1959), 172–3. The present text is based on a new photostat, and has been collated with the manuscript by Dr. A. I. Doyle. It differs from Miss Cooling's in transposing lines 32 and 33, as marks in the manuscript indicate, and in reading *ne* 3, *on* 20, *pat* 34, and *vp staithed* (emended) 36 instead of *ner*, *an*, *per*, and *wp staied* respectively. Professor J. A. W. Bennett, in a review of *The Middle English Miracles of the Virgin* edited by Beverly Boyd (1964) in *Medium Ævum*, xxxvi (1967), 93–5, drew attention to Miss Boyd's comment that the tail-rhyme version of the Theophilus legend which she printed (pp. 68–87) from MS. Rawl. poet. 225 had been thought to show traces of a dramatic original.[1] He noted the similarity of the theme of this legend to that of the Durham prologue,[2] and emphasized the importance of the prologue as evidence for the existence of 'a unique play about a miracle apparently not elsewhere described in English, French, or Latin'. In addition, he printed a passage of the *Legenda Aurea*, the source of the similar story about a knight and his wife in the *South English Legendary*,[3] which in some particulars closely resembles the prologue. It is perhaps worth adding that in a detail of vocabulary the Theophilus poem elucidates the prologue. The summary treatment of the story in the

---

[1] So W. Heuser, 'Eine neue mittelenglische Version der Theophilus-Sage', *Englische Studien*, xxxii (1903), 1–23; K. Plenzat, 'Die Theophiluslegende in den Dichtungen des Mittelalters', *Germanische Studien*, xliii (1926), 88.

[2] He said that the prologue was 'in the same metre' as the Theophilus text; but this is not so—the poem is indeed in tail-rhyme, but in the much commoner six-line stanza rhyming *aabccb*:

> Listenyth, bothe grete and smale:
> I wil yow tellen a litel tale
>   Of Tyofle the fre.
> Erchedekne he was yplyght,
> Wyse clerk and a man of myght,
>   And riche of gold and fee.

[3] Printed by B. Boyd, pp. 11–14, and C. D'Evelyn and A. J. Mill, E.E.T.S. 235 (1956), 231–4.

prologue does not describe the means by which Mary 'boured' the knight, so that the word seemed to Miss Cooling to have the developed sense of 'protected'. But in the poem the knight is taken to hell, and Mary goes there with the charter for his release written by Christ in his blood:

> Our Lady tok tho the ryght wey
> Into Helle, as I yow say,
> Tyofle out to *borwen*.   (511–13)

The verb here means 'redeem, rescue', and is clearly to be understood in the same sense in the prologue (cf. *M.E.D.* under *borwen*, 3).

Verse. The prologue consists of six six-line stanzas, rhyming *aaabab*, the *a* lines having four stresses and the *b* lines three. This arrangement of the rhyming lines is not common; and though it appears, for example, in the Towneley *Resurrection* and *Peregrini*, the short lines there usually have only two stresses.

Language. The rhymes are good, and the spelling usually conforms to them. The only exception of any consequence is *staithed* 36, which the rhyme with *plaied* shows to be incorrect, and which is in any case a distorted form probably miswritten under the influence of the preceding *sithen*. *O.E.D.* under *sty* v.¹ records variants such as *steȝede*, *steiȝed*, and in Scots *sticht*, but none with *-aith-*.

   The reflex of OE. *ā*, and *a* before a lengthening consonant group, is written *o*: *no* 5, *bold* 8, etc.; *sore* 13, *more* 15 rhyme on *before*.
   The reflex of OE. *ēo* is written *e* in *lede* 20, rhyming on *drede*.
   The reflex of OE. *y* before *nd* is written *e* in *mende* 24, rhyming on *ende*.
   The reflex of OE. *a* before a single nasal is written *a* in *gamen* 3, *man* 9, etc., *gan* 11; it does not appear in rhyme.
   In unstressed syllables the vowel is written *e* in *gamen* 3, *lyues* 22, *fendes* 29, *boured* 30, etc., but *i* in *sikirly* 6, 23, *mekill* 9, *knelid* 26, *nedis* 31.
   Final unstressed *-e* in historical positions is often not written, and the metre shows it to have been lost in some lines, e.g. 3, 8, 11, 23. On the other hand, pronunciation of *-e* in *saide* 19

makes a good line. Rhyme shows the loss of -e in the infins. *tell, dwell* 31, 33, the imper. pl. *ses* 2, the past sg. weak *light* 11.

Of verbal inflexions, pres. 3 sg. ends in -s in *nedis* 32; pl. has no ending, as *play* 5, *make* 7; imper. has no ending, as *stynt* 2.

Infin. has no -n, as *lett* 3, etc.; past part. has -n in *ben* 14.

Of the pronouns, *scho* is the fem. sg. nom. in 26, 30; *ʒe, ʒow* are used regularly as nom. and obl. respectively in 1, 2, 5, 31, 33, 35.

Forms and words of some regional significance are *gif* 27; *ʒon* 27; *mekill* 9; *pousté* 29; *sall* 21, 33, 34; *swilk* 11; *vntill* 17, which are to varying degrees northerly; *sikirly* 6, 23 and *till* 26 might be held to reinforce the group, but up to the fifteenth century they are so widespread (in Chaucer, for example) that they carry little weight.

The copy appears to have been made in a north-easterly dialect, from an original not significantly different; the rounded vowel in *sore*, etc., is out of keeping with the extreme north. In this region -e would be lost early, and composition can hardly be dated more closely than perhaps the late fourteenth or probably the early fifteenth century.

XII. THE ASHMOLE FRAGMENT

Manuscript. Bodleian MS. Ashmole 750, f. 168ʳ. The manuscript is a composite volume, made up of 205 leaves of paper with one of parchment at each end, containing 53 principal items written by many different fifteenth-century hands, and a large number of scattered scraps and scribbles. Item 37 in Black's Catalogue (1845), described as 'Sententiarum selectarum et versiculorum congeries, e Patribus plerumque desumpta', occupies ff. 160ʳ–168ʳ. It ends some two-thirds of the way down f. 168ʳ, and under it the dramatic fragment is written in a different hand of the late fifteenth century. The leaf measures about $8\frac{1}{4} \times 5\frac{7}{8}$ inches; the fragment begins about $3\frac{1}{4}$ inches from the foot of the page. On the verso are other disconnected notes. The writing of the fragment cannot be identified with any of the numerous hands elsewhere in the manuscript. The one complete stanza is fairly carefully written, with brackets linking the rhymes and the tail-lines written to the right in the usual

way; but the other half-stanza, which is crowded in at the very
foot of the page, is written continuously as if it were prose and
hastily scribbled with letters very ill-formed and sometimes
smudged.

The Catalogue describes the fragment, after item 37, as follows:
'At the end is written (by a less antient hand) a stanza of an old
Romance, beg. *Sur emperoure dred ye nothynge* (8 l.)'. R. H.
Robbins identified it as part of a play, and published it in *Anglia*,
lxxii (1954), 31–4 (with some errors of transcription and mis-
division of the second stanza). That it is dramatic, and not part of
a romance, is shown by the speech prefix 'Se*cun*dus Miles' and the
stage direction strangely miswritten 'To the hye trenite'; the words
'þou3 ye were', which are written above the stanza and to the right,
are evidently the cue at the end of the preceding speech. Robbins
says (p. 32), 'It would appear that the writer had a small part in
some mystery play and wrote it down, like the scribe of the Shrewsbury Fragments, on a blank half-sheet, introducing his own lines
by the catchwords of the preceding part.' The comparison with
the Shrewsbury Fragments is not happy because they were not
hastily written 'on a blank half-sheet' but carefully set out with
rubrics and music (see pp. xiv–xv above). Robbins observed that
declarations of loyalty of this kind by a knight to his lord can be
found in all the play cycles, with numerous verbal parallels including
references to Mahound. They are usually addressed to Herod, in
connection with the massacre of the Innocents, but in the Towneley
cycle by the messenger to 'Cesar Augustus';[1] and the address in
the present fragment to 'Sure Emperoure' implies that the lord
here is again Augustus.

There are two textual difficulties. In line 2 *frensche* is inappro-
priate unless the play were concerned with the Charlemagne
legends, which in view of the cycle parallels is most unlikely. The
word is presumably the result of scribal inadvertence. Epithets of
abuse associated with *gad(e)ling* include *false* (*Chester Plays* X
(*Innocents*) 237) and *foule* (*Robert of Sicily* 81, *Castle of Perseverance* 2369). It is more likely that the word here was *fresche*, in
the sense 'bold'—though this is usually laudatory it is not invariably
so. It might have been mistaken by someone writing hastily
and perhaps accustomed to applying such terms to the French.
The stage direction introducing the second stanza is still less

[1] Ed. England and Pollard, E.E.T.S., E.S. 71 (1897), IX. 115 ff.

appropriate: *trenite*, which is undoubtedly the form in the manuscript, must be an error, perhaps for *prest* as Robbins suggests.

Verse and Language. The complete stanza is in the common eight-line tail-rhyme form, rhyming *aaabcccb*, the longer lines of four stresses and the shorter of three. The remainder forms half a stanza of the same shape.

No conspicuous peculiarities of language appear. The rhymes are accurate and the spelling is mostly orthodox; the scattered exceptions—*Sure* 1, *sawle* 7, *lowuely* 10, *offur* 11, *gud* 12—permit no judgement of provenance.

XIII. THE REYNES EXTRACTS

Manuscript. Bodleian MS. Tanner 407, ff. 43^v–44^v. The manuscript is a commonplace book, for the most part compiled by Robert Reynes of Acle in Norfolk towards the end of the fifteenth century. It comprises 64 paper leaves, containing thirty miscellaneous items and some minor additions. The latest date mentioned in the book appears to be in a note on f. 38^r of a county court held at Norwich on 8 March 14 Henry VII, that is 1499; but this, though it may be by the same hand, is in a different style from the majority of the entries. These are in one hand, which, though varying to some extent in size and regularity, does so less than might have been expected in so many disconnected pieces no doubt entered at different times; it is as a rule agreeably clear and even. From the recurrence of the name Robert Reynes (usually written 'Roberd Reynys') in many of the documents copied into the book it would be reasonable to think that this main hand was his own; and this is confirmed by an entry in this hand on f. 48^r, an obit in Latin of Sir John Fastolf to which is appended the words 'qu*o*d Reynes'. The latest date certainly written in this hand is in another obit on the same page, recording the death of Master John Properchaunt,[1] sometime rector of Acle, on 2 March 1487. Various other entries copying legal documents and the like mention dates predominantly in the reign of Edward IV, and this was evidently the period of Reynes's principal concern with the book. His date of birth is not known, but records in the book show that he was married in 1471 and was churchwarden in 1474. His father John

[1] *O.E.D.* first records this word from Morley's *Introduction to practical musicke*, 1597.

was a carpenter, but also held some property—in 1477 (the year of his death) Robert bought from him his 'place' in the Market, with gardens and closes, and other land as well.

The items printed here are those numbered in Hackman's Catalogue of the Tanner manuscripts (1860, reprinted 1966) 21 'A poem on delight' and 22 'Epilogue to a miracle play'. The former occupies f. 43ᵛ and rather more than half of f. 44ʳ, the rest of which is blank; the latter is complete on f. 44ᵛ. Both were first printed by Iris G. Calderhead in *Modern Philology*, xiv (1916), 1–9. She rightly pointed out that the poem is not 'on' delight but a speech assigned to a character named Delight, and that it must be an extract from a morality; with its opening lines she compared the speech of 'Lust and Lykyng' in *Mundus et Infans*:

> A ha! now Lust and Lykyng is my name,
> I am as fresshe as flourys in Maye.

The last line of the first stanza, 'I hope not ful holy'—where *hope* has its northerly sense 'think, believe'—evidently does not belong to Delight but to a virtuous female character who disapproves of him; hence his rejoinder, 'Holy, quod *sche*?' Miss Calderhead observed also that since its language differs in some particulars from that of the Epilogue Reynes must have taken it from a different, apparently more northerly, source.

Reynes's interest in dramatic performances appears again on f. 32. On the recto of this are three quatrains on King Arthur, Charlemagne, and David, evidently from a pageant since the third is in the first person:

> I am Kyng Davyd that in my lyff
> lv maydenys and wyffves I had at my wylle,
> And afterward whan Golyas was styntyd of stryff
> I made the sawter my mercy to fullfyll;

and on the verso nine couplets headed 'IX Wurthy', which were printed by Ritson in 1783, and by Gollancz in Appendix XIII to his edition of *The Parlement of the Thre Ages* (London, 1915) under the heading 'Early Mumming-Play on the Nine Worthies' (*Index* and *Supplement*, 1929.5, 3666).

A. *A Speech of 'Delight'*

Verse. The text is not set out regularly in verse lines and stanzas. The stanzas are written separately and marked off by paragraph marks in the margin, and some lines are isolated, but generally the metrical structure must be deduced from the rhymes with some help from the rather uncertain rhythm. It emerges that there are ten six-line tail-rhyme stanzas, all rhyming *aabaab*. The length of line is very variable: the *a* lines usually have four stresses and the *b* lines three, but some *a* lines have only three and some *b* lines have two or four.

Language. There are no important discrepancies between rhymes and spellings, but the rhymes yield only a few significant points.

The reflex of OE. *ā* is written *o*, as *knowe* 4, *holsom*, *-sum* 25, 31, *hore* 37; *holy* 6 rhymes on *joly*.

The reflex of OE. *a* usually found before *ld* does not appear: *behelde* 14, *beheldand* 46 show the reflex of *ea*, but not in rhyme.

The reflex of OE. *y* is written *y*, as *myrthe* 9, *hyllys* 25; *thynne* 42 rhymes on *renne*, which in turn rhymes in 18 on *kenne*. But a rhyme between 'thin' and 'run' could be on either /i/ or /e/ (cf. the position in VI, p. lxxxii above).

Words containing earlier *iht* are usually written with *yght*: *lyght*, *bryght*, *nyght* 14, 16, 17 rhyme on *delyght*, *fyght* 36 on *whyte*; *yth* is used in *sythys*, *mythis* 55, 59, rhyming on *delyght is*. Evidently the fricative had been lost in the author's pronunciation.

In unstressed syllables, whatever the final consonant, the vowel is written *y* or *i* slightly more often than *e*: e.g. *huntyd* 38, *waltyr* 36, *sterrys* 15, *ascendys* 27, *ebbyt* 35, *refulsyth* 17, *mythis* 59, *flowit* 35; *glased* 47, *clowdes* 20, *semet* 13, *reioyceth* 10, 21. The quality of the vowel in noun plurals is shown by the rhymes in the last stanza, *sythys* 55: *delyght is* and *mythis* 59: *pyght is*; the numerous abbreviated forms are therefore expanded *-ys*. Final *-e* is not often written without historical justification, but it is sometimes omitted where it would have been in place and rhyme confirms its loss, as *plyght* 2, *delyght* 13, *spryng* 31, *sterte* 37.

The following spellings are not concerned in rhyme:

In some words *e* is written instead of *i*: *venys* 32, *lelyes* 33, *gledryng* 45.

The initial sound of words formerly beginning with *hw-* is usually written *wh*, as *what* 4, *wher* 25, but *qw* in *qwall* 36. On the other hand, *wh* is used for *w* in *whawys* 36.

The following are the main features of inflexion:

In verbs, the pres. indic. 3 sg. ends in -*th* in *reioyceth* 10, 21, *passeth* 54, *refulsyth* 17, *plesyth* 49; in -*t* in *semet* 13, 54, *ebbyt*, *flowit* 35; in -*s* in *ascendys* 27, *amendys* 30 (rhyming together). The pl. is without ending in *renne* 18, *rake* 19; in 32 there is a loop like an abbreviation of -*ys* at the end of *bryng*, but since this would spoil the rhyme it is presumably an error.[1] Infin. is without ending, as *knowe* 4, *behelde* 14, *renne* 39, and this is confirmed by rhyme in *be* 7, *see* 10, and probably in *kenne* 15 which rhymes on *renne* pl. Pres. part. ends in -*yng* in *rennyng* 24, 42, *gledryng* 45, *seyng* 55, and *seylyng* 34, *swymmyng* 35 confirmed by rhyme; but also in -*and* in *delyghtand* and three others 43–7. In 30 the verbal noun *syngang* is miswritten under the influence of this ending.

Of the personal pronouns, the fem. sg. nom. is *sche* 7; in 2 pl. *ʒe* and *ʒou* are used normally in 2 and 4; in 3 pl. the possessive is *þer*, *ther* 23, 26, 30, *her* 18, 19, obj. *hem* 56.

Characteristically northerly are the forms *mekyl* 30 and *warlde* 58, and the sense 'believe' of *hope* 6; *forant* 38, taken by Miss Calderhead to be the northern *farand* 'fine-looking', is more likely to be a variant of *ferra(u)nt* 'grey', used of horses but here of fallow deer (so *M.E.D.*). *Therke* 20, 27, after a few early appearances seems to be typically East Anglian— Lydgate, Bokenham, *Promptorium*, *Ludus Coventriae*, Sir Thomas Browne.

The author's aureate vocabulary includes not only established words such as *redolent* 26, *solacious* 55, but also *florent* 23, which *O.E.D.* records first in Udall (*M.E.D.* omits it, though this text was read), and *refulsyth* 17 which is not recorded at all.

B. *An Epilogue*

This text was printed, correctly divided into stanzas, by Miss Calderhead, pp. 7–8. R. H. Robbins printed it again as 'A Sixteenth Century English Mystery Fragment' in *English Studies*, xxx (1949), 134–6. He did not refer to Miss Calderhead's edition and seems not to have known of it, for he spoke of 'a new text', and did not set out the manuscript lines at the end of the second stanza into the rhyming triplet as she had done. In his introduction he said that the

[1] The same mark occurs otiosely at the end of *florent* 23.

epilogue was 'written *c.* 1555 in the hand of a Thomas Baxter'. This is not so; it is in the same hand as most of the Reynes commonplace book, none of which is nearly as late as 1555. The manuscript written at that date by Baxter is MS. Tanner 406, the description of which of course immediately precedes that of 407 in the Catalogue. It has nothing to do with Reynes.

Verse. There are two thirteen-line stanzas, the first rhyming *ababbcbcbdddb,* the second *ababbcbcdeeed,* followed by a quatrain *abab* in which the *b* rhyme is the same as that of the first stanza. The lines are for the most part written separately, but the last four lines of the second stanza are written as two. Rhymes are not bracketed. The lines are loosely constructed. In the first stanza the first eight lines, and probably the triplet also, have four stresses, and lines 9 and 13 have three; in the second the first eight have four stresses, the triplet probably three, and the short lines only two. The final quatrain has four stresses throughout.

Language. Indications of pronunciation are mostly unremarkable. The reflex of OE. *ā* in *also* 16 rhymes on *do.* Lowering of *i* is shown in the spelling of *sekerly* 17; probable loss of the fricative in *syth* 1, with which *ryght* rhymes.

In verbs, pres. 3 sg. forms are *causet* 16 (probably), *excedith* 30; pl. usually without ending but with -*n* in *syttyn* 1, *ben* 4, *han* 5, *arn* 24, *apperyn* 28. Infin. is usually without ending but with -*n* in *vtteryn* 19, *sen* 24, *ben* 29; pres. part. has -*yng* in *displesyng* 12, confirmed by rhyme; strong past part. has -*n* in *fowndyn* 15.

The pronoun of 2 pl. is regularly used: *ȝe* 5, 24; *ȝou, ȝow* 7, 20, 25. The form *euery ilke* is northerly. In so short a text the number of 'learned' words is noticeable, e.g. *abesyans, avysement, eloquensy, incressement, laudabyl, neglygensy,* the last of which *O.E.D.* does not record until 1800.

There is not enough material for a profitable comparison of A and B. So far as it goes, the only significant difference is the considerable sprinkling of -*n* forms in verbs in B and their complete absence in A. Miss Calderhead over-emphasized the peculiarity of A in saying that neither -*t* in 3 sg. nor initial *qw-* occur elsewhere in Reynes's work; both are in fact found sporadically. In a book of this kind it is not to be supposed that all the texts are of local origin; but both of these could well be East Anglian, of somewhat different date and precise locality.

SELECT BIBLIOGRAPHY

Bibliographies

BROWN, C., and ROBBINS, R. H., *The Index of Middle English Verse*. New York, 1943.

ROBBINS, R. H., and CUTLER, J. L., *Supplement to the Index of Middle English Verse*. Lexington, 1965.

STRATMAN, C. J., *Bibliography of Medieval Drama*. Berkeley and Los Angeles, 1954. [Entries 1299–1313 confound the Northampton play in the Dublin MS. with the Chester *Abraham and Isaac*.]

WELLS, J. E., *A Manual of the Writings in Middle English 1050–1400* (Chapter XIV). New Haven, 1916, and *First to Ninth Supplements*, 1919–51. (New edition ed. J. Burke Severs in progress.)

See also Chambers and Craig below.

General

BLAIR, L., 'A Note on the Relation of the Corpus Christi Procession to the Corpus Christi Play', *M.L.N.* lv (1940), 83–95.

CHAMBERS, E. K., *English Literature at the Close of the Middle Ages*. Oxford, 1945.

— *The Mediaeval Stage*. 2 vols., Oxford, 1903.

CRAIG, H., *English Religious Drama of the Middle Ages*. Oxford, 1955.

— 'The Corpus Christi Procession and the Corpus Christi Play', *J.E.G.P.* xiii (1914), 589–602.

CREIZENACH, W., *Geschichte des neueren Dramas*, i. Halle, 1893.

ECKHARDT, E., *Die lustige Person im älteren englischen Drama* (Palaestra xvii). Berlin, 1902.

HARDISON, O. B., Jr., *Christian Rite and Christian Drama in the Middle Ages*. Baltimore, 1965.

KOLVE, V. A., *The Play called Corpus Christi*. Stanford, 1966.

MACKENZIE, W. R. 'The Origin of the English Morality', *Washington University Studies*, ii (1915), 141–64.

MARSHALL, MARY H., 'Dramatic Tradition established by the Liturgical Play', *P.M.L.A.* lvi (1941), 962–91.

OWST, G. R., *Literature and Pulpit in Medieval England* (Chapter VIII). Cambridge, 1933; 2nd edn. Oxford, 1961.

PETIT DE JULLEVILLE, L., *Les Mystères*. 2 vols., Paris, 1880.

PROSSER, ELEANOR, *Drama and Religion in the English Mystery Plays. A Re-evaluation*. Stanford, 1961.

RAMSAY, R. L., introduction to Skelton's *Magnyfycence*. E.E.T.S., E.S. 98 (1908, repr. 1958).

SEYMOUR, ST. J. D., *Anglo-Irish Literature 1200–1582*. Cambridge, 1929.

THOMPSON, E. N. S., 'The English Moral Plays', *Transactions of the Connecticut Academy of Arts and Sciences*, xvi (1910), 293–414.

WICKHAM, G., *Early English Stages 1300–1600*, i. London, 1959.

WILLIAMS, A., *The Drama of Medieval England*. East Lancing, Michigan, 1961.

— 'The English Moral Play before 1500', *Annuale Mediaevale*, iv (1963), 5–22.

WILSON, F. P. (ed. G. K. HUNTER), *The English Drama 1485–1585* (Oxford History of English Literature). Oxford, 1968.

WILSON, R. M., *The Lost Literature of Medieval England* (Methuen's Old English Library). London, 1952.

YOUNG, K., *The Drama of the Medieval Church*. 2 vols., Oxford, 1933.

Collections of Texts

Chief Pre-Shakespearean Dramas, ed. J. Q. Adams. Boston, 1924.

English Miracle Plays, Moralities, and Interludes, ed. A. W. Pollard. Oxford, 1890; 8th edn. 1927.

Historical Poems of the XIVth and XVth Centuries, ed. R. H. Robbins. New York, 1959.

The Middle English Miracles of the Virgin, ed. Beverly Boyd. The Huntington Library, San Marino, 1964.

Le Mystére du Viel Testament, ed. J. de Rothschild. S.A.T.F., 6 vols., 1878–91.

The Non-Cycle Mystery Plays, together with the Croxton Play of the Sacrament and the Pride of Life, ed. O. Waterhouse. E.E.T.S., E.S. 104 (1909).

Quellen des weltlichen Dramas in England vor Shakespeare, ed. A. Brandl (Quellen und Forschungen lxxx). Strassburg, 1898.

Religious Lyrics of the XVth Century, ed. Carleton Brown. Oxford, 1939.

Specimens of the Pre-Shaksperean Drama, ed. J. M. Manly, i. Boston, 1897; 2nd edn. 1900.

Ten Miracle Plays, ed. R. G. Thomas (York Medieval Texts). London, 1966.

Two Coventry Corpus Christi Plays, ed. H. Craig. E.E.T.S., E.S. 87 (1902, 2nd edn. 1957).

Editions of Cycles

The Chester Plays, ed. H. Deimling and [J. B.] Matthews. E.E.T.S., E.S. 62 (1892, repr. 1926, 1959), 115 (1916, repr. 1935, 1959).

The Digby Plays, ed. F. J. Furnivall. New Shakspere Soc. 1882, repr. E.E.T.S., E.S. 70 (1896, repr. 1930, 1967).

Ludus Coventriae, or The Plaie called Corpus Christi, ed. K. S. Block. E.E.T.S., E.S. 120 (1922, repr. 1960).

The Macro Plays, ed. F. J. Furnivall and A. W. Pollard. E.E.T.S., E.S. 91 (1904, repr. 1924); ed. M. Eccles. E.E.T.S. 262 (1969).

The Towneley Plays, ed. G. England and A. W. Pollard. E.E.T.S., E.S. 71 (1897, repr. 1952).

The Wakefield Pageants in the Towneley Cycle, ed. A. C. Cawley. Manchester, 1958.

The York Plays, ed. Lucy Toulmin Smith. Oxford, 1885 (repr. 1963

Individual Plays

I. The Shrewsbury Fragments

Text: Skeat, Manly, Waterhouse, Adams, Young.

MILLER, FRANCES M., 'Metrical Affinities of the Shrewsbury *Officium Pastorum* and its York Correspondent', *M.L.N.* xxxiii (1918), 91–5.

SKEAT, W. W., 'Fragments of Yorkshire Mysteries', *The Academy*, 4 and 11 January 1890.

II. The Norwich Grocers' Play

Text: Fitch, Manly, Waterhouse, Adams.

DUSTOOR, P. E., 'Textual Notes on Three Non-Cycle Mystery Plays', *Modern Language Review*, xxiii (1928), 208–12. [Refers also to the two Abraham plays.]

FITCH, R., 'Norwich Pageants. The Grocers' Play', *Norfolk Archaeology*, v (1859), 8–31. Also issued separately, paginated 1–24, 'printed by Charles Muskett, Old Haymarket, 1856'.

HARROD, H., 'A few Particulars concerning early Norwich Pageants', *Norfolk Archaeology*, iii (1852), 3–18.

III. The Newcastle Play

Text: Bourne, Brand, Sharp, Holthausen, Brotanek, Waterhouse.

BOURNE, H., *The History of Newcastle upon Tyne; or, the Ancient and Present State of that Town.* Newcastle, 1736. [Play pp. 139–41.]

BRAND, J., *The History and Antiquities of the Town and County of the Town of Newcastle upon Tyne.* 2 vols., London, 1789. [Play ii. 373–9.]

BROTANEK, R., 'Noahs Arche. Ein Mysterium aus Newcastle upon Tyne', *Anglia*, xxi (1899), 165–200.

DUSTOOR, P. E., 'Notes on the Early English Text Society Edition of the Newcastle "Noah's Ark" ', *M.L.N.* xliii (1928), 252–5.

HOLTHAUSEN, F., 'Das Noahspiel von Newcastle on Tyne', *Göteborgs Högskolas Årsskrift* 1897, III. Also issued separately.

SHARP, T., *A Dissertation on the Pageants or Dramatic Mysteries anciently performed at Coventry.* Coventry, 1825.

IV. The Northampton *Abraham*

Text: Collier, Brotanek, Waterhouse.

BROTANEK, R., 'Abraham und Isaak: ein mittelenglisches Misterium aus einer Dubliner Handschrift', *Anglia*, xxi (1898), 21–55.

— *Mittelenglische Dichtungen aus der Handschrift 432 des Trinity College in Dublin.* Halle, 1940.

COLLIER, J. P., *Five Miracle Plays.* London, 1836.

WOOLF, ROSEMARY, 'The Effect of Typology on the English Mediaeval Plays of Abraham and Isaac', *Speculum*, xxxii (1957), 805–25. [Treats also the Brome play.]

V. The Brome *Abraham*

Text: Toulmin Smith (three editions), Manly, Waterhouse, Adams, and numerous other derived editions (see Stratman, nos. 1282–98).

FORT, MARGARET D., 'The Metres of the Brome and Chester Abraham and Isaac Plays', *P.M.L.A.* xli (1926), 832–9.

HARPER, CARRIE A., 'A Comparison between the Brome and Chester Plays of "Abraham and Isaac" ', in *Studies in English and Comparative Literature . . . presented to Agnes Irwin* (Radcliffe College Monographs xv), Boston, 1910.

HOHLFELD, A. R., 'Two old English Mystery Plays on the subject of Abraham's Sacrifice', *M.L.N.* v (1890), 111–19.

HOLTHAUSEN, F., 'Zu alt- und mittelenglischen Dichtungen', *Anglia*, xiii (1890), 357–62. [Play pp. 361–2.]

KAHRL, S. J., 'The Brome Hall Commonplace Book', *Theatre Notebook*, xxii (1968), 157–61; and note by N. DAVIS, ibid., xxiii (1970).

MARSTON, T. E., 'The Book of Brome', *Yale University Library Gazette*, xli, no. 4 (1967), 141–5.

SEVERS, J. B., 'The Relationship between the Brome and Chester Plays of "Abraham and Isaac" ', *M.P.* xlii (1945), 137–51.

SMITH, LUCY TOULMIN, 'Abraham and Isaac, a Mystery Play; from a Private Manuscript of the 15th Century', *Anglia*, vii (1884), 316–37.

— *A Common-place Book of the Fifteenth Century*. London, 1886.

— 'Notes on a Common-place Book of the Fifteenth Century, with a Religious Play of Abraham and Isaac', *The Norfolk Antiquarian Miscellany*, ed. W. Rye, iii (Norwich, 1887), 115–67.

VI. The Play of the Sacrament

Text: Stokes, Manly, Waterhouse, Adams.

BARNS, FLORENCE E., 'The Background and Sources of *The Croxton Play of the Sacrament*', *Abstracts of Theses, The University of Chicago, Humanistic Ser.* v, 1926–7 (Chicago, 1928), 443–6.

COLEMAN, E. D., *The Jew in English Drama. An Annotated Bibliography*. New York, 1943. [p. 24.]

CUTTS, CECILIA, 'The Croxton Play: an Anti-Lollard Piece', *M.L.Q.* v (1944), 45–60.

HOLTHAUSEN, F., 'Beiträge zur Erklärung und Textkritik alt- und mittelenglischer Denkmäler', III, *Englische Studien*, xvi (1892), 150–1; IV, *Anglia*, xv (1892), 187–203. [Play pp. 198–200.]

STOKES, W., 'The Play of the Sacrament', *Transactions of the Philological Society* 1860–1, Appendix, pp. 101–52.

VII. *The Pride of Life*

Text: Mills, Brandl, Holthausen, Waterhouse.

BROWN, C., 'The "Pride of Life" and the "Twelve Abuses" ', *Archiv*, cxxvii (1912), 72–8.

HEUSER, W., *Die Kildare–Gedichte* (Bonner Beiträge zur Anglistik xiv). Bonn, 1904.

HOLTHAUSEN, F., 'The Pride of Life', *Archiv*, cviii (1902), 34–48.

McIntosh, A., and Samuels, M. L., 'Prolegomena to a Study of Medi-æval Anglo-Irish', *Medium Ævum*, xxxvii (1968), 1–11.

Mackenzie, W. R., 'The Debate over the Soul in "The Pride of Life" ', *Washington University Studies*, ix (1922), 263–74.

Mills, J., *Account Roll of the Priory of the Holy Trinity, Dublin, 1337–1346, with the Middle English Moral Play 'The Pride of Life'*. Royal Society of Antiquaries of Ireland, Dublin, 1891.

VIII. *Dux Moraud*

Heuser, W., 'Dux Moraud, Einzelrolle aus einem verlorenen Drama des 14. Jahrhunderts', *Anglia*, xxx (1907), 180–208.

Also in Adams.

IX. The Cambridge Prologue

Robbins, R. H., 'An English Mystery Play Fragment', *M.L.N.* lxv (1950), 30–5.

Legge, M. Dominica, *Anglo-Norman Literature and its Background* (Oxford, 1963), pp. 328–31.

X. The Rickinghall Fragment

Brandl, A. L., 'Das Bibelstück-Fragment von Rickinghall Manor', *Archiv*, cxliv (1923), 255–6.

Gilson, J. P., 'A Fourteenth Century Fragment', *T.L.S.* 26 May 1921, pp. 340–1.

Greg, W. W., *T.L.S.* 2 June 1921, p. 356.

Studer, P., *T.L.S.* 9 June 1921, p. 373.

XI. The Durham Prologue

Cooling, June, 'An Unpublished Middle English Prologue', *R.E.S.*, n.s. x (1959), 172–3.

XII. The Ashmole Fragment

Robbins, R. H., 'A Dramatic Fragment from a Caesar Augustus Play', *Anglia*, lxxii (1954), 31–4.

XIII. The Reynes Extracts

A. Calderhead, Iris G., 'Morality Fragments from Norfolk', *M.P.* xiv (1916), 1–9.

B. Ibid., and Robbins, R. H., 'A Sixteenth Century English Mystery Fragment', *English Studies*, xxx (1949), 134–6.

ABBREVIATIONS

D.N.B.	*The Dictionary of National Biography*
D.O.S.T.	*A Dictionary of the Older Scottish Tongue*
E.D.D.	*The English Dialect Dictionary*
E.P.N.S.	English Place-Name Society
J.E.G.P.	*Journal of English and Germanic Philology*
ME.	Middle English
M.E.D.	*Middle English Dictionary* (Michigan)
M.L.N.	*Modern Language Notes*
M.L.Q.	*Modern Language Quarterly*
M.P.	*Modern Philology*
OE.	Old English
O.E.D.	*The Oxford English Dictionary*
OF.	Old French
ON.	Old Norse
P.M.L.A.	*Publications of the Modern Language Association of America*
R.E.S.	*The Review of English Studies*
S.A.T.F.	Société des Anciens Textes Français
T.L.S.	*The Times Literary Supplement*

THE TEXTS

In the texts of which manuscripts survive the spelling of the manuscripts is reproduced except for the correction of apparent errors. Emendations are indicated by footnotes, which give the forms in the manuscripts and the names of those who proposed the emendations. Scribal interlineations are printed in half-brackets; letters supplied to complete passages left defective by the scribe are in square brackets; conjectural restorations of passages illegible or lost through mutilation of the manuscript are in angle brackets. Abbreviations are expanded without notice according to the practice of the scribe when writing the same or similar words in full; except for the perennial question whether final flourishes may represent -*e* most offer no difficulty, and those which are doubtful are discussed in the introduction. When a scribe uses *y* in the function of *þ*, the form *þ* is printed. Word-division has been regularized, and capitals and punctuation introduced as in modern use; capital *I* and *J* are distinguished according to function. An acute accent is added to a final *e* when it stands for etymological *i* or Old French *é* (except in monosyllables). The structure of stanzas is indicated as far as possible by indenting rhyming lines. Speech prefixes, which are variously placed in the manuscripts, are uniformly brought to the beginnings of speeches.

NON-CYCLE PLAYS

I

THE SHREWSBURY FRAGMENTS

A. [Officium Pastorum]¹   f. 38ʳ

Pastores erant in regione eadem uigilantes et custodientes gregem suum. Et ecce angelus Domini astitit iuxta illos et timuerunt timore magno.

iijᵘˢ Pastor

[II. Pastor.]²	We, Tib!
III. Pastor. Telle on!	
[II. Pastor.]	þe nyght.

III. Pastor. Brether, what may þis be,
    þus bright to man and best?   5

[II. Pastor.] . . . . at hand.

III. Pastor.   Whi say ȝe so?

[II. Pastor.] . . . . warand.

III. Pastor. Suche siȝt was neuer sene
    Before in oure Jewery;   10
    Sum merueles wil hit mene
    þat mun be here in hy.

[II. Pastor.] . . . . a sang.

III. Pastor. Ȝe lye bothe, by þis liȝt,
    And raues as recheles royes!   15
    Hit was an angel briȝt
    þat made þis nobull noyes.

[II. Pastor.] . . . . of prophecy.

III. Pastor. He said a barn schuld be
    In þe burgh of Bedlem born;   20

¹ *No heading in MS., and no music for the opening Latin sentences.*
² *Speakers' names in brackets supplied by Skeat.*

And of þis, mynnes me,
Oure fadres fond beforn.

[II. PASTOR.] . . . .   Jewus kyng.

III. PASTOR. Now may we see þe same
Euen in oure pase puruayed;   25
þe angel nemed his name—
'Crist, Saueour,' he saied.

[II. PASTOR.] . . . .   not raue.

III. PASTOR. ʒone brightnes wil vs bring
Vnto þat blisful boure;   30
For solace schal we syng
To seke oure Saueour.
                                                  f. 38ᵛ

Transeamus usque Bethelem et uideamus hoc uerbum quod
factum est, quod fecit Dominus et ostendit nobis.¹

[II. PASTOR.] . . . .   to knawe.

III. PASTOR. For noþing thar vs drede,
But thank God of all gode;   35
þis light euer wil vs lede
To fynde þat frely fode.

[II. PASTOR.] . . . .   I mene.²

Saluatorem, Christum Dominum, infantem pannis inuolutum,
secundum sermonem angelicum.

III. PASTOR. A, loke to me, my Lord dere,
All if I put me noght in prese!   40
To suche a prince without[en] pere
Haue I no presand þat may plese.
But lo! a horn-spone haue I here
þat may herbar an hundrith pese:
þis gift I gif þe with gode chere,   45
Suche dayntese wil do no disese.
Farewele now, swete swayn,
God graunt þe lifyng lang!³   f. 39ʳ

¹ Accompanied by music. See Appendix.
² Under this a line across the page. Before l. 39 an asterisk refers to the Latin
passage here printed, which is written, with music, on f. 42ᵛ in a different hand.
³ Skeat adds from York Plays, XV. 130–1, assigning to the first shepherd:

And go we hame agayn,
And mak mirth as we gang!

B. [OFFICIUM RESURRECTIONIS][1]

Hic incipit Officium Resurreccionis in die Pasche.

III. MARIA.[2]　　Heu! Redemcio Israel,
　　　　　　　　Vt quid mortem sustinuit!

[II. MARIA.]　　. . . . .　payne.

III. MARIA.　　Allas! he þat men wend schuld by
　　　　　　　　　All Israel, bothe knyght and knaue,　　5
　　　　　　　　Why suffred he so forto dy,
　　　　　　　　　Sithe he may all sekenes saue?
　　　　　　　　　　Heu! cur ligno fixus clauis
　　　　　　　　　　Fuit doctor tam suauis?
　　　　　　　　　　Heu! cur fuit ille natus　　　10
　　　　　　　　　　Qui perfodit eius latus?

[II. MARIA.]　　. . . . .　is oght.

III. MARIA.　　Allas, þat we suche bale schuld bide
　　　　　　　　　þat sodayn sight so forto see,
　　　　　　　　　þe best techer in world wide　　15
　　　　　　　　　With nayles be tacched to a tre!
　　　　　　　　Allas, þat euer so schuld betyde,
　　　　　　　　　Or þat so bold mon born schuld be
　　　　　　　　For to assay oure Saueour side
　　　　　　　　　And open hit withoute pité!　　20

[ALL THREE.]　　Iam iam, ecce, iam properemus ad tumulum,[3]
　　　　　　　　Vnguentes[4] Dilecti corpus sanctissimum!　　f. 39[v]

Et appropiantes sepulcro cantent:

　　　　　　　　O Deus, quis reuoluet nobis lapidem
　　　　　　　　Ab hostio monumenti?

[II. MARIA.]　　. . . . .　him leid.　25

III. MARIA.　　He þat þus kyndely vs has kend
　　　　　　　　　Vnto þe hole where he was hid,
　　　　　　　　Sum socoure sone he wil vs send,
　　　　　　　　　At help to lift away þis lid.[5]

---

[1] *Title supplied from next line.*　　　[2] *MS. iij*[a] *m*[a] *at extreme right.*
[3] *Accompanied by music. The plural in the following stage direction doubtless applies to both passages.*
[4] *Skeat* vngentes; *but Young observes that* u *is rubbed but not erased.*
[5] *Young notes that the dialogue with the angel, beginning* Quem quæritis, *must*

III. MARIA.   Alleluya schal be oure song,   30
                Sithen Crist, oure Lord, by angellus steuen,
                Schewus him as mon here vs among
                And is Goddis Son, heghest in heuen.[1]

[II. MARIA.]   . . . . was gon.   f. 40ʳ

III. MARIA.   Surrexit Christus, spes nostra;   35
                Precedet vos in Galileam.
                Crist is rysen, wittenes we
                    By tokenes þat we haue sen þis morn!
                Oure hope, oure help, oure hele, is he,
                    And hase bene best, sithe we were born!   40
                If we wil seke him for to se,
                    Lettes noght þis lesson be forlorn;
                But gose euen vnto Galilee—
                    þere schal ȝe fynd him ȝow beforn![1]

                C. [OFFICIUM PEREGRINORUM][2]

Feria secunda in ebdomada Pasche discipuli insimul cantent:

[CHORUS.]   Infidelis incursum populi
                Fugiamus, Ihesu[3] discipuli!
                Suspenderunt Ihesum patibulo;
                Nul|li parcent eius discipulo.   f. 40ᵛ

[LUKE.]   . . . . fast to fle.[1]   5

[CLEOPHAS.]   But if we fle þai wil vs fang,
                    And ful felly þai wil vs flay;
                Agayn to Emause wil we gang,
                    And fonde to get þe gaynest way.
                And make in mynd euer vs amang   10
                    Of oure gode Maister, as we may,
                How he was put to paynes strang—
                    On þat he tristed con him betray!

[LUKE.]   . . . . but agayn.[4]

occur here; but MS. has no space, line, or cue, only paragraph mark for the next speech.
    [1] *Below this a red line across the page.*
    [2] *MS. has no heading; this supplied by Manly. Cf. Young, i. 688.*
    [3] *Skeat; MS. ihesum.*
    [4] *Speaker uncertain; Young assigns to Luke, Skeat and Manly to Jesus. Below this a red line across the page.*

[CLEOPHAS.]   By wymmen wordis wele wit may we   15
        Crist is risen vp in gode aray;
      For to oureself þe sothe say[d]¹ he,
        Where we went in þis world away
      þat he schuld dye and doluen be,
        And rise fro þe dethe þe thrid day.   20
      And þat we myȝt þat siȝt now se,
        He wisse vs, Lord, as he wele may!

[(?) LUKE.]   . . . .   resoun² riȝt.

[CLEOPHAS.]   Et quomodo tradiderunt eum summi sacerdotes
  et principes nostri in dampnacionem³ mortis et crucifixerunt
eum.

      Right is þat we reherce by raw
        þe materes þat we may on mene,   25
      How prestis and princes of oure lawe   f. 41ʳ
        Ful tenely toke him hom betwen,
      And dampned him, withouten awe,
        For to be dede with dele bedene;
      þai crucified him, wele we knaw,   30
        At Caluary, with caris kene.

[LUKE.]   . . . . wraist.

[(?) CLEOPHAS.] Dixerunt eciam se visionem angelorum vidisse, qui
dicunt eum viuere.

      þe wymmen gret, for he was gon;
        But ȝet þai told of meruales mo:
      þai saw angellus stondyng on þe ston,   35
        And sayn how he was farne hom fro.
      Sithen of oures went ful gode wone
        To se þat sight, and said right so.
      Herfore we murne and makis þis mon;
        Now wot þou wele of all oure wo.   40

[(?)JESUS.]   . . . . in pese.⁴

[CLEOPHAS AND LUKE.] Mane nobiscum, quoniam advesperascit
et inclinata est iam dies.   Alleluya!⁵

[JESUS]   . . . . wight.

---

¹ *Skeat.*   ² *MS.* rosoun.   ³ *MS.* daᵽnacõe.
⁴ *Below this a red line across the page.*   ⁵ *Accompanied by music.*

[CLEOPHAS.] Amend oure mournyng, Maister dere,
         And fonde oure freylnes for to fell!
         Herk, broþer! help to hold him here,   45
         Ful nobel talis wil he vs tell.

[LUKE.]   . . . . lent.   f. 41ᵛ

[CLEOPHAS.] And gode wyne schal vs wont non,
         For þerto schal I take entent.

[LUKE.]   . . . . he went.   50

[CLEOPHAS.] Went he is, and we ne wot how,
         For here is noght left in his sted.¹
         Allas! where were oure wittis now?
         With wo now walk we, wil of red.

[LUKE.]   . . . . oure bred.²   55

[CLEOPHAS.] Oure bred he brak and blessed hit;
         On mold were neuer so mased men
         When þat we saw him by vs sit,
         þat we couthe noght consayue him þen.

[LUKE.]   . . . . ay.   60

[CLEOPHAS AND LUKE.] Quid agamus uel dicamus,
           Ignorantes quo eamus,
           Qui doctorem sciencie
           Et patrem consolacionis
           Amisimus?³   65

[LUKE.]   . . . . gode state.   f. 42ʳ

[CLEOPHAS.] We schal hom tell, withouten trayn,
         Bothe word and werk, how hit was,
         I se hom sitt samyn in a playn.
         Forthe in apert dar I not pas.   70

[LUKE.]   . . . . and wife.²

[CLEOPHAS.] We saw him holl, hide and hewe;
         þerfore be still, and stint ʒoure strife.
         þat hit was Crist ful wele we knewe,
         He cutt oure bred withouten knyfe.   75

---

¹ *Skeat; MS.* stid.   ² *Below this a red line across the page.*
³ *Accompanied by music: see frontispiece.*

[CHORUS.]   Gloria tibi, Domine,
               Qui surrexisti a mortuis,
               Cum Patre et Sancto Spiritu,
               In sempiterna secula.   Amen.[1]

[CHORUS.]   Frater Thoma, causa | tristicie,   80 f. 42ᵛ
               Nobis tulit summa leticie![2]

---

[1] *Accompanied by music.*

[2] *Accompanied by music; remainder of f. 42ᵛ occupied by the words and music of the Latin passage following A. 38.*

II

THE NORWICH GROCERS' PLAY

[Text A]

The Story of the Creacion of Eve, with the expellyng of Adam and Eve out of Paradyce.

PATER. *Ego principium Alpha et O*[1] *in altissimis habito*:
    In the hevenly empery I am resydent.
Yt ys not semely for man, *sine adjutorio*,
    To be allone, nor very convenyent.
    I have plantyd an orcheyard most congruent   5
For hym to kepe and to tylle, by contemplacion:
Let us make an adjutory of our formacion

To hys symylutude, lyke in plasmacion.
    Into Paradyce I wyll nowe descende
With my mynysters angelicall of our creacion   10
    To assyst us in owr worke that we intende,
    A slepe into man be soporacion to sende.
A rybbe out of mannys syde I do here take;
    Bothe flesche and bone I do thys creatur blysse;
And a woman I fourme, to be his make,   15
    Semblable to man; beholde, here she ys.

ADAM. O my Lorde God, incomprehensyble, withowt mysse,
    Ys thy hyghe excellent magnyficens.
Thys creature to me ys *nunc ex ossibus meis*,
    And *virago* I call hyr in thy presens,   20
    Lyke onto me in natural preemynens.
Laude, honor, and glory to the I make.
Both father and mother man shall for hyr forsake.

PATER. Than my garden of plesure kepe thou suer.[2]
    Of all frutes and trees shall thou ete and fede,   25

---

[1] *MS. & ω. Latin quotations were underlined in MS.*
[2] *MS. first* sure, *then* suer *written above.*

Except thys tre of connyng, whyle ye bothe indure;
    Ye shall not touche yt, for that I forbede.
    ADAM. Thy precept, Lorde, in will, worde, and dede
Shall I observe, and thy request fulfyll
As thou hast commandyd, yt ys reason and skyll.   30
PATER. Thys tre ys callyd of connyng good and yll;
    That day that ye ete therof shall ye dye,
    Morte moriemini, yf that I do you aspye.

Showe thys to thy spowse nowe bye and bye.
    I shall me absent for a tyme and space;   35
A warned man may live: who can yt denye?
    I make the lord thereof; kepe wyll my place;
    If thou do thys, thou shall have my grace;
Into mortalité shall thou elles falle.
Looke thow be obedyent whan I the calle.   40

ADAM. Omnipotent God and hygh Lord of all,
    I am thy servante, bownde onder thyn obedyens,
And thou my creatour, one God eternall;
    What thou commandest, I shall do my dylygens.
    PATER. Here I leve the, to have experyens,   45
To use thys place in vertuse occupacion,
For nowe I wyll retorne to myn habitacion.

ADAM. O lovely spowse of Godes creacion,
    I leve the here alone, I shall not tary longe,
For I wyll walk a whyle for my recreacion   50
    And se over Paradyce, that ys so stronge.
    Nothyng may hurt us nor do us wronge;
God ys owr protectour and soverayn guyde;
In thys place non yll thyng may abyde.

SERPENS. O gemme of felicyté and femynyne love,   55
    Why hathe God under precept prohybyte thys frute,
That ye shuld not ete therof to your behofe?
    Thys tre ys plesant withowten refute.

EVA. *Ne forte* we shuld dye, and than be mortall;
    We may not towche yt, by Godes commandement.   60

SERPENS. *Nequaquam*, ye shall not dye perpetuall,
  But ye shuld be as godes[1] resydent,
Knowyng good and yll spyrytuall;
Nothyng can dere you þat ys carnall.[2]

EVA. For us than nowe what hold you best,   65
  That we do not owr God offende?
SERPENS. Eate of thys apple at my requeste.
  To the Almyghty God dyd me send.
EVA. Nowe wyll I take therof; and I entend
To please my spowse, therof to fede,   70
To knowe good and ylle for owr mede.

ADAM. I have walkyd abought for my solace;
  My spowse, howe do you? tell me.
EVA. An angell cam from Godes grace
  And gaffe me an apple of thys tre.   75
  Part therof I geffe to the;
Eate therof for thy pleasure,
For thys frute ys Godes own treasure.

PATER. Adam, Adam, wher art thou thys tyde?
  Byfore my presens why dost thou not apere? 80

[Gap in MS.]

Musick.

*Aftyr that Adam and Eve be drevyn owt of Paradyse they schall
speke thys foloyng:*

ADAM. O with dolorows sorowe we maye wayle and weepe!
  Alas, alas, whye ware we soo bolde?
By owr fowle presumpsyon we are cast full deepe,
  Fro pleasur to payn, with carys manyefold.
  EVA. With wonderous woo, alas! it cane not be told; 85
Fro Paradyse to ponyschment and bondage full strong.
  O wretches that we are, so euer we xall be inrollyd;
Therfor owr handes we may wrynge with most dullfull song.

---

[1] *Fitch and Waterhouse print capital* G *evidently from MS.*
[2] *Fitch; Waterhouse* casuall.

And so thei xall syng, walkyng together about the place, wryngyng
   ther handes.

Wythe dolorous sorowe, we maye wayle and wepe
Both[1] nyght and daye in sory sythys full depe.   90

N.B. These last 2 lines set to musick twice over and again, for a
chorus of 4 pts.[2]

[TEXT B]

The Storye of the Temptacion of Man in Paradyce, being therin
placyd, and the expellynge of Man and Woman from thence,
newely renvid and accordynge unto the Skripture, begon thys
yere Anno 1565, Anno 7. Eliz.

Item. Yt ys to be notyd that when the Grocers Pageant is played
   withowte eny other goenge befor yt then doth the Prolocutor say
   in this wise:

B¹ [First Prologue]

[PROLOCUTOR.] Lyke as yt chancyd befor this season,
   Owte of Godes scripture revealid in playes
Was dyvers stories sett furth by reason
   Of pageantes apparellyd in Wittson dayes;
   And lately be fal[l]en into decayes;   5
Which stories dependyd in theyr orders sett
By severall devices, much knowledge to gett.

Begynny[n]g in Genesis, that story repleate
   Of God his creacion of ech lyvynge thynge,
Of heaven and of erth, of fysh smalle and greate,   10
   Of fowles, herbe and tre, and of all bestes crepynge,
   Of angelles, of man, which of erth hath beynge,
And of the fall of angelles, in the Apocalips to se;
Which stories with the Skriptures most justly agree.

Then followed this owr pageant, which sheweth to be   15
   The Garden of Eden, which God dyd plante,
As in the seconde chapter of Genesis ye se;
   Wherin of frutes pleasant no kynde therof shulde wante;

---

[1] *Fitch* bothe *in preceding line.*
[2] *Manly notes that this note is apparently added by Fitch.*

In which God dyd putt man to cherish tre and plante,[1]
To dresse and kepe the grounde, and eate what frute hym lyste,   20
Exept the tre of Knoweledge, Godes high wyll[2] to resyste.

The story sheweth further that after man was blyste,
    The Lord did create woman owte of a ribbe of man;
Which woman was deceyvyd with the Serpentes darkned myste;
    By whose synn owr nature is so weak no good we can;   25
    Wherfor they were dejectyd, and caste from thence than
Unto dolloure and myseri and to traveyle and payne
Untyll Godes spright renvid; and so we ende certayne.

*Note that yf ther goeth eny other pageantes before yt, the Prolo-
cutor sayeth as ys on the other syde and leaveth owte this.*

B[2]. [Alternative Prologue]

THE PROLOCUTOR. As in theyr former pageantes is semblably
        declared
Of Godes mighty creacion in every lyvyng thynge,
As in the fyrst of Genesis to such it is prepared
    As lust they have to reade to memory to brynge
Of pride and fawle of angells that in Hell hath beinge;   5
In the seconde of Genesis of mankynde hys creacion
Unto this Garden Eden is made full preparacion.

And here begyneth owr pageant to make the declaracion,
    From the letter C. in the chapter before saide,
How God putt man in Paradyse to dresse yt in best fassion,   10
    And that no frute therof from hym shuld be denayed,
    Butt of the tre of lyffe that man shuld be afraide
To eate of, least that daye he eat that he shuld dye;
And of womanes creacion appering by and bye;

And of the deavilles temptacion, diseaivinge[3] with a lye   15
    The woman, beinge weakest, that cawsed man to tast.
That God dyd so offende, that even contynentlye
    Owte of the place of joye was man and woman caste,
    And into so great dolloure and misery browght at last;

---

[1] *Manly; MS.* taute, *Fitch* [him] taute.
[2] *Manly; Fitch and Waterhouse* wytt.
[3] *Fitch* discouvinge.

Butt that by God his spright was comforted ageyne.   20
This is of this owr pagent the some and effect playne.

B³. [CREATION AND FALL]

GOD THE FATHER. I am *Alpha et homega*, my *Apocalyps* doth
    testyfye,
  That made all of nothinge for man his sustentacion;
And of this pleasante garden that I have plant most goodlye
  I wyll hym make the dresser for his good recreacion.
  Therfor, Man, I gyve yt the, to have thy delectacion.   5
In eatyng thou shalt eate of every growenge tre,
Exepte the tre of knowledge, the which I forbydd the;

For in what daye soever thou eatest[1] thou shallt be
  Even as the childe of death; take hede: and thus I saye,
  I wyll the make an helper, to comforte the allwaye.   10
Beholde, therfore, a slepe I bryng this day on the,
  And oute of this thy ribbe, that here I do owte take,
  A creature for thy help behold I do the make.
  Aryse, and from thy slepe I wyll the nowe awake,
And take hyr unto the, that you both be as one   15
To comfort one th'other when from you I am gone.

And, as I saide before when that thou wert alone,
  In eatyng thow mayst eate of every tre here is,
Butt of the tre of knowledge of good and evyll eate non,
  Lest that thou dye the deth by doenge so amysse.   20
  I wyll departe now wher myne habytacion is.
  I leave you here . . . .[2]
Se that ye have my woordes in most high estymacion.

Then Man and Woman speke bothe.

[MAN AND WOMAN.] We thanke the, mighty God, and gyve the
    honoracion.

Man spekethe.

[MAN.] Oh bone of my bones and flesh of my flesh eke,   25
  Thow shalte be called Woman, bycaus thow art of me.

---

[1] *So Waterhouse as if from MS. Manly the same but as emendation of Fitch*
eaten.   [2] *Lacuna in MS.*

Oh gyfte of God most goodlye, that hath[1] us made so lyke,
  Most lovynge spowse, I muche do here rejoyce of the.
WOMAN. And I lykewyse, swete lover, do much reioyce of the.
God therefore be praised, such comforte have us gyve   30
That ech of us with other thus pleasantly do lyve.
MAN. To walke abowt this garden my fantasye me meve;
  I wyll the leave alone tyll that I turne ageyne;
Farewell, myn owne swete spouse, I leave the to remayne.
WOMAN. And farewell, my dere lover, whom my hart doth
  conteyn.   35

The Serpent speketh.

[SERPENT.] Nowe, nowe, of my purpos I dowght nott to atteyne;
  I can yt nott abyde in theis joyes they shulde be.
Naye, I wyll attempt them to syn unto theyr payne;
  By subtyllty to catch them the waye I do well se;
  Unto this, angell of lyght I shew mysylfe to be;   40
With hyr for to dyscemble, I fear yt nott at all,
Butt that unto my haight some waye I shall hyr call.
Oh lady of felicité, beholde my voyce so small!
  Why have God sayde to you, 'Eate nott of every tre
  That is within this garden?' Therein now awnswere me.   45

WOMAN. We eate of all the frutte that in the grounde we se,
  Exepte that in the myddest wherof we may nott taste,
For God hath yt forbydd, therfor yt may not be,
  Lest that we dye the deth and from this place be caste.
THE SERPENT. Ye shall not dye the deth; he make[2] you butt agaste;
Butt God doth know full well that when you eate of yt,   51
  Your eys shall then be openyd and you shall at the last
As godes[3] both good and evyll to knowe ye shal be fytt.
WOMAN. To be as God indede and in his place to sytt,
  Thereto for to agre my lust conceyve somewhatt;   55
Besydes the tre is pleasante to gett wysedome and wytt,
  And nothyng is to be comparyd unto that.
THE SERPENTE. Then take at my request, and eate, and fere yt natt.

---

[1] *Fitch and Waterhouse* hast; *Manly emends to* has.
[2] *Fitch* made.
[3] *Manly, who also prints* God *in next line; MS.* Godes *in both, Waterhouse* God *in both. Cf. A. 62.*

Here she takyth and eatyth, and Man cumyth in and sayeth unto hyr:

MAN. My love, for my solace, I have here walkyd longe.
 Howe ys yt nowe with you? I pray you do declare.   60
WOMAN. Indede, lovely lover, the Heavenly Kyng most stronge
 To eate of this apple his angell hath prepare;
Take therof at my hande th'other frutes emonge,
 For yt shall make you wyse and even as God to fare.

Then Man taketh and eatyth and sayethe:

[MAN.] Alack! alacke! my spouse, now se I nakid we ar;   65
 The presence of owr God we can yt nott abyde.
We have broke his precepte he gave us of to care;
 From God therfor in secrete in some place lett us hide.
 WOMAN. With fygge-leavis lett us cover us, of God we be nott
  spyede.
 THE FATHER. Adam! I saye Adam! Wher art thou nowe this tyde,
That here before my presence thou dost nott nowe apere?   71
 ADAM. I herde thy voyce, Oh Lorde, but yett I dyd me hide.
For that which I am naked I more greatly dyd feare.

THE FATHER. Why art thou then nakyd? Who so hath cawsyd the?
MAN. This woman, Lord and God, which thou hast gyven to me.
THE FATHER. Hast thou eat of the frute that I forbyd yt the? 76
 Thow woman, why hast thou done unto him thys trespace?
 WOMAN. The Serpente diseayvyd me with that his fayer face.
 THE FATHER. Thow Serpente, why dydst thou this wise prevente
  my grace,
My creatures and servantes in this maner to begyle?   80
 THE SERPENTE. My kind is so, thou knowest and that in every
  case—
Clene oute of this place theis persons to exile.[1]

THE FATHER. Cursed art for causynge my commandement to
  defyle,
 Above all cattell and beastes. Remayne thou in the fylde,
Crepe on thy belly and eate duste for this thy subtyll wyle;   85
 The womans sede shall overcome the, thus that[2] have I wylde.
 Thou, Woman, bryngyng chyldren with payne shall be dystylde,
And be subiect to thy husbonde, and thy lust shall pertayne
To hym: I hav determynyd this ever to remayne.

----

     [1] *Fitch* excite.   [2] *Fitch* y^t; *Manly* yt.

And to the, Man, for that my voyce thou didst disdayne,   90
  Cursed is the erth for ever for thy sake;
Thy lyvyng shall thou gett with swett unto thy payne,
  Tyll thou departe unto the erth [wherof]¹ I dyd the make.
  Beholde, theis letherin aprons unto yourselves now take.
Lo! Man as one of us hath bene, good and evyll to knowe;   95
  Therfor I wyll exempt hym from this place to aslake,
Lest of the tre of lyfe he eate and ever growe.
  Myne angell, now cum furth and kepe the waye and porte,
  Unto the tre of lyffe that they do not resorte.

THE AUNGELL. Departe from hence at onys from this place of
    comforte,   100
  No more to have axcesse or elles for to apere.
From this place I exile you, that you no more resorte,
  Nor even² do presume ageyne for to com here.

*Then Man and Woman departyth to the nether parte of the pageant
and Man sayeth:*

[MAN.] Alack! myn owne sweteharte, how am I stroke with feare,
  That from God am exiled, and browght to payne and woo. 105
Oh! what have we lost! Why dyd we no more care,
  And to what kynde of place shall³ we resort and goo?
  WOMAN. Indede into the worlde now must we to and fro,
And where or how to rest, I can nott say at all.
I am even as ye ar, what so ever me befall.   110

*Then cumeth Dolor and Myserye and taketh Man by both armys and
Dolor sayeth:*

[DOLOR.] Cum furth, O Man, take hold of me!
  Through envy hast lost thy heavenly lyght
By eatinge; in bondage from hence shall be.
  Now must thou me, Dolor, have allways in sight.
  MYSERYE. And also of me, Myserye, thou must taste and byte,
Of hardenes and of colde and eke of infirmitie;   116
  Accordinge to desarte thy portion is, of right,
To enjoy that in me that is withoute certentye.

---

¹ *Supplied by Manly.*
² *So Fitch and Waterhouse; Manly ever* without *comment.*
³ *Fitch* thatt.

ADAM. Thus troublyd, nowe I enter into dolor and miserie.
　　Nowe, Woman, must we lerne owr lyvynges to gett.   120
With labor and with travell; ther is no remedye,
　　Nor eny thyng therfrom we se that maye us lett.

Then cumyth in the Holy Ghost comforting Man and sayeth:

[HOLY GHOST.] Be of good cheare, Man, and sorowe no more.
　　This Dolor and Miserie that[1] thou hast taste,
Is nott in respect, layd up in store,   125
　　To the joyes for the that ever shall[2] last.
　　Thy God doth nott this the away to cast,
But to try the as gold is tryed in the fyer;
In the end, premonyshed, shalt have thy desyre.

Take owte of the Gospell that yt the requyre,   130
　　Fayth in Chryst Jhesu, and grace shall[3] ensewe.
I wyl be thy guyde and pay the thy hyer
　　For all thy good dylygence and doenge thy dewe.
　　Gyve eare unto me, Man, and than yt ys trewe,
Thou shalt kyll affectes that by lust in the reygne   135
And putt Dolor and Mysery and Envy to payne.

Theis armors ar preparyd, yf thou wylt turn ageyne,
　　To fyght wyth; take to the, and reach Woman the same;
The brest-plate of rightousnes Saynte Paule wyll the retayne;
　　The shylde of faythe to quench, thy fyrye dartes to tame;   140
　　The hellmett of salvacion the devyles wrath shall lame;
And the sworde of the Spright, which is the worde of God—
All theis ar nowe the offred to ease thy payne and rodd.

ADAM. Oh! prayse to The, Most Holye, that hast with me abode,
　　In mysery premonyshynge by this Thy Holy Spright.   145
Nowe[4] fele I such great comforte, my syns they be unlode
　　And layde on Chrystes back, which is my joye and lyght.
　　This Dolor and this Mysery I fele to me no wight;
No! Deth is overcum by forepredestinacion,
And we attayned wyth Chryst in heavenly consolacion.   150
Therfor, myne owne swett spous, withouten cavylacion,
　　Together lett us synge, and lett our hartes reioyse,
　　And gloryfye owr God wyth mynde, powre, and voyse. **Amen.**

Old Musick Triplex, Tenor, Medius, Bass:[1]

With hart and voyce
Let us reioyce   155
    And prayse the Lord alwaye
    For this our joyfull daye,
To se of this our God his maiestie,
Who hath[2] given himsellfe over us to raygne and to governe us.
Lett all our harte[s][3] reioyce together,   160
And lett us all lifte up our voyce, on of us with another.

  [1] *This direction evidently added by Fitch.*
  [2] *Manly's emendation of Fitch (and Waterhouse)* Who the hath. *These last lines can hardly be restored to regularity.*
  [3] *Manly.*

III

THE NEWCASTLE PLAY

A. BOURNE'S TEXT[1]

NOAH's ARK; or, The SHIPWRIGHTS ancient PLAY,
or DIRGE.

Deus incipitur.

*E*RE *was this World that I have wrought,*
No Marvel it is if I do ſhow;
Their Folk in Earth I made of Nought,
Now are they fully my Foe.
Vengeance now will I do   5
Of them that have grieved me ill,
Great Floods ſhall over them go,
And run over Hoope and Hill.
All Mankind dead ſhall be,
With Storms both ſtiff and ſteer;   10
All but Noah *my Darling free,*
His Children and their Wives,
Ever more yet they trow'd in me,
Save therefore I will their Lives.
Henceforth my Angel free,   15
Into Earth look what thou would,
Greet well Noah *in this Degree,*
Sleeping thou ſhalt him find:
Bid him go make a Ship
Of ſtiff Board and great,   20
Although he be not a Wright.
Therefore bid him not lett,
He ſhall have Wit at Will,
Be that he come thereto;
All Things I him fulfill,   25
Pitch, Tar, Seam and Rowe.
Bid him in any Manner of Thing,

[1] *Line numbers are those of the edited text.*

To Ship when he ſhall walk,
Of all kine Kind of Beaſt and Fowl,
The Male and Female with him he take.   30
Bid him go provey, ſay ſo,
In Ship that they not die,
Take with him Hay, Corn and Straw,
For his Fowl and his Fee.
Henceforth my Angel free   35
Tell him this for certain;
My Bleſſing with thee be,
While that thou come again.

Angelus dicat.

Waken Noah, to me take tent.
Noah bid, if thou hear this Thing,   40
Ever whilſt thou live thou ſhall repent.

Noah reſpondit.

What art thou for Heaven's King,
That wakens Noah off his Sleeping,
Away I would thou went.

Angelus dicat.

It is an Angel to thee ſent,   45
Noah, to tell thee hard Tiding;
For every Ilk a Wight for Warks wild,
And many fowled in Sins ſair,
And in Felony fowly filled;
Therefore a Ship thou dight to ſteer,   50
Of true Timber highly railed,
With thirty Cubits in Defence.
Look that ſhe draw when ſhe is dreſt,
And in her Side a Door thou ſhear,   55
With Feneſters full fitly feſt,
And make Chambers both more and leſs,
For a Flood that up ſhall burſt;
Such a Flood in Earth ſhall be,
That every like Life that hath Life-ward,   60
Beaſt and Body with Bone and Blood,
They ſhall be ſtormed through Streſs of Storm;

Albeit thou Noah *and thy Brood,*
And their three Wives in your Hand,
For you are full righteous and good, 65
You ſhall be ſaved by Sea and Land,
In the Ship ere you enter out,
You take with you both Ox and Cow;
Of ilk a Thing that Life has lent,
The Male and Female you take with you. 70
You fetch in Fother for your Freight,
And make good Purveiance for you prove,
That they periſh not in your Sight;
Do Noah *as I have bidden thee now.*

Noah reſpondit.

Lord be then in this Stead, 75
That me and mine will ſave and ſhield;
I am a Man no worth at Need,
For I am ſix hundred Winters old,
Unluſty I am to do ſuch a Deed,
Worklooms for to work and weeld 80
For I was never ſince I was born,
Of Kind of Craft to burthen a Boat,
For I have neither Ryff nor Ruff,
Spyer, Sprund, Spront, no Sprot.
Chriſt be the Shaper of this Ship, 85
For a Ship need make I muſt.
Even wo worth thou fouled Sin,
For all too dear thou muſt be bought,
God for Thanks he made Mankind,
Or with his Hands that he them wrought; 90
Therefore or ever you blind,
You mind your Wife, and turn your Thought,
For of my Work I will begin,
So well were me were all forth brought.

Deabolus intrat.

Put off Harro, and wele away, 95
That ever I uproſe this Day;
So may I ſmile and ſay,
I went, there has been none alive,

Man, Beaſt, Child nor Wife,
But my Servants were they;   100
All this I have heard ſay,
A Ship that made ſhould be,
For to ſave with owten Nay,
Noah and his Meenye;
Yet trow I they ſhall be,   105
Thereto I make a Vow,
If they be never ſo ſlee,
To taynt them yet I trow.
To Noah's Wife will I wynd,
Gare her believe in me;   110
In Faith ſhe is my Friend,
She is both whunt and ſlee,
Reſt well, reſt well, my own Dereday.

Uxor Noah dicat.

Welcome, fewſthere, what is thy Name,
Tyte that thou tell me.   115

Deabolus dicat.

To tell my Name I were full loath,
I come to warn thee of thy Skaith,
I tell thee ſecretly,
And thou do after thy Husband read,
Thou and thy Children will all be dead,   120
And that right haſtily.

Uxor dicat.

Go Devil, how ſay, for Shame.

Deabolus dicat.

Yes, hold thee ſtill le Dame,
And I ſhall tell how;
I ſwear thee by my crooked Snout,   125
All that thy Husband goes about
Is little for thy Profit;
Yet ſhall I tell thee how,
Thou ſhall weet all his Will;
Do as I ſhall bid thee now,   130

Thou ſhalt weet every Deal.
Have here a Drink full good,
That is made of a mightful Main,
Be he hath drunken a Drink of this,
No longer ſhall he learn.   135
Believe, believe, my own dear Dame,
I may no longer bide,
To Ship when thou ſhall ſayre,
I ſhall be thy Side.

Noah dicat.

This Labour is full great   140
For like an old Man as me,
Lo, lo, faſt I ſweat,
It trickles at our myn ee;
Now Home will I wende,
My weary Bones for to reſt,   145
For ſuch Good as God hath ſent,
There I get of the beſt.
Reſt well Day, what Chear with thee.

Uxor dicat.

Welcome, Noah, *as might I thee*
Welcome to thine own Wayns.   150
Sit down here beſide me,
Thou haſt full weary Baynes:
Have eaten, Noah, *as might I thee,*
And ſoon a Drink I ſhall give thee,
Such Drink thou never none afore.   155

Noah dicat.

What the Devil what Drink is it,
By my Father's Soul I have nere loſt my Wit.

Uxor dicat.

Noah, *bode you tell me whereabout you wends,*   160
I give God a Vow, we two ſhall nere be Friends.

Noah dicat.

O Yes Dame could thou layne
I would thee tell my Wit.   165

How Good of Heaven an Angel ſent,
And bad me make a Ship,
This World he will fore doe
With Storms both ſtiff and ſteer fell,
All but thee and me, our Children and Wifes.   170

Uxor dicat.

Who Devil made thee a Wright,
God give him Evil to fayre
Of Hand to have ſuch ſlight,
To make Ship leſs or more perfect,   175
Men ſhould have heard wide where
When you began to ſmite.

Noah dicat.

Yes Dame it is God's will,
Let be ſo thou not ſay,
Go make an End I will,   180
And come again full throng.

Uxor dicat.

By my Faith I no rake
Whether thou be Friend or Foe,
The Devil of Hell thee ſpeed,
To ſhip when thou ſhalt go.   185

Noah dicat.

God ſend me Help in high,
To clink you Nail too
God ſend me help in high,
Your Hand to hold again,
That all may well be done,   190
My Strokes be not in Vain.

Angelus dicat.

God hath thee Help hither ſend,
Thereof be thou right bold,
Thy Strokes ſhall fair be kend,
For thou thy Wife has cowld.   195

Noah dicat.

Now is this Ship well made
within and without thinks me,
Now home then will I wend
To fetch in my Money,
Have good day both old and young,   200
My Bleſſing with you be.

Deabolus dicat.

All that is gathered in this Stead,
That will not believe in me,
I pray to Dolphin Prince of dead,
Scald you all in his Lead   205
That never a one of you thrive, nor thee.

FINIS. Amen.

B. EDITED TEXT[1]

Noah's Ark; or The Shipwrights' Ancient
Play or Dirge

Deus incipitur. *Me rewes*[2] this world that I have wrought;
    No marvel *if* I do *sae.*[3]
Their folk in earth I made of nought;
    Now are they fully my *fae.*
Vengeance now will I *tae*[4]   5
    Of them that have grieved me ill.
Great floods shall over them *gae,*[4]
    And run over hoope and hill.

All mankind dead shall be
    With storms both *steer* and *stiff,*[5]   10
All but Noah, my darling free,
    His children and their *wifes;*
Evermore yet they trow'd in me,
    Save therefore I will their *life.*

---

[1] *In this text departures from Bourne are printed in italics.*
[2] *Bradley; Holthausen and Waterhouse* Fre was.
[3] *Bradley* so; *Brotanek and Waterhouse* it destroy.
[4] *Brotanek* ta, ga.
[5] *Holthausen; Brotanek* that both stere and stiff [is]; *cf.* 169–71.

Hence forth, my angel free,   15
    Into earth look *that* thou *wind.*
Greet well Noah in *his*[1] degree—
    Sleeping thou shalt him find.

Bid him go make a ship
    Of stiff board and great;   20
Although he be not a wright,
    Therefore bid him not lett.

He shall have wit at will
    Be that he come thereto;
All things I him fulfill—   25
    Pitch, tar, seam, and rowe.

Bid him in any manner of thing,
    To ship when he shall walk,
Of *alkin* beast and fowl *with wing*[2]
    The male and female with him he take.   30

Bid him go provey, say *sae,*
    In ship that they not *dee;*
Take with him hay, corn, and *strae*
    For his fowl and his fee.
Hence forth, my angel free,   35
    Tell him this for certain.
My blessing with thee be
    While that thou come again.

ANGELUS DICAT. Waken, Noah, to me take tent!
    Noah, *but* if thou hear this thing   40
Ever whilst thou live thou shall repent.
    NOAH RESPONDIT. What art thou, for Heaven's King,
—*Away,* [*away*] *I would thou went—*
    That wakens Noah off his sleeping?[3]
ANGELUS DICAT. It is an angel to thee sent,   45
    Noah, to tell thee hard tiding.

For every ilk a wight *does* warks wild,
    And many *sowled* in sins *seir*

---

[1] *Holthausen.*
[2] *Brotanek* Of alkin best and [bird with wing]; *Holthausen* Of allkine kind of beasts living.   [3] *Transposed by Holthausen.*

And in felony fowly filled.
    Therefore a ship thou dight to steer,   50

Of true timber highly railed,
    With thirty cubits in defence[1]

.   .   .   .
    Look that she draw when she is drest.
And in her side a door thou shear,   55
    With fenesters full fitly fest;
And make chambers both *less* and *mair*
    For a flood that up shall *brest*.

In earth shall be such a flood
    That every *ilke thing* that hath life *form*,   60
Beast and body with bone and blood,
    They shall be *stroied*[2] through stress of storm;
Albeit thou, Noah, and thy brood,
    And their three wives in your hand,
For you are full righteous and good   65
    You shall be saved by sea and land.

In the ship ere you *entent*[2]
    You take with you both ox and cow;
Of ilk a thing that life has lent
    The male and female you take with you.   70
You fetch in fother for your freight
    And make good purveiance for *your prow*,[3]
That they perish not in your sight.
    Do, Noah, as I have bidden thee now.

NOAH RESPONDIT. Lord, be then in this stead,   75
    That me and mine will save and shield.
I am a man no worth at need,
    For I am six hundred winters *of eld*.[4]
Unlusty I am to do such a deed,
    Worklooms for to work and weeld.   80

---

[1] *Though both sense and rhyme are defective, and no simple emendation is apparent, this seems a likely structure of this imperfect stanza; but more than one line may have been lost. Brotanek and Holthausen assume loss of two lines after 51.*
[2] *Holthausen.*
[3] *Brotanek; Holthausen prowe.*
[4] *Holthausen winters eld; Brotanek wintir of eld.*

For I was never *in my life*
    Of kind *or*[1] craft to burthen a boat;
For I have neither *ruff* nor *ryff*,
    Spyer, sprund, *sprout, nor* sprot.[2]
Christ be the shaper of this ship,   85
    For a ship need make I *mot*.[3]

Even wo worth *the*, fouled sin,
    For all too dear thou must be bought.
God *forthinks* he made *mankin*[4]
    Or with his hands that he them wrought.   90
Therefore, [*men*], or ever you *blin*,
    You *mend* your *life*[3] and turn your thought,
For of my work I will begin.
    So well were me were all forth brought.

DEABOLUS INTRAT. *Out, out*, harro, and *welaway*   95
That ever I uprose this day!
    So may I smile and say,
I *wene* there has been none alive,
Man, beast, child, nor wife,
    But my servants were they.   100

All this I have heard say,
    A ship that made should be
For to save, withowten nay,
    Noah and his meenye.

Yet trow I they shall *dee*—   105
    Thereto I make a vow:
If they be never so slee,
    To taynt them yet I trow.

To Noah's wife will I wynd,
    Gare her believe in me;   110
In faith she is my friend,
    She is both whunt and slee.

Rest well, rest well, my own dere *dame*![3]
UXOR NOAH DICAT. Welcome, *bewschere*;[3] what is thy name?
    Tyte that thou tell me.   115

---

  [1] *Brotanek.*
  [2] *Holthausen* [Nor] spyer [nor] sprund [nor] sprout no[r] sprot.
  [3] *Holthausen.*   [4] *Holthausen, with* blin 91; *Waterhouse follows Bourne.*

DEABOLUS DICAT. To tell my name I were full *laith*.[1]
I come to warn thee of thy skaith:
    I tell thee secretly,
And thou do after thy husband read
Thou and thy children will all be dead,   120
    And that right hastily.

UXOR DICAT. Go, devil, how say, for shame!
DEABOLUS DICAT. Yes, hold the still, *lo* dame,
    And I shall tell [*thee*][1] how.
I swear thee by my crooked snout,   125
All that thy husband goes about
    Is little for thy *prow*.

Yet shall I tell thee how
    Thou shall weet all his will.
Do as I bid thee now,   130
    Thou shalt weet every deal.

Have here a drink full good, [*iwis*],[1]
    That is made of a mightful main.
Be he hath drunken a drink of this
    No longer shall he *lain*.   135

Believe, believe, my own *dame dere*,
    I may no longer bide.
To ship when thow shall *fayre*,
    I shall be [*by*][2] thy side.

NOAH DICAT. This labour is full great   140
    For *slike*[3] an old man as me.
Lo, lo, fast I sweat,
    It trickles atour myn ee.

Now home will I wende
    My weary bones for to rest,   145
For such good as God hath sent
    There I get of the best.

Rest well, *dame*,[4] what chear with thee?
UXOR DICAT. Welcome, Noah, as might I thee,
    Welcome to thine own wayns!   150

[1] *Holthausen.*   [2] *Brand.*
[3] *Holthausen; Waterhouse follows Bourne.*   [4] *Brotanek.*

Sit down here beside me,
 Thou hast full weary baynes.
Have eaten, Noah, as might I thee,
And soon a drink I shall give thee,
 Such *drank* thou never *ayns*.   155

NOAH DICAT. What the devil!
 What drink is it?
By my father's soul,
 I have nere lost my wit!

UXOR DICAT. Noah, *bot thou* tell me [*now*] 160
 Whereabout *thou* wends,
I give God [*in Heaven*] a vow
 We two shall nere be friends.[1]

NOAH DICAT. O yes, dame, could thou *a laint*,
 I would thee tell my wit—   165
How *God* of Heaven an angel sent
 And bad me make a ship.

This world foredoe *will he*
 With storms both *steer* and *stiff*,[2]
All but thee and me,   170
 Our children and [*their*] wifes.[3]

UXOR DICAT. Who devil made thee a wright?
 God give him evil to fayre—
Of hand to have such slight
 To make ship less or *mair*.   175
When thou *began to smite*
 Men should have heard wide-where.[4]

NOAH DICAT. Yes, dame, it is God's will;
 Let be, so thou not say.
Go make an end I will,   180
 And come again full *thrae*.

UXOR DICAT. By my faith, I no rake
 Whether thou be friend or foe.

---

[1] *These two stanzas printed by Bourne as four long lines. Holthausen, Brotanek,
and Waterhouse offer different reconstructions.*
[2] *Holthausen; Brotanek* stere and stiff [is].
[3] *Cf.* 10–12 *above.*   [4] *Transposed by Brotanek.*

The devil of hell thee *take*[1]
    To ship when thou shalt go.   185

NOAH DICAT. God send me help in *hy*
    To clink *yon nails twain*;
God send me help in *hy*
    Your hand to hold again.
That all *well done may be*   190
    My strokes be not in vain.

ANGELUS DICAT. God hath thee help hither send,
    Thereof be thou right bold.
Thy strokes shall fair be kend,
    For thou thy wife has *told*.   195

NOAH DICAT. Now is this ship well *yare*,[2]
    Within and without, thinks me.
Now home then will I *fare*
    To fetch in my *meenye*.[3]
Have good day, both *less* and *mair*;   200
    My blessing with you be.

DEABOLUS DICAT. All that is gathered in this stead
    That will not believe in me,
I pray to Dolphin, prince of dead,
Scald you all in his lead,   205
    That never a one of you thrive nor thee.
                Finis.   AMEN.

[1] *Brotanek.*
[2] *Holthausen* gare, *with* fare 198; *Brotanek* ginned, wend.
[3] *Cf.* 104 *above.*

IV

THE NORTHAMPTON PLAY
OF *ABRAHAM AND ISAAC*

DEUS. Of all þing þer euer was I am þe begynnere,   f. 74ᵛ
  Boþe hevenly and erthly, and of hem þat ben in hell;
At my bidding was wrought boþe goode man and synnere,
  All in ioy to haue dwellid, tyl Adam to syn fell.
  His vnkindnes haþe displesid me, truþe for to tell,   5
For many a þing made I for his ioy and daliaunce.
  Whi sholde he displese me þat I loued so well,
And comaunded hym but on þing and ȝit he forfetid my
  pleasaunce.
But ȝit siþ he haþ displesid me, I haue made proviaunce
  þat anodre of his kynd shal plese me ayeyne,   10
þe which haþe euer be my seruaunt in al manere obseruaunce:
  Abraham is his name, my man þat cannot feyne,
    But evyr hathe be trewe.
    Herebefore he requryed me hye
    To haue a childe of his body,   15
    And I grauntid hym and haþe on redely,
    Isaac ful feyre of hewe.

Of al þing erthely, I wot wel, he loueþ him best;
  Now he shuld loue me moste, as reson wold and skylle,
And so I wot well he doþe, I dyd it neuer mystrest.   20
  But ȝit, for to preue hym, þe truþe wol I fele.
  Myne aungel, go to Abraham þat I loue riȝt wele,
And say þat I comaunded and charged hym aboue all þinge,
  The furst dede þat he doþe, or mete ouþer mele,¹
To make sacrifise vnto me of Isaac his son ȝynge.   25
ANGELUS. O, blessid Lord, I am redy at þi bidding
  To do þat shal plese þe in hevyn, erþe, and helle;
For all þese owen to þe obedience aboue all þing.
  þis message vnto Abraham þi seruaunt I wol go telle.

---

¹ *Brotanek; MS.* ouþer mete or mele.

DEUS. Then hye the þat þou were on grounde.   f. 76ʳ
I do not but to assay hym,   31
And if he do it I wol not dismay hym;
Of his sorow I shal delay hym,
   And for on childe encrese hym a þusunde.[1]

   Et vadit angelus ad terram et expectat usque dum
                Habraham dicit:

ABRAHAM. O gret God on hye þat al þe worlde madest,   35
   And lendist vs oure leving here to do þi plesaunce,
With swete counfort of þe erþe all oure hertys gladest,
   To þe be honoure, to þe be ioy and all dewe obesaunce;
   And hily, Lord, I þank þe þat so makest my purviaunce
To provide or I dye a childe of myne owne body.   40
   To reioyse þat þou gaue me in erþe to my daliaunce
And to plese þe, souereigne Lord, I shall charge hym perfitly,
      Isaac, my son so dere.
I haue ben out all day:
Now shal I go home to my wif I say,[2]   45
þere shal I fynde bothe tway,
      Sara and Isaac infere.

   Et vadit et in eundo obruat ei angelus et dicit:

ANGELUS. Abraham, Abraham!
ABRAHAM. Al redy, who calleþ? lo, here I am.
Who is þere, in þe hye Lordes name,   50
   þat al þing shope of nought?
ANGELUS. I am here, a messangere
Of þat souereigne Lord entere,
þerfore herkyn now and here
   What message I haue brought.   55

þe goode Lord of al hevenes hye
Comaundeþ þe to take and sacrifye
Isaac þi son þat þou louest so hertlye
   To his souerenté and plesaunce blyve.   59
Farewele, for my message I haue þe sayde.   f. 77ᵛ
HABRAHAM. Aungel, as God wol, I am right wele payde;
For of me his wille shal neuer be withnayde
   Whil I am on lyve;

      [1] *MS.* m¹.   [2] *MS. and* to my wif ⌜*and*⌝ say.

And hardly, aungell, trust thereto,
For doughtles it shal be do.   65
ANGELUS. Farewele þan, for I wol go
    To bring oure Lord relacion.
HABRAHAM. Now, goode Lord, graunt me hert þeretylle,
þat I may do that is thy wille:
And be my trouþe, I shal it fulfille   70
    Without fraude outher cauelacion.

Et vadit angelus et dicit Habraham:

A goode Lord, what is now best to do?
Home to my wif I most nedis go
For þer is Isaac and I trowe she wol be ful wo,
    If she know þe case.   75
For she haþe hym and no mo,
And if I telle her þat it is so,
þat God wol haue hym to deþe ido,
    She faileþ not of sorowes trase.

No forse, I haue levyr þat she displesid be,   80
Than þat God be wrothe with me.
Now doughtles I shal go and se
    How prevely that I can it do.
Vndo þese yates! Hey, who is here?
SARA. None but I and my son dere.   85
Welcom my lord, welcom my fere,
    Welcom my counfort also.

A, ye haue walkid ferre aboute!
Howȝ haue ye fare whil ye haue be oute?
Without fayle, I haue had gret doute   90
    Last any thinge did you grevaunce.
HABRAHAM. Nay, I thanke the goode Lorde,
All thing and I done wel acorde,
Saving þis: my goode Lord haþ sent me worde,
    That I moste nedis go do his plesaunce: 95

I most do sacrifyse vpon þat hille on hye.   f. 78ʳ
And þerfore, sirs, makeþ myne asse redye,
And Isaac, son, þou neuer ȝit me sye
    Do no soche obseruaunce.

þerfore aray the and go with me,   100
And lerne how God shuld plesid be;
For, son, and euer þou þenke to the,
   Put euer God to honowraunce.

ISAAC. So shal I, fadir, and euer haue do,
As ye haue taught me and my moder also.   105
Loke, when euer þat ye wol go,
   I shal not be behynde.
SARA. Ye, but I pray you, gentil fere,
As euer ye haue loued me dere,
Lat Isaac abide at home here,   110
   For I kept not he went in þe wynde.

HABRAHAM. Peese dame, lat be, do way.
þou wost wele, I wax right gray,
And þis childe neuer ȝit say
   How God shuld be plesid;   115
And þerfore now he shal go with me
And þer he shal boþe know and se
How þat God shal plesid be
   And myne hert i-esid.

SARA. Then, siþe ye wol haue forthe my childe,   120
Goode, loke þat his horse be not to wilde,
And sirs, wayte on hym, þat he be not defilde
   With neiþer cley nor fen.
And loke wele þat his horse go rownde
And þat he stumbel not for no pownde.   125
Now, goode hert, God send þe home sownde,
   þi fadir and all his men!

HABRAHAM. Gete hidre oure horses and let vs go hen,
Boþe I and Isaac and these two men;
And loke we haue fyre and stikkes to bren!   130
   Lepiþ vp, haue ido anon!
SARA. All þing is redy, I you say;
But, gentil hert, I you pray,
Tary as litel while out as ye may,
   Because of Isaac, my son.   135

Et equitat et equitando Habraham dicit: f. 78ᵛ

HABRAHAM. Now, sirs, abide here ye two,
Takeþ here my horse and Isaac also:
For he and I most a litel farþer go
    To do this sacrifyse.
And I charge you þat ye abide here in deede,   140
And þat ye remeve not from þis stede,
Whil Isaac and I go do this dede
    To God in oure best wise.

Come hidre, Isaac, my son goode,
Take vp þis fyre and þis wode,   145
Spare not þi cloþes, geue me þi hode,
    I shal not combre the sore.
ISAAC. Now gawe, fader, þat þis dede were hyed,
For þis wode on my bak is wel tyed.
But where is þat quyk best þat shal be sacrified—   150
    Behynde vs, or afore?

HABRAHAM. Son, care not þerfore on neuer a side,
But let God alone þerwith þis tyde,
And for oure wey he shal provyde
    And defend vs from fere.   155
A, son, I haue aspyed þe place,
þat God haþe provided vs of his grace.
Come on, son, a riȝt goode pace
    And hye vs þat we were þere.

Now Isaac, son, I may no lengre refrayne,   160
But I most tell þe truthe certayne,
And þerfore loke þou be not þeragayne,
    But do it with all þi wille.
þe hye God, þat all haþe wrought,
Comaunded me þat hidre þou shuldest be brought,   165
And here þi body shal be brouȝt to nought
    Vnto sacrifise on this hille.

Lay downe þat wode on þat auter there,
And fast delyuer þe and do of þi gere.
ISAAC. Alas, gentyl fader, why put ye me in þis fere?   170
    Haue I displesid you any thing?

3if I haue trespast, I cry you mercy;
And, gentil fader, lat me not dye!
Alas, is þer none oþer beste but I
    þat may plese þat hy King?   175

HABRAHAM. Nay, son, to me þou hast do no trespas,
But þou hast my blessing in euery place;
But I may not forfet þat Lordes grace,
    þat al þing haþe me sent.
For and it shuld be affter me,   180
I had leuer haue slayne al my bestes þan þe.
But his wille nedys fulfilled most be,
    And truly so is myn entent.

ISAAC. Alas, what haue I displesid þis Lord of blisse,
þat I shal be martyred in þis mysse?   185
But, gentil fader, wot my modre of þis,
    þat I shal be dede?
HABRAHAM. She? Mary, son, Crist forbede!
Nay, to telle her it is no nede;
For whan þat euer she knoweþ þis dede,   190
    She wol ete affter but litel brede.

ISAAC. In feiþe, for my moder I dar wel say,
And she had wist of this aray
I had not riden out from her þis day,
    But she had riden also.   195
HABRAHAM. Ye, son, God most be serued ay,
þi modre may not haue hir wille all way.
I loue þe as wele as she doþe, in fay,
    And 3it þis dede most be do.

ISAAC. A, fader, þen do of my gowne,   200
Vngirde me and take hem with you to towne;
For I may not. I falle in swowne,
    Deþe haþe enbrasid myn hert.
But on þing, fader, I pray you þus:
Let neuer my moder se my cloþus;   205
For and¹ she do, withouten othus,
    It wol greue her to smert.

¹ *MS.* a.

HABRAHAM. A, dere hert, what shal I do by þe?
Wo is me þat shal sle the!
With all my goodes I wold by þe,   210
    And God wold assent þerto.
ISAAC. A, fader, do now what euer ye lyst,   f. 79ᵛ
For of my modre, I wot wel, I shal be myst.
Many a tyme haþ she me clipt and kyst,
    But farewel nowe, for þat is do.   215

She was wont to calle me hir tresoure and hir store;
But farewel now, she shal no more.
Here I shal be dede and wot neuer wherefore,
    Saue þat God most haue his wille.
Fader, shal my hed of also?   220
HABRAHAM. Ye, forsoþe, son, þat most nedis be do.
Alas, goode hert, þat me is wo
    þat euer I shuld þe þus spille!

ISAAC. þen, fader, bynde myne handes and my legges fast,
And yeue me a gret stroke, þat my peynes were past;   225
For last I shrinke I am riȝt sore agast,
    And þan ye wol smyte me in a noþer place;
Then is my peyne so moche the more.
A, soffte, gentil fader; ye bynde me sore.
HABRAHAM. A, dere hert, wo is me therefore,   230
    My mynde is worse than evyr it was.

ISAAC. A, fadir, ley me downe sofft and feyre
And haue ido nowe, and sle youre eyre.
For I am hampred and in dispeyre
    And almost at my lives ende.   235
HABRAHAM. A, fayre hert-rote, leue þi crye!
þi sore langage goþe myne hert ful nye.
þer is no man þerfore so wo as I,
    For here shal I sle my frende.

þe hye Lord bad me to do þis dede,   240
But my hert gruccheþ, so God me spede,
My blode aborreþ to se my son blede,
    For all on blode it is.

Alas, þat my hert is wondre sore,
For I am now riȝt olde and hore;   245
But God haþe chose þe for his owne store
   In counfor of al my mys,

And to be offerd to hym þat is Lord an hye.
And þerfore, son, take it pacientlye.
Parauenture in batayle or oþer myschef þou myȝtest dye,   250
   Or ellis in anoþer vngoodely veniaunce.[1]
ISAAC. Now, fader, þen siþe it is so,   f. 80ʳ
With al my hert I assent þerto.
Strecche out my nek, anon haue do,
   And put me out of penaunce.   255
HABRAHAM. Now kisse me furst, hert-rote;
Now ly downe, strecche out þi þrote!
This takeþ me ful nye, God wote,
   Goode Lord, to do þi plesaunce!

   Et extendit manum ut inmolaret eum et dicit angelus:

ANGELUS. Habraham, leue of and do not smyte;   260
   Withdrawe þyn hond, it is Goddes wille!
Take vp Isaac, þi son so whyte,
   For God wol not þat þou hym spille.
He seeþe þat þou art redy for to fulfille
His comaundement, in wele and wo;   265
   And þerfore now he sent me the tylle
And bad þat Isaac shuld not be sacrified so.
      And as for þi sacrifise,
   Turne þe and take þat wedyr there,
   And sacrifye hym on þat awtere,   270
   And loke þat Isaac haue no dere,
      I charge þe in all wise.

HABRAHAM. A, sufferen Lord, þi wille be fulfilled
   In hevyn, in erþe, in watyr and clay!
And Lord, I þank þe þat Isaac is not killed.   275
   Now, Lord, I know wele þou dydest but asay
   What I wold sey þerto, ouþer ye or nay.
þou knowest myne hert now, and so þou didest afore;
   Haddest not sent þyn aungil, Isaac had died þis day.

      [1] *Written after* wyse *struck out.*

But, goode Lord, saue þi plesaunce, þis pref was riȝt sore,   280
    But ȝit I þanke þe hye
    þat I haue my sones lyve.
    Gawe, son, do on þi cloþes blyve,
    And let not þi moder wete of þis stryve,
      I pray þe, son, hertly.   285

DEUS. Habraham, loke vp and herkyn to me.
Siþe þou woldest haue done þat I charged þe,
And sparedist not to sle Isaac, þi son so fre,
    The chef tresoure that thow haste,
Be myn owne self I swere certeyn,   f. 80ᵛ
þi goode wille I shal quyte ayeyn: 291
þat shal be worship vnto you tweyn
    While þe world shal last.

For þou sparedist not þi son for me.
Go and novmbre þe gravel in þe see,   295
Ouþer motes in þe sunne, and it wol be
    By any estimacion;
And as þik as gravel in þe see doþe ly,
As þik þy sede shal multiply,
And oon shal be borne of þi progeny   300
    þat to all shal cause saluacion.

HABRAHAM. A, lord, ithanked euer be thy myght,
By tyme, by tyde, by day and nyght.
Now Isaac, son, let vs hens dight
    To oure horses and oure men.   305
Gawe! þei ben here fast by.
Hey, sirs! bring þens oure horses in hy
And let vs lepe vp here lightly,
    Fast þat we were hen.

Lepe vp, son, and fast haue ido.   310
ISAAC. All redy, fadre, I am here, lo;
Ye shal not be let whan euer ye go.
    Mi modre I wolde fayne se.
And ȝit, that owre I sawe þis day!
I wend I shuld haue gone my way.   315
HABRAHAM. Ye, blessid be þat Lord þat so can ⌈a⌉say
    His servaund in euery degré!

Et equitat versus Saram et dicit Sara:

SARA. A, welcom souereigne, withouten doute;
How haue ye fared whils ye haue ben oute?
And, Isaac, son, in all þis rowte?   320
 Hertly welcome home be ye!
HABRAHAM. Gramercy, wif, fayre most you befalle.
Com þens, wif, out of youre halle,
And let vs go walke and I wol telle you alle,
 How God haþe sped þis day with me.   325

Wif, I went for to sacrifye;
But how trowe you, telle me verylye?
SARA. Forsoþe, souereigne, I wot not I,   f. 81ʳ
 Parauenture som quyk best?
HABRAHAM. Quyk? Ye forsoþe, quyk it was!   330
As wel I may tel you al þe case
As anoþer þat was in þe same place,
 For I wote wel it wol be wist.

Almighty God, þat sitteth on hye,
Bad me take Isaac, þi son, þerbye   335
And smyte of his hed and bren hym veralye,
 Aboue vpon yondre hille.
And when I had made fyre and smoke,
And drowe my knyf to yeve hym a stroke,
An aungel cam and my wille broke,   340
 And seid oure Lord alowed my wylle.

SARA. Alas, all þen had gone to wrake!
Wold ye haue slayne¹ my son Isaac?
Nay, þan al my ioy had me forsake!
 Alas, where was your mynde?   345
HABRAHAM. My mynde? Vpon þe goode Lord on hy!
Nay, and he bid me, trust it verayly,
Þouȝ it had be þiself and I,
 It shuld not haue ben left behynde.

God gave hym betwix vs tweyne,   350
And now he asked hym of vs ageyne.
Shuld I say nay? Nay, in certeyne,
 Not for al þe world wide.

       ¹ *MS.* slayme.

Now he knoweþ my hert verayly;
Isaac haþe his blessing and also I,   355
And haþe blessid also all oure progeny,
    For euer to abide.

SARA. Now blessid be þat Lorde souereigne
þat so likeþ to say to you tweyne;
And what þat euer he lust, I say not þeragayne,   360
    But his wille be fulfilled.

[HABRAHAM.] Isaac haþe no harme, but in maner I was sory;
And ȝit I haue wonne his love truly.
And euermore, goode Lord, gramercy
    þat my childe is not kylled.   365

Now ye þat haue sene þis aray,
I warne you all, boþe nyȝt and day,
What God comaundeþ say not nay,
    For ye shal not lese þerby.

V

THE BROME PLAY OF
ABRAHAM AND ISAAC

ABRAHAM. Fader of Heuyn Omnipotent, f. 15ʳ
   Wyth all my hart to the I call;
Thow hast ȝoffe me both lond and rent,
And my lyvelod thow hast me sent;
   I thanke the heyly euermore of all.   5

Fyrst off the erth þou madyst Adam,
   And Eue also to be hys wyffe;
All other creaturys of them too cam;
And now thow hast grant to me, Abraham,
   Her in thys lond to lede my lyffe.   10

In my age þou hast grantyd me thys,
   That thys ȝowng chyld wyth me schall won;
I love no thyng so myche, iwysse,
Excepe þin owyn selffe, der Fader of blysse,
   As Ysaac her, my owyn swete son.   15

I haue dyuerse chyldryn moo,
   The wych I love not halffe so wyll;
Thys fayer swet chyld, he schereys me soo,
In euery place wer that I goo,
   That noo dessece her may I fell.   20

And ther� ⌐for⌐, Fadyr of Heuyn, I the prey,
   For hys helth and also for hys grace;
Now, Lord, kepe hym both nygth and day
That neuer dessese nor noo fray
   Cume to my chyld in noo place.   25

Now cum on, Ysaac, my owyn swet chyld;
   Goo we hom and take owre rest.

YSAAC. Abraham, myn owyn fader so myld,
   To folowe ʒow I am full prest,[1]
     Bothe erly and late.[2]   30
ABRAHAM. Cume on, swete chyld, I love the best   f. 15ᵛ
   Off all the chyldryn that euer I begat.

DEUS. Myn angell, fast hey the thy wey,
   And onto medyll-erth anon þou goo;
Abrams hart now wyll I asay,   35
   Wethere that he be stedfast or noo.

Sey I commaw[n]dyd[3] hym for to take
   Ysaac, hys ʒowng sonne, þat he love so wyll,
And wyth hys blood sacryfyce he make,
   Yffe ony off my freynchepe[4] he wyll fell.   40

Schow hym the wey onto the hylle
   Wer that hys sacryffyce schall be;
I schall asay now hys good wyll,
   Whether he lovyth[5] better hys chyld or me.
All men schall take exampyll hym be[6]   45
My commawmentys how they schall fulfyll.[7]

ABRAHAM. Now, Fader of Heuyn, þat formyd all thyng,
   My preyerys I make to the aʒeyn,
For thys day my tender offryng
   Here mvst I ʒeve to the, certeyn.   50
A! Lord God, Allmyty Kyng,
   Wat maner best woll make þe most fayn?
Yff I had therof very knoyng,
   Yt schuld be don wyth all my mayn
     Full sone anon.   55
To don thy plesyng on an hyll,
Verely yt ys my wyll,
   Dere Fader, God alon.[8]

THE ANGELL. Abraham, Abraham, wyll þou rest!
   Owre Lord comandyth þe for to take   60

---

[1] *Manly; MS.* glad, *which is bracketed with* rest *as if rhyming, though another* (? *later*) *bracket links it to* myld.
[2] *This line outside brackets to right.*
[3] *MS. regularly omits* n *in this word.*
[4] *Manly; MS.* yf *before* he.   [5] *MS.* lovyd; *Manly* lovyþ.
[6] *MS.* be hym.   [7] *MS.* kepe.   [8] *MS.* in trenyte; *cf.* 354.

Ysaac, thy ȝowng son that thow lovyst best,   f. 16ʳ
   And wyth hys blod sacryfyce þat thow make.

Into the Lond of V[y]syon¹ thow goo,
   And offer thy chyld onto thy Lord—
I schall the lede—and schow all-soo   65
   Vnto Goddys hest, Abraham, acord,
      And folow me vpon thys gren.
     ABRAHAM. Wollecom to me be my Lordys sond,
     And hys hest I wyll not wythstond;
     ȝyt Ysaac, my ȝowng sonne in lond,   70
      A full dere chyld to me haue byn.

I had lever, yf God had be plesyd
   For to a forbore all þe good þat I haue,
Than Ysaac my son schuld a be desessyd,
   So God in Heuyn my sowll mot saue!   75

I lovyd neuer thyng soo mych in erde,²
   And now I mvst the chyld goo kyll.
A! Lord God, my conseons ys stronly steryd,
And ȝyt my dere Lord, I am sore aferd
   To groche ony thyng aȝens ȝowre wyll.   80

I love my chyld as my lyffe,
   But ȝyt I love my God myche more,
For thow my hart woold make ony stryffe,
ȝyt wyll I not spare for chyld nor wyffe,
   But don after my Lordys lore.   85

Thow I love my sonne neuer so wyll,
   ȝyt smyth of hys hed sone I schall.
A! Fader of Heuyn, to the I knell,
An hard deth my son schall fell
   For to honore the, Lord, wythall.   90

THE ANGELL. Abraham, Abraham, thys ys wyll seyd,   f. 16ᵛ
   And all thys comamentys loke þat þou saue;³
But in thy hart be nothyng dysmayd.⁴
ABRAHAM. Nay, nay, forsoth, I hold me wyll payd,⁵
   To plesse⁶ my God wyth the best þat I haue;   95

¹ *Emended by Holthausen.*   ² *Manly; MS.* erthe.
³ *MS.* kepe.   ⁴ *Holthausen; MS.* dysmasyd.
⁵ *Manly suggests* a-payd*; MS.* plesyd.   ⁶ *MS.* pelsse.

For thow my hart be heuely sett
  To see the blood of my owyn dere son,
3yt for all thys I wyll not lett,
But Ysaac, my son, I wyll goo fett,
  And cum asse fast as euer we con.[1]   100

Now, Ysaac, my owyn son dere,
  Wer art thow, chyld? Speke to me.
YSAAC. My fayer swet fader, I am here,
  And make my preyrys to þe Trenyté.

ABRAHAM. Rysse vp, my chyld, and fast cum heder,   105
  My gentyll barn þat art so wysse,
For we to, chyld, must goo to-geder,
  And onto my Lord make sacryffyce.

YSAAC. I am full redy, my fader, loo!
  3evyn[2] at 3owr handys I stand rygth here,   110
And watsoeuer 3e byd me doo,
  Yt schall be don with glad chere,
    Full wyll and fyne.
ABRAHAM. A! Ysaac, my owyn son soo dere,
  Godys blyssyng I 3yffe the, and myn.   115

Hold thys fagot vpon þi bake,
  And her myselffe fyere schall bryng.
YSAAC. Fader, all thys her wyll I packe;
  I am full fayn to do 3owre bedyng.
ABRAHAM. A! Lord of Heuyn, my handys I wryng,   f. 17ʳ
Thys chyldys wordys all towond my harte.   121

Now, Ysaac, son, goo we owr wey
  Onto 3on mownte, wyth all owr mayn.
YSAAC. Gowe, my dere fader, as fast as I may
  To folow 3ow I am full fayn,   125
    Allthow I be slendyr.
ABRAHAM. A! Lord, my hart brekyth on tweyn,[3]
  Thys chyldys wordys, they be so tender.

A! Ysaac, son, anon ley yt down,
  No lenger vpon þi backe yt hold;[4]   130

---

[1] *MS.* can.   [2] *MS.* 3ovyn.
[3] *Smith; MS.* tewyn.   [4] *Manly, quoting Kittredge (cf.* 116); *MS.* bere.

For I mvst make me redy bon
　To honowre my Lord God as I schuld.

YSAAC. Loo, my dere fader, wer yt ys!
　To cher ȝow allwey I draw me nere;
But, fader, I mervell sore of thys,　　　　　　　135
　Wy þat ȝe make thys heuy chere;

And also, fader, euermore dred I:
　Wer ys ȝowr qweke best þat ȝe schuld kyll?
Both fyer and wood we haue redy,
　But queke best haue we non on þis hyll.　　　140

A qwyke best, I wot wyll, must be ded,
　Ȝowr sacryfyce for to make.[1]
ABRAHAM. Dred the nowgth, my chyld, I the red,
Owre Lord wyll send me onto thys sted
　Summ maner a best for to take,　　　　　　　145
　　Throw his swet sond.
　YSAAC. Ȝa, fader, but my hart begynnyth to quake,
　To ⌈se⌉ þat scharpe sword in ȝowre hond.

Wy bere ȝe ȝowre sword drawyn soo?
　Off ȝowre contenaunce[2] I haue mych wonder.　f. 17ᵛ
ABRAHAM. A! Fader of Heuyn, so[3] I am woo!　　151
　Thys chyld her brekyth[4] my harte onsonder.[5]

YSAAC. Tell me, my dere fader, or that ȝe ses,
　Bere ȝe ȝowr sword draw for me?
ABRAHAM. A! Ysaac, swet son, pes! pes!　　　155
　For iwys thow breke my harte on thre.

YSAAC. Now trewly, sumwat, fader, ȝe thynke
　That ȝe morne thus more and more.
ABRAHAM. A! Lord of Heuyn, thy grace let synke,
　For my hart wos neuer halffe so sore.　　　　160

YSAAC. I preye ȝow, fader, þat ȝe wyll let me yt wyt,
　Wyther schall I haue ony harme or noo?
ABRAHAM. Iwys, swet son, I may not tell the ȝyt,
　My hart ys now soo full of woo.

---

[1] *Smith; MS. transposes these two lines.*　　　[2] *MS.* cōwnaŭs.
[3] *Smith; MS.* os.　　[4] *MS.* brekyd, -d *written over another letter.*
[5] *Holthausen, after Chester; MS.* on too.

Ysaac. Dere fader, I prey ȝow, hydygth[1] not fro me,   165
　　But sum of ȝowr thowt[2] þat ȝe tell on.[3]
Abraham. A! Ysaac, Ysaac! I must kyll the.
　　Ysaac. Kyll me, fader? alasse! wat haue I don?

Yff I haue trespassyd aȝens ȝow owt,
　　With a ȝard ȝe may make me full myld;   170
And wyth ȝowre scharp sword kyll me nogth,
　　For iwys, fader, I am but a chyld.

Abraham. I am full sory, son, thy blood for to spyll,
　　But truly, my chyld, I may not chese.
Ysaac. Now I wold to God ⌈my⌉ moder were her on þis hyll!
　　Sche woold knele for me on both hyre kneys   176
　　　　To save my lyffe.
　　And sythyn that my moder ys not here,
　　I prey ȝow, fader, schonge ȝowr chere,
　　　　And kyll me not wyth ȝowyre knyffe.   180

Abraham. Forsothe, son, but ȝyf I the kyll,   f. 18ʳ
　　I schuld greve God rygth sore, I drede;
Yt ys hys commawment and also hys wyll
　　That I schuld do thys same dede.

He commawndyd me, son, for serteyn,   185
　　To make my sacryfyce wyth thy blood.
Ysaac. And ys yt Goddys wyll þat I schuld be slayn?
　　Abraham. Ȝa, truly, Ysaac, my son soo good,
　　　　And therfor my handys I wryng.
　　Ysaac. Now, fader, aȝens my Lordys wyll   190
　　I wyll neuer groche, lowd nor styll;
　　He mygth a sent me a better desteny
　　　　Yf yt had a be hys plecer.[4]

Abraham. Forsothe, son, but yf I ded þis dede,
　　Grevosly dysplessyd owre Lord wyll be.   195
Ysaac. Nay, nay, fader. God forbede
　　That euer ȝe schuld greve hym for me.

Ȝe haue other chyldryn, on or too,
　　The wyche ȝe schuld love wyll be kynd;

---

[1] *Cf.* 304.　　[2] *MS.* thowᵗ, *also* owᵗ 169 *and* 202.　　[3] *MS.* me.
[4] *These two lines apparently replace original lines with rhymes on* -ill *and* -ing; *cf.* 219–27.

I prey ʒow, fader, make ʒe no woo,   200
For, be I onys ded and fro ʒow goo,
   I schall be sone owt of ʒowre mynd.

Therfor doo owre Lordys byddyng,
   And wan I am ded, than prey for me;
But, good fader, tell ʒe my moder nothyng,   205
Sey þat I am in another cuntré dwellyng.[1]
   ABRAHAM. A! Ysaac, Ysaac, blyssyd mot thow be!

My hart begynnyth[2] stronly to rysse,
   To see the blood off thy blyssyd body.
YSAAC. Fadyr, syn yt may be noo other wysse,   210
   Let yt passe ouer as wyll as I.

But, fader, or I goo onto my deth,   f. 18ᵛ
   I prey ʒow blysse me wyth ʒowre hand.
ABRAHAM. Now, Ysaac, wyth all my breth,
   My blyssyng I ʒeve þe vpon thys lond,   215
      And Godys also therto, iwys.
   A, Ysaac, Ysaac, son, vp thow stond,
      Thy fayere swete mowthe þat I may kys.

YSAAC. Now, forwyll, my owyn fader so fyn,
   And grete wyll my moder in erde.[3]   220
But I prey ʒow, fader, to hyd my eyne,
   That I se not þe stroke of ʒowr scharpe swerd,[4]
      That my fleysse schall defyle.
   ABRAHAM. Son, thy wordys make me to wepe full sore;
   Now, my dere son Ysaac, speke no more.   225
   YSAAC. A, my owyn dere fader, werefore?
      We schall speke togedyr her but a wylle.

And sythyn that I must nedysse be ded,
   ʒyt, my dere fader, to ʒow I prey,
Smyth but fewe[5] strokys at my hed,   230
   And make an end as sone as ʒe may,
      And tery not to longe.
   ABRAHAM. Thy meke wordys, chyld, make me afray;[6]
      So welawey may be my songe,

---

[1] *Smith; MS.* dewllyng.   [2] *Manly; MS.* begynnyd.
[3] *Manly; MS.* erthe.   [4] *Manly; MS.* sword.
[5] *Manly; MS.* feve.   [6] *Manly; MS.* afrayed.

Excepe alonly Godys wyll.   235
   A! Ysaac, my owyn swete chyld,
3yt kysse me a3en vpon thys hyll!
   In all thys ward ys ⌈non⌉ soo myld.

Ysaac. Now, truly, fader, all thys teryyng
   Yt doth my hart but harme;   240
I prey 3ow, fader, make an enddyng.
   Abraham. Cume vp, swet son, onto my arme.

I must bynd thy handys too
   Allthow thow be neuer soo myld.
Ysaac. A, mercy, fader! Wy schuld 3e do soo?   245
   Abraham. That thow schuldyst not let [me], my chyld. f. 19ʳ

Ysaac. Nay, iwysse, fader, I wyll not let 3ow;
   Do on for me 3owre wyll,
And on the purpos that 3e haue set 3ow,
   For Godys love kepe yt forthe styll.   250

I am full sory thys day to dey,
   But 3yt I kepe not my God to greve;
Do on 3owre lyst for me hardly,
   My fayer swete fader, I 3effe 3ow leve.

But, fader, I prey 3ow euermore,   255
   Tell 3e my moder no dell;
Yffe sche wost yt, sche wold wepe full sore,
   For iwysse, fader, sche lovyt me full wyll;
      Goddys blyssyng haue mot sche![1]
   Now forwyll, my moder so swete,   260
We too be leke no mor to mete.
   Abraham. A, Ysaac, Ysaac! son, þou makyst me to gret,
   And wyth thy wordys thow dystempurst me.

Ysaac. Iwysse, swete fader, I am sory to greve 3ow,
   I cry 3ow mercy of that I haue donne,   265
And of all trespasse þat euer I ded meve 3ow;
   Now, dere fader, for3yffe me þat I haue donne.[2]
     God of Heuyn be wyth me!

---

[1] *Holthausen; MS.* mot sche haue.
[2] *MS. has three minims for* nn.

ABRAHAM. A, dere chyld, lefe of thy monys;
In all thy lyffe thow grevyd me neuer onys;   270
Now blyssyd be thow, body and bonys,
    That thow were bred and born to me![1]

Thow hast be to me chyld full good;
    But iwysse, chyld, thow I morne neuer so fast,
    3yt must I nedys here at the last   275
In thys place sched all thy blood.

Therfor, my dere son, here schall þou lye,
    Onto my warke I must me stede,
Iwysse I had as leve myselffe to dey,
    Yffe God wyll be plecyd wyth my dede,   f. 19ᵛ
        And myn owyn body for to offere.   281
    YSAAC. A, mercy, fader, morne 3e no more,
    3owr wepyng make my hart sore
        As my owyn deth that I schall suffere.

3owre kerche, fader, abowt my eyn 3e wynd!   285
    ABRAHAM. So I schall, my swettest chyld in erde.[2]
YSAAC. Now 3yt, good fader, haue thys in mynd,
    And smyth me not oftyn wyth 3owr scharp swerd,[3]
        But hastely that yt be sped.

Here Abraham leyd a cloth ouer Ysaacys face, thus seyyng:[4]

ABRAHAM. Now, forewyll, my chyld, so full of grace.   290
YSAAC. A, fader, fader, torne downgward my face,
    For of 3owre scharpe sword I am euer adred.

ABRAHAM. To don thys dede I am full sory,
    But, Lord, thyn hest I wyll not wythstond.
YSAAC. A, Fader of Heuyn, to the I crye,   295
    Lord, reseyve me into thy hand!

ABRAHAM. Loo, now ys the tyme cum, certeyn,
    That my sword in hys necke schall bite.[5]

---

[1] *MS.* That eu*e*r thow wer*e* bred and born.
[2] *Manly; MS.* erthe.   [3] *Manly; MS.* sword.
[4] *This direction written as if part of the text, opposite the speaker's name in two lines, the second beginning* Ouer.
[5] *Holthausen; MS.* synke.

A! Lord, my hart reysyth therageyn,
   I may not fyndygth[1] in my harte to smygth;   300
      My hart wyll not now thertoo,
   Ʒyt fayn I woold warke my Lordys wyll;
   But thys Ʒowng innosent lygth so styll,
   I may not fyndygth in my hart hym to kyll.
      O, Fader of Heuyn! what schall I doo?   305

YSAAC. A, mercy, fader, wy tery Ʒe so,
   And let me ley thus longe on þis heth?
Now I wold to God þe stroke were doo.
Fader, I prey yow hartely, schorte me of my woo,
   And let me not loke thus after my degth.   310

ABRAHAM. Now, hart, wy wolddyst not thow breke on thre?
   Ʒyt schall þou ⌈not⌉ make me to my God onmyld.   f. 20ʳ
I wyll no lenger let for the,
For that my God agrevyd wold be.
   Now hoold the[2] stroke, my owyn dere chyld.   315

Her Abraham drew hys stroke and þe angell toke the sword in hys
hond soddenly.[3]

THE ANGELL. I am an angell, thow mayist be blythe,
   That fro heuyn to the ys senth;
Owre Lord thanke the an hundyrd[4] sythe
   For the kepyng of hys commawment.

He knowyt þi wyll and also thy harte,   320
   That thow dredyst hym above all thyng,
And sum of thy hevynes for to departe
   A fayyr ram Ʒynder I gan brynge;

He standyth teyed, loo! among þe brerys.
   Now, Abraham, amend thy mood,   325
For Ysaac, thy Ʒowng son þat her ys,
   Thys day schall not sched hys blood;

Goo, make thy sacryfece wyth Ʒon rame,
   For onto heuyn I goo now hom.

---

[1] *Cf.* 304.   [2] *MS.* tha.
[3] *This direction written as if part of the text in two lines, the second beginning*
And.   [4] *MS.* .C.

Now forwyll, blyssyd Abraham,[1]   330
  The wey ys full gayn [that I mot gon].
    Take up thy son soo free.
  ABRAHAM. A! Lord, I thanke the of thy gret grace,
  Now am I yeþed[2] on dyuers wysse.
  Arysse vp, Ysaac, my dere sunne, arysse,   335
    Arysse vp, swete chyld, and cum to me.

YSAAC. A, mercy, fader, wy smygth ȝe nowt?[3]
  A, smygth on, fader, onys wyth ȝowre knyffe!
ABRAHAM. Pesse, my swet sun, and take no thowt,
  For owre Lord of Heuyn hath grant þi lyffe,   340
    Be hys angell now,[4]

That þou schalt not dey þis ⌐day⌐, sunne, truly.
YSAAC. A, fader, full glad than wer I,   f. 20ᵛ
  Iwys, fader, I sey iwys,
Yf thys tall wer trew!   345
ABRAHAM. An hundyrd tymys, my son fayer of hew,
  For joy þi mowth now wyll I kys.

YSAAC. A! my dere fader, Abraham,
  Wyll not God be wroth þat we do thus?
ABRAHAM. Noo, noo! harly, my swyt son,   350
For he hath sent vs ȝyn same rame[5]
  Hethyr down to vs.

Ȝyn best schall dey here in þi sted,
  In the worþchup[6] of owr Lord alon;
Goo, fet hym hethyre, my chyld, inded.   355
YSAAC. Fader, I wyll goo hent hym be the hed,
  And bryng ȝon best wyth me anon.

  A, scheppe, scheppe! blyssyd mot þou be
    That euer thow were sent down heder!
  Thow schall thys day dey for me,   360

---

[1] *MS. transposes these two lines.*
[2] *MS.* yeyed.   [3] *Holthausen; MS.* not ȝyt.
[4] *The lack of a rhyme to this line, and the irregular pattern of the following lines,*
indicate some loss.
[5] *Holthausen; MS.* For ȝyn same rame he hath vs sent.
[6] *MS.* worþchup.

In the worchup of the Holy Trynyté.
  Now cum fast and goowe togeder
    To my fader in hy;[1]
  Thow þou be neuer so jentyll and good,
  3yt had I leuer thow schedyst þi blood,   365
    Iwysse, scheppe, than I.

Loo, fader, I haue browt here full smerte
  Thys jentyll scheppe, and hym to 3ow I 3yffe:[2]
But, Lord God, I thank þe with all my hart,
  For I am glad that ⌜I⌝ schall leve,   370
    And kys onys my dere moder.
ABRAHAM. Now be rygth myry, my swete chylld,
For thys qwyke best that ys so myld,
    Here I schall present[3] before all othere.   f. 21ʳ

YSAAC. And I wyll fast begynne to blowe,   375
  Thys fyere schall brene a full good spyd.
But fader, wyll I stowppe down lowe,
  3e wyll not kyll me with 3owre sword, I trowe?
    ABRAHAM. Noo, harly, swet son, haue no dred,
      My mornyng ys past.   380
    YSAAC. 3a! but I woold þat sword were in a gled,[4]
      For iwys, fader, yt make me full yll agast.

   Here Abraham mad hys offryng, knelyng and seyyng thus:[5]
ABRAHAM. Now, Lord God of Hevyn, in Trynyté,
  Allmyty God Omnipotent,
Myn offeryng I make in the worchope of the,   385
  And wyth thys qweke best I the present.
  Lord, reseyve thow myn intent,
    As [thow] art God and grownd of owr gre.[6]

DEUS. Abraham, Abraham, wyll mot thow sped,
  And Ysaac, þi 3owng son the by!   390
Trvly Abraham, for thys dede
I schall mvltyplye 3owrys botherys sede

---

[1] *Manly's suggestion; MS.* of heuyn.
[2] *Manly; MS. writes* And hym to 3ow I 3yffe *as separate line.*
[3] *MS.* present.   [4] *Manly; MS.* glad.
[5] *This direction written as if part of the text in two lines, the second beginning* Knelyng.   [6] *MS.* grace.

As thyke as sterrys be in the skye,
   Bothe more and lesse;
    And as thyke as gravell in the see, 395
     So thyke mvltyplyed ʒowre sede schall be;
      Thys grant I ʒow for ʒowre goodnesse.

Off ʒow schall cume frewte gret [won]¹
And euer be in blysse wythowt ʒynd,
For ʒe drede me as God alon 400
And kepe my commawmentys eueryschon.
    My blyssyng I ʒeffe, wersoeuer ʒe wend.²

ABRAHAM. Loo! Ysaac, my son, how thynke ʒe
   Be thys warke that we haue wrogth?
Full glad and blythe we may be, f. 21ᵛ
   Aʒens ⌈þe⌉ wyll of God þat we grucched³ nott, 406
    Vpon thys fayere hetth.
YSAAC. A, fader, I thanke owre Lord euery dell,
That my wyt servyd me so wyll,
   For to drede God more than my detth. 410

ABRAHAM. Why! derewordy son, wer thow adred?
   Hardely, chyld, tell me thy lore.
YSAAC. ʒa! be my feyth, fader, now haue⁴ I red,
   I wos neuer soo afrayd before
    As I haue byn at ʒyn hyll. 415
   But, be my feyth, fader, I swere
   I wyll neuermore cume there
    But yt be aʒens my wyll.

ABRAHAM. ʒa, cum on wyth me, my owyn swet son,
   And homward fast now let vs goon. 420
YSAAC. Be my feyth, fader, therto I vn,⁵
   I had neuer so good wyll to gon hom,
    And to speke wyth my dere moder.
     ABRAHAM. A! Lord of Heuyn, I thanke the,
    For now may I led hom wyth me 425
    Ysaac, my ʒownge son soo fre,
     The gentyllest chyld above all other.⁶

¹ *Inserted by Manly.*   ² *Holthausen; MS.* goo.
³ *MS.* grutthed.   ⁴ *Manly; MS.* hath.
⁵ *MS.* grant; *rhyme requires* vn *though it is not recorded elsewhere after c. 1330.*
⁶ *Smith; MS.* erthe.

Now goo we forthe, my blyssyd son.
YSAAC. I grant, fader, and let vs gon,
  For be my trowthe, wer I at home   430
I wold neuer gon owt vnder that forme,
    Thys may I wyll avoee.[1]
    I pray God ȝeffe vs grace euermo,
And all thow that we be holdyng to.

DOCTOR. Lo! sovereyns and sorys, now haue we schewyd,[2]   435
    Thys solom story[3] to gret and[4] smale;
It ys good lernyng to lernd and lewyd,
And þe wysest of vs all,
    Wythowtyn ony berryng.   f. 22ʳ
For thys story schoyt ȝowe [her][5]   440
How we schuld kepe to owr po[we]re[5]
    Goddys commawmentys wythowt grochyng.

Trowe ȝe, sorys, and God sent an angell
  And commawndyd ȝow ȝowre chyld to slayn,[6]
Be ȝowre trowthe ys ther ony of ȝow   445
  That eyther wold ⌈groche⌉ or stryve therageyn?

How thyngke ȝe now, sorys, therby?
  I trow ther be thre ore a fowr[7] or moo;
And thys women that wepe so sorowfully
  Whan that hyr chyldryn dey them froo,   450
    As nater woll,[8] and kynd;
Yt ys but folly, I may wyll awooe,
To groche aȝens God or to greve ȝow,
For ȝe schall neuer se hym myschevyd, wyll I know,
  Be lond nor watyr, haue thys in mynd.   455

And groche not aȝens owre Lord God,
  In welthe or woo, wether that he ȝow send,
Thow ȝe be neuer so hard bestad,
  For whan he wyll, he may yt amend.

---

[1] *MS. has this line after 427, where it does not fit.*
[2] *MS.* schowyd.   [3] *MS. has here* hath schowyd.
[4] *MS.* a.   [5] *Emended by Manly.*
[6] *Holthausen; MS.* to smygth of ȝowre chyldys hed.
[7] *MS.* iij ore a iiij.   [8] *MS. repeats* woll.

Hys comawmentys trevly yf ȝe kepe wyth goo[d] hart,   460
     As thys story hath now schovyd ȝow befor[n]e,¹
And feytheffully serve hym qwyll ȝe be qvart,
     That ȝe may plece God bothe euyn and morne.
Now Jhesu, that weryt the crown of thorne,
     Bryng vs all to heuyn-blysse!   465

Finis.

¹ *Emended by Holthausen.*

VI

THE PLAY OF THE SACRAMENT

PRIMUS VEXILLATOR. Now þe Father and þe Sune and þe Holy
    Goste, f. 338^r

  That all þis wyde worlde hat wrowght,

Save ⌐all¬ thes semely, bothe leste and moste,

  And bryn[g]e yow to þe blysse þat he hath yow to bowght!

    We be ful purposed with hart and with thowght   5

Off our mater to tell þe entent,

  Off þe marvellys þat wer wondursely wrowght

Off þe holi and blyssed¹ Sacrament.

SECUNDUS [VEXILLATOR]. S[o]uereyns, and yt lyke yow to here þe
    purpoos of þis play

  That [ys] representyd now in yower syght,   10

Whych in Aragon was doon, þe sothe to saye,

  In Eraclea, that famous cyté, aryght—

    Therin wonneth a merchaunte off mekyll myght,

Syr Arystorye was called hys name,

  Kend full fere with mani a wyght,   15

Full ⌐fer¬ in þe worlde sprong hys fame.

PRIMUS. Anon to hym² ther cam a Jewe,

  With grete rychesse for the nonys,

And wonneth in þe cyté of Surrey—þis full trewe—

  þe wyche hade gret plenté³ off precyous stonys.   20

Off þis Cristen merchaunte he freyned⁴ sore,

  Wane he wolde haue had hys entente.

Twenti pownd⁵ and merchaundyse mor

  He proferyd for þe Holy Sacrament.

SECUNDUS. But þe Cristen marchaunte theroff sed nay,   25

  Because hys profer was of so lityll valewe;

---

¹ *MS.* blbyssed *with second* b *blotted.*   ² *MS.* hyn.

³ *These five words interlined, above the first four words of the next line wrongly
written here and struck out.*

⁴ *MS.* freynend.   ⁵ *MS.* xxti li.

An hundder pownd[1] but he wolde pay
  No lenger theron he shuld pursewe.

But mor off ther purpos they gunne speke,   f. 338ᵛ
  The Holi Sacramente for to bey;[2]   30
And all for þe wolde[3] be wreke,
  A gret sume off gold begune down ley.
PRIMUS. Thys Crysten merchante consentyd, þe sothe to sey,
And in þe nyght affter made hym delyueraunce.

  Thes Jewes all grete joye made they;   35
But off thys betyde a straunger chaunce:

They grevid our Lord gretly on grownd,
  And put hym to a new[4] passyoun;
With daggers gouen hym[5] many a greuyos wound;
  Nayled hym to a pyller, with pynsons plukked hym doune.   40

SECUNDUS. And sythe thay toke þat blysed brede so sownde
  And in a cawdron they ded hym boyle.[6]
In a clothe full just they yt wounde,
  And so they ded hym sethe in oyle;

And than thay putt hym to a new turmentry,   45
  In an hoote[7] ouyn speryd hym fast.
There he appyred with woundys blody;
  The ovyn rofe asondre and all tobrast.
PRIMUS. Thus in our lawe they wer made stedfast;
The Holy Sacrament sheuyd them grette fauour;   50
  In contrycyon thyr hertys wer cast
And went and shewyd ther lyues to a confesour.

Thus be maracle off þe Kyng of Hevyn,
  And by myght and power govyn to þe prestys mowthe,
In an howshold wer conuertyd[8] iwys elevyn.[9]   55
  At Rome þis myracle ys knowen welle kowthe.

SECUNDUS. Thys marycle at Rome was presented, forsothe,
  Yn the yere of our[10] Lord, a thowsand fowr hundder sixty and
    on,[11]

---

[1] *MS.* C. li. (*cf.* 288).   [2] *MS.* bye.   [3] *MS.* woldr.
[4] *Manly; MS.* nell (*cf.* 933).   [5] *First hand ends.*
[6] *Stokes; MS.* boylde.   [7] *MS.* ob *before* ouyn.
[8] *Stokes; MS.* counteryd.   [9] *MS.* I wyll wys xj *with* wyll *partly struck out.*
[10] *Manly; MS.* youʳ.   [11] *MS.* M¹cccc.c.lxj—*the fifth* c *expuncted.*

That þe Jewes with Holy Sa[c]rament dyd woth,[1]
  In the forest seyd of Aragon.   60

Loo,[2] thus God at a tyme shovyd hym there,   f. 339ʳ
  Thorwhe hys mercy and hys mekyll myght;
Vnto the Jewes he gan[3] appere
  That þei shuld nat lesse hys hevenly lyght.
    PRIMUS. Therfor, frendys, with all your myght   65
Vnto youer gostly father shewe your synne;
  Beth in no wanhope daye nor nyght.
No maner off dowghtys þat Lord put in.

For þat þe dowghtys þe Jewys than in stode—
  As ye shall se pleyd, both more and lesse—   70
Was yff þe Sacrament were flesshe and blode;
  Therfor they put yt to suche dystresse.
    SECUNDUS. And yt place yow, thys gaderyng þat here ys,
At Croxston on Monday yt shall be sen;
  To see the conclusyon of þis lytell processe   75
Hertely welcum shall yow bene.

Now Jhesu yow sawe from[4] trey[5] and tene,
  To send vs hys hyhe ioyes of hevyne;[6]
There myght ys withouton mynd to mene.
  Now, mynstrell, blow vp with a mery stevyn.   80
                            Explicit.

Here after foloweth þe Play of þe Conuersyon of Ser Jonathas þe Jewe by Myracle of þe Blyssed Sacrament.

ARISTORIUS MERCATOR. Now Cryst, þat ys our Creatour, from
  shame he cure vs;
He[7] maynteyn vs with myrth þat meve vpon þe mold;
Vnto hys en[d]elesse joye myghtly he restore vs,
  All tho þat in hys[8] name in peas well them hold;
  For of a merchante most myght therof my tale ys told,   85

---

[1] *MS.* wᵗ.   [2] *MS.* be *struck out before this, and* thy *after it.*
[3] *Manly; MS.* gayn.   [4] *MS.* fron.   [5] *Holthausen; MS.* treyn.
[6] *Last four words interlined, above the last four words of the next line written here and struck out; the next line crowded in.*
[7] *Stokes; MS.* be.   [8] *Manly; MS.* thys.

In Eraclea ys non suche, woso wyll vnderstond,
      For off all Aragon I am most myghty of syluer and of gold—
For and yt wer a countré to by, now wold I nat wond.

Syr Arystory ys my name,   f. 339ᵛ
      A merchaunte myghty of a royall araye;   90
Ful wyde in þis worlde spryngyth my fame,
      Fere kend and knowen, þe sothe for to saye,
      In all maner of londys, without ony naye,
My merchaundyse renneth, þe sothe for to tell;
      In Gene and in Jenyse and in Genewaye,   95
In Surrey¹ and in Saby and in Salern I sell;

In Antyoche and in Almayn moch ys my myght,
      In Braban and in Brytayn I am full bold,
In Calabre and in Coleyn þer rynge² I full ryght,³
      In Dordrede and in Denmark be þe clyffys⁴ cold;   100
      In Alysander I haue abundaw[n]se in the wyde world.
In France and in Farre fresshe be my flower[ys],
      In Gyldre and in Galys haue I bowght and sold,
In Hamborowhe and in Holond moch⁵ merchantdyse ys owrys;

In Jerusalem and in Jherico among the Jewes jentle,   105
      Amo[n]g the Caldeys and Cattlyngys kend ys my komyng;
In Raynes and in Rome to Seynt Petyrs temple,
      I am knowen certenly for bying and sellyng;

In Mayn and in Melan full mery haue I be;⁶
      Owt of Navern to Naples moch good ys þat I bryng;   110
In Pondere and in Portyngale moche ys my gle;
      In Spayne and in Spruce moche ys my spedyng;
      In Lombardy and in Lachborn there ledde ys my lykyng;
In Taryse and in Turkey there told ys my tale;
      And in þe dukedom of Oryon moche have I in weldyng: 115
And thus thorowght all þis world sett ys my sale.

No man in thys world may weld more rychesse;   f. 340ʳ
      All I thank God of hys grace, for he þat me sent;

¹ *Manly; MS.* surgery.   ² *MS.* ryng *with final loop.*
³ *Last six words interlined above* demark by the clyffys cold *which is struck out.*
⁴ *MS.* chyffys.
⁵ Holond *interlined above* Jherico *struck out;* moch *corrected from* among
(*copied from next line*).   ⁶ *First written* ben, n *struck out.*

And as a lordys pere thus lyve I in worthynesse.
　My curat wayteth¹ vpon me to knowe myn entent,　　　120
　And men at my weldyng, and all ys me lent
My well for to worke in thys world so wyde.
　Me dare they not dysplese by no condescent.
And who so doth, he ys not able to abyde.

PRESBYTER. No man shall you tary ne t[r]owble thys tyde,　　125
　But euery man delygently shall do yow plesance;
And I vnto my connyng² to þe best shall hem guyde
　Vnto Godys plesyng to serue yow to attrueaunce.

For ye be worthy and notable in substance of good,
　Off merchauntys of Aragon ye have no pere—　　　130
And therof thank God þat dyed on þe roode,
　That was your makere and hath yow dere.

ARISTORIUS. Forsoth, syr pryst, yower talkyng ⌜ys⌝ good;
　And therfor affter your talkyng I wyll atteyn
To wourshyppe my God that dyed on þe roode,　　　135
　Neuer whyll þat I lyve ageyn þat wyll I seyn.
But, Petyr Powle, my clark, I praye the goo wele pleyn
Thorowght all Eraclea, that thow ne wonde,
　And wytte yff ony merchaunte be come to þis reyn
Of Surrey or of Sabé or of Shelysdown.　　　140

CLERICUS. At your wyll for to walke I wyl not say nay,
　Smertly to go serche at þe waterys syde;
Yff ony plesaunt bargyn be to your paye,
　As swyftly as I can I shall hym to yow guyde.
Now wyll I walke by thes pathes wyde,　　　f. 340ᵛ
And seke the haven both vp and down,　　　146
　To wette yff ony onkowth³ shyppes therin do ryde
Of Surrey or of Saby [or] of Shelysdown.

Now shall þe merchantys man withdrawe hym and þe Jewe Jonathas
*shall make hys bost.*⁴

JONATHAS. Now, almyghty Machomet, marke in þi magesté,
　Whose⁵ lawes tendrely I have to fulfyll,　　　150

---

¹ *MS.* waytheth.　　² *MS.* comnyng.　　³ *Stokes; MS.* onknowth.
⁴ *Manly; MS.* best.　　　　　⁵ *Manly; MS.* whoses.

After my dethe bryng me to thy hyhe see,
  My sowle for to save yff yt be thy wyll;
  For myn entent ys for to fulfyll,
As my gloryus God the to honer,[1]
  To do agen thy entent yt shuld grue me yll,   155
Or agen thyn lawe for to reporte.

For I thanke þe hayly þat hast me sent
  Gold,[2] syluer, and presyous stonys,
And abu[n]ddaunce of spycys þou hast me lent,
  A[s] I shall reherse before yow onys: 160
  I have amatystys, ryche for þe nonys,
And baryllys that be bryght of ble;
  And saphyre semely, I may show yow attonys,
And crystalys clere for to se;

I haue dyamantys derewourthy to[3] dresse,   165
  And emerawdys, ryche I trow they be,
Onyx and achatys[4] both more and lesse,
  Topazyouns, smaragdys of grete degré,
  Perlys precyous grete plenté;
Of rubés ryche I have grete renown;   170
  Crepawdys and calcedonyes semely to se,
A[nd] curyous carbunclys here ye fynd mown;

Spycys I hawe both grete and smale   f. 341ʳ
  In my shyppes, the sothe for to saye,
Gyngere, lycoresse and cannyngalle,   175
  And fygys fatte to plese yow to paye;
Peper and saffyron and spycys smale,
  And datys wole dulcett for to dresse,
Almundys and rys,[5] full euery male,
  And reysones both more and lesse: 180

Clowys, greynis,[6] and gynger grene,
  Mace, mastyk that myght ys,
Synymone, suger, as yow may sene,
  Long peper and Indas lycorys;

---

[1] *Failure of rhyme, and lack of an object of* fulfyll, *show this passage to be corrupt.
Perhaps the rhyme was originally between* thy (bi)hest *and* resist.
[2] *Manly; MS.* godd.   [3] *Preceded by* do *with* d *struck out.*
[4] *MS.* Machatys.   [5] *Uncertain;* y *apparently written over* e.
[6] *Stokes; MS.* grenyis.

Orengys a[nd] apples of grete apryce,   185
    Pungarnetys and many other spycys,—
To tell yow all I haue now, iwyse,
    And moche other merchandyse of[1] sondry spycys.[2]

Jew Jonathas ys my name,
    Jazon and Jazdon þei waytyn on my wyll,   190
Masfat and Malchus they do the same,
    As ye may knowe yt ys bothe rycht and skyll.
I tell yow all, bi dal and by hylle,
In Eraclea[3] ys noon so moche of myght.
    Werfor ye owe tenderli to tende me tyll,   195
For I am chefe merchaunte of Jewes, I tell yow be ryght.

But Jazon and Jazdon, a mater wollde I mene—
    Mervelously yt ys ment in mynde—
þe beleve of thes Cristen men ys false, as I wene;
    For þe beleue on a cake—me thynk yt ys onkynd.   200
And all they seye how þe prest dothe yt bynd,[4]   f. 341ᵛ
And be þe myght of hys word make yt flessh and blode—
    And thus be a conceyte þe wolde make vs blynd—
And how þat yt shuld be he þat deyed upon þe rode.

JASON. Yea, yea, master, a strawe for talis!   205
    That ma not fale in my beleve;
But myt we yt gete onys within our pales,
    I trowe we shuld sone affter putt yt in a preve.[5]
    JAZDON. Now, be Machomete so myghty, þat ye doon of meue,
I wold I wyste how þat we myght yt gete;   210
    I swer[6] be my grete god, and ellys mote I nat cheue
But wyghtly the[r]on wold I be wreke.

MASPHAT. Yea, I dare sey feythfulli þat ther feyth [ys fals:][7]
    That was neuer he that on Caluery was kyld,
Or in bred for to be blode yt ys ontrewe als;   215
    But yet with ther wyles þei wold we were wyld.

---

[1] *Followed by* ey *with* er *abbr. above, apparently not cancelled.*
[2] *Second hand ends, first resumes.*   [3] *MS.* graclea.
[4] *First part of this line written at foot of recto, then struck out and repeated here.*
[5] *Stokes; MS.* in a praye *interlined above* in a pye *struck out.*
[6] *Manly; MS.* seuer.   [7] *Manly's suggestion; no sign of loss in MS.*

MALCHUS. Yea, I am myghty Malchus, þat boldly am byld;
That brede for to bete byggly am I bent.
   Onys out of ther handys and yt myght be exyled,
To helpe castyn yt in care wold I counsent.   220

JONATAS. Well, syrse, than kype cunsel, I cummande yow all,
   And no word of all thys be wyst.
But let us walke to see Arystories hall,
   And affterward more counsell among vs shall caste.
   With hym to bey and to sel I am of powere prest: 225
A bargyn with hym to make I wyll assaye;
   For gold and syluer I am nothyng agast
But þat we shall get þat cake to ower paye.

*Her shall Ser Ysodyr þe prest speke ont[o] Ser Arystori,[1] seyng on
   thys wyse to hym; and Jonatas goo don of his stage.*

PRESBITER. Syr, be yowr leue, I may [no] lengere dwell;
   Yt ys fer paste none, yt ys tyme to go to cherche,   230
There to saye myn evynsong, forsothe as I yow tell,
   And syth coume home ageyne, as I am wont to werche.

ARISTORIUS. Sir Isydor, I praye yow wallke at yowr wyll,   f. 342ʳ
   For to serfe God yt ys well doune,
And syt com agen and ye shall suppe your fyll,   235
   And walke than to your chamber as ye are wont to doon.

Her shall the marchant men mete with þe Jewes.

JONATAS. A! Petre Powle, good daye and wele imett!
   Wer ys thy[2] master, as I the pray?
CLERICUS. Lon[g] from hym haue I not lett
   Syt I cam from hym, þe sothe for to saye.   240
   Wat tidyng with yow, ser, I yow praye,
Affter my master þat ye doo frayne?
   Haue ye ony bargen þat wer to hys paye?
Let me haue knowlech; I shall wete hym to seyn.

JHONATTAS. I haue bargenes[3] royall and ry[c]h   245
   For a marchaunt with to bye and sell;
In all thys lond is ther non lyke
   Off aboundaunce of good, as I will tell.

---

¹ *MS.* acrystori.   ² *Manly; MS.* they.   ³ *MS.* bargened.

Her shall þe clerk goon to Ser Aristori, saluting him thus:

CLERICUS. All hayll, master, and wel mot[1] yow be!
　Now tydyngys can I yow tell:　　　　　　　　　　　250
þe grettest marchante in all Surré
　Ys come with yow to bey and sell:
　　This tal ryght wele he me told.[2]
Sir Jonatas ys hys nam,
　A marchant of ryght gret fame;　　　　　　　　　255
He wolld sell yow, without blame,
　P[l]enté of clothe of golde.[3]

ARISTORIUS. Petre Powle, I can þe thanke!
　I prey þe rychely araye myn hall
As owyth for a marchant of þe banke;　　　　　　260
　Lete non defawte be fownd at all.
　CLERICUS. Sekyrly, master, no m[o]re ther shall!
Styffly about I thynke to stere,
　Hasterli to hange your parlowr with pall,
As longeth for a lordis pere.　　　　　　　　　265

*Here shall þe Jewe merchaunt and his men come to þe Cristen
merchaunte.*　　　　　　　　　　　　　　　　　f. 342ᵛ

JONATHAS. All haylle, Syr Aristorye, semelé to se,
　The myghtyest merchaunte off Arigon!
Off yower welfare fayn wet wold we,
　And to bargeyn with you þis day am[4] I boun.

ARISTORIUS. Sir Jonathas, ye be wellcum vnto myn hall!　　270
　I pray yow come vp and sit bi me,
And tell me wat good ye haue to sell,
　And yf ony bargeny mad may be.

JONATHAS. I haue clothe of gold, precyous stons and spycys plenté.
　Wyth yow a bargen wold I make—　　　　　　　275
I wold bartre[5] wyth yow in pryvyté
　On lytell thyng, [þat] ye wyll me yt take

---

　[1] *Corrected from* moste.
　[2] *MS. first* tell, e *altered to* o. *This line written to the right, outside the rhyme-brackets, opposite* 251-2; *cf.* 257.　　　　　[3] *To right, opposite* 255-6.
　[4] *MS.* an.　　　　　[5] *MS.* vartre *following* bar *struck out.*

Preuely in þis stownd;[1]
And I woll sure yow be thys lyght,
Neuer dystre[n] yow daye nor nyght,   280
But be sworn to yow full ryght
    And geve yow twenti pownd.[2]

ARISTORIUS. Sir Jonathas, sey me for my sake,
    What man[er] of marchandis ys þat ⌐ye⌐ mene?
JONATHAS. Yowr God, þat ys full mytheti, in a cake,   285
    And thys good anoon shall yow seen.
    [ARISTORIUS.] Nay, in feyth, þat shall not bene.
I woll not for an hundder pownd
    To stond in fere my Lord to tene;
And for so lytell a walew in conscyen[c]e to stond bownd.   290

JONATHAS. Sir, þe entent ys, if I myght knowe or vndertake
    Yf þat he were God allmyght,
Off all my mys I woll amende make,
    And doon hym wourshepe bothe day and nyght.

ARISTORIUS. Jonathas, trowth I shall þe tell: f. 343ʳ
    I stond in gret dowght to do þat dede,   296
To yow þat dere[3] all for to sell
    I fere me þat I shuld stond in drede;
    For and I vnto þe chyrche yede,
And preste or clerke myght me aspye,   300
    To þe bysshope þei wolde go tell þat dede
And apeche me of eresye.[4]

JONATHAS. Sir, as for þat, good shyffte may ye make,
    And, for a vaylle, to walkyn on a nyght
Wan prest and clerk to rest ben take;   305
    Than shall ye be spyde of no wyght.
    ARISTORIUS. Now sey me, Jonathas, be this lyght!
Wat payment þerfor wollde yow me make?
    JONATHAS. Forty pownd,[5] and pay yt ful ryght,
Evyn for þat Lorde sake.   310

ARISTORIUS. Nay, nay, Jonathas, there-ageyn;[6]
    I w[o]ld not for an hundder[7] pownd.

---

[1] *This line and 282 to right, as other tail-lines.*   [2] *MS.* xxᵗⁱ li.
[3] *MS.* bere.   [4] *MS.* tresye.   [5] *MS.* xl. li.   [6] *MS.* -agen.
[7] *MS.* C.

JONATHAS. Sir, hir ys [yo]wr askyng toolde pleyn,
　I shall yt tell in this stownd.

Here is an hundder pownd,[1] neyther mor nor lasse,[2]　　　315
　Of dokettys good, I dar well saye;
Tell yt ere yow from me passe;
　Me thynketh yt a royall araye.

But fyrst, I pray yow, tell me thys:
　Off thys thyng whan shall I hafe delyuerance?　　　320
ARISTORI[US]. To-morowe betymes; I shall not myse;
　This nyght therfor I shall make purveaunce.

Syr Isodyr he ys now at chyrch,　　　f. 343ᵛ
　There seyng hys evynsong,
As yt ys[3] worshepe for to werche;　　　325
　He shall sone cum home, he wyll nat be long,[4]
　　Hys sopere for to eate;
And when he ys buskyd to hys bedde,
Ryght sone hereafter he shalbe spedd.
No speche among yow there be spredd;　　　330
　To kepe yowr toungys ye nott lett.

JONATHAS. Syr, almyghty Machomyght be with yow!
　And I shall cum agayn ryght sone.
ARYSTORIUS. Jonathas, ye wott what I haue sayd, and how
　I shall walke for that we haue to doun.　　　335

　　　Here goeth þe Jewys away and þe preste commyth home.

PRESBITER. Syr, Almyghty God mott be yowr gyde
　And glad yow wheresoo ye rest!
ARISTORIUS. Syr, ye be welcom home thys tyde.
　Now, Peter, gett vs wyne of the best.

CLERICUS. Syr, here ys a drawte of Romney red,　　　340
　Ther ys no better in Aragon,
And a lofe of lyght bred—
　Yt ys holesom as sayeth þe fesycyon.

ARYSTORIUS. Drynke of, Ser Isoder, and be of good chere!
　Thys Romney ys good to goo with to reste;　　　345

---

¹ *MS.* C. li.　　　　　　² *MS.* lesse.
³ *MS.* hys.　　⁴ *First hand ends, third follows.*

Ther ys no precyouser fer nor nere,
  For all wykkyd metys yt wyll degest.

PRESBITER. Syr, thys wyne ys good at a taste,
  And therof haue I drunke ryght well.
To bed to gone thus haue I cast,   350
  Euyn strayt after thys mery mele.

Now, Ser, I pray to God send yow good nyght.[1]   f. 344^r
  For to my chambere now wyll I gonne.
ARISTORIUS. Ser, with yow be God almyght,[2]
  And sheld yow euer from yowr fone.   355

    Here shall Aristorius call hys clarke to hys presens.

Howe, Peter! In the ys all my trust,
  In especyall to kepe my counsell:
For a lytyll waye walkyn I must.[3]
  I wyll not be long; trust as I the tell.

Now preuely wyll I preue my pace,   360
  My bargayn thys nyght for to fulfyll.
Ser Isoder shall nott know of thys case,
  For he hath oftyn sacred as yt ys skyll.
    The chyrche key ys at my wyll;
Ther ys no thyng þat me shall tary,   365
  I wyll nott abyde by dale nor hyll
Tyll yt be wrowght, by Saynt Mary!

    Here shal he enter þe chyrche and take þe Hoost.

Ah! now haue I all myn entent;
  Vnto Jonathas now wyll I fare;
To fullfyll my bargayn haue I ment,   370
  For þat mony wyll amend my fare,
    As thynkyth me.
But now wyll I passe by thes pathes playne;
  To mete with Jonathas I wold fayne.
Ah! yonder he commytht in certayn;   375
  Me thynkyth I hym see.

---

[1] *Holthausen; MS.* rest.
[2] *Written* almyghty, -y *erased.*
[3] *Preceded by* wyll *struck out.*

Welcom, Jonathas, gentyll and trew,
   For well and trwly þou kepyst thyn howre;
Here ys þe Host, sacred newe,
   Now wyll I home to halle and bowre.   380

JONATHAS. And I shall kepe thys trusty treasure   f. 344ᵛ
   As I wold doo my gold and fee.
Now in thys clothe I shall the cure[1]
   That no wyght shall the see.

Here shall Arystory goo hys waye and Jonathas and hys seruauntys
shall goo to þe tabyll þus sayng:

JONATHAS. Now, Jason and Jasdon, ye be Jewys jentyll,   385
   Masfatt and Malchus, that myghty arn in mynd,
Thys merchant from the Crysten temple
   Hathe gett vs thys bred that make vs thus blynd.
Now, Jason, as jentyll as euer was the lynde,
Into the forsayd parlowr preuely take thy pase;   390
   Sprede a clothe on the tabyll þat ye shall þer fynd,
And we shall folow after to carpe of thys case.

Now þe Jewys goon and lay the Ost on þe tabyll, sayng:

JONATHAS. Syrys, I praye yow all, harkyn to my sawe!
   Thes Crysten men carpyn of a mervelows case;
They say þat þis ys Jhesu þat was attayntyd in owr lawe   395
   And þat thys ys he þat crwcyfyed was.

On thes wordys ther law growndyd hath he
   That he sayd on Shere Thursday at hys sopere:
He brake the brede and sayd *Accipite*,
   And gave hys dyscyplys them for to chere: 400
   And more he sayd to them there,
Whyle they were all togethere and sum,
   Syttyng at the table soo clere,
Comedite Corpus meum.

And thys powre he gaue Peter to proclame,   f. 345
   And how the same shuld be suffycyent to all prechors;   406
The bysshoppys and curatys saye the same,
   And soo, as I vnderstond, do all hys progenytors.[2]

---

[1] *MS.* cure *struck out and replaced by* couere.
[2] *Reading certain, but evidently an error.*

JASON. Yea, sum men in þat law reherse another:
　They say of a maydyn borne was hee,　　　　　　　　410
And how Joachyms dowghter shuld be hys mother,
　And how Gabrell apperyd and sayd 'Aue';
　And with þat worde she shuld conceyuyd be,
And þat in hyr shuld lyght the Holy Gost.
　Ageyns owr law thys ys false heresy,　　　　　　　415
And yett they saye he ys of myghtys most.

JASDON. They saye þat Jhesu to be owr kyng,
　But I wene he bowght þat full dere.
But they make a royall aray of hys vprysyng;
　And that in euery place ys prechyd farre and nere.　　420
　And how he to hys dyscyples agayn dyd appere,
To Thomas and to Mary Mawdelen,
　And syth how he styed by hys own power;[1]
And thys, ye know well, ys heresy full playn.

MASPHAT. Yea, and also they say he sent them wytt and wysdom
　For to vnderstond euery langwage;　　　　　　　426
When þe Holy Gost to them come,[2]
　They faryd as dronk men of pymente[3] or vernage;
　And sythen how þat he lykenyd hymself a lord of parage,
On hys fatherys ryght hond he hym sett.　　　　　430
　They hold hym wyser þan euer was Syble sage,
And strenger than Alexander, þat all þe worde ded gett.

MALCHUS. Yea, yet they saye as fals, I dare laye my hedde, f. 345ᵛ
　How they that be ded shall com agayn to Judgement,
And owr dredfull Judge shalbe thys same brede,　　435
　And how lyfe euerlastyng them shuld be lent.
　And thus they hold, all at on consent,
Because that Phylyppe sayd for a lytyll gᵀᵀosse—
　To turne vs from owr beleve ys ther entent—
For that he sayd, '*judecare viuos et mortuos*'.　　　440

JONATHAS. Now, serys, ye haue rehersyd the substance of ther[4]
　lawe,
　But thys bred I wold myght be put in a prefe
Whether þis be he that in Bosra of vs had awe.
　Ther staynyd were hys clothys, þis may we belefe;

---

[1] *MS.* powre.　　　[2] *MS.* came.　　　[3] -e *repr. by loop.*　　　[4] *Stokes; MS.* oʳ.

Thys may we know, ther had he grefe,   445
For owr old bookys veryfy thus.

Theron he was jugett to be hangyd as a thefe—
Tinctis Bosra vestibus.

JASON. Yff þat thys be he that on Caluery was mad red,
    Onto my mynd, I shall kenne yow a conceyt good: 450
Surely with owr daggars we shall ses on thys bredde,
    And so with clowtys we shall know yf[1] he haue eny blood.
    JASDON. Now, by Machomyth so myghty, þat meuyth in my
       mode!
Thys ys masterly ment, thys matter thus to meue:
    And with owr strokys we shall fray hym as he was on þe rood,
That he was on don with grett repreue.   456

MASPHAT. Yea, I pray yow, smyte ye in the myddys of þe
       cake,   f. 346ʳ
    And so shall we smyte þeron woundys fyve.
We wyll not spare to wyrke yt wrake,
    To prove in thys brede yf þer be eny lyfe.   460

MALCHUS. Yea, goowe to, than, and take owr[2] space,
    And looke owr daggarys be sharpe and kene:
And when eche man a stroke smytte hase,
    In þe mydyll part thereof owr master shall bene.
    JONATHAS. When ye haue all smytyn, my stroke shalbe sene;
With þis same dagger that ys so styf and strong,   466
    In þe myddys of thys prynt I thynke for to prene;
On lashe I shall hyme lende or yt be long.

Here shall þe iiij Jewys pryk þer daggerys in iiij quarters, þus sayng:
JASON. Haue at yt! Haue at yt, with all my myght!
    Thys syde I hope for to sese!   470
JASDON. And I shall with thys blade so bryght
    Thys other syde freshely afeze!
    MASPHAT. And I yow plyght I shall hym not please,
For with thys punche I shall hym pryke.
    MALCHUS. And with thys augur[3] I shall hym not ease,   475
Another buffett shall he lykke.

---

[1] *Stokes; MS.* ys.   [2] *Stokes; MS.* yowʳ.   [3] *MS.* augus.

JONATHAS. Now am I bold with batayle hym to bleyke,
   þe mydle part alle for to prene;
A stowte stroke also for to stryke—
   In þe myddys yt shalbe sene!   480

Here þe Ost must blede.

Ah! owt! owt! harrow! what deuyll ys thys?
   Of thys wyrk I am in were;
Yt bledyth as yt were woode, iwys;
   But yf ye helpe, I shall dyspayre.[1]

JASON. A fyre! a fyre! and that in hast!   f. 346^v
   Anoon a cawdron full of oyle!   486
JASDON. And I shalle helpe yt were in cast,
   All þe thre[2] howrys fo[r] to boyle!

MASPHAT. Ye,[3] here is a furneys stowte and strong,
And a cawdron therin dothe hong.   490
Malcus, wher ⌐art⌐ thow so long,
   To helpe thys dede were dyght?
MALCUS. Loo, here ys fowr[4] galouns off oyle clere.
Haue doon fast! blowe up þe fere!
Syr, bryng that ylke cake nere,   495
   Manly, with all yowre my⌐g⌐the.

JANATHAS. And I shall bryng þat ylke cak
And throwe yt in, I undertake.
Out! Out! yt werketh me w⌐r⌐ake!
   I may not awoyd yt owt of my hond.   500
I wylle goo drenche me in a lake.
And in woodnesse I gynne to wake!
   I renne, I lepe ouer þis lond.

Her he renneth wood, with þe Ost in hys hond.

JASON. Renne, felawes, renne,[5] for Cokkys peyn,
Fast we had owr mayster ageyne![6]   505
Hold prestly on thys pleyn
   And faste bynd hyme to a poste.

---

[1] *Third hand ends, first resumes.*   [2] *MS.* iij.
[3] *Written* yea, a *struck out.*   [4] *MS.* iiij.
[5] *MS.* reme.   [6] *MS.* agene.

JASDON. Here is an hamer and naylys thre,[1] I s[e]ye;
Lyffte vp hys armys, felawe, ⌈o⌉n hey,
Whyll I dryue þes nayles, I yow praye,   510
  With strong strokys fast.

MASPHAT.[2] Now set on, felouse, with mayne and myght,
And pluke hys armes awey in fyght!
Wat yfe he twycche, felovse, aryght!
  Alas, balys breweth ryght badde!   515

Heres hall thay pluke þe arme, and þe hond shall hang[3] styll with þe
                              Sacrament.   f. 347ʳ

MALCHAS. Alas, alas, what deuyll ys thys?
Now hat he but oon hand iwyse!
Forsothe, mayster, ryght woo me is
  þat ye þis harme hawe hadde.

JANATHAS. Ther ys no more; I must enduer!   520
  Now hastely to owr chamber lete us gon;[4]
Tyll I may get me sum recuer;
  And therfor charge yow euerychoon
  That yt be counsell that we haue doon.

    Here shall þe lechys man come into þe place sayng:

COLLE. Aha! here ys a fayer felawshyppe,   525
Thewh I be nat sh[a]pyn, I lyst to sleppe:
I haue a master I wolld he had þe pyppe,
  I tell yow in counsel.
He ys a man off all syence,
But off thryffte—I may with yow dyspence!   530
He syttyth[5] with sum tapstere in þe spence:
  Hys hoode there wyll he sell.

Mayster Brendyche of Braban,
I tell yow he ys þat same man,
Called þe most famous phesy[cy]an   535
  þat euer sawe vryne.
He seeth as wele at noone as at nyght,
And sumtyme by a candelleyt
Can gyff a judgyment[6] aryght—
  As he þat hathe noon eyn.   540

---

[1] *MS.* iij.   [2] *Stokes; MS.* Malspas.   [3] *MS.* sang.
[4] n *smudged and uncertain.*   [5] *MS.* sytthyt.   [6] *MS.* judyyment.

He ys allso a boone-setter;
I knowe no man go þe better;
In euery tauerne he ys detter;
   þat ys a good tokenyng.
But euer I wonder he ys so long;   545
I fere ther gooth ⌜sumthyng⌝¹ awrong,
For he hath dysa[rv]yde to be hong—
   God send neuer wurse tydyng!

He had a lady late in cure;   f. 347ᵛ
I wot² be þis she ys full sᵘre;   550
There shall neuer Cristen creature
   Here hyr tell no tale.
And I stode here tyll mydnyght,
I cowde not declare aryght
My masteris cunyng insyght—   555
   þat he hat in good ale.

But³ what deuyll ayleth⁴ hym, so long to taré!
A seekman myght soone myscary.
Now alle þe deuyllys of hell hym wari;
   God grante me my boon!   560
I trowe best, we mak a crye:
Yf any man can hym⁵ aspye
Led hym to þe pylleri.
   In fayth, yt shall be don.

Here shall he stond vp and make proclamacion, seyng thys:

COLLE. Yff ther be eyther man or woman   565
That sawe Master Brundyche of Braban,
Or owyht of hym tel can,
   Shall wele be quit hys med;⁶
He hath a cut⁷ berd and a flatte noose,
A therde-bare gowne and a rent hoose;   570
He spekyt neuer good matere nor purpoose;
   To þe pylleré ye hym led!

---

¹ *Interlined by the third hand.*   ² *MS.* wotr.
³ *Stokes; MS.* By.   ⁴ *Manly; MS.* dyleth.
⁵ *Stokes; MS.* cam I.   ⁶ *Abbr.* md *with stroke above.*   ⁷ *MS.* tut.

MASTER BRUNDYCHE. What, thu boye, what janglest here?
COLL. A! master, master, but to your reuerence![1]
I wend neuer to a seen yowr goodly chere,   575
    Ye taréd hens so long.
MASTER BRUNDYCHE.[2] What hast thow sayd in my absense?
COLL. Nothyng, master, but to yowr reuerence
I haue told all þis audiense—
    And some lyes among.   580

But, master, I pray yow, how dothe yowr pa[c]yent
That ye had last vnder yowr medycament?
MASTER BRUNDYCHE. I waraunt she neuer fele anoyment.[3]
    COLL. Why, ys she in hyr graue?
MASTER BRUNDYCHE. I haue gyven hyr a drynke made full
    well   f. 348ʳ
Wyth scamoly and with oxennell,   586
Letwyce, sawge and pympernelle.
    COLLE. Nay, than she ys full saue,

For, ⌈now⌉ ye ar cum, I dare well saye
Betuyn Douyr and Calyce þe ryght wey   590
Dwellth non so cunnyng, be my fey,
    In my judgyment.
MASTER BRUNDYCHE. Cunnyng? Yea, yea, and with pratt[y]ffe;
I haue sauid many a mannys lyfe.[4]
COLLE. On wydowes, maydese and wyfe[5]   595
    Yowr connyng yow haue nyhe spent.

MASTER BRUNDYCHE. Were ys [my] bowg[e]tt with drynk profyt-
    able?
    COLL. Here master, master, ware how ye tugg.[6]
The devyll I trowe within shrugge,[7]
For yt gooth rebyll rable.   600

MASTER BRUNDYCHE. Here ys a grete congregacyon,
And all be not hole, without negacyon;
I wold haue certyfycacyon:

---

    [1] *Evidently copied in error from 578.*
    [2] *Abbr. here and later by flourished* M *and* B.
    [3] *Manly; MS.* anoyntment.
    [4] *After this lines 597–8 written and struck out;* 597 *runs:* wer ys my bowget wᵗ
drynke profetabyll.   [5] *MS.* wyse.
    [6] *First written* tugges, es *struck out.*   [7] *Final loop may be intended for* -ys.

Stond vp and make a proclamacion.

Haue do faste, and make no pausa[c]yon,   605

But wyghtly mak a declaracion

    To all people þat helpe w[o]lde haue.

        Hic interim proclamacionem faciet.

COLL. All manar off men þat haue any syknes,

    To Master Brentberecly loke þat yow redresse.

    What dysease or syknesse þat euer ye haue,   f. 348ᵛ

    He wyll neuer leue yow tyll ye be in yow[r] graue.   611

    Who hat þe canker, þe collyke, or þe laxe,

    The tercyan, þe quartan, or þe brynny[n]g axs—

    For wormys, for gnawyng, gᴿrᴸyndy[n]g in þe wombe or in þe

        boldyro—

    All maner red eyn, bleryd eyn, and þe myegrym also,   615

    For hedache, bonache, and therto þe tothache—

    The colt-euyll,[1] and þe brostyn men he wyll undertak,

    All tho þat [haue] þe poose, þe sneke, or þe tyseke—

    Thowh a man w[e]re ryght heyle, he cowd soone make hym sek.

    Inquyre to þe colkote, for ther ys hys loggyng,   620

    A lytyll besyde Babwell Myll, yf ye wyll haue und[er]stondyn[g].

MASTER BRUNDYCHE. ⌜Now⌝,[2] yff ther be ether man or woman

That nedethe helpe of a phesyscian—[3]

COLL. Mary, master, þat I tell can,

    And ye wyll vnderstond.   625

MASTER BRUNDYCHE. Knoest any abut þis plase?

COLL. Ye, þat I do, mastᴿrᴸe, so haue [I] grase;

Here ys a Jewe, hyght Jonathas,

    Hath lost hys ryght hond.

MASTER BRUNDYCHE. Fast to hym I wold inquere.   630

COLL. For God, master, þe gate ys hyre.

MASTER BRUNDYCHE. Than to hym I wyll go nere.

    My master, wele mot yow be!

JONATHAS. What doost here, felawe? what woldest thu hanne?

MASTER BRUNDYCHE. Syr, yf yow nede ony surgeon or physycyan,

Off yow[r] dyse[se] help yow welle I cane,   636

    What hurtys or hermes[4] so-euer they be.

---

[1] *O.E.D.; MS.* Coltugll.   [2] *Inserted by third hand.*

[3] *MS.* phesyscion.   [4] *MS.* hermet.

JONATHAS. Syr, thu art ontawght to come in thus homly,[1]   f. 349ʳ
Or to pere in my presence thus malepertly.
Voydoth from my syght, and þat wyghtly,   640
    For ye be mysse-avysed.
COLL. Syr, þe hurt of yowr hand ys knowen full ryfe,
And my maste[r] haue ⌐sauyd⌐[2] many a manes lyfe.
JONATHAS. I trowe ye ⌐be⌐ cum to make sum stryfe.[3]
    Hens fast, lest þat ye be chastysed.   645

COLL. Syr, ye know well yt can nott mysse;
    Men that be masters of scyens be profytable.
In a pott yf yt please yow to pysse,
    He can tell yf yow be curable.
[JONATHAS.] Avoyde, fealows, I loue not yowr bable!   650
Brushe them hens bothe and that anon!
Gyff them ther reward þat they were gone!

            Here shall þe iiij Jewys bett away þe leche and hys man.

JONATHAS. Now haue don, felawys, and that anon,
    For dowte of drede what after befall!
I am nere masyd, my wytte[4] ys gon;   655
    Therfor of helpe I pray yow all.

And take yowre pynsonys þat ar so sure,
    And pluck owt the naylys won and won;
Also in a clothe ye yt cure
    And throw yt in þe cawdron, and þat anon.   660

Here shall Jason pluck owt the naylys and shake þe hond into þe
                        cawdron.

JASON. And I shall rape me redely anon   f. 349ᵛ
To plucke owt the naylys that stond so fast,
    And beare thys bred and also thys bone
And into the cawdron I wyll yt cast.

JASDON. And I shall with thys dagger so stowte   665
    Putt yt down that yt myght plawe,
And steare the clothe rounde abowte
    That nothyng therof shalbe rawe.

---

¹ m *lacks a minim.*   ² *Interlined by third hand.*
³ *First hand ends, third resumes and writes to end.*
⁴ -e *represented by final loop.*

MASPHAT. And I shall manly, with all my myght,
  Make the fyre to blase and brynne,[1]   670
And sett thervnder suche a lyght
  That yt shall make yt ryght thynne.

    Here shall þe cawdron byle, apperyng to be as blood.

MALCHAS. Owt and harow! what deuyll ys herein?
All thys oyle waxyth redde as blood,
  And owt of the cawdron yt begynnyth to rin.[2]   675
I am so aferd I am nere woode.

    Here shall Jason and hys compeny goo to Ser Jonathas sayng:

JASON. Ah! master, master, what chere ys with yow?
  I can nott see owr werke wyll avayle;
I beseche yow avance yow now
  Sumwhatt with yowr counsayle.   680

JONATHAS. The best counsayle that I now wott,
  That I can deme, farre and nere,
Ys[3] to make an ovyn as redd hott
  As euer yt can be made with fere;
  And when ye see yt soo hott appere,   685
Then throw yt into the ovyn fast—
  Sone shall he stanche hys bledyng chere.
When ye haue donne, stoppe yt—be not agast!

JASDON. Be my fayth, yt shalbe wrowgh[t],   f. 350ʳ
  And that anon, in gret hast.   690
Bryng on fyryng, serys, here ye nowght?
  To hete thys ovyn be nott agast.

MASPHAT. Here ys straw and thornys kene:
  Com on, Malchas, and bryng on fere,[4]
For that shall hete yt well, I wene;   695
    Here þei kyndyll þe fyre.
  Blow on fast, that done yt were!
MALCHAS. Ah, how thys fyre gynnyth to brenne clere!
Thys ovyn ryght hotte I thynk to make.
  Now, Jason, to the cawdron þat ye stere
And fast fetche hether that ylke cake.   700

      [1] *MS.* brenne.   [2] *Stokes* rinn; *MS.* run.
      [3] *Written in preceding line.*   [4] *MS.* fyre.

Here shall Jason goo to þe cawdron and take owt the Ost with hys
pynsonys and cast yt into the ovyn.

JASON. I shall with thes pynsonys withowt dowt,
    Shake thys cake owt of thys clothe,[1]
And to the ovyn I shall yt rowte
    And stoppe hym there, thow he be loth.
    The cake I haue cawght here in good sothe—   705
The hand ys soden, the fleshe from þe bonys—
    Now into the ouyn I wyll therwith.
Stoppe yt, Jasdon, for the nonys!

JASDON. I stoppe thys ovyn, wythowtyn dowte,
    With clay I clome yt vppe ryght fast,   710
That non heat shall cum owtte.
    I trow there shall he hete and drye in hast!

Here the owyn must ryve asunder and blede owt at þe cranys, and an
image appere owt with woundys bledyng.

MASPHAT. Owt! owt! here ys a grete wondere!   f. 350ᵛ
    Thys ovyn b[l]edyth owt on euery syde!
MALCHAS. Yea, þe ovyn on peacys gynnyth to ryve asundre; 715
    Thys ys a mervelows case thys tyde.

    Here shall þe image speke to the Juys sayng thus:

JHESUS. *O mirabiles Judei, attendite et videte*
    Si est dolor sicut[2] dolor meus.

Oh ye merveylows Jewys,
    Why ar ye to yowr kyng onkynd,   720
And [I] so bytterly bowt yow to my blysse?
    Why fare ye thus fule with yowre frende?
    Why peyne yow me and straytly me pynde,
And I yowr loue so derely haue bowght?
    Why are ye so vnstedfast in yowr mynde?   725
Why wrath ye me? I greve yow nowght.
Why wyll ye nott beleue that I haue tawght,
    And forsake yowr fowle neclygence,
And kepe my commandementys in yowr thowght,
    And vnto my godhed to take credence?   730

---

[1] *Preceded by* clowte *struck out.*   [2] *MS.* similis.

Why blaspheme yow me? Why do ye thus?
  Why put yow me to a newe tormentry,
And I dyed for yow on the crosse?
  Why consyder not yow what I dyd crye?
  Whyle that I was with yow, ye ded me velanye.   735
    Why remember ye nott my bytter chaunce,
    How yowr kynne dyd me awance
    For claymyng of myn enherytaunce?
    I shew yow the streytnesse of my greuaunce,
And all to meue yow to my mercy.   740

JONATHAS. *Tu es protector vite mee; a quo trepidabo?*   f. 351ʳ
  O thu, Lord, whyche art my defendowr,
    For dred of the I trymble and quake.
  Of thy gret mercy lett vs receyue þe showre;
    And mekely I aske mercy, amendys to make.   745

     Here shall they knele down all on ther kneys, sayng:

JASON. Ah! Lord, with sorow and care and grete wepyng
  All we felawys lett vs saye thus,
With condolent harte and grete sorowyng:
  Lacrimis nostris conscienciam nostram baptizemus!

JASDON. Oh thow blyssyd Lord of mykyll myght,   750
  Of thy gret mercy, thou hast shewyd vs þe path,
Lord, owt of grevous slepe and owt of dyrknes to lyght,
  Ne grauis sompnus irruat.

MASPHAT. Oh Lord, I was very cursyd, for I wold know þi crede.
  I can no menys make but crye to the thus: 755
O gracyows Lorde, forgyfe me my mysdede!
  With lamentable hart: *miserere mei, Deus!*

MALCHAS. Lord, I haue offendyd the in many a sundry vyse,
  That styckyth at my hart as hard as a core.
Lord, by þe water of contrycion lett me aryse: 760
  Asparges me, Domine, ysopo, et mundabor.

JHESUS. All ye that desyryn my seruauntys for to be
  And to fullfyll þe preceptys of my lawys,

The intent of my commandement knowe ye:
   Ite et ostendite vos sacerdotibus meis.   765

To all yow þat desyre in eny wyse
   To aske mercy, to graunt yt redy I am.
Remember and lett yowr wyttys suffyce,
   Et tunc non auertam a vobis faciem meam.

No, Jonathas, on thyn hand thow art but lame,   f. 351ᵛ
   And ys thorow thyn own cruelnesse.   771
For thyn hurt þou mayest þiselfe blame,
   Thow woldyst preve thy powre me to oppresse;
   But now I consydre thy necesse;
Thow wasshest thyn hart with grete contrycion;   775
   Go to the cawdron—þi care shalbe the lesse—
And towche thyn hand to thy saluacion.

Here shall Ser Jonathas put hys hand into þe cawdron, and yt shalbe
                 hole agayn; and then say as fo[l]wyth:

JONATHAS. Oh thow my Lord God and Sauyowr, osanna!
   Thow Kyng of Jewys and of Jerusalem!
O thow myghty, strong Lyon of Juda,   780
   Blyssyd be the tyme þat þou were in Bedlem!
Oh þou myghty, strong, gloryows, and gracyows oyle streme,
Thow myghty conquerrowr of infernall tene,
   I am quyt of moche combrance thorowgh thy meane,
That euer blyssyd mott þou bene!   785

Alas, þat euer I dyd agaynst thy wyll,
   In my wytt to be soo wood
That I so ongoodly wyrk shuld soo gryll!
   Aʒens my mysgouernaunce thow gladdyst me with good:
   I was soo prowde to prove the on þe Roode,   790
And þou haste sent me lyghtyng þat late was lame;
   To bete the and boyle the I was myghty in moode,
And now þou hast put me from duresse and dysfame.

But, Lord, I take my leve at thy hygh presens,
   And put me in thy myghty mercy;   795
The bysshoppe wyll I goo fetche to se owr offens,
   And onto hym shew owr lyfe, how þat we be gylty.

Here shall þe master Jew goo to þe byshopp and hys men knele
                    styll.   f. 352ʳ

JONATHAS. Hayle, father of grace! I knele vpon my knee,
    Hertely besechyng yow and interely,
A swemfull syght all for to see   800
    In my howse apperyng verely:
    The holy Sacrament, þe whyche we haue done tormentry,
And ther we haue putt hym to a newe passyon,
    A chyld apperyng with wondys blody:
A swemfull syght yt ys to looke vpon.   805

EPISCOPUS. Oh Jhesu, Lord, full of goodnesse!
    With the wyll I walke with all my myght.
Now, all my pepull, with me ye dresse
    For to goo see that swymfull syght.

Now, all ye peple that here are,   810
    I commande yow, euery man,
On yowr feet for to goo bare,
    In the devoutest wyse that ye can.

    Here shall þe bysshope entere into þe Jewys howse and say:
O *Jhesu fili Dei,*
    How thys paynfull passyon rancheth myn hart!   815
Lord, I crye to the, *miserere mei,*
    From thys rufull syght þou wylt reuerte.
    Lord, we all with sorowys smert,
For thys vnlefull work we lyue in langowr;
    Now, good Lord, in thy grace let vs be gert,¹   820
And of thy souerreyn marcy send vs thy socowr;
And for thy holy grace forgyfe vs owr errowr.
    Now lett thy peté spryng and sprede;
Thowgh we haue be vnrygh[t]full, forgyf vs owr rygore,
    And of owr lamentable hartys, good Lord, take hed.   825

    Here shall þe im[a]ge change agayn into brede.   f. 352ᵛ
EPISCOPUS. Oh thu largyfluent Lord, most of lyghtnesse,
    Onto owr prayers thow hast applyed:
Thu hast receyuyd them with grett swettnesse,
    For all owr dredfull dedys þou hast not vs denyed.

                    ¹ *Stokes; MS.* grett.

Full mykyll owte thy name for to be magnyfyed   830
With mansuete myrth and gret swettnes,
    And as owr gracyows God for to be gloryfyed,[1]
For thu shewyst vs gret gladnes.

Now wyll I take thys Holy Sacrament
    With humble hart and gret devocion,   835
And all we wyll gon with on consent
    And beare yt to chyrche with sole[m]pne processyon;

Now folow me, all and summe,
    And all tho that bene here, both more and lesse,
Thys holy song, *O sacrum*[2] *Conuiuium*,[3]   840
    Lett vs syng all with grett swetnesse.

Here shall þe pryst, Ser Isoder, aske hys master what þis menyth.

[PRESBITER.] Ser Arystory, I pray yow, what menyth all thys?
    Sum myracle, I hope, ys wrowght be Goddys myght;
The bysshope commyth processyon with a gret meny of Jewys;
    I hope sum myracle ys shewyd to hys syght.   845
    To chyrche in hast wyll I rune full ryght,
For thether, me thynk, he begynnyth to take hys pace.
    The Sacrament so semly ys borne in syght,
I hope that God hath shewyd of hys grace.

ARYSTORIUS. To tell yow the trowth I wyll nott lett: 850
    Alas þat euer thys dede was dyght!
An onlefull bargayn [I] began for to beat;   f. 353ʳ
    I sold yon same Jewys owr Lord full ryght
For couytyse of good, as a cursyd wyght.
Woo the whyle that bargayn I dyd euer make!   855
    But yow be my defensour in owr dyocesans syght,
For an heretyke I feare he wyll me take.

PRESBITER. For sothe, nothyng well-avysed was yowr wytt;
    Wondrely was yt wrowght of a man of dyscrescion
In suche perayle yowr solle for to pytt;[4]   860
    But I wyll labor for yowr absolucyon.

---

[1] *Preceded by* magnyfyed *struck out.*   [2] *Stokes; MS.* scacrum.
[3] *So MS., hitherto misread* Dominum.   [4] *MS.* putt.

Lett vs hye vs fast that we were hens,
   And beseche hym of hys benygne grace
That he wyll shew vs hys benyvolens
   To make a menys¹ for yowr trespas.   865

*Here shall þe merchant and hys prest go to þe chyrche and þe bysshop
shall entre þe chyrche and lay þe Ost on² þe auter, sayng thus:*

EPISCOPUS. *Estote forte⌈s⌉ in bello et pugnate cum³ antico serpente,
   Et accipite regnum eternum, et cetera.*

My chyldern, ye be strong in batayll gostly
   For to fyght agayn the fell serpent,
That nyght and day ys euer besy;   870
   To dystroy owr sollys ys hys intent.
   Look ye be not slow nor neclygent
To arme yow in the vertues seuyn;
   Of synnys fo[r]gotyn⁴ take good avysement,
And knowlege them to yowr confessor full euyn;   875

For that serpent, the deuyll, ys full strong,
   Meruelows myschevos for man to mene;
But that the Passyon of Cryst ys meynt vs among,
   And that ys in dyspyte of hys infernall tene.⁵
   Beseche owr Lord and Sauyowr so kene   f. 353ᵛ
To put doun that serpent, cumberer of man,   881
   To withdraw hys furyous froward doctryn bydene,
Fulfyllyd of þe fend callyd Leuyathan.

Gyff lawrell to that Lord of myght
   That he may bryng vs to the joyows fruycion,   885
Form vs to put the fend to flyght,
   That neuer he dystroy vs by hys temptacion.

PRESBITER. My father vnder God, I knele vnto yowr kne,
   In yowr myhty mysericord to tak vs in remembrance;
As ye be materyall to owr degré,   890
   We put vs in yowr moderat ordynaunce,
   Yff yt lyke yowr hyghnes to here owr greuaunce:
We haue offenddyd sorowfully in a syn mortall,

---

¹ *MS.* menyn.   ² *MS.* of non.   ³ *Stokes; MS.* co.
⁴ *Second* o *written over* y.   ⁵ *Written below* payne *struck out.*

Wherfor we fere vs owr Lord wyll take vengaunce
For owr synnes both grete and small.   895

EPISCOPUS. And in fatherhed that longyth to my dygnyté,
    Vnto yowr grefe I wyll gyf credens.
Say what ye wyll, in þe name of þe Trynyté,
    Agayn[s]t God yf ye haue wroght eny inconuenyens.

ARISTORIUS. Holy father, I knele to yow vnder *benedycite*.   900
    I haue offendyd in the syn of couytys:
I sold owr Lordys body for lucre of mony
    And delyueryd to the wyckyd with cursyd advyce.
    And for that pres[u]mpcion gretly I agryse
That I presumed to go to the autere   905
    There to handyll þe holy sacryfyce—
I were worthy to be putt in brennyng fere.[1]

But, gracyous lord, I can no more,   f. 354ʳ
    But put me to Goddys mercy and to yowr grace:
My cursyd werkys for to restore,   910
    I aske penaunce now in thys place.

EPISCOPUS. Now for thys offence that þou hast donne
    Aȝens the Kyng of Hevyn and Emperowr of Hell,
Euer whyll þou lyuest good dedys for to done
    And neuermore for to bye nor sell: 915
    Chastys thy body as I shall the tell,
With fastyng and prayng and other good wyrk,
    To withstond the temtacyon of fendys of hell;
And to call to God for grace looke þou neuer be irke.

Also, þou preste, for thy neclygens,   920
    That thou were no wyser in thyn office,
Thou art worthy inpresu[n]ment for thyn offence;
    But beware euer herafter and be more wyse.

And all yow creaturys[2] and curatys that here be,
    Off thys dede yow may take example   925
How that yowr pyxys lockyd ye shuld see,
    And be ware of the key of Goddys temple.

---

[1] *MS.* fyre.   [2] *Manly suggests* vicarys *or* prechorys, *comparing* 406.

JONATHAS. And I aske Crystendom with great devocion,
   With repentant hart in all degrees,
I aske for vs all a generall absolucion.   930

   Here þe ⌐Juys¬ must knele al down.

For that we knele all vpon owr knees;
For we haue greuyd owr Lord on grovnd
And put hym to a new paynfull passioun:
With daggars styckyd hym with greuos wo[u]nde,[1]
   New naylyd hym to a post and with pynsonys pluckyd hym
   down.   935

JASON. And syth we toke that blyssyd bred so sownd   f. 354ᵛ
   And in a cawdron we dyd hym boyle,
In a clothe full just we hym wounde[2]
And so dyd we seth hym in oyle.

JASDON. And for þat we myght not ouercom hym with tormentry,
   In an hott ovyn we speryd hym fast,   941
There he apperyd with wondys all bloody:
   The ovyn rave asunder and all tobrast.
MASPHAT. In hys law to make vs stedfast,
There spake he to vs woordys of grete favore;   945
   In contrycyon owr hartys he cast
And ⌐bad¬[3] take vs to a confessore.

MALCHUS. And, therfor, all we with on consent
   Knele onto yowr hygh souereynté,
For to be crystenyd ys owr intent;   950
   Now all owr dedys to yow shewyd haue we.

   Here shall þe bysshoppe crysten þe Jewys with gret solempnyté.
EPISCOPUS. Now the Holy Gost at thys tyme mot yow blysse
   As ye knele all now in hys name,
And with the water of baptyme I shall yow blysse
   To saue yow all from the fendys blame.   955
   Now, that fendys powre for to make lame,
In þe name of þe Father, þe Son and þe Holy Gost,
   To saue yow from the deuyllys flame,
I crysten yow all, both lest and most.

   [1] *Final loop may be intended for* -ys.
   [2] *Preceded by* bownd *struck out.*   [3] *Interlined above* vs *struck out.*

SER JONATHAS. Now owr father and byshoppe þat we well knaw,[1]
   We thank yow interly, both lest and most.   961
Now ar we bownd to kepe Crystys lawe
   And to serue þe Father, þe Son and þe Holy Gost.
Now wyll we walke by contré and cost,   f. 355ʳ
Owr wyckyd lyuyng for to restore: 965
   And trust in God, of myghtys most,
Neuer[2] to offend as we haue don befor.[3]

Now we take owr lea[v]e at lesse and mare[4]—
   Forward on owr vyage we wyll vs dresse;
God send yow all as good welfare   970
   As hart can thynke or towng expresse.

ARYSTORIUS. Into my contré now wyll I fare
   For to amende myn wyckyd lyfe,
And to kep þe[5] people owt of care
   I wyll teache thys lesson to man and wyfe.   975

Now take I my leave in thys place,
   I wyll go walke my penaunce to fullfyll;
Now, God, aʒens whom I haue done thys trespas,
   Graunt me forgyfnesse yf yt be thy wyll!

PRESBITER. For joy of thys me thynke my hart do wepe,   980
   That yow haue gyuyn yow all Crystys seruauntys to be,
⌐And⌐[6] hym for to serue with hart full meke—
   God, full of pacyens and humylyté—

And the conuersacion of all thes fayre men,
   With hartys stedfastly knett in on,   985
Goddys lawys to kepe and hym to serue bydene,
   As faythfull Crystyanys euermore for to gone.

EPISCOPUS. God Omnypotent euermore looke ye serue
   With deuocion and prayre whyll þat ye may;
Dowt yt not he wyll yow preserue   990
   For eche good prayer þat ye sey to hys pay;
   And therfor in euery dew tyme loke ye nat delay
For to serue the Holy Trynyté,

---

[1] MS. know.   [2] MS. Neuerer.   [3] MS. befer.
[4] MS. more.   [5] Preceded by my struck out.   [6] In margin.

And also Mary, that swete may,   f. 355ᵛ
And kepe yow in perfyte loue and charyté.   995

Crystys commandementys ten[1] there bee;
    Kepe well them; doo as I yow tell.
Almyght ⌜God⌝ shall yow please in euery degré,
    And so shall ye saue yowr sollys from hell.
    For there ys payn and sorow cruell,   1000
And in heuyn ther ys both joy and blysse,
    More then eny towng can tell,
There angellys syng with grett swetnesse;

To the whyche blysse he bryng vs
    Whoys name ys callyd Jhesus,   1005
And in wyrshyppe of thys name gloryows
    To syng to hys honore *Te Deum Laudamus.*

Finis.

Thus endyth the Play of the Blyssyd Sacrament, whyche myracle was don in the forest of Aragon, in the famous cité Eraclea, the yere of owr Lord God M[1] cccc. lxj, to whom ⌜be⌝ honowr, Amen.

The namys[2] and numbere[3] of the players: f. 356ʳ

Jh[es]us   Jason, Judeus ijᵘˢ
Episcopus   Jasdon, Judeus iijᵘˢ
Aristorius, Christianus mercator   Masphat, Judeus iiijᵘˢ
[Isoder, presbiter]   Malchus, Judeus vᵗᵘˢ
Clericus   Magister phisicus
Jonathas, Judeus jᵐᵘˢ Magister   Coll, seruus

IX may play yt at ease.

R.C.

¹ *MS.* x.   ² *MS.* nanys.   ³ *MS. begins with only five minims.*

VII

THE PRIDE OF LIFE

[Prolocutor.]

Pees, and herkynt hal ifer,
⟨Ric⟩[1] and por, yong and hold,
Men and wemen þat bet her,
Bot lerit and leut, stout and bold.

Lordinge[s] and ladiis þat beth hende,   5
Herkenith al with mylde mode
⟨How ou⟩re[2] gam schal gyn and ende.
Lorde us wel spede þat sched his blode!

Now stondith stil and beth hende,
⟨And ter⟩yith[3] al for þe weder,   10
⟨And⟩ ʒe schal or ʒe hennis wende
Be glad þat ʒe come hidir.

Here ʒe schullin here spelle
Of mirth and eke of kare;
Herkenith and I wol ʒou telle   15
⟨How þis oure gam⟩[4] schal fare.

⟨Of þe Kyng of⟩[5] Lif I wol ʒou telle;
⟨He stondith⟩ first biffore
⟨All men þat beth⟩[6] of flessch and fel
⟨And of woman i⟩[6]bore.   20

⟨He is, forsoth, ful⟩[4] stronge to stond,
⟨And is⟩[6] bycomin of kinge,
⟨ʒiveth⟩[6] lawis in eche a londe,
⟨And nis⟩[7] dradd of no thinge.

⟨In⟩[7] pride and likinge his lif he ledith,   25
Lordlich he lokith with eye;

---

[1] Mills.
[2] Holthausen (cf. 111); MS. . . . ke; Brandl A menske; Waterhouse Swillke.
[3] Brandl; Waterhouse prayith.   [4] Holthausen.
[5] Brandl (cf. 76).   [6] Holthausen, based on Brandl.   [7] Brandl.

⟨Prin⟩ce[1] and dukis, he seith, him dredith,
 ⟨He⟩[1] dredith no deth for to deye.

⟨He⟩[1] hath a lady louelich al at likinge,
 Ne may he of no mirth mene ne misse; 30
He seith in swetnisse he wol set his likinge
 And bringe his bale boun into blisse.

Knytis[2] he[3] hat cumlic
 In bred and in leint;
Not I neuir non suc 35
 Of stotey ne off strynt.

Wat helpit[4] to yilp mucil of his mit
 Or bost to mucil of his blys?
⟨For⟩[1] sorou may sit on is sit
 ⟨And⟩ myrt⟨h m⟩ay[5] he[3] not miss. 40

⟨Her ek is þe⟩ ladi of lond,
 ⟨þe fa⟩inist a lord for[6] to led;
⟨Glad⟩[1] may he[3] be fort to stond
 ⟨And b⟩ehold þat blisful bled.

⟨þa⟩t ladi is lettrit in lor 45
 As cumli becomit for a quen,
And munit[7] hir mac euirmor,
 As a dar for dred him to ten.

Ho bid him bewar or he[3] smert,[8]
 ⟨F⟩or in his lond Det wol alend;[9] 50
⟨As⟩ ho louit[10] him gostlic in hert
 ⟨Ho b⟩it him bewar of his hend.

⟨Ho⟩ begynit to charp of char
 þes wordis wytout lesing:
'Det dot not spar 55
 Knytis,[2] cayser, ne kyng.

---

[1] *Brandl.*   [2] *MS.* kyntis.
[3] *Holthausen; MS.* ʒe.   [4] *Mills; MS.* lelpit.
[5] *Holthausen; MS.* . . . mryt . . . ay.   [6] *Holthausen; MS.* sort to.
[7] *Holthausen; Mills* tun mit; *Skeat* tuinnit; *Brandl* tuin uit.
[8] *Brandl* (cf. 63); *Mills* smrt; *Skeat* snirt.
[9] *Holthausen; Brandl* alende, *reporting MS.* alond.
[10] *Skeat, Brandl; Mills, Waterhouse* leuit.

Nou lord, leu þi likynd
    Wyc bringit þeᴵ soul gret bal.'²
þis answer ho had of þeᴵ kyng;
    'ʒe, þis a womanis tal.'   60

þeᴵ kyng hit ne toke not to hert
    For hit was a womanis spec,
⟨And y⟩et³ hit mad him to smert
    ⟨W⟩an⁴ him mit help no lec.

⟨þe⟩⁴ quen yit can hir undirstond   65
    Wat help þar mit be,
And sent aftir þeᴵ bicop of þeᴵ lond
    For he chout mor þan he.ᴵ

Heᴵ cham and precit al þat heᴵ couþe,
    And warnit him hal of his hind;   70
⟨H⟩it saurit not in þeᴵ kyngis mout,
    Bot hom heᴵ bad him wynd.

Wan⁵ þeᴵ bicop is þan⁶ wend
    Fram þat k[e]ne stryf
⟨To Det a me⟩ssenger⁷ þan send   75
    ⟨Hat⟩⁸ þeᴵ King of Lif.

⟨For he⟩ him wold do undirston[d]
    ⟨þat al⟩ heᴵ may del and dit:
⟨He⟩ wold cum into his ouin lond
    On him to kyt his mit.   80

Deth comith, he⁹ dremith a dredfful dreme—
    Welle aʒte al carye;
And slow fader and moder and þen heme:
    He ne wold none sparye.

Sone affter hit befel þat Deth and Life   85
    Beth togeder itaken;¹⁰
And ginnith and striuith a sterne strife
    [þe]¹¹ King of Life to wrake.

---

¹ *Holthausen, based on Brandl; MS.* ʒe.   ² *Brandl; MS.* bas.
³ *Holthausen* ʒet; *Brandl* set (=seþ).   ⁴ *Brandl.*
⁵ *MS.* wand.   ⁶ *MS.* yam; *Holthausen* hom *based on Brandl.*
⁷ *Holthausen so reconstructs on the basis of 457 ff.*   ⁸ *Holthausen* Is by.
⁹ *Holthausen; MS.* &.   ¹⁰ *Brandl; Waterhouse* itake.
¹¹ *Supplied by Holthausen.*

With¹ him driuith adoun to grounde,
    He dredith nothing his kniʒtis;   90
And delith him depe deþis wounde
    And kith on him his miʒtis.

Qwhen þe body is doun ibroʒt
    þe soule sorow awakith;
þe bodyis pride is dere aboʒt,   95
    þe soule þe fendis takith.

And throgh priere of Oure Lady mylde
    þe soule and body schul dispyte;²
Scho wol prey her son so mylde,
    Al godenisse scho wol qwyte.   100

þe cors þat nere knewe of care,
    No more þen stone in weye,
Schal wit³ of sorow and sore care
    And þrawe⁴ betwene ham tweye.

þe soule þeron schal be weye   105
    þat þe fendis haue ikaʒte;
And Oure Lady schal þerfor preye
    So þat with her he schal be lafte.

Nou beith in pes and beith hende,
    And distourbith noʒt oure place,   110
For þis oure game schal gin and ende
    Throgh Jhesu Cristis swete grace.

REX VIUUS INCIPIET SIC DICENDUM:

Pes, now, ʒe princis of powere so prowde,
    ʒe kingis, ʒe kempis, ʒe kniʒtis ikorne,
ʒe barons bolde, þat beith me obowte;   115
    ⟨Sem⟩⁵ schal ʒu my sawe, swaynis i[s]worne.

Sqwieris stoute, stondit now stille,
    And lestenith to my hestis, I hote ʒu now her,
Or [I] schal wirch ʒu wo with werkis of wil
    And doun schal ʒe drive, be ʒe neuer so dere.   120

¹ *MS.* wᵗ.   ² *Holthausen so transposes MS. lines 98 and* 100.   ³ *Skeat* wᵗ.
⁴ *Read by Waterhouse only; earlier editors leave blank, Holthausen conjectures*
tremble.   ⁵ *Holthausen.*

King ic am, kinde of kingis ikorre,
   Al þe worlde wide to welde at my wil;
Nas þer neuer no man of woman iborre
   Oȝein me withstonde þat I nold him spille.

Lordis of lond beith at my ledinge,   125
   Al men schal abow in hal and in bowr;

  ·   ·   ·   ·   ·   ·   ·

[REGINA.] Baldli þou art mi bot,
   Tristili and ful treu;
Of al mi rast þou art rot,
   I nil chong fer no new.[1]   130

REX. Al in wel ic am biwent,
   May no[2] grisful þing me grou;
Likyng is wyt me bilent,[3]
   Alyng is it mi behou.

Strent and Hel, knytis[4] kete,   135
   [Douti],[5] derrist[6] in ded,
Lok þat[7] for no[8] þing ȝe let
   Smartli to me sped.

Bringit wyt ȝou[9] brit brondis,
   Helmis brit and schen;[10]   140
For ic am lord ofir al londis
   And þat is uel isen.

PRIMUS MILES, FORTITUDO. Lord, in truþe þou mit trist
   Feþfuli to stond,
þou mit liu as þe[11] list,   145
   For wonschildis þu fond.

Ic am Strent, stif and strong,
   Neuar is suc non,
In al þis world brod and long,
   Imad of blod and bon.   150

---

[1] *This stanza assigned to* Regina *by Brandl.*   [2] *MS.* ne.
[3] *Skeat; Mills* bil . . ut.   [4] *MS.* kyntis.
[5] *Supplied by Holthausen (cf. 260).*   [6] *Manly; MS.* det rift.
[7] *Manly, based on Skeat* lok y.   [8] *Skeat; Brandl* ne.
[9] *MS.* þou.   [10] *MS.* schend.   [11] *MS.* ȝe.

Hau no dout of no þing
  þat euir may befal;
Ic am Streynt[1] þi derling
  Flour of knitis al.

SECUNDUS MILES, SANITAS. King of Lif, þat berist
  þe croun,   155
  As hit is skil and riȝte,
I am Hele icom to toun,
  þi kinde curteyse kniȝte.

þou art lord of lim and life,
  And king withouten ende;   160
Stif and strong and sterne in strif,
  In londe qwher þou wende.

þou nast no nede to sike sore
  For no thing on lyue;
þou schal lyue euermore: 165
  Qwho dar with þe striue?

REX. Striue? Nay, to me qwho is so gode?
  Hit were bot folye;
þer is no man þat me dur bode
  Any vileynye.   170

Qwherof schuld I drede
  Qwhen I am King of Life?
Ful evil schuld he spede
  To me þat wroȝt[2] striue.

I schal lyue evermo   175
  And croun ber as kinge;
I ne may neuer wit of wo,
  I lyue at my likinge.

REGINA. Sire, þou saist as þe liste,
  þou liuist at þi wille;   180
Bot somthing þou miste,
  And þerfor hold þe stille.

Thinke, þou haddist beginninge
  Qwhen þou were ibore;

---

[1] *MS.* strenyt.   [2] *Brandl* worth; *Waterhouse* werch.

And bot þou mak god endinge 185
þi sowle is forlore.

Loue God and Holy Chirche,
And haue of him som eye;
Fonde his werkis for to wirch
And thinke þat þou schal deye. 190

REX. Douce dam, qwhi seistou so?
þou spekis noȝt as þe sleye.
I schal lyue euermo
For boþe two þin eye.

Woldistou þat I were dede 195
þat þou miȝt haue a new?
Hore, þe deuil gird of þi hede
Bot þat worde schal þe rewe!

REGINA. Dede, sire? Nay, God wote my wil,
þat ne kepte I noȝte; 200
Hit wolde like me full ille
Were hit þareto broȝte.

⟨Ȝet⟩ þogh þou be kinge
Nede schalt haue ende;
Deth ouercomith al thinge 205
Hou-so-euer we wende.

REX. Ȝe, dam, þou hast wordis fale,
Hit comith þe of kinde;
þis nis bot women tale,
And þat I wol þe finde. 210

I ne schal neuer deye
For I am King of Life;
Deth is vndir myne eye
And þerfor leue þi strife.

þou dost bot mak myn hert sore, 215
For hit nel noȝt helpe;
I prey þe spek of him no more.
Qwhat wolte of him ȝelpe?

REGINA. Ȝilpe, sire? Ney, so mot I the;
    I sigge hit noȝt therfore,[1]   220
Bot kinde techith boþe þe and me,
    First qwhen we were bore,

For dowte of Dethis maistri,
    To wepe and make sorowe;
Holy writ and prophecye   225
    þerof I take to borowe.

þerfor, qwhile ȝe have miȝte
    And þe worlde at wille,
I rede ȝe serue God Almiȝte
    Boþe loude and stille.   230

þis world is bot fantasye
    And ful of trechurye;
Gode sire, for ȝoure curteysye
    Take þis for no folye.

For, God wot[2] þe soþe,   235
    I ne sey hit for no fabil;
Deth wol smyte to þe,
    In feith loke þou be stabil.

REX. Qwhat prechistou of Dethis miȝt
    And of his maistrye?   240
He ne durst onis with me fiȝt
    For his boþe eye.

Streinth and Hele, qwhat say ȝe,
    My kinde korin[3] kniȝtis?
Schal Deth be lord ouer me   245
    And reue me of miȝtis?

I MILES. Mi lord, so brouke I my bronde,
    God þat me forbede
þat Deth schold do þe wronge
    Qwhile I am in þi þede.[4]   250

---

[1] *Holthausen; MS.* qwher-.
[2] *Skeat* wol; *Brandl* wel; *Holthausen* [wot] wel.
[3] *Holthausen; MS.* kornin.   [4] *Holthausen; MS.* ȝede.

I wol withstonde him with strife
    And make his sidis blede,
And tel him þat þou art King of Life
    And lorde of londe and lede.

II MILES. May I him onis mete   255
    With þis longe launce,
In felde oþer in strete,
    I wol him ȝiue mischaunce.

REX. ȝe, þes be kniȝtis of curteisye
    And doghti men of dede;   260
Of Deth ne of his maistrie
    Ne have I no drede.

Qwher is Mirth my messager,
    Swifte so lefe on lynde?
He is a nobil bachelere   265
    þat rennis bi þe wynde.

Mirth and solas he can make
    And ren so þe ro;
Liȝtly lepe oure þe lake
    Qwher-so-euer he go.   270

Com and her my talente
    Anone and hy þe blyue:
Qwher any man, as þou hast wente,
    Dorst with me to striue?

NUNCIUS. King of Lif and lord of londe,   275
    As þou sittis on þi se
And florresschist with þi briȝt bronde,
    To þe I sit on kne.

I am Mirth, wel þou wost,
    þi mery messagere;   280
þat wostou wel, withoute bost
    þer nas neuer my pere

Doȝtely to done a dede
    þat ȝe haue for to done,
Hen to Berewik opon Twede   285
    And com oȝein ful sone;

þer is nothing þe iliche
 In al þis worlde wide;
Of gold and siluer and robis riche
 And hei hors on to ryde.   290

I haue ben boþe fer and nere
 In bataile and in strife;
Ocke þer was neuer þy pere,
 For þou art King of Life.

REX. Aha! Solas, now þou seist so, 295
 þou miriest me in my mode;
þou schal, boy, ar þou hennis go
 Be auaunsyd, bi þe rode.

þou schal haue for þi gode wil
 To þin auauncemente,   300
þe castel of Gailispire on þe Hil,
 And þe erldom of Kente.

Draw þe cord, Sire Streynth,
 Rest I wol now take;
On erth in brede ne leynth   305
 Ne was nere ȝet my make.

Et tunc clauso tentorio dicet Regina secrete nuncio:[1]

REGINA. Messager, I pray þe nowe
 For þi curteysye,
Go to þe bisschop, for þi prowe,
 And byd him hydir to hye.   310

Bid him be ware before,
 Sey him þat he most preche;
My lord þe King is ney lore
 Bot he wol be his leche.

Sey him þat he wol leue noȝt 315
 þat euer he schal deye;
He is in siche errour broȝte
 Of God stont him non eye.

----

[1] *MS. had this s.d. and the word* Regina *before the preceding stanza.*

NUNCIUS. Madam, I make no tariyng
    With softe wordis mo;   320
For I am Solas, I most singe
    Oueral qwher I go.   *Et cantat.*

Sire Bisschop, þou sittist on þi se
    With þi mitir on þi heuede;
My lady þe Qwen preyith þe   325
    Hit schold noȝt be bileuyd.

.   .   .   .

[EPISCOPUS.][1] þe[2] world is nou, so wo-lo-wo,
    In suc bal ibound
þat dred of God is al ago
    And treut is go to ground.   330

Med is mad a demisma[n],
    Streyint betit þe[3] lau;
Geyl is mad a cepman
    And truyt is don of dau.

Wyt is nou al trecri,   335
    Oþis fals and gret;
Lou is nou al lecuri[4]
    And corteysi is let.

Play is nou uileni,
    Cildrin bet onlerit,   340
Halliday is glotuni—
    þis lauis bet irerit.

Slet men bet[5] bleynd
    And lokit al amis;
He bicomit onkynd   345
    And þat is reut, iuis.

Frend may no man find
    Of fremit[6] ne of sib;
þe[2] ded bet out of mind,
    Gret soru it is to lib.   350

---

[1] *Supplied by Mills.*   [2] *MS.* ȝe.
[3] *MS.* bet it ȝe.   [4] *MS. transposes 337 and 339.*
[5] *MS.* blet.   [6] *Waterhouse alone* frouer.

þes ricmen bet reuþyles,
  þe[1] por got to ground,
And fals men bet schamles,[2]
  þe sot ic hau ifound.

It is wrong þe ric knyt[3]   355
  Al þat þe por dot;
Far þat is sen day and nit
  Wosa wol sig sot.

Paraventur men halt me a fol
  To sig þat sot[4] tal;   360
þai farit as ficis in a pol—
  þe[1] gret eteit þe[1] smal.

Ricmen spart for no þing
  To do þe[1] por wrong;[5]
þai þingit not on hir[6] ending   365
  Ne on Det þat is so strong.

Noþer þai louit God ne dredit
  Noþer him no his lauis;
Touart hel fast him spedit[7]
  Ayeins har ending-daus.   370

Bot God of his godnis
  Yif ham gras to amend,
Into þe[1] delful derknys[8]
  þe got wytout hend.

þer is dred and sorow   375
  And wo wytoutin wel;
No man may oþir borou
  Be þer neuir so fel.

þer ne fallit no[9] maynpris,
  Ne supersidias;   380
þay he[10] be kyng or iustis,
  He[1] passit not þe[1] pas.

[1] *MS.* ʒe.   [2] *MS.* schanles.   [3] *Brandl; MS.* ʒe ric kynyit it is wrong.
[4] *Waterhouse; Brandl reports MS.* fot.   [5] *MS.* worng.
[6] *Waterhouse; others report MS.* hen.   [7] *Brandl; MS.* draut.
[8] *MS.* derkyns.   [9] *Holthausen; MS.* ne.   [10] *Holthausen; MS.* þayt þe.

Lord, þat for his manhed
And also for his god,
þat for lou and not for dred
Deit oppon þe¹ rod,   385

Yif ou gras or lif to led
þat be ȝour soulis to bot;
God of Heuin for his godhed
Leu þat hit so mot.   Amen.   390

Tunc dicet regi:

Schir Kyng, þing oppon þin end
And hou þat þou schalt dey,
Wat uey þat þou schalt wend
Bot þou be bisey.

And² eke þat þou art lenust man,   395
And haddist begyning,
And euirmor hau þout opon
þi dredful ending.

þou schalt þing þanne—
And mac þe¹ euir yar³—   400
þat Det is not þe¹ man
For noþing þe¹ uil spar.

þou schalt⁴ do dedis of rit⁵
And lernen Cristis lor,
And lib in heuin-lit   405
To sauy þi soul fro⁶ sor.

Rex. Wat! bissop, byssop babler,
Schold y of Det hau dred?
þou art bot a chagler—
Go hom þi wey, I red.   410

Wat! com þou þerfor hidir
Wit⁷ Deþ⁸ me to afer?

---

¹ *MS.* ȝe.   ² *Waterhouse only.*
³ *Brandl; MS.* þyar.   ⁴ *MS.* scholt.
⁵ *Brandl; MS.* charite.   ⁶ *Skeat; others* fre.
⁷ *Mills; MS.* wet.   ⁸ *Holthausen; MS.* deþt.

þat[1] þou and he bot[2] togidir
　Into þe[3] se scot[4] uer.

Go[5] hom, God yif þe[3] sorow,　　　415
　þou ureist me in my mod.
War woltou prec tomorou?
　þou nost ner, bi þe[3] rod!

Troust þou I uold[6] be ded
　In mi ȝyng[7] lif?　　　420
þou lisst, screu, bolhed;
　Euil mot[8] þou t[h]riwe.

Wat schold I do at churg, wat?
　Schir bisop, wostou er?
Nay, churc nis no wyl cat,[9]　　　425
　Hit wol abid þer.

I wool let car away,
　And go on mi pleying.[10]
To hontyng and to o[þ]ir play
　For al þi long prechyng.　　　430

I am ȝyng,[11] as þou mit se,
　And hau no ned to char
þe wyle þe[3] Quen and ⟨mi me⟩iné
　About me bet yar.

EPISCOPUS. Thynk, Schir Kyng, one oþir trist—　　　435
　þat tyng misst son.
þot þou leu nou as þe[3] list,
　Det wol cum rit son,

And ȝiue þe dethis wounde
　For þin outrage;　　　440
Within a litil stounde
　þen artou but a page.

---

[1] *Holthausen; MS.* þit.　　　[2] *Holthausen; MS.* wer bot.
[3] *MS.* ȝe.　　　[4] *Brandl reports MS.* irot, *Waterhouse* igot.
[5] *MS.* I go.　　　[6] *Holthausen* wold; *Brandl, Waterhouse* nold.
[7] *MS.* þyng.　　　[8] *Brandl; Waterhouse* met.
[9] *Holthausen; MS.* cot; *Waterhouse* coot.
[10] *MS.* pelying; *Brandl* petying; *Holthausen* plesing.
[11] *Brandl; MS.* þyng (*cf.* 420); *Mills conj.* king.

Qwhen þou art grauen on grene,
  þer metis fleys[1] and molde,
þen helpith litil, I wene,   445
  þi gay croun of golde.

Sire Kyng, haue goday,
  Crist I ȝou beteche.
Rex. Fare wel, bisschop, þi way,
  And lerne bet to preche.   450

                                         Hic adde

Nou, mafay,[2] hit schal be sene,
  I trow, ȝit to-daye,
Qwher Deth me durst tene
  And mete in þe waye.

Qwher artou, my messagere,   455
  Solas bi þi name?
Loke þat þou go fer and nere,
  As þou wolt haue no blame,

My banis for to crye
  By dayis and bi niȝte;   460
And loke þat þou aspye,
  Ȝe, bi al þi miȝte,

Of Deth and of his maistrye
  Qwher he durst com in siȝte,
Oȝeynis me and my meyné   465
  With force and armis to fiȝte.

Loke þat þou go both est and west
  And com oȝeyne anone;[3]
Nuncius. Lorde, to wende I am prest,
  Lo, now I am gone.   470

                     Et eat pla⟨team.⟩

Pes and listenith to my sawe,
  Boþe ȝonge and olde;
As ȝe wol noȝt ben aslawe
  Be ȝe neuer so bolde.

---

[1] *Waterhouse; Mills and Brandl report MS.* þᵗ mete is ffeyt & moide.
[2] *MS.* maifay.   [3] *Waterhouse; Brandl reports MS.* on one.

I am a messager isente 475
  From þe King of Life;
þat ȝe schal fulfil his talente[1]
  On peyne of lym and lif.

His hestis to hold and his lawe
  Vche[2] a man on honde; 480
Lest ȝe be henge and todraw,
  Or kast in hard bonde.

Ȝe wittin[3] wel þat he is king
  And lord of al londis,
Kepere and maister of al thing 485
  Within se and sondis.

I am sente for to enquer
  Oboute ferre and nere,
Ȝif any man dar werre arere
  Aȝein suche a bachelere. 490

To wroþer hele he was ibore
  þat wold with him stryue;
Be him sikir he is ilore
  As here in þis lyue,

þegh hit wer þe[4] King of Deth 495
  And he so hardy were;
Bot he ne hath miȝt ne meth
  þe King of Lif to afere;

Be he so hardy or so wode
  In his londe to aryue, 500
He wol se his herte-blode
  And he with him stryue.

[1] *Mills; Waterhouse* entente.
[2] *Waterhouse alone* yche.
[3] *Waterhouse; Brandl reports* withiṇ.
[4] *Waterhouse omits.*

VIII

DUX MORAUD

I. Emperourys and kyngys be kende,
　　Erlys and barunnys bolde,
　　Bachelerys and knytys to mende,
　　Sueyerys and ȝemen to holde,
　　Knauys and pagys to sende,　　　　　　　　　5
　　So parfyt þat aryn to be solde,
　　I prey ȝow, lordyngys so hende,
　　　　No yangelyngys ȝe mak in þis folde
　　　　To-day;
　　　　　Als ȝe are louely in fas,　　　　　　10
　　　　　Set ȝow alle semly in plas,
　　　　　And I xal withoutyn falas
　　　　　　Schewe resounus here to ȝoure pay.

Welthys I welde at my wylle,
　　In word I am knowyn ful wyde,　　　　　　15
I aue hert and hynd vpon hille,
　　I am gay on grounde for to glyde;
Semly þer I syt vpon sille,
　　My wyf and my mené be my syde.
I [commaund]¹ ȝow tende me tylle,　　　　　　20
　　Or ellys I xal bate ȝowre pride
　　　　Wyt dynt,
　　　And þerfor I warne ȝow infere
　　　þat ȝe mak neyþer criyng ne bere.
　　　If ȝe do, withoutyn duere,　　　　　　25
　　　　Strokys at ȝow xal I mynt.

Duk Morawd I hot be name,
　　Korteyser lord may be none,
Wol fer þan rengnyt my fame,
　　To be comly korownyt from one.　　　　　　30

¹ *Supplied by Adams.*

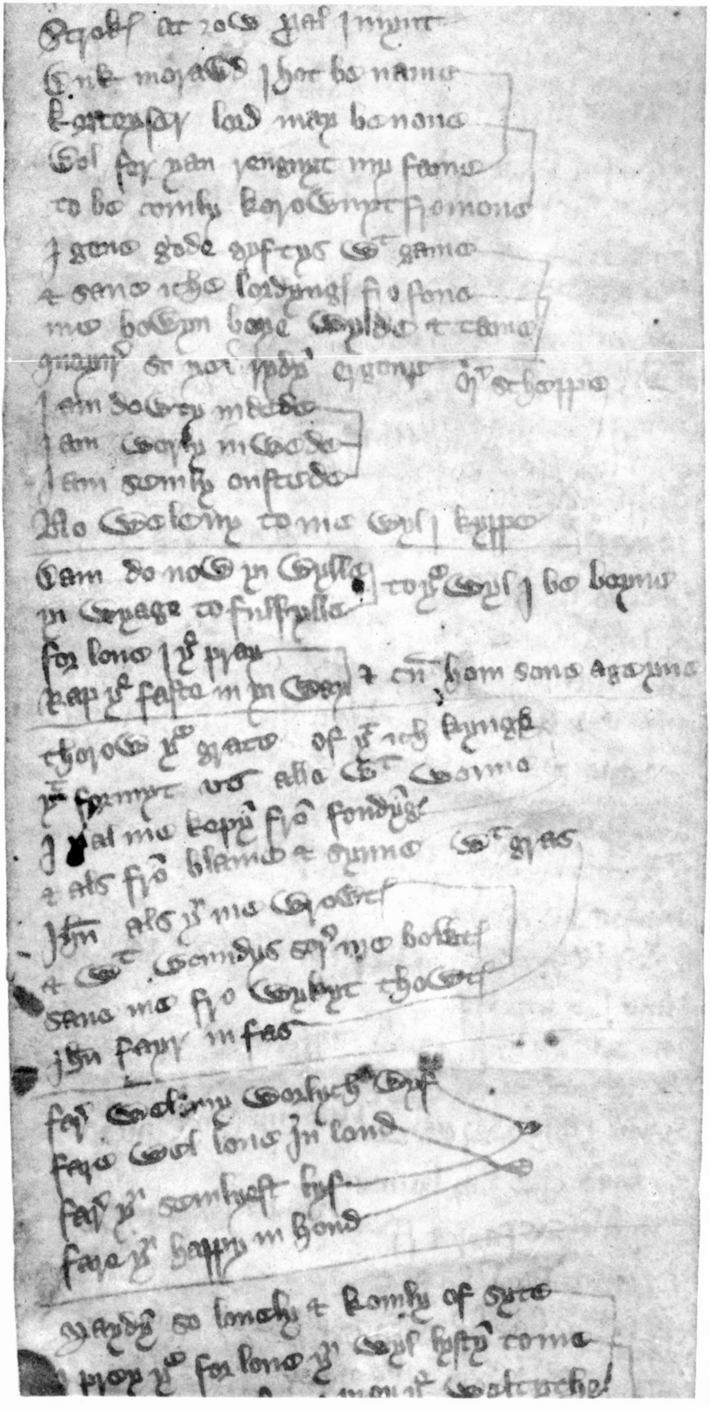

PLATE IV

Part of Bodleian MS. Eng. Poet. f. 2 (R)
(*Dux Moraud*, lines 26-61)

I geue gode gyftys with game
And saue iche lordyng[1] fro fone,
Me bowyn boþe wylde and tame,
Queþire so þei rydyn er gone
  Ore scheppe.   35
 I am dowty in dede,
 I am worly in wede,
 I am semly on stede,
  No weleny to me wyl I kyppe.

II. Dam, do now þi wylle   40
 þi wyage to fulfylle,
  To þe wyl I be beyne.
 For loue I þe pray:
 Rap þe faste in þi way,
  And cum hom sone ageyne.   45

III. Thorow þe grace of þat ich Kyngk
 þat formyt vs alle with wenne,
 I xal me kepyn from fondyng
 And als from blame and synne
  With gras.   50
 Jhesu, als þou me wrowtys
 And with woundys sore me bowtys,
 Saue me fro wykyt thowtys,
  Jhesu, fayr in fas!

IV. Fare wel, my worlych wyf,   55
 Fare wel, loue jn lond,
 Fare þou, semlyest lyf,
 Fare þou happy in hond!

V. Maydyn so louely and komly of syte,
 I prey þe for loue þou wyl lystyn to me; 60
 To here my resun I prey þe wel tythe,
 Loue so deryn me most schewe to þe;
 My loue to þi body is castyn so bryth,
 My wyl me most aue of þe.
 þou art louely to leykyn and brythest with ryth, 65
 I loue[2] þe in thowt, þou semly of ble,
  Be name.

---

[1] *Loop at end like -ys abbreviation.*   [2] *Heuser; MS.* leue.

~~þou maydyn þat moryst þi merthis with~~ myth,
Derne dedys me most do be day and be nyth
Be þe worþiest woundyn, wytthest wyt—   70
The soþe tale I telle withoutyn ony blame.

VI. My fere so graciouse in gras,
   Thanc þou xalt auen of me,
For þou art louely in fas
   And þerto bryth berende of ble.   75
Now wyl I makyn solas,
   For my deryn loue xalt þou be.
Kys me now par amour in plas,
   Als þou art worly to se
     In syte.   80
   Damysel, fayrest to fonde,
   Als þou art semly to stonde,
   Rap we vs to wendyn in honde
     To þi chambyr þat is so louely of lythe.

VII. A! I am wondyn in gret dolour,   85
   With danger and tene I am bownde.
To me þou geue tent par amowr,
   And lystne quat I sey þis stounde![1]
ȝon traytowr xal bewrey vs þis oure,
   I telle þe, semly on grownde;   90
þan xul we aue no socowr,
   But carys to vs xal be fownde,
     Iwys.
   I ne may neuer be fawe[2]
   Tyl yon traytowr be slaw   95
   þat is so rebel in sawe;
     Sorows mot ay to her kys.[3]

VIII. ⟨A⟩ues⟨to⟩w now slayne, be þi fay,
   þe fol þat dede vs þat tene?

IX. A! Now am I mery þis stound,   100
   þat che is browt to þat ded,
For che suld a wreyd vs on grownd,
   þat ilke old schrewed qued,

---

[1] *Roll originally cut and stitched under this line, now joined by cloth strip.*
[2] *So MS., though Heuser reports* before.   [3] *Heuser; MS.* herkys.

To sorowe che xuld vs a found—
   þat adde ben to vs an ewyl red; 105
In care forsoþe is che wownd,
   And þerfor I am mery to led
     And gay.
  ⟨D⟩amysel, lo⌐ue⌐ly[1] of chere,
  Mak we mery here, 110
  For care, withoutyn duere,
    Is went awey for ay.

X. A! Aue I begotyn þis stownd
   A schyld so louely of þe,
  I am in sorows wownd, 115
   For care me most fle.
  I prey þe in welth[2] now wownd,
   þat fot in syt myth I se.[3]

XI. Aa, ⟨byrd⟩[4] fayr and bryt,
   Do ⌐it⌐ out of my syt, 120
    For thowt I am ny sclawe!
  ⟨S⟩clo it in present—
  þat is my cowmaundement—
    Fast bry[n]g it of dawe!

For al þis lond I wold nowt 125
þat lordys of þis lond ad yt thowt,
   þat I ad synd be þe.
For serow and care þat we xuld drywe
We xuld led euer lyf ful rywe
    And þeron ay to be. 130

þerfor I prey þe,
For ⟨þi⟩ loue of me,
   Slo yt with þin hond!
þa⟨n⟩ xul we ben in pes,
Withoutyn ony lees, 135
   And auyn merth in lond.

XII. ⟨In es . . . al . . .⟩[5] syng
   þer I sytte louely in thowr,

---

[1] *Corr. from* (?) *lowely.*   [2] *Heuser; MS.* weltys.
[3] fot *and* syt *partly decayed, uncertain.*   [4] *Traces of all four letters visible.*
[5] *Much of the surface lost; traces suggest some such reading.*

I thang þe, louely þ[i]ng,
For þi w⟨e⟩rkyngys þis oure.   140
For þat parfyt tydyng
I geue þe allys and bowr,
For þou, withoutyn lesyng,
Pottyst me fro scham and dolowr.

XIII. In to kontré¹ I wyl wend,   145
þer to plete boþe fer and hend,
With god d⟨edys⟩ boun.
þer as it comyt in my mend
For to mete with lordys kynd
Boþe in fylde and toun.   150

XIV. Betyd me god⟨   ⟩,²   Verso.
Into contré ⟨   ⟩³
⟨   ⟩
But I prey þe þis oure,
My der ⟨   ⟩⁴ paramowre,   155
⟨   ⟩⁵
I xal no more þat ⟨   ⟩⁶
But sertys I xal fond
Withoutyn ⟨   ⟩⁷
⟨Ha god⟩day, worlych wyth!   160
Ha godday, louely in lyth!
Par⟨   ⟩⁸ semly in syth,
⟨   ⟩⁹ comly ⟨   ⟩.

XV. I am mythful and mery markyd¹⁰ in mynd,
I am flour fayrest be fryt for to fare,   165
I am fayrest in fas, ferly to fynd,
I am loueliche in lond, lyttest in lare,
I am comly and curteys and crafty of kynd,
I am comly castyn fro knottys of care,

---

¹ *MS.* konrte.
² *This and the next twelve lines almost illegible, the readings given uncertain.*
Heuser read here [or ille].
³ *Heuser* [fle I wylle].   ⁴ *Heuser* swet.
⁵ *Heuser* [Tak it to   ].   ⁶ *Heuser* no [onore stond].
⁷ *Heuser* [to com].   ⁸ *Heuser* þou xal [sittyn].
⁹ *Heuser* [So].   ¹⁰ *Heuser; MS.* mankyd.

I am lordly to leykyn lyt vndyr lynd,   170
  I am semly to syttun syttys so sare,
    I wyl pres me in pride!
Quan alle þe lordys of þis lond are gadered infere,
I am flour of hem alle withoutyn duere,
And ellys I were woxyn[1] of blamys ryt here   175
But I be ryal in rayis forto ryde.

XVI. A! now I here
A belle ryngant ful nere,
  ჳendyr in þe kyrk.
þeþer I wyl fare,   180
For I am in gret care
  þer sum god ded to werk.

XVII. A synful kaytyf I am,
Synfully I aue wrowt blam
  Be gret tyme of my lyfe.   185
Now, Cryst, ast þou me bowt;
Forgeue me þat blam þat I aue wrowt,[2]
  And mak me sumquat blyþe!

For in þis werd may be none,
þat euer tok lyf with flesch and bone,   190
  þat auyt so gret blam.
But I aue gras and help of þe,
I am lost fro þe so fre,
  In helle to be be nam.[3]

A prest now me most aue,   195
If [I] xal be saue
  Ageynus Cryst of myth,
To telle hym my blam
þat I aue wrowt be nam,
  þat is my thowt now tyth   200
    To-day!
Jhesu, heuene-flowr,
Pot me from dolour,
And geue me gras þis o[u]re
  A prest to auyn, I say!   205

[1] -n *lacks a minim.*   [2] *MS.* worwt.   [3] -m *partly lost.*

XVIII. A! Blyssyd be þou ay,
 þat þou com to-day
  To here my dedly syn!
 Quylys we are infere,
 I wyl schrywe me here,   210
  For now wil I begyn.

 I aue led my lyf
 In sorow and in stryf,
  With cursydnessys and care;
 ʒet is more in my th[o]wt,   215
 Synnus I aue wrowt
  Be my douter in lare.

 And chyld che bar be me,
 Quyk was fayr and fre
  Boþe in body and fas,   220
 And I myt neuer be fawe
 Tyl we had hym sclawe—
  I sey þe soþe cas!

 ʒet more I wyl telle now.
 My wyf þer che sclow   225
  Thowr egment of me.
 And þus is my lyf spend—
 Lord omnipotent,
  Grant me my synnus to fle.

XIX. I wyl blely, my leue frend,   230
 Do penawns boþe fer and hend,
  To saue my sowle fro wrat⟨h⟩.[1]

XX. Heyl douter, louely of syt.
 Heyl, louely leuende to-day,
 Cryst þat is mytty in myt   235
 Saue þe ermor and ay!

XXI. Lat be, my douter dere,
 Lat be, louely in lere,
 I aue forsakyn here
  My blam and my syn.   240

    [1] *At edge.*

My syn I aue forsake,
And to penawns I aue me take,
For þat wykkyd wrake
    Now is time to blyn.

And þerfor I prey þe,   245
Sertys with herte fre,
þat þou mak not[1] me
    To falle in nomor blam!
Now wyl I don away
My tresorys rych and gay,   250
And traueylyn I wyl ay
    For my wykyt fam.

XXII. Now my lyf wyl passe
    Fro me þis i⌈l⌉k stonde,
I am smetyn in þe fas   255
    With carful strokys and rownde.
Jhesu ful of gras
Forgeue ⌈þe⌉ þis trespas
    þat þou ast don to me,
And geue þe gras to blyn   260
Of þat wykyd syn
    Quylk þou ast don so fre.

My tyme comyt faste to
þat I xal pas ȝow fro,
    In oþir plas to duelle.   265
In manus tuas, domine!
Jhesu haue mercy on me,
    And saue my sowle fro helle.

[1] -t *apparently written over* w.

IX

THE CAMBRIDGE PROLOGUE

Oez, seygnur, oez, oez!
Escoutez tant cum wus poez![1]
Escutez ben, pur uostre honur,
Le ban de nostre enperrur.
Aset luy deuez grenur fey[2]   5
Ke nul autre, par ma ley.
Fetes place e tene'us coy,
E si entendet ben a moy.
S'il i a nul que noyse face,
V que entre en cet[e] place   10
Pur nostre iu ren desturber,
Prendre le frun saunz demorrer
E jucer ley[n]s en la prisun.
Ja quit n'ert pur nul ransun
Que el ne seyt mut haut[3] pendu,   15
V suuiaus nun mult ben batu.
Fey ke[4] io doy a mun seygnur,
C'est la ban l'enpereur;
E pus que c'est sun comandement,
Fet serra mut[5] ignelement.   20
Si m'ait Mahun, io n'ay regard
Que nul me turne de coard.[6]

[1] *Followed by* escoutez ben tant cum wus poe *struck out.*
[2] *First written* fay, *then a subpuncted and* e *written above.*
[3] *Interlined above* sayt *struck out.*   [4] *MS.* que ke.
[5] *MS. has a minim too few.*   [6] *MS.* de co coard.

Nu sittet stille and herkint[1] alle,
þat[2] hur no mis þing ev bifalle;
And sittet rume and wel[3] atwo[4]
þat men moȝt[5] among ev go.
þey þat beut igadert fale,   5
Ne makiet naȝt[6] to lude tale—
Hit uer ev bot muchel scame
For to lette hure game,
And ek I scuerie bi this day
And bi Mahun and bi his lay,   10
If ani his so hardi man
þat stille ber him ne can,
þ'amperur hat þat men awonge
And so uyt him men anhonge,
Bot hit bu child other vitles man[7]   15
þat nones mannes wit ne can.
And ȝet[8] he hat men sal him[9] binde
And hym bete and sore swenge.[10]
So ich mote heuer Mahun soe,
Als ich sege eu[11] so it sal bu.   20
Ȝet[12] tes lordes pays ich grede;
Nu sittet stille, bi mine rede! Amen.

---

[1] *Accent on the first minim.*
[2] *Here and elsewhere* þ *usually represented by z.*
[3] *Followed by* athuoe *struck out.*   [4] *MS.* atwe.
[5] *MS.* moþt.   [6] *MS.* naþt.   [7] *MS.* mam.
[8] *MS.* zet.   [9] *MS.* zu.   [10] *MS.* sowenge
[11] *MS.* ue *and a minim, written at an angle, evidently inserted later.*
[12] *MS.* þet.

X

THE RICKINGHALL
(BURY ST. EDMUNDS) FRAGMENT

Assit principio Sancta Maria meo. Coruum perfidie da[m]pnant
animalia queque.

Ore escotez, seignurs cheris,
Cuntis e barouns e chiualeris,
   E tus qui sunt en cour.
Ben le sauez pur verité
Ke ieo su rey coronné   5
   E vostre couernour.

Pur ceo ieo voil ke moun barnage,
Tretus ke sunt de grant parage,
   Ke i veniunt a moy;
Kar ieo voil ou eus parler   10
E ma resoun demonstrer
   Saun acun delay.

Tunc dicet nuncio:
Venet sa, moun messager,
Vous dirray, pur turney
I vous couent tout aler.   15

Lordinges

   wytouten lesinge,
Ye weten wel þat I am kinge   5
 Her of al þis lond.

þerfore I wile þat min barnage,
Ye þat ben of gret parage,
 þat he comin to min wil;
For al þat arn in burw or toun   10
I wile he witen mi resoun,
 And þat is richt and schil.

XI

THE DURHAM PROLOGUE

Pes, lordyngs, I prai ȝow pes,
And of ȝour noys ȝe stynt and ses,
Oure gamen to lett ne cry in pres
    For ȝour courtasy.
þat we ȝow play it is no les,   5
    Godmen, sikirly.

Oure myrth we make of a knyght
þat in his tyme was bold and wyght,
Rich of rent, man mekill of myght,
    Proper and aupert.   10
Swilk hap gan fall þat on him light
    þat put him to pouert.

þan he sight full wondre sore,
þat so rich had ben before,
And had nothyng to leue on more;   15
    His hert was full of grefe.
þe fende apierd vntill him þor[1]
    As man at his myschiefe.

He saide, 'Man, lat be þi drede,
þou leue on me and my lede   20
And þou sall haue all þat þe nede
    Vntill þi lyues ende.'
Bot sikirly, als we cone rede,
    Of Mary milde þan was his mende.

Mary had of him pité,   25
And till hir son scho knelid on kne,
Sayd, 'Son, ȝon body gif me.
    I chalange be right.'
þus fro þe fendes pousté
    Boured scho þe knyght.   30

[1] *MS. þer.*

Me nedis ʒow no more to tell
O þis thing how it befell;[1]
Bot ʒe sall her, and ʒe will dwell,
   How þat it sall be plaied.
He kep ʒow all þat herid hell,   35
   And sithen vp staied.[2]

---

[1] *This line written after 33, but correct order indicated by marginal* a *and* b *opposite 31 and 32.*   [2] *MS.* staithed.

XII

THE ASHMOLE FRAGMENT

SECUNDUS MILES.

Sure emperoure, dred ye no thynge!
Yff there be any fresche[1] gedling
That wold yow greue with any thyng,
    In word or in dede,
By þe berd I schall hym schake,   5
That ys skulle schall al tocrake,
And hys sawle from hym tak,
    And rost hym ouer[2] a glede.

To the[3] hye prest:[4]
O Mahound, þou grete god and tru,
Lowuely and also meke of hew,   10
Offur to þe I wyll newe
    A daggar þat ys gud and fyne.

[1] *MS.* ffrensche.   [2] *Above line over* on *apparently not cancelled.*
[3] *Followed by* y *struck out.*   [4] *Robbins; MS.* trenite.

XIII

THE REYNES EXTRACTS

A. A SPEECH OF 'DELIGHT'

Lo, here is a ladde lyght,   f. 43ᵛ
Al fresch I ʒou plyght,
   Galant and joly.
Wyl ʒe knowe what I hyght?
My name, serys, is Delyght.   5
   [I hope not ful holy.]

Holy, quod sche? Nay, let be!
Be Crist, it acordyth not with me,
   But sporte, myrthe, and play
Me reioyceth for to see;   10
þe worldys wunderys and vanyté,
   Therinne delyght I ay.

For me semet it is to delyght
To behelde þe firmament lyght,
   The cours of sterrys to kenne,   15
The sunne with his bemys bryght,
þe mone how he refulsyth[1] þe nyght,
   The planetys in her circumferens renne.

The skyes in her coloures rake,
þe therke sladdes of clowdes blake—   20
   This reioyceth me above.
Than of the erthe delyght I take
To see the florent[2] wodys þer leves shake,
   The ryverys rennyng by þerinne dyuers fysshes move.

I se these hey hyllys wher is the holsom ayer;   25
Benethe, the redolent medowes with ther flowres fayer,
   þe therke mystes how it ascendys.

---

[1] r- *written over incomplete* f.
[2] *Loop at end like* -ys *abbreviation.*

In the valeys of the cornys ylke ayer
I se dyuers fowlys to þe wodes repayer—
þer swetly syngang me mekyl amendys.   30

I se in these gay gardeynes wher holsum erbys spryng
þese pererys, þe pomerys, þe venys þat swete frutys bryng,[1]
The reed rosys and the lelyes whyte.
I se in þe gret see ther shyppys euer seylyng,
Also how it ebbyt and flowit and fysshes þerin swymmyng,   35
The whawys how they waltyr, and se the qwall fyght.

In þe hore hethys I se the hare sterte,   f. 44ʳ
The forant dere huntyd, the bukke and the harte,
And the swyfte grefoundes renne;
The foxe huntyd with howndes in þe gret couerte,   40
The swyfte flyght of hawkes, þe fowlys reuerte,
The fawkonerys rennyng throw thykke and throwe thynne.

Also I am gretly delyghtand
In fayer courses swyftly renand,
In harneys gledryng bryght;   45
Stately howsys beheldand
Glased with storys glasand,
Pynnakelys ful of fanys gloriously dyght.

Precyos aray, that plesyth me gretly,
The swet musy[ci]auns in dyuers melody,   50
The cumlynesse of iche creature;
And þe bewté of women specyaly,
With ther whyte pappys poppyd vp prately—
þat passeth al other, as me semet in sure.

Me seyng now these solacious sythys,   55
Therfor in hem al my delyght is
So souereynlyche abouen alle.
This warlde so preciously pyght is,
þerinne delyght I with alle myn mythis,
As for wele most speciall.   60

[1] *Loop at end like -ys abbreviation.*

B. AN EPILOGUE

Now, wursheppful souereyns þat syttyn here in syth,
  Lordys and ladyes and frankelens in fay,
With alle maner of abesyans we recomaunde vs ryght
  Plesantly to ʒour persones that present ben in play;
  And for ʒour soferyng sylens that ʒe han kept þis day   5
    In pleyng of oure play withowte ony resystens
  Derely we thank ʒow with myght as we may,
    And for ʒour laudabyl lystenyng in good audiens
· That we haue had this day.
      And if we haue passyd ony poynt in oure pleyng,   10
      Or moved ony materys in oure seyng
      That schuld be to ʒoure personys displesyng,
  We beseche ʒou reporte it not away.

For trewly oure entent was wel to do,
  And if ony fawte be þer fowndyn it is oure neglygensy;   15
And short tyme avysement causet also,
  For lytell tyme of lernyng we haue had sekerly,
  And euery man is not expert in eloquensy
    To vtteryn his mater gayly onto ʒour audiens.
  Wherfor we beseche ʒou of ʒoure gret gentry   20
    The best to reporte of vs in oure absens
      In euery ilke a place.
    Souereyns alle insame,
    ʒe that arn come to sen oure game,
    We pray ʒou alle in Goddys name   25
      To drynke ar ʒe pas;[1]

For an ale is here ordeyned be a comely assent
  For alle maner of people þat apperyn here þis day,
Vnto holy chirche to ben incressement
  Alle that excedith þe costys of our play.   30

---

[1] *Botched, apparently corr. from* pl.

APPENDIX

NOTES ON THE MUSIC IN THE SHREWSBURY LITURGICAL PLAYS

by FRANK LL. HARRISON

MUSIC is provided for words sung by two or three characters. With the possible exception of the words at the beginning of the *Officium Nativitatis* (*Pastorum*), words written in the manuscript in red are sung by the character whose part this is, though the music is not given. The possible exception is the quotation from St. Luke's account of the nativity, which may have been sung to the Gospel tone:[1]

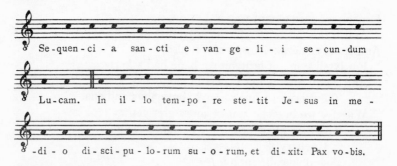

Se - quen - ci - a san - cti e - van - ge - li - i se - cun - dum

Lu - cam. In il - lo tem - po - re ste - tit Je - sus in me -

-di - o di - sci - pu - lo - rum su - o - rum, et di - xit: Pax vo - bis.

To judge from the music for *Transeamus usque Bethelem . . . nobis*, the three opening words are sung in free rhythm by the shepherd whose part this is. All three shepherds then sing the remainder. The music is related to the plainsong for the same words in Rouen.[2] The music of the first three words corresponds quite closely, while the rest of the Shrewsbury music is a measured paraphrase of a hypothetical plainsong model similar to the Rouen plainsong. It differs most at the three cadence points at the words *verbum*, *Dominus*, and *nobis*. Each cadence is made by a rise of one tone, which is something of a thematic motif in the melody as a whole.

Young pointed out that *Salvatorem Christum Dominum* on folio 42ᵛ should be inserted at the asterisk on f. 38ᵛ, and this has been done in the

[1] W. H. Frere, *The Use of Sarum*, i (Cambridge, 1898), 266–7.
[2] H. Loriquet, *Le Graduel de l'église cathédrale de Rouen au xiiie siècle*, facsimile (Rouen, 1907), f. 12.

present edition. This text is also in Rouen; the Shrewsbury music is related to the Rouen plainsong in the same way as that of *Transeamus*, though the correspondence is less close. It is not possible to say with any certainty what the other shepherds sang in these two pieces. There are three possibilities: (1) that the surviving music was sung in unison by all three; (2) that it is the middle part of a three-part polyphonic piece; or (3) that it is the middle part of a piece in faburden, beginning:

The last possibility is more convincing for the first piece than for the second. The two pieces were not necessarily treated in the same way, though it is likely that they were.

In the *Officium Resurrectionis* the Latin lines written in red were sung alone by Mary Magdalene, whose part this is, either in plainsong or in measured monophony. *Heu redemcio . . . sustinuit* has music elsewhere; this is the Fleury chant:

The second text in red, *Heu cur ligno . . . latus*, does not seem to occur in the other plays of the Resurrection. The third, *Surrexit Christus*, is a verse from the sequence *Victime paschali laudes*, which was sung in dialogue at this point in the play. In the sequence it has this music:

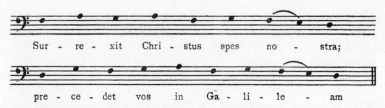

Sur - re - xit Chri - stus spes no - stra;

pre - ce - det vos in Ga - li - le - am

The two pieces for which music is provided are sung by the three Marys. They are not apt for faburden, but are most likely either measured monophonies or the highest parts of three-part pieces. The setting of *Jam, jam ecce* may possibly have had as its middle (and perhaps occasionally lowest) part a form of the plainsong melody for these words in the Dublin processional:

Jam, jam ec - ce jam pro - pe - re - mus ad tu - mu - lum

un - guen - tes di - le - cti cor - pus san - ctis - si - mum.

The Fleury melody for these words is quite different.[1] The setting of *O Deus, quis revolvet* may be an ornamented paraphrase of the Rouen plainsong, which does not, however, have the first two words:

Quis re - vol - vet no - bis la - pi - dem

ab ho - sti - o mo - nu - men - ti?

Of the five pieces for which music is given in the *Officium Peregrinorum*, the first three are sung by the two disciples, Luke and (probably) Cleophas. Like those in the other plays they may be monophonic, or more likely the upper parts of two-part pieces. That they are upper and not lower parts is certain from their final cadences. *Mane nobiscum* is in Fleury as part of a longer piece; the music there has no apparent connection with this setting.

[1] C. E. H. de Courremaker, *Drames liturgiques au moyen âge* (Paris, 1861), p. 187.

The Latin speech, written here in red, has music in Fleury.[1]

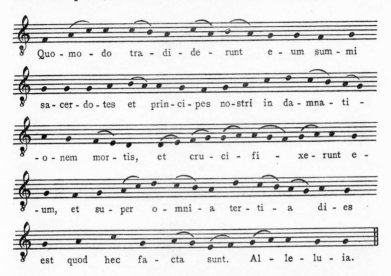

Quo - mo - do tra - di - de - runt e - um sum - mi sa - cer - do - tes et prin - ci - pes no - stri in da - mna - ti - o - nem mor - tis, et cru - ci - fi - xe - runt e - um, et su - per o - mni - a ter - ti - a di - es est quod hec fa - cta sunt. Al - le - lu - ia.

The other Latin speech of this disciple, *Dixerunt eciam*, does not occur with music in the other usual versions. The two final pieces are sung by all three characters, presumably including Jesus. *Gloria tibi Domine* is the doxology verse of office hymns from Easter to the Ascension. The music here has no clear connection with that of any of the hymns of this season, though it may possibly be an elaboration of the faburden of the Compline hymn *Jesu Salvator seculi*.[2] The last piece, *Frater Thoma*, does not seem to occur elsewhere.

Apart from the short *Propheta* play in the Palm Sunday procession, of which I have given an account with transcriptions of the two musical pieces,[3] the Shrewsbury music appears to be the only music which has survived for liturgical plays in the British Isles.

[1] Ibid., p. 196, as part of *De Jesu Nazareno*, sung by both disciples.
[2] See my article 'Faburden in Practice', *Musica Disciplina*, xvi (1962), 11.
[3] In *Annales musicologiques*, vi (1957), 124–8.

SHREWSBURY MUSIC

Trans-e-a-mus us-que Be-the-lem, et vi-de-a - mus hoc ver - bum quod fa - ctum est, quod fe - cit Do - mi - nus et o - sten - dit no - - bis.

Jam, jam, ec-ce jam pro-pe-re-mus ad tu-mu-lum, un-guen-tes di - - le - cti cor-pus san - - ctis - si - - - - mum.

O De - - - us! Quis re - vol - - vet no - bis la - pi - dem ab ho - sti - o mo - nu- men - ti?

Sal - va - to - rem, Chri - stum Do - - mi - num, in - fan - tem pan - nis in - vo - lu - tum se - cun - dum ser - mo - nem an - ge - li - - - - cum.

In - fi - de - lis
in - cur - sum
po - pu - li
Fu - gi - a - mus,
Jhe - su di - sci - pu -
- li! Su - spen - de -
- runt Jhe - sum
pa - - - - ti - bu -
- - - lo; Nul - -
- li par - cent e -
- - ius di - sci - -
- - pu - - - lo.

Ma - ne no - bis - cum, quo - ni - am ad - ve - sper - a - scit, et in - cli - na - ta est jam di - es, Al - le - lu - - - - - ya.

Quid a - ga - mus, vel di - ca - mus. I - gno - ran - tes quo e - a - mus, Qui do - cto - rem sci - en - ci - e Et pa - trem con - so - la - ci - o - nis A - mi - si - - mus?

Glo - ri - a ti - bi, Do - mi - ne, Qui sur - re - xi - sti a mor - tu - is, Cum Pa - tre et San - - cto Spi - ri - tu In sem - pi - ter - - na se - cu - la. A - - - - men.

Fra - - - ter
Tho - ma, cau -
- sa tri - - - sti -
- ci - e No - - - -
- - - - - bis
tu - lit sum - - - -
- - - - ma
le - ti - ci - e.

GLOSSARY

The glossary is intended to explain only words and senses now unfamiliar. Senses current today are therefore not usually recorded except as a background to special uses, but a few unusual spellings of commonplace words are included because they might check a modern reader. In addition, inflexional forms of possible interest are given, and set phrases in which some common words appear are collected; see for example *do(o)*, *hau(e)*, *mak(e)*.

In the arrangement, ȝ follows g, but þ is treated as *th*; vocalic *y* is treated as *i*, consonantal *y* has its usual place; consonantal *i* is treated as *j*; *u* and *v* are separated according to function. The sign ∼ stands for the headword in any of its forms.

References are selective, not a complete record. The numbers refer to the number of the text and its line; 's.d.' means the stage direction following the line-number given. The subdivisions of the text of the Norwich Grocers' Play—Text A, and the First Prologue, Alternative Prologue, and Text of Text B—are for brevity referred to as 2a, b, c, d. Emended forms are marked by asterisks.

a see **haue, ho.**
abesyans see **obesaunce.**
abid(e), abyde v. endure 2d/37, 66; continue 4/357, 6/124; delay 6/366; stay 7/426. **abode** *pp.* remained 2d/144.
aboȝt *pp.* paid for 7/95. Cf. **by.**
aborreþ *pr. 3 sg.* abhors, dreads 4/242.
about *adv.* in *goes* ∼ is busy with 3/126; **oboute** about, around 7/488.
abouen *prep.* above 13a/57.
abow v. submit 7/126.
achatys n. *pl.* agates *6/167.
acord n. acquiescence 5/66.
acordyth *pr. 3 sg.* agrees: ∼ *with* suits 13a/8.
adde see **haue.**
adjutory n. helper 2a/7.
adred *adj.* afraid 5/292, 411.
afer(e) v. frighten 7/412, 498. **aferd** *pp. adj.* afraid 5/79, 6/676.
afeze v. strike 6/472.
affectes n. *pl.* passions 2d/135.
afore *prep.* in front (of) 4/151.

afray n. fear *5/233.
af(f)ter, aftir *prep.* according to 3/119, 5/85, 6/134; dependent on 4/180; about 6/242; *sent* ∼ sent for 7/67.
agayn *adv.* back 1c/8, 6/333; **ageyne** 4/351, 8/45; **agen(e)** 6/235, 505 (MS.). Cf. **aȝeyn.**
agast(e) *adj.* afraid 2d/50, 4/226, 5/382, 6/688; *I am nothyng* ∼ *but þat* I do not doubt that 6/227.
ageyn *prep.* against 6/136; **agen** 6/155, 156. **ageynus** towards, in the sight of 8/197.
ago *pp.* gone, departed 7/329.
agrevyd *pp.* offended, angry 5/314.
agryse *pr. 1 sg.* feel horror 6/904.
aȝeyn *adv.* again 5/48; **aȝen** 5/237; **ayeyn(e)** 4/10; back, in return 4/291; **oȝein(e)** back 7/286, 468. Cf. **agayn.**
aȝens *prep.* against 5/190, 406, 6/978; in return for 6/789; **oȝeynis** 7/465; **ayeins** approaching, before 7/370.

aȝte see owe.

ay *adv.* always 1c/60, 8/97, 251; *for* ∼ for ever 8/112.

ayer *n.* air 13a/25; *ylke* ∼ (?) everywhere 13a/28.

ayleth *pr. 3 sg.* troubles, is the matter with *6/557.

ayns see onis.

al(1) *adj.* every 4/1, 23, 5/47; hal all 7/1; ∼ *and sum(me)* one and all 6/402, 838; ∼ *thing(e)* everything 4/51, 93, 7/205, 485.

al(1) *adv.* altogether, completely 7/131; ∼ *if* even though 1a/40; see for; hal thoroughly 7/70.

ale *n.* ale-party 13b/27.

alend *v.* arrive, come *7/50.

alyng *adv.* in every way, altogether 7/134.

alkin *adj.* every kind of 3/29.

al(1)myght, -miȝte *adj.* almighty 6/292, 354, 998, 7/229.

allys *n. pl.* halls 8/142.

allwey *adv.* always 5/134.

alonly *adv.* alone, only 5/235.

alowed *pa. t.* commended, was pleased with 4/341.

als *adv.* also 6/215, 8/49.

als *conj.* as 8/10, 82, 11/23.

amang see among.

amatystis *n. pl.* amethysts 6/161.

amend *v.* remedy 5/459; improve 6/371. amendys *pr. 3 sg.* cheers 13a/30. amend *imp.* relieve, assuage 1c/43; change (for the better): ∼ *thy mood* be happier 5/325.

amende *n.* amends, restitution 6/293. amendys *pl.* 6/745.

amis *adv.* badly 7/344.

among *prep.* (postponed) among, between 1b/32; amang 1c/10; emonge 2d/63.

and *conj.* if 3/119, 4/102, 180, 211, 6/9, 219, 299, 11/33.

anhonge *pr. subj.* hang 9/14.

anoyment *n.* trouble, pain *6/583 (emendation seems required by sense, but MS. anoyntment perhaps possible in meaning 'extreme unction').

anon(e) *adv.* at once, quickly 4/131, 5/55, 6/651, 7/272, 468.

another *pron.* something else 6/409; anodre another 4/10.

apeche *v.* accuse 6/302.

apert *adj.* open: *in* ∼ openly 1c/70; aupert accomplished 11/10.

apparellyd *pp.* prepared, arranged 2b/4.

appyred *pa. t. sg.* appeared 6/47.

applyed (onto) *pp.* complied (with) 6/827.

apryce *n.* value, excellence 6/185.

ar see or.

aray(e) *n.* state, condition 1c/16, 6/90; state of things, circumstance 4/193; series of events, happening 4/366; display 6/318, 419; furnishings or clothing 13a/49.

aray(e) *imp.* adorn, decorate 6/259; *refl.* get ready 4/100.

ar(e) see be.

arere *v.* raise, instigate 7/489.

aryght *adv.* properly 6/514, 539; indeed, assuredly 6/12.

aryn, arn see be.

aryue *v.* come to land 7/500.

as *adv.* pleonastic with adv., ∼ *here* 7/494.

as(s)ay(e) *v.* attack 1b/19; test 4/31, 276; try 6/226.

askyng *n.* demand 6/313.

aslake *v.* grow weaker 2d/96.

aslawe *pp.* killed 7/473. Cf. sle.

aspye *v.* see 2a/33, 6/300, 562. *pr. subj.* find out 7/461. aspyed *pp.* perceived 4/156.

assent *n.* agreement 13b/27.

at *prep. introd. infin.* to 1b/29.

atour *prep.* over 3/143.

attayned *pp.* reconciled 2d/150.

attayntyd *pp.* condemned 6/395.

atteyn *v.* achieve; almost pleonastic in *I wyll* ∼ *to wourshyppe* I will indeed worship 6/134.

attempt *v.* tempt 2d/38.

attonys *adv.* at once 6/163.

attrueaunce *n.* instruction; *to* ∼ at your command 6/128.

atwo *adv.* separately *9/3.

audiens *n.* hearing 13b/19.

aupert see apert.

auter, awtere *n.* altar 4/168, 270.

avayle *v.* do good 6/678.

avance, awance *v.* help 6/737. *imp.* put forward 6/679. auaunsyd *pp.* promoted 7/298.

auauncemente *n.* promotion 7/300.
aue(n), auestow, etc., see **haue.**
avysement *n.* consideration 6/874
(see **take**); planning, preparation
13b/16.
avoee *v.* declare 5/432; awooe 5/452.
awoyd *v. tr.* remove, get rid of 6/500.
avoyde *intr. imp.* go away 6/650.
awonge *pr. subj.* seize 9/13. Cf. **fang.**
awakith *pr. 3 sg.* arises 7/94.
awe *n.* fear, respect 1c/28, 6/443.
awrong *adv.* wrong, out of order
6/546.
axs *n. pl.* pains 6/613.
ayeyn(e), ayeins see a3eyn, a3ens.

bachelere *n.* young knight 7/265, 490.
bachelerys *pl.* 8/3.
baynes *n. pl.* bones 3/152.
bal(e) *n.* sorrow, pain 1b/13, 7/32, 58,
328. balys *pl.* disasters, evils 6/515.
baldli *adv.* assuredly 7/127.
banis *n. pl.* banns, proclamation
7/459.
baptyme *n.* baptism 6/954.
bar see **ber.**
bargen, bargeny *n.* bargain 6/273,
275.
baryllys *n. pl.* beryls 6/162.
barn *n.* child 1a/19, 5/106.
barnage *n.* baronage, barons 10/7.
bate *v.* subdue, reduce 8/21.
be *v.* be 1a/4; ben(e) 6/76, 8/134; bu
9/20. artou *pr. 2 sg.* with suffixed
pron. 7/442, 455. ar(e) *pl.* 2a/87,
2d/65, 6/657, 720, 8/10; aryn 8/6;
arn 6/386, 10/10, 13b/24; be(e) 2b/5,
5/462, 6/5, 996; ben(e) 4/2, 6/839,
10/8; bet(h) 7/3, 5; beith 7/115; beut
9/5. bu *subj.* 9/15. beth *imp. pl.* 6/67,
7/9; beith 7/109. be *pp.* 5/193, 6/109;
ben(e) 1b/40, 4/44; byn 5/71.
be, by *prep.* about, concerning 5/404;
beside (postponed) 5/390; with 4/208,
8/70, 127, (along) with 7/266; from
(postponed) 5/45; during, for (of
time) 8/185; according to 9/22; ~
þis by now 6/550; see **nam.** *conj.* by
the time that, when 3/134; ~ *that*
3/24.
beat *v.* strike (a bargain) 6/852.
bedene see **bydene.**
bedyng see **byddyng.**

befal(le) *v.* happen 7/152; befall,
come to: *fayre most you* ~ may good
fortune be yours 4/322. *pr. subj.*
6/654, 9/2. befel(l) *pa. t. sg.* happened
7/85, 11/32.
beforn *prep.* (postponed) before 1b/44.
beforne *adv.* before *5/461.
began *pa. t. sg.* as *auxil.* did 6/852.
begune *pl.* 6/32. Cf. **gin.**
begyle *v.* deceive 2d/80.
behelde *v.* look at, contemplate 13a/14.
beheldand *pr. p.* 13a/46.
behynde *adv.* behind; *left* ~
neglected, left undone 4/349.
behofe *n.* advantage, benefit, good
2a/57; behou 7/134.
bey see **by.**
beyne *adj.* compliant, obedient 8/42.
beleve *n.* belief, credence 6/206; see
fale.
benedycite *n.* blessing 6/900.
bent *pp. adj.* intent, determined
6/218.
ber *v.* wear 7/176; *refl.* behave 9/12.
bar *pa. t. sg.* bore (child) 8/218. bore
pp. 7/222.
bere *n.* noise, clamour 8/24.
berende *pr. p. adj.* possessing; *bryth*
~ *of ble* endowed with a fair complexion 8/75.
berryng *n.* barring, exclusion; *wyth-*
owtyn ony ~ without doubt 5/439.
best *adj. sup.* best; *to þe* ~ in the
best way 6/127.
bestad *pp.* placed: *hard* ~ hard
pressed, in difficulties 5/458.
bet *adv. comp.* better 7/450.
beteche *pr. 1 sg.* entrust, commend
7/448.
betyd(e) *v.* happen 1b/17. *pr. subj.*
befall 8/151. *pa. t.* 6/36.
betymes *adv.* early 6/321.
betwen *prep.* (postponed) between
1c/27 (see **take**).
betwix *prep.* between 4/350.
beut see **be.**
bewar *v.* take care 7/49, 52.
bewrey *v.* inform against, betray
8/89. Cf. **wreyd.**
bewschere *n.* (in address) fair sir
(= *beau sire*) *3/114.
by *v.* buy 6/88; redeem 1b/4, 4/210;
bey buy 6/*30, 225. bowght *pa. t.*

paid for 6/418; **bowt** 6/721. **bowtys**
2 *sg.* didst redeem 8/52. **bowght** *pp.*
6/4; **bowt** 8/186.
by see **be**.
by(e) and bye *adv.* at once 2a/34,
2c/14.
bycomin *pp.* descended 7/22.
bid *pr. 3 sg.* commands 7/49; **bit**
*7/52. *subj.* 4/347. **bad** *pa. t.* 4/240,
6/947, 7/72.
byddyng *n.* bidding, what someone
commands 5/203; **bedyng** 5/119.
bide *v.* endure 1b/13; stay 3/137. Cf.
abid(e).
bydene, bedene *adv.* at once 1c/29,
6/882; (tag) indeed 6/986.
byggly *adv.* strongly, firmly 6/218.
byld *pp.* created, made 6/217.
byle *v.* boil 6/672 s.d.
bilent *pp.* arrived: *wyt me* ～ come to
me 7/133.
bileuyd *pp.* omitted, neglected 7/326.
byn see **be**.
binde *v.* tie up 9/17. **ibound** *pp.*
fettered 7/328.
byrd *n.* lady *8/119.
bisey *pp.* of **bise(n)**, in passive *be* ～
look to yourself, take care 7/394.
bytterly *adv.* painfully 6/721.
biwent *pp.* become 7/131; see **wel(e)**.
blam(e) *n.* fault, dishonesty 6/256;
wrong, sin 8/184, 187; reproach
6/955, 8/191. **blamys** *pl.* in *of* ～ to
blame, blameworthy 8/175.
ble *n.* colour 6/162; complexion 8/66,
75.
bled *n.* scion, creature 7/44.
bleyke *v.* cause to turn pale, terrify
6/477.
blely *adv.* gladly 8/230.
bleryd *pp. adj.* inflamed 6/615.
blyn *v.* cease, end 8/244; ～ *of* cease
from 8/260. **blin** *pr. pl.* *3/91.
blisful *adj.* happy, blessed 1a/30;
beautiful 7/44.
blysse *v.* bless 2a/14, 5/213, 6/952.
blys(s)ed, blyssyd *pp.* 6/8, 41,
5/207, 8/206; **blyste** 2b/22.
blyþe, blythe *adj.* happy, content
5/316, 8/188.
blyve *adv.* at once 4/59, 283, 7/272.
blod *n.* blood: *imad of* ～ *and bon*
created 7/150.

board *n.* timber, planking 3/20.
bode *v.* threaten 7/169.
body *n.* body; person 11/27; ～ *and*
bonys entirely 5/271.
boy(e) *n.* servant 7/297; knave, rogue
6/573.
bold *adj.* confident, assured 3/193.
boldyro *n.* some bodily organ 6/614.
bolhed *n.* 'bull-head', (?) stubborn
fool 7/421.
bon see **boun**.
bonde *n.* fetters, chains 7/482.
boon *n.* prayer 6/560.
bore see **ber**.
borou *v.* rescue, redeem 7/377.
boured *pa. t.* 11/30.
borowe *n.* surety, guarantee 7/226;
see **take**.
bost *n.* boasting 7/281.
bot *n.* help, protector 7/127; *to* ～ for
the good of 7/388.
bot *adv.* both 9/7.
bot see **but**.
botherys *pron. gen.* of both: *ȝowrys*
～ of both of you 5/392.
boun *adj.* ready, prepared 6/269,
8/147; **bon** in *redy* ～ quite ready
5/131.
boun *adv.* readily, quickly 7/32.
boure, bowr(e) *n.* dwelling 1a/30;
bedroom, in *halle and* ～ house,
home 6/380, *allys and* ～ 8/142; *in*
hal and in ～ everywhere 7/126.
boured see **borou**.
bowgett *n.* bag *6/597.
bowght, bowt(ys) see **by**.
bowyn *pr. pl.* submit (to) 8/33.
brak *pa. t. sg.* broke 1c/56; **broke**
destroyed, prevented 4/340.
bred(e) *n.* breadth: *in* ～ *and in leint*
in every feature 7/34; *in* ～ *ne leynth*
anywhere 7/305.
bren(e) *v.* burn 4/130, 336, 5/376;
brenne 6/670(MS.), 697. **brennyng,**
brynnyng *pr. p. adj.* 6/*613, 907.
brest *v.* burst: *up* ～ break out *3/58.
brether *n. pl.* brothers 1a/4.
breweth *pr. pl.* are imminent 6/515.
bryng *imp.* bring, put *8/124; see **day**.
broȝte *pp.* brought 7/317; *þareto* ～
come to that 7/202; **brought,**
brouȝt: *forth* ～ made, completed
3/94; ～ *to nought* destroyed 4/166;

bryng (*cont.*):
  browt: ～ *to þat ded* killed in that way 8/101.
brynnyng see **bren(e)**.
bryth *adj.* bright, radiant, beautiful 8/63. **brythest** *sup.* 8/65.
brod *adj.* broad: *in al þis world ～ and long* throughout the length and breadth of the world 7/149.
broȝte see **bryng**.
broke see **brak**.
bronde *n.* sword 7/247, 277. **brondis** *pl.* 7/139.
brostyn *pp.* ruptured, suffering from hernia 6/617.
brought, brouȝt see **bryng**.
brouke *pr. subj.* use, enjoy; in asseveration *so ～ I my bronde* as I may use my sword 7/247.
brushe *imp.* drive out 6/651.
bu see **be**.
burgh *n.* city, town 1a/20; **burw** 10/10.
burthen *v.* equip 3/82.
buskyd *pp.* hastened 6/328.
but, bot *prep.* except: *not ～ only* 4/31. *adv.* only 7/168. *conj.* unless, if . . . not 3/160, 5/418, 6/27, 7/185, 198, 314, 371, 8/192, 9/15; correl. with **ellys** 6/211, 8/176; ～ *if, ȝyf* unless 1c/6, *3/40, 5/181, 194, 6/484.

cayser *n.* emperor 7/56.
calcedonyes *n. pl.* chalcedonies 6/171.
Caldeys *n. pl.* Chaldees 6/106.
cam see **cum**.
can[1] *pr. 1, 3 sg.* am capable of 6/908; ～ *thanke* am grateful (see **thanc**) 6/258; ～ *wit* possesses intelligence 9/16. **can** *pl.* 2b/25; **con** *5/100. **couþe, couthe** *pa. t.* could 1c/59, 7/69; **chout** knew 7/68.
can[2] *auxil. of pa. t.* did 7/65; **con** 1c/13. **cone** *pl.* 11/23. Cf. **ȝan** under **gin**.
canker *n.* cancer 6/612.
cannyngalle *n.* galingale 6/175.
car(e), kare *n.* trouble, pain 6/220, 776, 974, 7/14, 427, 8/106, 169; anxiety 8/181; attention 2d/106; **char** 7/53. **caris** *pl.* pains 1c/31; troubles 8/92. See **caste**.
care *v.* care: *of to ～* to attend to, observe 2d/67; **carye** be anxious

7/82; **char** 7/432. **care** *imp.* be anxious 4/152.
carful *adj.* painful 8/256.
carpe *v.* speak 6/392; **charp** 7/53. **carpyn** *pr. pl.* 6/394.
cas(e) *n.* circumstances 4/75, 331, 8/223; happening, affair 6/362, 392.
caste, castyn *v.* cast, throw: ～ *in care* bring to sorrow 6/220; consider 6/224. **cast** *pp.* turned, moved 6/51; decided 6/350; **castyn** inclined, set 8/63; released 8/169.
Cattlyngys *n. pl.* (?) Catalans 6/106.
cavylacion, cauelacion *n.* objection 2d/151, 4/71.
cawght *pp.* seized 6/705.
cepman *n.* merchant 7/333.
certayne, certeyn *adv.* certainly, for certain 2b/28, 4/290, 5/50, 297.
certeyne *n.* certainty: *in ～* certainly 4/352.
certyfycacyon *n.* notice 6/603.
chagler *n.* 'cackler', idle talker, windbag 7/409.
chalange *pr. 1 sg.* claim 11/28.
cham see **cum**.
char see **car(e)**.
charp see **carpe**.
chaunce *n.* fate 6/736.
che see **sche**.
cher(e) *v.* cheer, make happy 5/134; encourage 6/400. **schereys** *pr. 3 sg.* 5/18.
chere *n.* face 6/575, 8/109; bearing, behaviour 5/136, see **mak(e)**; *with gode, glad ～* willingly 1a/45, 5/112; *schonge ȝowr ～* change your mind 5/179; *bledyng ～* flow of blood 6/687.
chese *v.* choose 5/174.
cheue *v.* succeed, prosper 6/211.
chyldern *n. pl.* children 6/868; **cildrin** 7/340.
chong *v.* change 7/130. **schonge** *imp.* 5/179.
chout see **can**[1].
circumferens *n.* (?*pl.*) orbit(s) 13a/18.
clark, clerk *n.* clerk, secretary 6/137; cleric 6/300.
clere *adj.* beautiful, fine 6/403.
clink *v.* clinch 3/187.
clipt *pp.* embraced 4/214.
clome *pr. 1 sg.* plaster, seal 6/710.
clowtys *n. pl.* cloths 6/452.

Cokkys *n. gen.* colloquial or vulgar corruption of *God's* 6/504.

colkote *n.* (char)coal shed 6/620.

colt-euyll *n.* a swelling of the penis (especially in horses) *6/617.

combrance *n.* distress 6/784.

combre *v.* burden 4/147.

com(e) see **cum.**

com(e)ly see **cumli, cumlic.**

commawment *n.* commandment 5/183. **comamentys, commawmentys** *pl.* 5/46, 92.

con(e) see **can.**

conceyte *n.* notion, idea 6/203; plan 6/450.

conceyve see **consayue.**

condescent *n.* manner: *by no* ~ in no way 6/123.

condolent *adj.* contrite 6/748.

congruent *adj.* appropriate 2a/5.

connyng *n.* knowledge 2a/26; skill 6/*127 (see **unto**), 596; (with obj.) knowing 2a/31. Cf. **cun(n)yng.**

consayue *v.* comprehend 1c/59. **conceyve** *pr. 3 sg.* inclines 2d/55.

consent *n.* consensus, agreement: *at, with, on* ~ unanimously 6/437, 836, 948.

conteyn *v.* hold 2d/35.

contemplacion *n.* in *bi* ~ out of consideration (for him) 2a/6.

contenaunce *n.* bearing, behaviour 5/150.

contynentlye *adv.* without interval 2c/17.

contré, kontré *n.* country, land; *by* ~ *and cost* through all the world 6/964; region outside a city or town 8/*145, 152.

convenyent *adj.* suitable, fitting 2a/4.

conuersacion *n.* association, company 6/984.

core *n.* core (of fruit) 6/759.

cornys *n. pl.* cornfields 13a/28.

cors *n.* body 7/101.

corteysi, courtasy, curteysye *n.* courtesy, graciousness, kindness: *for þi, 3our* ~ kindly 7/308, 338, 11/4.

counfor, counfort *n.* alleviation, remedy 4/247; enjoyment 4/37.

counsayle, counsell, cunsell *n.* advice 6/680; deliberation: *caste* ~ deliberate 6/224; private information,

secret 6/524; *kepe, kype* ~ say nothing 6/221, keep [my] secret 6/357; *in* ~ in confidence 6/528.

courses *n. pl.* charges (of armed knights) 13a/44.

couþe, couthe see **can¹.**

couytys(e) *n.* greed 6/854; avarice 6/901.

craft *n.* skill 3/82.

crafty *adj.* skilful, intelligent 8/168.

creaturys *n. pl.* persons 6/924.

credence *n.* belief 6/730; see **take.**

crepawdys *n. pl.* toadstones 6/171.

cry(e) *v.* announce 7/459. *pr. 1 sg.* beg for [mercy] 4/172, 5/265.

crye *n.* crying 4/236; proclamation 6/561.

Cristen, Crysten *adj.* Christian 6/25, 33.

Crystendom *n.* Christianity, christening 6/928.

cum *v.* come 7/79; **com** 7/286. **comith** *pr. 3 sg.* 7/81; **comyt:** ~ *to* approaches 8/264. **comin** *subj. pl.* 10/9. **cam** *pa. t.* 6/17; **cham** 7/69. **com** *2 sg.* 7/411, 8/207. **cam** *pl.* 5/8; **come** 7/12. **cum** *pp.* 5/297, 6/589; **come** 6/139; **icom** 7/157.

cumberer *n.* ensnarer 6/881.

cumli *adv.* fittingly 7/46; **comly** 8/30; well 8/169.

cumlic *adj.* handsome 7/33; **comely** fitting 13b/27; **komly** beautiful 8/59.

cun(n)yng *adj.* skilled, expert 6/555, 591. Cf. **connyng.**

curat *n.* priest in charge of a parish 6/120. **curatys** *pl.* 6/924.

cure *n.* care; *in* ~ under treatment 6/549.

cure *v.* cover *6/383. *pr. subj.* protect 6/81. *imp.* 6/659.

curyous *adj.* skilfully worked 6/172.

cursyd *adj.* wicked, evil 6/754, 903.

cursydnessys *n. pl.* wickednesses, abominations 8/214.

curteysye see **corteysi.**

day *n.* day, in ~ *and nit* 7/357. **dayis** orig. *gen.* in *by* ~ in the daytime 7/460. **daus** *pl.* in *ending-* ~ 7/370. **dau** orig. *dat.* in *don of* ~ put to death 7/334; **dawe** in *bryng of* ~ 8/124.

dayntese *n. pl.* valuable things 1a/46.
dal(e) *n.* valley; *bi* ∼ *and by hylle* everywhere 6/193; *by* ∼ *nor hyll* anywhere 6/366.
daliaunce *n.* pleasure 4/6, 41.
dam(e) *n.* lady; in address 3/*113, 123, 7/191, 8/40.
damysel *n.* maiden, girl 8/109.
dampned *pa. t.* condemned 1c/28.
dar *pr. 3 sg.* dares 7/48, 166, 489. **dur** *subj.* 7/169. **durst** *pa. t. subj.* would dare 7/241, 453; **dorst** 7/274.
dau(s), dawe see **day.**
deal *n.* part 3/131; **dell** in *no* ∼ nothing 5/256; *euery* ∼ in every way 5/408.
declare *v.* describe 6/554.
ded *n.* deed, action 7/136; see **do(o).**
ded(e) *n.* death 5/280, 8/101. Cf. **deth(e).**
ded(e) *adj.* dead; *be* ∼ die 1c/29, 3/120, 5/141, 228, 7/419.
dedly *adj.* mortal 8/208.
dee *v.* die *3/105; **dey(e)** 7/28, 211. *pr. pl.* 5/450 (see **fro(o)**). **dee** *subj.* *3/32; **dye** in ∼ *the deth* 2d/20, 49. **deit** *pa. t.* 7/386.
defawte *n.* defect, fault 6/261.
defence *n.* 3/52 *evidently corrupt since neither sense nor rhyme is appropriate.*
defensour *n.* defender 6/856.
defyle *v. intr.* be violated 2d/83. *tr.* destroy 5/223.
degre(e) *n.* quality 6/168; condition, state 6/890; *in his* ∼ as befits his position 3/17; *in all degrees* in every way 6/929.
dejectyd *pp.* rejected 2b/26.
del *v.* dispose; ∼ *and dit* govern, be master of 7/78.
delay *v.* relieve 4/33.
dele *n.* sorrow, pain 1c/29.
delful *adj.* painful 7/373; **dullfull** mournful 2a/88.
delyght *n.* delight, enjoyment 13a/5; see **take.**
delyght *v.* enjoy; *to* ∼ to be enjoyed, delightful 13a/13. **delyghtand** *pr. p.* taking pleasure 13a/43.
delyuer *v. refl.* submit 4/169.
delyuerance *n.* delivery: *haue* ∼ receive 6/320; see **mak(e).**
dell see **deal.**

deme *v.* judge, think of 6/682.
demisman *n.* judge 7/331.
denayed *pp.* withheld 2c/11.
departe *v.* remove, dispel 5/322.
dere *n.* harm 4/271.
dere *v.* harm 2a/64.
dere *adj.*[1] dear; *hath* ∼ holds dear, loves 6/132; as *n.* loved one *6/297.
dere *adj.*[2] fierce, courageous 7/120.
derrist *sup.* *7/136.
dere *adv.* dearly, at a high price 6/418, 7/95.
derely *adv.* cordially 13b/7.
derewordy, -wourthy *adj.* beloved 5/411; precious 6/165.
deryn, derne *adj.* secret 8/62, 77; dark 8/69.
derling *n.* favourite 7/153.
dessece, dessese see **disese.**
desessyd *pp. adj.* dead 5/74.
deth(e) *n.* death 1c/20, 7/81. **deþis, dethis** *gen.* death's, mortal 7/91, 439.
devil, deuyll *n.* intensive in *who* ∼ who the devil? 3/172; *what* ∼ 6/481, 516.
dewe *n.* duty 2d/133.
dight, dyght *v.* arrange; *dit* 7/78, see **del.** *imp.* make ready, prepare 3/50. *intr.* go 4/304. *pp.* done 6/492, 851; made 13a/48.
dygnyté *n.* high office 6/896.
dylygens *n.* endeavour 2a/44; see **do(o).**
dynt *n.* blow, force 8/22.
dyrknes *n.* darkness 6/752.
disese *n.* discomfort, harm 1a/46; **dessece, dessese** uneasiness, disquiet 5/20, 24.
dysfame *n.* reproach, shame 6/793.
dyspence *v.* in ∼ *with* grant dispensation to, excuse 6/530.
dyspyte *n.* spite 6/879.
dispyte *v.* dispute, contend 7/98.
dystempurst *pr. 2 sg.* distress 5/263.
dystylde *pp.* (?) infused 2d/87.
distourbith *imp. pl.* disturb 7/110.
dystren *v.* compel, constrain *6/280.
dit see **dight.**
do(o) *v.* (1) do, perform, commit 1a/46, 2a/38, 3/2, 4/24, 5/54, 8/262; **don(e)** 5/56, 6/914, 7/283; **doon, doun** 6/236, 335; ∼ [someone's]

byddyng 5/119, 203; ∼ [one's] *wylle*
do as one likes 8/40; ∼ *care* give
attention 2d/106; ∼ [one's] *dylygens*
endeavour 2a/44; ∼ *obseruaunce* perform a ritual 4/99; ∼ *penawns* 8/231;
∼ *sacrifyse* make sacrifice 4/96; ∼
[someone] *plesance* please 6/126; ∼
[someone] *grevaunce* 4/91, *harme*
5/240, *offence* 6/912, *tene* 8/99, *trespas*
2d/77, 4/176, 6/978, 8/259; *tormentry*
6/802; *velanye* 6/735; *wronge* 2a/52,
7/249, 364; ∼ (*a, the*) *dede*(*s*) 3/79,
4/142, 199, 240, 5/184, 194, 293,
6/296, 914, 7/283, 403, 8/69; ∼ *on*
proceed to do 5/248, 253. (2) finish,
in *pp*. (i)don(e) etc. 5/308, 6/696, esp.
haue ∼ make an end, finish 4/131,
233, 254, 310, 6/494, 605, 653. (3) put,
place, set 6/456, 8/120, 249; ∼ *of* take
off 4/169, 200; ∼ *on* put on 4/283; ∼
of dau kill 7/334; ∼ *to depe* kill 4/78;
∼ *way* stop 4/112. (4) make, cause;
∼ *undirstond* inform 7/77. (5) intr.
act 5/85, 349, 6/155, 731, 13b/14;
fare, get on 2a/73, 6/581. (6) representing another verb 4/20, 104, 6/124,
236, 382, 8/25. (7) auxil. forming with
infin. periphrastic tense, pres. or
past, 2a/13, 14, 68, 2b/introd., 4/20,
93, 298, 5/266, 6/42, 147, 7/55. **dost**
pr. 2 sg. 2a/80, **doost** 6/634. **doth**(e),
dope *3 sg.* 2b/introd., 4/20, 6/124,
490; **dot** 7/55, 356. **do**(o) *pl.* 6/147,
242; **done** 4/93; **doon** 6/209. **doo**
imp. 6/997. **did, dyd** *pa. t.* 2b/16, 23,
6/421, 734; **ded**(e) 5/194, 266, 6/42,
8/99. **do**(o) *pp.* 4/254, 5/308; **don**(e)
2d/77, 5/112, 6/456; **donne** 5/265,
6/688, 912; **doon** 6/11, 524; **ido**
4/131, 233.
doʒtely *adv.* bravely 7/283.
doghti, douti *adj.* valiant 7/260,
*137; **dowty** 8/36.
dokettys *n. pl.* ducats 6/316.
dolour, dolowr *n.* pain, grief 8/85,
144; **dolloure** 2c/19.
doluen *pp.* buried 1c/19.
dorst see **dar**.
douce *adj.* sweet 7/191.
doughtles *adv.* without question
4/65.
dout(e), **dowt**(e) *n.* fear 4/90, 7/151,
223; **dowght** 6/296, doubt 6/701,

709; ∼ *of drede* fear 6/654. **dowghtys**
pl. doubts 6/68, 69.
dowty see **doghti**.
dradd *pp. adj.* afraid 7/24; see
dred(e) *v.*
draw *v.* measure (*not* 'require a certain depth of water') 3/54. *refl., pr. 1
sg.* come 5/134. **drowe** *pa. t.* drew
4/339. **drawyn** *pp.* 5/149; **draw**
5/154.
dred(e) *n.* fear 6/654, 743, 7/262;
for ∼ *him to ten* for fear of angering
him 7/48.
dred(e) *v.* be afraid 1a/34, (with *of*)
7/171. *pr. 1 sg.* 5/137. *refl. imp.* 5/143.
dredith *pr. 3 sg.* 7/28. *pl.* fear 7/27.
dredfull *adj.* awesome 6/435; to be
feared 7/398.
drenche *v.* drown 6/501.
dresse *v.* cultivate 2b/20; arrange, set
6/165, 178. *intr. imp.* prepare 6/808.
refl. set out 6/969. **drest** *pp.* equipped
3/54.
dresser *n.* cultivator 2d/4.
drive *v. intr.* go, fall 7/120. *tr.*
suffer 8/128. **driuith** *pr. 3 sg.* in ∼
with thrusts 7/89. **drevyn** *pp.* 2a/80
s.d.
dulcett *adj.* sweet 6/178.
dullfull see **delful**.
dur, durst see **dar**.
duresse *n.* affliction 6/793.
duere *n.* doubt; *withoutyn* ∼ certainly 8/25, 111, 174.
dwell *v.* stay, wait 6/229, 11/33.

eat *pa. t.* ate 2c/13. *pp.* eaten 2d/76.
eche *adj.* each, every; ∼ *a* every
7/23; **iche** 8/32; **vche** 7/480.
ee *n.* eye 3/143. **eye** *pl.* 7/194, 242;
eyn(e) 5/221, 285, 6/540, 615.
egment *n.* incitement 8/226.
eye *n.* fear, awe 7/188, 318 (see **stont**);
vndir myne ∼ in awe of me 7/213.
eyre *n.* heir, son 4/233.
ek(e) *adv.* also 2d/25, 7/14, 9/9.
eld *n.* age *3/78.
ellys *adv.* else 8/21; ∼ . . . *bot, but*
unless 6/211, 8/175.
emerawdys *n. pl.* emeralds 6/166.
emonge see **among**.
empery *n.* empire 2a/2.
enbrasid *pp.* seized 4/203.

encrese *v.* provide by multiplying 4/34.

end *n.* death 7/391; **hend** 7/374; **hind** 7/70; **ȝynd** end 5/399.

ending(e) *n.* death 7/185, 365.

ending-daus *n. pl.* last days, death 7/370.

enherytaunce *n.* inheritance 6/738.

entent(e) *n.* heed 1c/49, see **take**; sense, import 6/6; intention 6/291, 13b/14; will 6/22, 155.

entent *pr. pl.* intend to go *3/67.

entere *adj.* perfect 4/53.

er *adv.* ever, at all 7/424.

er *conj.* or 8/34.

erde *n.* earth; *in* ~ (tag) there *5/76, 220, 286.

eresye *n.* heresy *6/302.

ermor see **euermore**.

estimacion *n.* calculation 4/297.

ev see **ȝe**.

euer *adv.* always, continually 1c/10, 8/129.

euerychoon, eueryschon *pron.* every one 5/401, 6/523.

euery ilk(e) *adj.* every *3/60; ~ *a* 3/47, 13b/22.

euermo *adv.* always 5/433; for ever 7/175.

euermore, euirmor *adv.* always 5/5, 7/397; for ever 4/364, 7/165; still 5/137, 255; **ermor** 8/236.

evil *adv.* ill, badly 7/173, 422.

euyn *adv.* exactly 6/875.

excepe *prep.* except (for) 5/14, 235.

exempt *v.* remove 2d/96.

exyled *pp.* removed 6/219.

experyens *n.* in *have* ~ observe, explore 2a/45.

fabil *n.* fiction, myth 7/236.

fae see **fone**.

fay *n.* faith; *in* ~ on my word 4/198, faithful, honest 13b/2; *be þi* ~ 8/98; **fey** 6/591.

fayle *n.* in *without* ~ certainly, truly 4/90.

faileþ *pr. 3 sg.* will lack 4/79.

fayn(e) *adj.* pleased, glad 5/52, 119; **fawe** 8/94; satisfied 8/221. *adv.* gladly; *wold(e)* ~ should be glad to, wish to 4/313, 6/268, 374.

fair *adv.* (probably) far 3/194.

fayre *adj.* good, fortunate; as *n.* good fortune 4/322.

fayre see **fare**.

falas *n.* deception 8/12.

fale, fall *v.* come about, happen 11/11; ~ *in my beleve* come within my credence 6/206. **fallit** *pr. 3 sg.* comes into question 7/379.

fale see **fel**.

fals *adv.* falsely 6/433.

fam *n.* repute 8/252.

fang *v.* seize, capture 1c/6.

fanys *n. pl.* flags 13a/48.

fantasye *n.* inclination 2d/32.

far(re) see **fer(e)**.

fare *n.* way of life, position 6/371.

fare *v.* go *3/198, 6/369, 7/16, 8/165, 180; **fayre** *3/138; fare, do 3/173. **fare** *pr. pl.* behave 6/722; **farit** 7/361. **fare** *tr. imp.* in ~ *wel þi way* 7/449. **faryd** *pa. t.* behaved 6/428. **fare** *pp.* fared 4/89; **farne** gone 1c/36.

fast(e) *adv.* firmly 6/46, 507; hard 5/375; earnestly 5/274; ~ *by* close at hand 4/306; quickly 4/309, 5/105, 362, 6/505, 8/44.

fatherhed *n.* fatherhood, fatherly function 6/896.

fawe see **fayn(e)**.

fawle *n.* fall 2c/5.

fee *n.* cattle 3/34; property, wealth 6/382.

fey see **fay**.

fel *n.* skin, in *flessch and* ~ 7/19.

fel *adj.* many 7/378; **fale** 7/207; in great number 9/5.

felawe *n.* friend, comrade 6/509; knave, rascal 6/634. **felawes, felawys** *pl.* comrades 6/504, 653; **felouse** 6/512, 514; **fealows** villains 6/650.

felawshyppe *n.* company 6/525.

felde *n.* field, open country; *in* ~ *oþer in strete* anywhere 7/257; **fylde** in *in the* ~ excluded from society 2d/84; *in* ~ *and toun* everywhere 8/150.

fele *v.* test, seek to discover 4/21; **fell** feel 5/20, 40.

fell *v.* overcome 1c/44; kill 5/89.

felly *adv.* cruelly 1c/7.

fen *n.* mud 4/123.

fendys *n. gen.* Devil's 6/955, 956. **fendis** *pl.* devils 7/96, 106.

fenesters *n. pl.* windows 3/56.

fer(e), ferre *adv.* far 6/230; far and wide 4/88, 6/15, 92, 8/29; **far(re)** 6/682, 7/357, ~ *and nere* everywhere 6/420, 7/291, 457, anywhere 6/682; *boþe* ~ *and hend* 8/146, 231.

fere *n.*[1] companion; husband 4/86, 108; mistress 8/72.

fere *n.*[2] fire 6/494, 684, *694, *907.

fere *refl., pr. 1 sg.* fear 6/298.

ferly *adj.* wonderful 8/166.

fesycyon *n.* physician 6/343.

fest *pp.* set, fixed 3/56.

fet(t) *v.* fetch, bring 5/99. *imp.* 5/355.

feþfully *adv.* steadily, firmly 7/144.

fylde see **felde**.

filled *pp.* defiled 3/49.

fyn *adj.* excellent 5/219.

finde, fynde *v.* find 1a/37; show 7/210. **fond** *pa. t. 2 sg.* have found 7/146. *pl.* found out 1a/22. **found, fownde** *pp.* provided, made 8/92; set (as to school, etc.) 8/104; **ifound** discovered 7/354.

fyndygth = *fynd yt* find it 5/300, 304.

fyne *adv.* thoroughly; *wyll and* ~ 5/113.

fyryng *n.* firewood 6/691.

flay *v.* terrify 1c/7.

fle *v.* escape from 8/229.

fleysse *n.* flesh 5/223; **fleys** *7/444.

florent *adj.* flourishing 13a/23.

florresschist *pr. 2 sg.* in ~ *with* brandish 7/277.

fode *n.* child 1a/37; **fot** *8/118.

fol *n.* fool, villain 8/99.

folde *n.* earth, world; *in þis* ~ at all 8/8.

fond see **finde**.

fond(e) *v.* try 1c/9, 8/158; experience, know 8/81. *imp.* 1c/44, 7/189.

fondyng *n.* temptation 8/48.

fone *n. pl.* enemies 6/355, 8/32. **fae** in *my* ~ hostile to me *3/4.

for *prep.*[1] for the sake of 5/84; instead of 5/360; because of 8/252; ~ *me* for my part 5/248; in spite of 7/194, 242, *al* ~ 7/10, ~ *al* 7/430. *conj.* because 3/65, 6/31; ~ *that* 5/314, 6/69.

for *prep.*[2] before (in asseveration): ~ *God* 6/631.

forant *adj.* (?) fallow 13a/38 (see p. cxxiii).

forbede *pr. subj.* forbid 7/248. **forbyd** *pa. t.* 2d/76.

forbore *pp.* done without 5/73.

force, forse *n.* strength, power: *no* ~ it is no matter 4/80; violence: *with* ~ *and armis* renders Lat. phrase *vi et armis* 7/466.

foredoe *v.* destroy 3/168.

forepredestinacion *n.* predestination 2d/149.

forgyf(e) *imp.* forgive 6/756, 824; **forȝyffe** 5/267.

forlore *pp.* lost 7/186; **forlorn** forgotten 1b/42.

form *v.* instruct 6/886.

forme *n.* way: *vnder that* ~ in that way 5/431.

forsake, forsakyn *pp.* left 4/344; given up 8/239, 241.

forse see **force**.

forsoth(e), forsoþe *adv.* in truth, truly, indeed 4/328, 330, 5/94, 194, 6/57, 7/21, 8/106. Cf. **sothe**.

forthe *adv.* away 1c/70, 4/120; forward: *kepe* ~ pursue 5/250.

forthinks *pr. 3 sg.* repents *3/89.

forwyll *adv.* farewell 5/219, 260, 330; **forewyll** 5/290.

fot see **fode**.

fother *n.* fodder 3/71.

fouled *pp. adj.* foul, filthy 3/87.

found see **finde**.

fowle *adj.* wicked 6/728.

fray *n.* fear, terror 5/24.

fray *v.* attack 6/455.

frayne *v.* ask (*after*) 6/242. **freyned** *pa. t.* inquired of, asked 6/21.

frankelens *n. pl.* freemen, gentlemen 13b/2.

fre(e) *adj.* noble 3/11, 15, 35, 4/288, 5/332, 8/193; sincere 8/246; *fayr and* ~ 8/219.

fre *adv.* freely, willingly 8/262.

freight *n.* cargo 3/71.

freylnes *n.* frailty 1c/44.

freyned see **frayne**.

frely *adj.* noble, high-born 1a/37.

fremit *adj.* as *n.* person not related: ~ *ne sib* nobody 7/348.

frend(e) *n.* friend 7/347; kinsman 4/239.

fresch *adj.* lively, gay 13a/2.

freshely *adv.* vigorously 6/472.

fryt *n.* wood 8/165.

fro(o) *prep.* from 5/165, 201, 8/32, 11/29, (postponed) 1c/36, 8/264; *dey them* ~ die and are lost to them 5/450.

from *prep.* by 8/30.

froward *adj.* perverse, evil 6/882.

fruycion *n.* enjoyment, bliss 6/885.

ful(l) *adv.* very, completely 1c/7, 3/116, 4/17, 5/109, 13a/6.

fule *adv.* foully, wickedly 6/722; Cf. **fowle.**

fulfill, ful(l)fyll(e) *v.* observe 6/150; perform 6/977, 7/477, 8/41. *pr. 1 sg.* provide amply 3/25. **fulfyllyd** *pp.* performed 6/883.

gadered *pp.* assembled 8/173.

gaderyng *n.* company 6/73.

gae see **go(o).**

gaffe see **geve.**

gay *adj.* happy 8/17.

gayn *adj.* straight, short 5/331. **gaynest** *sup.* quickest 1c/9.

galant *adj.* gay, merry 13a/3.

gam(e) *n.* play 7/7, 111, 9/8, 13b/24; **gamen** 11/3; pleasure 8/31.

gan see **gin.**

gang *v.* go 1c/8.

gare *v.* make, cause to 3/110.

gawe see **go(o).**

gedling *n.* rascal, rogue 12/2.

geyl *n.* guile, deceit 7/333.

gentil(l), jentyll *adj.* noble, courteous 4/108, 6/377; dear 4/133, 170.

gentry *n.* kindness 13b/20.

gere *n.* clothing 4/169.

gert *pp.* girded, clothed *6/820.

gett *v.* acquire, conquer 6/432. *pp.* got 6/388.

geve *v.* give 6/282; **gyff** 6/539. **geue** *pr. 1 sg.* 8/31; **geffe** 2a/76. **give** *subj.* grant 3/173. **geue** *imp.* 8/87, 204; **gif** 11/27; **gyff** 6/652. **gaffe** *pa. t. sg.* 2a/75. **gouen** *pl.* 6/39. **gyve** *pp.* 2d/30; **gyuyn** 6/981; **govyn** 6/54. Cf. **ȝiue.**

gin *v. intr.* begin 7/7, 111. **gyn(ne)** *pr. 1 sg.* begin 6/502. **ginnith, gynnyth,** *3 sg.* 6/697, 715. *pl.* 7/87. **gan** *pa. t.* as *auxil.,* did: ~ *brynge* have brought 5/323; similarly 6/63, 11/11. **gunne** *pl.* 6/29.

gird *pr. subj.* strike 7/197.

glad *pr. subj.* cause pleasure to 6/337. **gladest, gladdyst** *2 sg.* 4/37, 6/789.

glasand *pr. p. adj.* in glass: *storys* ~ representations of narratives in stained glass 13a/47.

glased *pp. adj.* fitted with glass windows 13a/47.

gle *n.* entertainment, pleasure 6/111.

gled(e) *n.* fire *5/381, 12/8.

gledryng *pr. p. adj.* glittering 13a/45.

glyde *v.* go, travel 8/17.

glosse *n.* comment 6/438.

go(o) *v.* go 2d/107, 4/29; **gon(n)e** 5/422, 6/350, 353; be, live 6/987; **goon** 5/420, 6/248 s.d.; **gae** *3/7. **goeth** *pr. pl.* 6/335 s.d.; **got** 7/352. **gone** *subj. pl.* walk 8/34. **gawe** *1 pl. subj.* (with suffixed pron.) let us go, come 4/148, 283, 306; **go(o)we** 5/124, 362; ~ *to* let us set about it 6/461. **gose** *imp. pl.* go 1b/43. **go(o)** *pp.* gone 5/201, 7/330; **gon(e)** 1c/33, 2d/16, 4/315; *I am* ~ I'm off 7/470.

god(e) *n.* that which is good 1a/35; goodness 7/384; **good** possessions 5/73, 6/129, 248; benefit 6/789; goods 6/272; **goode** (in address) good sir 4/121.

go(d)day *n.* good-day; *ha(ue)* ~ goodbye 7/447, 8/*160, 161.

godhed *n.*[1] divinity 6/730.

godhed *n.*[2] goodness 7/389.

godmen *n. pl.* masters (of household) 11/6.

goodly *adj.* pleasant, kindly 6/575.

goodlye *adv.* excellently 2d/3.

gostly *adj.* spiritual 6/66, 868.

gostlic *adv.* in spirit, profoundly 7/51.

gouen, gouyn see **geve.**

gramercy *n.* thanks 4/322, 364.

grant *pr. 1 sg.* assent, agree 5/429. *pp.* granted 5/9, 340; **grantyd** 5/11.

grauen *pp.* buried 7/443.

gre *n.* grace, favour *5/388.

grede *pr. 1 sg.* call for, request (with double obj. of thing and person) 9/21.

grefe *n.* distress 6/445, 897.

grefoundes *n. pl.* greyhounds 13a/39.

greynis *n. pl.* grains of Paradise, the spice *Amomum Meleguetta* *6/181.

grene *n.* grass, ground 5/67, 7/443.

gret *v.* weep 5/262. *pa. t. pl.* 1c/33.

gret *adj.* powerful: ~ *and smale* everyone 5/436.

grevaunce *n.* injury, harm 4/91, 6/739; offence, sin 6/892.

greve *v.* offend 5/182, 252, 12/3; injure 6/726. *refl.* grieve, distress oneself 5/453. grevyd *pa. t. 2 sg.* offended 5/270. grevid *pl.* harmed, injured 6/37.

grevous *adj.* noxious 6/752.

gryll *adv.* cruelly 6/788.

grisful *adj.* frightening, terrible 7/132.

groche *v.* complain (*against*) 5/80, 191, 453. gruccheþ *pr. 3 sg.* is reluctant, resists 4/241. groche *imp.* 5/456. grucched *pa. t.* *5/406.

grochyng *n.* complaint 5/442.

grou *v.* frighten 7/132; grue in *yt shuld* ~ *me yll* I should be much afraid 6/155 (but possibly an error for *greue*).

ground(e), grownd *n.* the earth 4/30; foundation 5/388; *on* ~ (tag) there 6/37, in the world, here 6/932, 8/17, 90, 102; *got to* ~ perish 7/352; *go to* ~ laid low 7/330.

grownded *pp.* founded 6/397.

grucche- see groche.

grue see grou.

gunne see gin.

3a *adv.* yea, yes 5/147, 188; 3e 7/462; ye 4/108, 316, 6/627.

3ard *n.* rod 5/170.

3e *pron. 2 pl.* you 1a/7, b/44, 5/111, 11/2; ye 2a/27, b/17, 4/88. you, yow *nom.* 2a/73, 3/65, 4/327, 6/76, 183. 3ow *acc. and dat.* 1b/44, 5/29, 8/7, 11/1; you, yow 2d/44, 4/140, 6/4; ou 7/387; eu, ev 9/2, 4, *20. 3our(e), 3owr(e) *poss.* 5/110, 8/13, 11/2; your(e) 4/233, 6/65; youer 6/66; or 7/387; 3owrys 5/392.

3effe, 3eve see 3iue.

3elpe *v.* speak favourably 7/218; 3ilpe 7/219; yilp boast 7/37.

3emen *n. pl.* attendants 8/4.

3endyr *adv.* over there 8/179; 3ynder 5/323.

3evyn *adv.* even, just *5/110.

C 6409

3if, 3yf *conj.* if 4/172, 5/181; see but.

3yn see 3on(e).

3ynd see end.

3ynder see 3endyr.

3yng(e) *adj.* young 4/25, *7/420.

3it, 3yt *adv.* (of time) yet 4/98; (of concession) yet, nevertheless 4/8, 9, 5/79; yit 7/65; even 7/452; 3et further, again 9/17. *conj.* though 5/70.

3iue *v.* give 7/439; 3effe 5/433; yeve 4/339. 3yffe *pr. 1 sg.* 5/115, 368; 3effe 5/254, 402; 3eve 5/215. 3iveth *3 sg.* *7/23. yif *subj.* 7/372, 415. yeue *imp.* 4/225. 3offe *pp.* 5/3. Cf. geve.

3on(e) *adj. dem.* that 1a/29, 5/123, 328, 8/89, 11/27; yon 6/853; 3yn 5/351, 353, 415.

habitacion *n.* dwelling 2a/47, 2d/21.

haight *n.* command 2d/42.

hayly see hily.

halliday *n.* holiday, feast day 7/341.

halt see hold(e).

ham see he.

hampred *pp.* harassed, distressed 4/234.

hap *n.* fortune, fate 11/11.

happy *adj.* fortunate; *fare þou* ~ good fortune attend you 8/58.

hardely *adv.* confidently, without hesitation 5/412; hardly 4/64, 5/253; harly certainly 5/350, 379.

hardi, hardy *adj.* bold, brave 7/496, 9/11.

harneys *n.* armour 13a/45.

harro, har(r)ow *interj.* of distress 3/95, 6/481, 673.

hast *n.* haste: *in* ~ quickly 6/712.

hasterly *adv.* speedily 6/264; hastily 3/121.

hat see hot(e).

hau(e) *v.* have 4/4; hanne 6/634; aue(n) 8/64, 73; a *3/164, 5/73, 192, 193, 6/575, 8/102, 104; ~ *dout of fear* 7/151; ~ *dred of fear* 7/408; ~ *ned* need 7/432; ~ *pité of* take pity on 11/25; ~ *þout opon* consider 7/397; ~ *wordis* speak 7/207. hast *pr. 2 sg.* 7/207; auestow (with suffixed pron.) *8/98. hath *pl.* 2c/5. haue *imp.* in ~ *at yt* let me get at it 6/469; ha in ~ *godday* goodbye 8/161; see do(o). had *pa. t. subj.* would

L

hau(e) (*cont.*):
have 4/342, 344; (so that we) might have 6/505; **adde** would have 8/105.
he *pron. pl.* they 7/345, 10/9, 11. **hem** *acc.* and *dat.* them, those 4/2, 201, 6/127; **hom** 1c/27, 36, 67; **ham** 7/104, 372. **her** *poss.* 13a/18, **hyr** 5/450; **har** 7/370. Cf. **þai.**
hear *pr. subj.* obey 3/40.
heder see **hider.**
hey see **hy(e).**
heyl(e) *adj.* healthy, well 6/619; as greeting 8/233-4.
heyly see **hily.**
hel(e) *n.* health 7/135, 157; salvation 1b/39; *to wroþer ~* to misfortune 7/491.
hem see **he.**
heme (= *eme*) *n.* uncle 7/83.
hen *adv.* hence, away 4/128, 309; from here 7/285. Cf. **hens.**
hend *adv.* at hand, near 8/146, 231; see **fer(e).**
hend see **end.**
hend(e) *adj.* gracious, courteous 7/5, 9, 109, 8/7.
henge *pp.* hanged 7/481.
hens *adv.* away from here 4/304, 6/576; as *imp.* 6/645; **hennis** 7/11, 297.
hent *v.* seize 5/356.
her see **he.**
herbar *v.* hold 1a/44.
hereafter *adv.* after this 6/329.
herebefore *adv.* before now 4/14.
herein *adv.* in this 6/673.
herfore *adv.* for this reason 1c/39.
herid *pa. t.* harrowed (of Christ's 'harrowing of hell') 11/35.
herkyn *imp. pl.* listen 4/54, 286; **herkint, herkynt** 9/1, 7/1; **herkenith** 7/6, 15.
hert *n.*[1] courage 4/68; feelings 5/83; (in address) beloved 4/133, 208; disposition, intent 4/354; **hart** 5/35; *hit ne toke not to ~* did not attend to it 7/61.
hert *n.*[2] stag 8/16.
herte-blode *n.* life-blood: *se his ~* kill him 7/501.
hertly(e) *adv.* cordially, deeply 4/58, 321.
hert-rote *n.* (bottom of the heart), beloved 4/236, 256.

hest *n.* command, order 5/66, 69, 294. **hestis** *pl.* 7/118, 479.
hete *v. intr.* grow hot 6/712.
heuede *n.* head 7/324.
heuely *adv.* grievously: *~ sett* afflicted with grief 5/96.
heuene-flowr *n.* flower of heaven 8/202.
heuy *adj.* sad, sorrowful 5/136.
heuyn-blysse *n.* joy of heaven 5/465.
hevynes *n.* sadness, grief 5/322.
hevin-lit *n.* light of heaven 7/405.
hew(e) *n.* colour, complexion 1c/72, 4/17, 5/346; aspect 12/10.
hy *n.* haste: *in ~* quickly 1a/12, *3/186, 188, 4/307, *5/363.
hy(e) *adj.* high, exalted 4/50, 164; as *n.* in *on ~* in heaven 4/35, high up 4/96; up 6/509; **hey** 6/509.
hy(e) *v. intr.* hasten 7/310. *refl. imp.* 4/30, 7/272; **hey** 5/33. *pr. subj.* 4/159. *tr. pp.* **hyed** quickly done 4/148.
hide *n.* skin; *~ and hewe* from head to foot 1c/72.
hider, hidir, hydir *adv.* here 7/12, 310, 411; **hidre** 4/165; **heder** 5/105, 359; **hether, hethyre** 6/700, 5/355.
hydygth = *hyd yt* hide it 5/165.
hye *adv.* earnestly 4/14, 281.
hyght see **hot(e).**
hily *adv.* exceedingly 4/39; **heyly, hayly** 5/5, 6/157.
hille *n.* hill, in tag *vpon ~* on my land 8/16.
hind see **end.**
hir, hyre *adv.* here 6/313, 631.
his, hys *adj. poss.* forming *gen.* (erroneously): *God his* 2b/9, *man-kynde hys* 2c/6, *man his* 2d/2.
hit *pron.* it 1b/20, c/74, 7/61, 426, 9/7; as indef. subject 7/201.
ho *pron.* she 7/49; a 7/48. Cf. **sche.**
hold(e) *v.* hold, maintain, keep 8/4; *~ on honde* observe 7/479. **halt** *pr. pl.* hold, regard as 7/359. **ho(o)ld** *imp.* take 5/315; keep 6/506; *refl.* keep 7/182. **holdyng** *pr. p.* associated (with) 5/434.
hole *n.* sepulchre 1b/27.
holl *adj.* whole, complete 1c/72; **hole** healthy 6/602.
holsom, holsum *adj.* health-giving, salubrious 13a/25, 31.
hom see **he.**

homly *adv.* too familiarly, impudently *6/638.

hond(e) *n.* hand; *in* ~ (tag) (?) in your possessions 8/58, (?) hand in hand 8/83; *on* ~ firmly 7/480.

honoracion *n.* honour 2d/24.

honowraunce *n.* honour; *put to* ~ worship 4/103.

hoope *n.* valley; ~ *and hill* 3/8.

hope *pr. 1 sg.* think, believe 6/843, 849, 13a/6.

hore *n.* whore 7/197.

hore *adj.* grey, bare 13a/37; grey-haired 4/245.

horn-spone *n.* spoon made of horn 1a/43.

hot(e) *pr. 1 sg.* command 7/118; am called 8/27; **hyght** 13a/4. **hat** *3 sg.* commands 9/13, 17. **hyght** *pp.* called 6/628.

howe *interj.* ho! 6/356.

howre *n.* appointment 6/378; **owre** time, experience 4/314.

hundrith *n.* hundred 1a/44; **hundder** 6/288.

hur *adv.* here 9/2 (perhaps a genuine form, found also in Vespasian homilies; see *M.E.D.*).

hure *adj. poss.* our 9/8.

husband *n. gen.* husband's 3/119.

ibor(r)e *pp. adj.* born 7/20, 123.

ibound see **binde**.

ibroзt *pp.* brought: *doun* ~ laid low, destroyed 7/93. see **bryng**.

ic *pron.* I 7/121, 131; **ich** 9/19, 20.

ich see **ilke**.

iche see **eche**.

icom see **cum**.

i-esid *pp.* eased, comforted 4/119.

ifer *adv.* together 7/1. Cf. **infere**.

ifound see **finde**.

igadert *pp.* assembled 9/5.

ikaзte *pp.* caught 7/106.

ikorne, ikorre *pp. adj.* chosen, excellent, famous 7/114, 121. Cf. **korin**.

iliche *adj.* like 7/287.

ilke, ylke *adj.*[1] same (after *that*) 6/495, 497, 700, 8/103; very 8/254; **ich** 8/46.

ylke *adj.*[2] every 13a/28; **ilk a** 3/69. See **euery**.

yll *adv.* painfully 5/382, 6/155.

ilore *pp.* lost, ruined 7/493. Cf. **lese**.

imad see **mak(e)**.

imett see **metis**.

inconuenyens *n.* impropriety, offence 6/899.

incressement *n.* benefit, profit 13b/29.

Indas *adj.* Indian 6/184.

indure *v.* survive 2a/26.

infere *adv.* together 4/47, 8/173, 209; all together 8/23. Cf. **ifer**.

inquere *v.* ask: ~ *to* ask the way to 6/630.

inrollyd *pp.* recorded 2a/87.

insame *adv.* in company 13b/23. Cf. **samyn**.

insyght *n.* understanding 6/555.

intent *n.* intention 5/387.

inter(e)ly *adv.* completely, sincerely 6/799, 961.

irerit *pp.* set up 7/342.

irke *adj.* weary 6/919.

isen *adj.* apparent, clear 7/142.

isente see **send**.

isworne *pp. adj.* sworn, pledged *7/116.

itaken see **take**.

iwys(e) *adv.* indeed, certainly *3/132, 5/13, 156, 6/55, 483, 517; **iuis** 7/346.

janglest *pr. 2 sg.* babble, chatter 6/573.

jentyll see **gentil(l)**.

Jewe *n.* Jew 6/17. **Jewes** *pl.* 6/59 etc. **Jewus** *gen.* 1a/23.

Jewery *n.* Jewish land 1a/10.

judgyment *n.* judgement, opinion 6/592; diagnosis *6/539.

just *adv.* tightly 6/43, 938.

iustis *n.* justice, judge 7/381.

kaytyf *n.* wretch 8/183.

kare see **car(e)**.

kempis *n. pl.* warriors, champions 7/114.

kende see **kind(e)**.

kene *adj.* severe 1c/31; sharp 6/693; mighty 6/880.

kenne *v.* make known 6/450; know 13a/15. **kend** *pp.* 3/194; known 6/15, 92; directed 1b/26.

kepe, kepyn *v.* look after 2b/20; protect, defend 8/48; hold (tongue) 6/331; **kyppe** in *to me* ∼ accept 8/39. **kepe** *pr. 1 sg.* wish 5/252. **kep** *subj.* preserve 11/35. **kype** *imp.* 6/221. **kept(e)** *pa. t. subj.* should not wish 4/111, 7/200.

kerche *n.* kerchief 5/285.

kete *adj.* bold, brave 7/135.

kind(e), kynd *n.* nature 2d/81, 5/451, 7/208, 221; natural ability 3/82, 8/168; race 4/10; **kende** lineage 8/1; *be* ∼ by natural affection 5/199.

kynd, kinde *adj.* of the race, descended 7/121; gracious 7/158, 244, 8/149.

kyndely *adv.* in accordance with his nature, generously 1b/26.

kinge *n.*, orig. *dat. pl.* kings 7/22.

kyp(p)e see **kepe**.

kyrk *n.* church 8/179.

kys *v.* kiss; *to her* ∼ embrace her 8/97.

kyt *v.* make known, show, manifest 7/80. **kith** *pr. 3 sg.* 7/92.

knaue *n.* servant: *knyght and* ∼ 1b/5. **knauys** *pl.* 8/5.

knaw(e) *v.* know 1a/33. *pr. pl.* 1c/30. **knewe** *pa. t.* 1c/74, 7/101. **knowen, knowyn** *pp.* 6/92, 8/15.

knett, *pp.* tied, united 6/985.

knoyng *n.* knowledge 5/53.

knottys *n. pl.* bonds 8/169.

knowlech *n.* knowledge; *have* ∼ know 6/244.

knowlege *imp.* acknowledge 6/875.

komly see **cumlic**.

korin *pp. adj.* chosen, excellent *7/244. Cf. **ikorne**.

korownyt *pp.* crowned 8/30.

korteyser *adj. comp.* more gracious 8/28.

kowthe *adv.* familiarly, well 6/56.

lafte see **leue**.

lay *n.* law, religion 9/10. Cf. **lawe**.

laye *v.* wager, stake 6/433.

lain *v.* conceal, keep secret *3/135. **laint** *pp.* *3/164.

laith see **loth**.

lake *n.* stream (*O.E.D.* lake *sb.*³) 7/269.

lame *adj.* crippled 6/770, 791; impotent 6/956.

lamentable *adj.* sorrowful 6/757, 825.

lang *adj.* long 1a/48.

langage *n.* words 4/237.

langowr *n.* distress, affliction 6/819.

lare see **lor(e)**.

largyfluent *adj.* generous, bounteous 6/826.

lashe *n.* stroke 6/468.

lasse see **less(e)**.

last *conj.* lest 4/91, 226.

lat see **let**.

lawe *n.* religion 1c/26, 6/397, 441. Cf. **lay**.

laxe *n.* diarrhoea 6/612.

lead *n.* cauldron 3/205.

leche *n.* physician 7/314; **lec** 7/64. **lechys** *gen.* 6/524 s.d.

lecuri *n.* lechery 7/337.

led *v.* escort 7/42; accompany 8/107; live (life) 8/129. **ledde** *pp.* pursued 6/113.

lede *n.* people 7/254; followers 11/20.

ledinge *n.* control, command 7/125.

le(e)s *n.* falsehood 11/5; *withoutyn ony* ∼ truly, assuredly 8/135.

lefe see **leue**.

leykyn *v.* play, sport 8/65, 170.

leint *n.* length, height 7/34; **leynth** 7/305.

leke *adj.* likely 5/261.

lelyes *n. pl.* lilies 13a/33.

lende *v.* give 6/468. **lendist** *pa. t. 2 sg.* granted 4/36. **lent** *pp.* granted 3/69, 6/121, 159, 436.

lenger(e) *adv. comp.* longer 5/130, 6/28, 229.

lenust *adj. sup.* frailest 7/395.

lepiþ *imp. pl.* spring 4/131.

lere *n.* face 8/238.

lerit *pp. adj.* learned 7/4.

lernyng *n.* lesson 5/437.

les see **le(e)s**.

lese *v.* lose 4/369; **lesse** 6/64.

lesing(e) *n.* falsehood 7/54; *withoutyn* ∼ truly, assuredly 8/143, 10/4.

less(e) *adj. comp.* smaller; ∼ *and mare* of various sizes *3/57, one and all *3/200, 6/968; ∼ *or mair* of any size *3/175; *more and* ∼ 5/394, 6/70; **lasse** in *neyther mor nor* ∼ *6/315. **lest(e)** *sup.*: ∼ *and most(e)* of all ranks 6/3, 959, 961.

lestenith see **lystne**.

let *v.*[1] leave, let go 2d/122, 7/427; cause, make: ~ *wyt* tell 5/161. *imp.* cause 5/159; let 4/173; ~ *be* stop, leave it alone 3/179, 13a/7; ~ *God alone þerwith* leave it to God 4/153; lat in ~ *be* 4/112, enough! 8/237, 238, cast aside 11/19. lettes *imp. pl.* let 1b/42. lett *pp.* parted 6/239.

let(t), lette *v.*[2] hinder 5/246, 247, 9/8, 11/3; omit, refrain 3/22, 5/98, 313, 6/850, 7/137. *imp.* 6/331. *pp.* hindered 4/312, 7/338.

lettrit *adj.* educated, learned 7/45.

letwyce *n.* lettuce 6/587.

leu *pr. subj.* grant 7/390.

leu see lib.

leue *imp.* give up 7/214; lefe of stop 5/269. lafte *pp.* left 7/108.

leue *v.* believe 7/315. *imp.* 11/20.

leue *adj.* dear 8/230. leuer, levyr *comp.* more pleasing; *I haue* ~ I prefer 4/80; *I had* ~ I would rather 4/181, 5/72.

leuende *n.* creature 8/234.

leving see lifyng.

lewyd *adj.* unlettered; *lernd and* ~ everyone 5/437; leut in *lerit and* ~ 7/4.

lib *v.* live 7/350, 405; leue 11/15. leu *pr. subj.* 7/437.

lif(e), lyf *n.* life; creature 3/60, 8/57; lyve 4/282, *on* ~ alive 4/63, in the world 7/164. lives *gen.* of life 4/235, 11/22.

lifyng *n.* life 1a/48; leving 4/36.

lyght *adj.* cheerful, gay 13a/1; lyt light, nimble 8/170. lyttest *sup.* (?) quickest 8/167.

light *pa. t.* alighted, fell 11/11.

lyghtyng *n.* alleviation, relief 6/791.

lyghtnesse *n.* brightness, radiance 6/826.

like *v.* please 7/201. likeþ *pr. 3 sg.* is pleased 4/359.

lykenyd *refl., pa. t.* made himself like 6/429.

lykyng, likinge *n.* pleasure 6/113, 7/25, 133; *at* ~ as he wishes 7/29; likynd 7/57.

lykke *v.* take 6/476.

lynd(e) *n.* linden, lime 6/389, 7/264, 8/170.

lisst *pr. 2 sg.* lie 7/421.

lyst *n.* pleasure, what one pleases 5/253. Cf. lust.

list(e), lyst *pr. 1 sg.* wish 6/526. *pl.* 4/212. *3 sg. impers.:* þe ~ please 7/145, 179, 437. lust *3 sg.* pleases 4/360. lyste *pa. t.* pleased 2b/20.

lystne *imp. sg.* listen to 8/88. lestenith *pl.* 7/118.

lyt see lyght.

lyth *n.* light; in tag *louely in* ~ beautiful to see 8/161.

lyvelod *n.* means of living, sustenance 5/4.

lo(o) *interj.* see, look 4/49, 5/133, 6/61.

lo(o)ke *v.* look: ~ *after* wait anxiously for 5/310; *imp.:* ~ *to* attend to 1a/39; see to it 4/121, 124, 271, 5/92, 6/919, 7/137, 238. *pr. pl. subj.* (let us) see 6/462. lokit *pr. pl.* see 7/344.

lond *n.* land; *in* ~ (tag) in the world 8/56.

longeth, longyth *pr. 3 sg.* is fitting 6/265; belongs 6/896.

lor(e) *n.* learning 7/45; instruction 5/85; lesson 5/412; teaching 7/404; lare (?) wit (in tag) 8/167; *in* ~ at my instigation 8/217.

lording(e)s *n. pl.* sirs, masters 7/5, 8/7, 11/1.

lordly *adj.* masterful 8/170.

lordlich *adv.* masterfully 7/26.

lore *pp.* lost 7/313. Cf. lese.

loth *adj.* reluctant 6/704; laith *3/116.

loude, lowd *adv.* loudly 5/191; publicly 7/230; ~ *and, nor, still(e)* in any way 5/191, in all circumstances 7/230.

loue *n.* beloved 8/56, 77.

louelich *adj.* lovely, beautiful 7/29; lowuely handsome 12/10.

lucre *n.* gain, profit 6/902.

lust *n.* pleasure, liking, desire 2c/4, d/55, 88; passion 2d/135.

lust see lyst.

mac see make.

madam *n.* (in address) my lady 7/319.

mafay *interj.* on my word *7/451.

may *n.* maiden 6/994.

may *pr. 3 sg.* can 1b/7; **ma** 6/206. **mit**
2 sg. 7/143, 431. **mown** *pl.* may 6/172.
mit *pa. t.* 7/64. **myt** *subj. pl.* could
6/207; **moȝt** *9/4.
main, mayn(e) *n.* strength 3/133,
5/54, 123, 6/512.
maynpris *n.* mainprize, bail 7/379.
mair see **more.**
maistri(e), maistrye *n.* power
7/223, 240.
mak(e), makyn *v.* make, do, cause;
~ (*dat.*) *afray* frighten 5/233; ~ *bere*
cry out, shout 8/24; ~ *delyueraunce*
hand over 6/34; ~ *god endinge* come
to a good end 7/185; ~ *heuy chere* be
sad 5/136; ~ *in mynd of* recall 1c/10;
~ *joye, mirth, solas* rejoice 6/35,
7/267, 8/76, ~ *mery* 8/110; ~ *laude*
do honour 2a/22; ~ (*a*) *menys* appeal
for help 6/755, intercede 6/865; ~
mon, sorowe, wo(o) lament, grieve
1c/39, 7/224, 5/200; ~ *sacryfyce*
5/62; ~ *tale* talk 9/6; ~ *tariyng*
delay 7/319. **make** *pr. 3 sg.* 6/388.
makeþ *imp. pl.* 4/97; **makiet** 9/6.
mad *pa. t.* caused 7/63. **imad** *pp.*
created 7/150.
make *n.* match, equal 7/306; mate
2a/15; **mac** husband 7/47.
male *n.* bag, sack 6/179.
malepertly *adv.* impertinently 6/639.
man *n.* man: ~ *and best* 1a/5.
manhed *n.* human form: *for his* ~ in
his incarnation 7/383.
mankin *n.* mankind *3/89.
manly *adv.* bravely, strongly 6/496,
669.
man(n)er(e) *n.* kind: *al* ~ every
kind of 4/11; *in any* ~ *of thing* by all
means 3/27; *no* ~ *off* no kind of 6/68;
summ ~ *a best* an animal of some kind
5/145; *wat* ~ what kind of 5/52; *in* ~
(?) in behaviour 4/362.
mansuete *adj.* gentle, mild 6/831.
maracle, marycle *n.* miracle 6/53, 57.
mare see **more.**
marke *n.* as *adj.* distinguished 6/149.
markyd *pp. adj.* formed, disposed
*8/164.
mased, masyd *pp. adj.* stupefied,
bewildered 1c/57, 6/655.
masterly *adv.* in a masterly way
6/454.

mastyk *n.* mastic gum, *Pistachia
lentiscus* 6/182.
materyall *adj.* important 6/890.
meane *n.* agency; *thorowgh thy* ~ by
means of thee 6/784. **menys** *pl.*
intercession, influence 6/755, *865;
see **mak(e).**
med(e) *n.* reward 2a/71, 6/568; gain
7/331.
medycament *n.* treatment 6/582.
medyll-erth *n.* the earth 5/34.
meenye *n.* household 3/104, *199;
meny company 6/844; **meiné,
meyné** 7/*433, 465; **mené** 8/19.
meynt *pp.* mingled, blended 6/878.
meke *adj.* kind 12/10.
mekill, mekyll *adj.* great 6/13, 62,
11/9; **mykyll** 6/750.
mekyl *adv.* greatly 13a/30; **mykyll**
6/830.
mele *n.* meal 4/24.
men *pron. indef.* one 9/13, 14, 17.
mend *imp.* reform *3/92.
mende (= *mynde*) *v.* keep in mind,
remember 8/3.
mende see **mind.**
mene *v.*[1] signify 1a/11; mention, tell
of 6/79, 197; plan, intend 6/877; ~
on remember 1c/25. **ment** *pp.* intended 6/370; planned 6/454; ~ *in
mynde* remembered 6/198.
mene *v.*[2] complain (of) 7/30.
mené, meny see **meenye.**
menys see **meane.**
merth see **myrth.**
meruales, merueles *n. pl.* wonders
1c/34, 1a/11.
merveylows *adj.* to be wondered at
6/719.
mervell *pr. 1 sg.* wonder (*of*, at)
5/135.
meruelows *adv.* wonderfully 6/877.
messager *n.* messenger 7/263, 280.
mete *n.* food 4/24. **metys** *pl.* 6/347.
meth *n.* capacity 7/497.
metis *pr.* (?) *pl.* meet, come together
*7/444. **imett** *pp.* in *wele* ~ 6/237.
meve *v.* cause 5/266; propose 6/454;
move, bring 6/740. *pr. 3 sg.* moves
2d/32; **meuyth** *intr.* acts, works
6/453. **meve** *pl.* live 6/82; ~ *of*
speak of 6/209. **moved** *pp.* brought
up 13b/11.

mych(e) *adv.* much 5/13, 76; **mucil** 7/37, 38. Cf. **moch(e)**, **mekyl**.

myddys *n.* midst, middle 6/480.

myegrym *n.* headache, migraine 6/615.

myght, miȝte *n.* strength, power 7/227, 462, 11/9; **mit, myt** 7/80, 8/235; **myth** in *with* ∼ strongly 8/68; *of* ∼ mighty 8/197; *with* ∼ *as we may* to the best of our ability 13b/7. **miȝtis** *pl.* 7/92.

myght *adj.* powerful 6/85; strong, pungent 6/182.

mightful *adj.* powerful 3/133; **myth-ful** 8/164.

myghty *adj.* in ∼ *in moode* bold, arrogant 6/792; **mytheti** mighty 6/285; **mytty** 8/235.

myghtly *adv.* with power 6/83.

mykyll see **mekyl(l)**.

myld(e) *adj.* submissive 5/170, 244; gentle 5/238; kind 7/6.

mind, mynd(e) *n.* remembrance (see **mak(e)**) 1c/10; state of mind 4/231; **mende** thought 11/24; *with-outon* ∼ beyond the power of intellect 6/79; *out of* ∼ forgotten 7/349.

mynnes *pr. 3 sg. impers.* in ∼ *me* I remember 1a/21. **munit** *pers.* reminds, warns *7/47.

mynt *v.* aim, direct 8/26.

miriest *pr. 2 sg.* make happy 7/296.

myrth *n.* happiness 6/82, 7/14; entertainment 11/7; **merth** 8/136. **merthis** *pl.* pleasures 8/68.

mis *adj.* bad 9/2.

mys(se) *n.* error: *withowt* ∼ certainly 2a/17; wrong: *in þis* ∼ so unjustly 4/185; wrongdoing 4/247, 6/293.

myscary *v.* come to grief, die 6/558.

mischaunce *n.* ill fortune, defeat 7/258.

myschef, myschiefe *n.* disaster 4/250; *at his* ∼ in misfortune, ruin 11/18.

myschevyd *pp.* injured, discomfited 5/454.

myschevos *adj.* harmful, injurious 6/877.

mys(s)e, miss *v.* fail 6/321, 646; lack 7/40. **miste** *pr. 2 sg.* omit 7/181. **misst** *3 sg.* will fail 7/436.

mysericord *n.* mercy 6/889.

mysgouernaunce *n.* wrongdoing 6/789.

mysse-avysed *pp. adj.* ill-advised, misguided 6/641.

mystrest *v.* doubt 4/20.

mit, myt(h) see **may, myght**.

mytheti see **myghty**.

mo(o) *adj. comp.* more (in number) 1c/34, 4/76, 5/16, 448, 7/320. Cf. **more**.

moch(e) *adj.* great 6/97, 194; **muchel** 9/7; **mych** 5/150. Cf. **mekill**.

mod, mo(o)de *n.* mind, heart 6/453, 792, 7/296, 416; *with mylde* ∼ kindly 7/6.

moderat *adj.* judicious, just 6/891.

moȝt see **may**.

mold(e) *n.* earth 1c/57, 6/82, *7/444.

mon *n.* lament 1c/39. **monys** *pl.* complaints 5/269.

more *adj. comp.* greater 4/228; see **less(e)**; **mair** *3/57, 175; **mare** 6/968. **most(e)** *sup.* greatest 6/3, 416, 826, 966. Cf. **mo(o)**.

moryst *pr. 2 sg.* increase 8/68.

morne *pr. 1 sg.* grieve 5/274. *pl.* are sad 5/158.

mornyng *n.* grief, pain 5/380.

most(e) see **more**.

most *pr. 1, 3 sg.* must 4/161, 182, 7/312, 321; *impers.* in *me* ∼ I must 8/62, 64. *pl.* 4/138. *subj. sg.* may 4/322.

mot(e), mott *pr. 1, 3 sg.* may 5/75, 259, 6/211, 249, 7/219, 9/19; may be 7/390; must *3/86. *2 sg.* 5/207, 389, 6/785, 7/422.

moved see **meve**.

mown see **may**.

muchel see **moch(e)**.

mucil see **mych(e)**.

mun *pr. pl.* shall 1a/12.

munit see **mynnes**.

naȝt see **noȝt(e)**.

nay(e) *adv.* no 13a/7; as *n.* in *with-owten (ony)* ∼ without contradiction, certainly 3/103, 6/93.

nam *n.* name: *be* ∼ (tag) especially, specifically, notably 8/*194, 199.

nas see **nis**.

nast *pr. 2 sg.* have not 7/163.

nat(t) see **noȝt(e)**.

ne *adv.* (preceding vb.) not 7/177, 236, 9/12.

ne *conj.* nor 11/3.

necesse *n.* necessity 6/774.

neclygence *n.* indifference, unbelief 6/728; negligence 6/920.

nede *adv.* of necessity 3/86, 7/204; **nedes, nedis, nedys(se)** 4/182, 221, 5/228, 275.

nedis *pr. 3 sg. impers.* is necessary: *me* ~ I need 11/31. **nede** *subj.* 11/21.

negacyon *n.* contradiction; *without* ~ for certain 6/602.

neglygensy *n.* omission, inadequate preparation 13b/15.

ney see **ny(e)**.

nemed *pa. t.* named 1a/26.

nere *adv.* near 8/178; nearly 6/655.

neuer *adv.* never; ~ *a* no 4/152; **ner(e)** 3/163, 7/101; not at all 7/418.

neuermore *adv.* never again 5/417.

newe *adv.* newly 6/379, 12/11.

ny(e) *adv.* near 4/237, 258 (see **take**); nearly 8/121; **ney** 7/313.

nil *pr. 1 sg.* will not 7/130. **nel** *3 sg.* 7/216. **nold** *pa. t. subj.* would not 7/124.

nis *pr. 3 sg.* is not; ~ *bot* is nothing but 7/209. **nas** *pa. t.* 7/123, 282.

no *adv.* not at all 3/182; nor 7/368.

noght *n.* nothing 1c/52; **nought** 4/51; **nott** 2d/125; *brou3t to* ~ destroyed 4/166.

no3t(e), noght *adv.* not at all 7/200; not 1a/40, c59, 7/216, 315; **nowght** 6/726; **nowt** 8/125; **na3t** *9/6; **nat(t)** 2d/58, 6/88.

nold see **nil**.

nonys *quasi-n.* in tag *for the* ~ then, indeed 6/18, 161; now 6/708.

not *pr. 1 sg.* do not know 7/35; see **wit. nost** *2 sg.* 7/418.

noþer *adv.* neither; ~ . . . *ne, no* neither . . . nor 7/367, 368.

nothing, nothyng *adv.* not at all, by no means 5/93, 6/227, 858, 7/90.

nought, nowght, nowt see **noght, no3t(e)**.

obesaunce *n.* homage 4/38; **abesyans** respect, deference 13b/3.

obowte *prep.* (postponed) about, around 7/115. See **about**.

ocke *conj.* but 7/293.

of(f) *prep.* by 4/62, 213, 6/8, 306, 859; from 6/36, 8/192; in, as regards 6/248; about 7/463.

oght *n.* anything 1b/12; **owyht** 6/567; **owt** as *adv.* in any way 5/169.

o3ein *prep.* against 7/124. See **a3eyn**.

o3eynis see **a3ens**.

on *adj.* one 4/204; the same 4/243.

on *pron.* one, a man 1c/13; one (object) 6/985; **won** in ~ *and* ~ one by one 6/658.

on *prep.* in ~ *a nyght* at night 6/304.

ongoodly *adv.* wickedly 6/788.

onis, onys *adv.* once 5/270, 6/160, 7/241, 255; *be I* ~ *ded* once I am dead 5/201; **ayns** *3/155.

onkynd *adj.* unnatural 6/200; cruel 6/720, 7/345.

onkowth *adj.* unknown, foreign *6/147.

onlefull see **vnlefull**.

onlerit *pp. adj.* untaught 7/340.

onmyld *adj.* rebellious 5/312.

onsonder *adv.* apart *5/152.

ontawght *pp. adj.* ill-bred, uncivil 6/638.

onto see **unto**.

ontrewe *adj.* untrue 6/215.

or *prep.* before 4/24. *conj.* 6/468, 7/11; **ar** 7/297, 13b/26; ~ *that* 5/153.

or see **3e**.

ordeyned *pp.* arranged 13b/27.

ordynaunce *n.* control 6/891.

oþir *pron.* other; another 7/377; *one* ~ another thing, something different 7/435.

othus *n. pl.* oaths; *withouten* ~ without (need for) oaths 4/206.

ou see **3e**.

oures *pron. poss.* ours: *of* ~ of our people 1c/37.

oureself *pron. pl.* ourselves, us 1c/17.

out(e), owt *adv.* away from home 4/319; as *interj.* alas! 6/481, 499.

ouþer *adv.* either 4/277, 296.

outrage *n.* presumption, insolence 7/440.

oueral *adv.* everywhere 7/322.

owe *pr. pl.* ought, are bound to 6/195.

owyth *pr. 3 sg.* is proper 6/260. **owte** *orig. pa. t. subj.* ought 6/830; **a3te** 7/82.

owyht, owt see oght.

owre see howre.

oxennell *n.* oxymel, a compound of vinegar and honey 6/586.

pace *n.* step: *preue my* ∼, *take thy* ∼ go 6/360, 390, 847; speed 4/158; pase (way of) life 1a/25.

packe *v.* carry in a bundle 5/118.

pay(e) *n.* pleasure: *to* (*3oure*) ∼ to (your) satisfaction 6/143, 176, 8/13; *to ower* ∼ as we wish 6/228.

payd(e) *pp.* pleased 4/61, *5/94.

payne *n.* punishment 2d/38; *putt to* ∼ defeat 2d/136; peyne in *on* ∼ *of* on pain of losing 7/478. paynes *pl.* tortures 1c/12.

pays see pes(se).

pales *n. pl.* boundaries, precincts 6/207.

pall *n.* rich cloth 6/264.

pappys *n. pl.* breasts 13a/53.

parage *n.* high birth, lineage 6/429, 10/8.

par amour, amowr *adv.* as a lover, passionately 8/78; for love 8/87.

paramowre *n.* mistress 8/155.

parauentur(e) *adv.* perhaps 4/250, 329, 7/359.

parfyt *adj.* perfect, fine 8/6.

pas *n.* passage 7/382.

pas *v.* go 1c/70. *pr. pl.* 13b/26.

pase see pace.

passeth *pr. 3 sg.* surpasses 13a/54; passit passes through 7/382. passyd *pp.* touched on 13b/10.

pausacyon *n.* delay *6/605.

peese see pes(se).

peyne *pr. pl.* torture 6/723.

peyne see payne.

penaunce *n.* suffering 4/255; penawns penance 8/231.

peper *n.* pepper: *long* ∼ a variety of pepper made from *Piper officinarum* 6/184.

pere *n.* peer, equal 1a/41, 6/119, 265, 7/282.

pere *v.* appear 6/639.

pererys *n. pl.* pear-trees 13a/32.

pes(se) *n.* peace, silence 6/84, 7/109; pays 9/21; peace of mind 8/134; as *interj.* be quiet 5/155, 339, 7/1, 113, 471, 11/1; peese 4/112.

pese *n. coll.* peas 1a/44.

peté see pité.

pyght *pp.* set, placed 13a/58.

pymente *n.* spiced wine 6/428.

pynde *pr. pl.* shut up, confine 6/723.

pynsons, -ys *n. pl.* pincers 6/40, 657.

pyppe *n.* an indeterminate disease (technically an ailment of birds) 6/527.

pité *n.* pity 11/25; peté 6/823.

pytt *v.* put *6/860.

pyxys *n. pl.* pyxes, vessels in which consecrated bread is kept 6/926.

place *pr. subj.* please 6/73.

play *n.* sport, amusement 7/429; *in* ∼ for entertainment 13b/4; play 13b/6.

play *pr. pl.* play (a drama) 11/5. plaied *pp.* 11/34.

playn(e) *adj.* open 6/373; clear: *in a* ∼ clearly 1c/69.

plant *pp.* planted 2d/3.

plas *n.* place: *in* ∼ here 8/78.

plasmacion *n.* formation 2a/8.

plawe *v.* boil 6/666.

pleying *n.* entertainment, pleasure *7/428. Cf. play.

pleyn *n.* ground 6/506.

pleyn *adv.* completely, in full 6/137, 313.

plesantly *adv.* with good will 13b/4.

plesa(u)nce *n.* pleasure, satisfaction 4/8, 36, 59, 6/126.

plesyng *n.* pleasure, will 5/56.

plete *v.* plead (as at law), appeal 8/146.

plyght *pr. 1 sg.* pledge 6/473; promise, assure 13a/2.

pomerys *n. pl.* orchards 13a/32.

poose *n.* cold in the head, catarrh 6/618.

poppyd vp *pp.* (?) prominently supported 13a/53.

porte *n.* gate 2d/98.

pot see put.

pousté *n.* power 11/29.

pouert *n.* penury 11/12.

powere *n.* ability; *to owr* ∼ as well as we can *5/441.

pownde *n.* pound (of money): *for no* ∼ on no account 4/125.

prately *adv.* prettily 13a/53.

prattyffe *n.* practice, action: *with* ~ *6/593.

prec *v.* preach 7/417. **prechistou** *pr. 2 sg.* (with suffixed pron.) do you preach 7/239. **precit** *pa. t.* preached 7/69.

preciously *adv.* splendidly 13a/58.

pref(e) *n.* test 4/280; *in a* ~ to the test 6/442; **preve** *6/208.

premonyshed *pp.* forewarned 2d/129. **premonyshynge** *pr. p.* 2d/145.

prene *v.* stab, pierce 6/467, 478.

prepare *n.* preparation; *hath* ~ (?) proposes 2d/62.

pres *v. refl.* thrust myself forward 8/172.

pres(e) *n.* exertion: *put me in* ~ put myself forward 1a/40; crowd: *in* ~ together 11/3.

presand *n.* present, gift 1a/42.

present *n.* present: *in* ~ now 8/122.

present *v.* offer 5/374; present 5/386. **presented** *pp.* formally reported 6/57.

prest *adj.* ready *5/29, 7/469; *of powere* ~ ready and able 6/225.

prestly *adv.* vigorously 6/506.

preue *v.* test, try 4/21, 6/360, 773; prove 6/460, 790.

preve see **pref(e)**.

prevely *adv.* privately 4/83; secretly 6/278, 360.

prevente *v.* frustrate 2d/79.

priere *n.* prayer 7/97.

prynt *n.* impression, stamp 6/467.

pryvyté *n.* privacy, secrecy 6/276.

processe *n.* narrative, account 6/75.

profytable *adj.* beneficial 6/597, 647.

progenytors *n. pl.*; *apparently an error for a word meaning 'followers'* 6/408.

prohybyte *pp.* forbidden 2a/56.

prolocutor *n.* speaker of a prologue 2b, c/introd.

proper *adj.* handsome, admirable 11/10.

prove see **preue**.

provey *v.* provide 3/31.

proviaunce *n.* provision 4/9. Cf. **purveiance**.

prow(e) *n.* profit, advantage *3/72, 127, 7/309.

punche *n.* dagger 6/474.

pungarnetys *n. pl.* pomegranates 6/186.

purpoos(e) *n.* purport 6/9; sense 6/571.

purposed *adj.* in *be* ~ intend 6/5.

puruayed *pp.* provided, furnished 1a/25.

purveiance *n.* provision 3/72; **purveaunce, purviaunce** 6/322, *my* ~ provision for me 4/39.

put *v. refl.* submit 6/909. *pr. 1 sg.* see **pres(e)**. **pottyst** *tr. 2 sg.* remove, free 8/144. **pot** *imp.* 8/203. **put** *pp.* subjected 1c/12.

quan *conj.* when 8/173; **qwhen** 7/93.

qvart *adj.* in good health 5/462.

quartan *n.* quartan fever (recurring every three days) 6/613.

quat *pron.* what 8/88.

qued *n.* evil person, villain 8/103.

queþire so *adv.* whether 8/34.

quyk *adj.* living, live 4/150, 329, 330; **queke, qweke** 5/138, 140.

quyk, quylk see **which**.

quylys see **whils**.

quyte, qwyte *v.* repay 4/291; reward 7/100. **quit, quyt** *pp.* paid 6/568; rid 6/784.

quod *pa. t.* said 13a/7.

qwall *n. coll.* whale(s), porpoises 13a/36.

qwhat see **what**.

qwhen see **quan**.

qwher *adv.* where 7/455.

qwher *conj.* whether 7/453, 464. *adv.* introducing question 7/273.

qwherof *adv.* of what 7/171.

qwhile see **while**.

qwho *pron.* who 7/166, 167.

rayis *n. pl.* kinds of striped cloth 8/176.

railed *pp.* set, arranged 3/51.

rake¹ *pr. 1 sg.* care 3/182.

rake² *pr. pl.* move quickly, change 13a/19.

rancheth *pr. 3 sg.* tears, wounds 6/815.

rap(e) *v. refl.* hasten 6/661. *pr. subj. 1 pl.* 8/83. *imp.* 8/44.

rast *n.* rest, comfort 7/129.

raue *v.* talk foolishly 1a/28. **raues** *pr.
pl.* 1a/15.

rave see **ryve.**

raw *n.* row; *by* ∼ in order 1c/24.

reach *imp.* hand, give 2d/138.

read see **red(e).**

rebel *adj.* disobedient, rebellious
8/96.

rebyll rable *adv.* in *gooth* ∼ rattles
6/600.

recheles *adj.* thoughtless, senseless
1a/15.

recomaunde *refl.*, *pr. 1 pl.* commend
ourselves 13b/3.

recuer *n.* remedy 6/522.

red(e) *n.* advice, plan 1c/54, 9/22;
course of action 8/105; **read** 3/119;
opinion: *haue I* ∼ I believe 5/413.

red(e) *pr. 1 sg.* advise 5/143, 7/229,
410.

redely *adv.* without delay 4/16, 6/661.

redolent *adj.* fragrant 13a/26.

redresse *pr. subj. pl.* address yourselves 6/609.

refulsyth *pr. 3 sg.* makes radiant
13a/17.

refute *n.* refutation; *withowten* ∼
undeniably 2a/58.

reherce, reherse *v.* repeat, recall
1c/24; describe 6/160. *pr. pl.* relate,
tell 6/409.

reyn *n.* realm, country 6/139.

reysyth see **rysse.**

reysones *n. pl.* raisins 6/180.

reioyceth *pr. 3 sg.* delights 13a/10,
21.

relacion *n.* report 4/67.

remeve *pr. subj.* move 4/141.

ren(ne) *v.* run 7/268, 13a/39; **rin**
*6/675. **renne** *pr. 1 sg.* 6/503. **renneth**
3 sg. is current 6/94; runs 6/503 s.d.;
rennis 7/266. **renne** *pl.* 13a/18. *imp.*
6/504. **rennyng** *pr. p.* 13a/42; renand 13a/44.

rengnyt *pr. 3 sg.* reigns, extends 8/29.

rent *n.* income (from land) 5/3, 11/9.

renvid *pa. t. intr.* changed 2b/28. *pp.*
revised 2b/introd.

repayer *v.* make (their) way 13a/29.

repleate *adj.* complete 2b/8.

reporte *v.* (?) speak (*but failure of
rhyme indicates corruption*) 6/156.

repreue *n.* shame, ignominy 6/456.

requryed *pa. t.* begged 4/14.

reseyve *imp.* accept 5/387.

resystens *n.* adverse criticism 13b/6.

resounus see **resun.**

respect *n.* in *in* ∼ *to* in comparison
with 2d/125.

rest *imp.* in ∼ *well*, a greeting 3/113,
148, 5/59.

restore *v.* atone for 6/910, 965.

resun *n.* statement, what one has to
say 8/61; **resoun** 10/11. **resounus**
pl. considerations; *schewe* ∼ give an
account of things 8/13.

reut *n.* pity 7/346.

reuþyles *adj.* ruthless, cruel 7/351.

reue *v.* deprive, rob 7/246.

reuerence *n.* honour 6/574, 578.

reuerte *v.* return to a former state,
change 6/817; turn back 13a/41.

rewe *v.* cause to regret 7/198. **rewes**
pr. 3 sg. impers. in *me* ∼ I repent
*3/1.

ryal *adj.* royal, kingly 8/176.

rychesse *n.* wealth 6/18, 117.

ricmen *n. pl.* powerful men, mag-
nates 7/351.

ryfe *adv.* widely 6/642.

ryff *n.* reef (part of) sail 3/83.

ryght *adj.* straight, shortest 6/590;
richt just 10/12.

right, rygth *adv.* just, exactly 1c/38;
equitably 6/281; very 3/121, 4/22,
5/372, 6/329; **rit, ryt** 7/438, 8/175;
ful ∼ at once, quickly 6/309, 846,
853.

rygore *n.* cruelty 6/824.

rin see **ren(ne).**

ryngant *pr. p.* ringing 8/178.

rynge *pr. 1 sg.* move, travel 6/99.

rys *n.* rice 6/179.

rysse *v.* rise, rebel, revolt 5/208.
reysyth *pr. 3 sg.* 5/299.

ryth *n.* right, justice; *with* ∼ justly
(called) 8/65.

ryve *v.* split 6/712 s.d., 715. **rofe**
pa. t. 6/48; **rave** 6/943.

rywe *adj.* regretful, sad 8/129.

ro *n.* roe(buck) 7/268.

rod, ro(o)de *n.* cross 6/131, 135,
7/386; (in oath) 7/298, 418.

rodd *n.* punishment 2d/143.

royes *n. pl.* (?) fellows (see *O.E.D.*
roy *sb.*²) 1a/15.

Romney *n.* Rumney, a sweet wine of Greek origin 6/340.

rot *n.* root, source 7/129.

rowe *n.* plate or ring ('burr') into which the point of a nail (**seam**) is clinched 3/26.

rownde *adj.* heavy, severe 8/256.

rownde *adv.* with easy motion 4/124.

rowte *n.* company 4/320.

rowte *v.* throw 6/703.

ruff *n.* (?) rough-tree, spar 3/83.

rufull *adj.* sorrowful, painful 6/817.

rume *adv.* wide apart 9/3.

sacred *pp.* consecrated (the Host) 6/363, 379.

sacrifye *v.* sacrifice 4/57. **sacrified** *pp.* 4/150.

sae *adv.* so *3/2, 31; (?) say 3/122.

say see **se(e)**.

sayn see **sig**.

sale *n.* sail 6/116.

saluacion *n.* cure 6/777.

samyn *adv.* together 1c/69. Cf. **insame**.

sang *n.* song 1a/13.

sare see **sore**.

saue *adj.* safe, unimpaired; saving, in ∼ *þi plesaunce* with due respect for thy pleasure 4/280; out of danger 6/588 (cf. **sure**).

saue *v.* cure, remedy 1b/7; **sauy** save 7/406; observe, keep *5/92. *pr. subj.* preserve, save 8/236.

saurit *pa. t.* savoured, tasted pleasant 7/71.

sawe *n.* something said, words 6/393, 7/116, 471, 8/96.

scamoly *n.* scammony, a gum-resin used as a purge 6/586.

schal *pr. sg.* shall 1b/30; *pl.* 1a/31. **xal** *sg.* 8/21, 48; *pl.* 2a/87, 8/92. **schul** *pl.* 7/98; **schullin** 7/13; **xul** 8/91. **shuld** *pa. t. subj.* (in uncertified report): ∼ *be* was 1a/19, is said to be 6/204; similarly 6/411, 413; **xuld** 8/104; **suld** would 8/102.

sche *pron.* she 5/257–9 etc.; **che** 8/101, 102; **scho** 7/99, 100, 11/26, 30. Cf. **ho**.

schen *adj.* bright, beautiful 7/140.

scheppe *pr. pl. subj.* go by ship, sail 8/35.

schereys see **cher(e)**.

schewe see **showe**.

schil see **skil**.

schyld *n.* child 8/114.

schir see **ser**.

scho see **sche**.

schonge see **chong**.

schorte *imp.* shorten: ∼ *me of my woo* shorten my misery for me 5/309.

schrewed *adj.* malicious, wicked 8/103. Cf. **screu**.

schrywe *v. refl.* confess 8/210.

schul see **schal**.

scyens, syence *n.* learning, science 6/529, 647.

sclawe, sclo(w) see **sle**.

scot *pp.* thrown *7/414 (cf. *O.E.D.* shoot *v.* 11, quot. *a.* 1340).

screu *n.* villain 7/421.

scuerie *pr. 1 sg.* swear 9/9.

se(e) *n.* seat 6/151; throne 7/276, 323.

se(e) *v.* see 1a/24, 1b/14; **seen** 6/286; **soe** 9/19. **sawe** *pa. t. 1, 3 sg.* 4/314, 6/536; **say** 4/114. **sye** *2 sg.* 4/98. **saw** *pl.* 1c/35, 58. **sen(e)** *pp.* 1a/9, b/38, 4/366, 6/74, 7/357.

seam *n.* nail or rivet fastening the strakes of a clinker-built boat 3/26.

seekman *n.* sick man 6/558.

sege see **sig**.

seir *adj.* various, manifold *3/48.

sekenes *n.* illness, infirmity 1b/7.

sekyrly see **sikirly**.

sem *v.* suit, please *7/116.

semblable *adj.* similar 2a/16.

semblably *adv.* similarly 2c/1.

semelé, semely *adj.* beautiful, handsome 6/163, 266; **semly** 8/18, 38; capable, fit 8/171; as *n. pl.* worthy people 6/3. **semlyest** *sup.* fairest 8/57.

semly *adv.* reverently 6/848; decorously 8/11.

send *pp.* sent 3/192, 7/75. **isente** 7/475.

ser, sir, syr *n.* sir, used as title of a priest 6/228 s.d., 233, 323, etc.; **schir** in address 7/424, 435; **sure** 12/1. **sorys** *pl.* 5/435, 443; **syrse** 6/221.

serow *n.* grief, pain 8/128.

sertys *adv.* certainly, assuredly 8/246.

ses¹ *pr. pl.* cease, end 5/153.

ses(e)² *v.* strike 6/451, 470.
set *v. refl.* sit down 8/11.
seth(e) *v.* boil 6/44, 939. soden *pp.* 6/706.
shapyn *pp. adj.* (naturally) fitted, competent *6/526.
shear *imp.* cut 3/55.
Shere Thursday *n.* the Thursday in Holy Week, Maundy Thursday 6/398.
shew(e) see showe.
shyffte *n.* in *make good* ~ find good means 6/303.
shope *pa. t.* created 4/51.
showe *v.* make known, explain 2a/34; schewe declare 8/62; shew in ~ *our lyfe* confess 6/797. shewe *imp.* confess 6/66. shewyd (*lyues*) *pa. t.* 6/52. shewyd *pp.* 6/951; revealed 6/849.
shrugge *pr. subj. sg.* is moving about 6/599.
shuld see schal.
sib *adj.* as *n.* relative 7/348.
siche *adj.* such 7/317; swilk 11/11. Cf. slike.
side *n.* in *on neuer a* ~ (with neg.) anywhere 4/152.
sye see se(e).
syence see scyens.
sig *v.* say, tell 7/358, 360; sege 9/20; sayn 1c/36. sigge *pr. 1 sg.* 7/220.
sike *v.* sigh 7/163. sight *pa. t.* 11/13.
sikir *adj.* sure: *be him* ~ let it be sure for him, let him be assured 7/493.
sikirly *adv.* certainly 11/6, 23; sekerly, sekyrly 6/262, 13b/17.
sille *n.* floor (of a hall): *vpon* ~ in hall 8/18.
symylutude *n.* likeness: *to hys* ~ like him 2a/8.
synke *v.* come down, descend 5/159.
synymone *n.* cinnamon 6/183.
sit, syt(h) *n.* sight 8/120; aspect 7/39 (2nd); *in* ~ (tag) 8/80, with my own eyes 8/118, before me 13b/1.
sit *v.* sit; dwell, rest 7/39; syttun endure, bear 8/171. sit *pr. 1 sg.* in ~ *on kne* kneel 7/278.
syt(h) *adv.* afterwards 6/232, 235; sithen, sythen 1c/37, 6/429, 11/36.
sythe *n. pl.* times 5/318.

sithe, siþe *conj.* since 1b/7, 40, 4/120, 252; syt 6/240; sithen, sythyn 1b/31, 5/228.
sythys *n. pl.* sighs 2a/90.
syttys *n. pl.* cares, troubles 8/171.
skaith *n.* harm, injury 3/117.
skil, skyll(e) *n.* reason, what is reasonable or right 6/363; *reason and* ~ 2a/30, 4/19; ~ *and riȝte* 7/156; *rycht and* ~ 6/192, schil 10/12.
sladdes *n. pl.* hollows, valleys 13a/20.
sle *v.* kill 4/239, 288. *imp.* 4/233; slo 8/133; sclo *8/122. slow *pa. t.* 7/83; sclow 8/225. slayne *pp.* 4/181, 8/98; slaw 8/95; sclawe 8/121, 222.
slee *adj.* clever, skilful 3/107, 112; sleye as *n.* wise man 7/192.
sleppe *v.* slip off, escape 6/526.
slet *adj.* wise 7/343.
slight *n.* skill 3/174.
slike *adj.* such *3/141. Cf. siche.
slo, slow see sle.
smaragdys *n. pl.* emeralds 6/168.
smartli see smertly.
smert *v.* suffer pain 7/63. *pr. pl.* 6/818. *subj. sg.* *7/49.
smert(e) *adv.* painfully 4/207; quickly 5/367.
smertly *adv.* quickly 6/142; smartli 7/138.
smyte *v.* strike (with *to*, 'at') 7/237. smytte *pp.* 6/463; smytyn 6/465; smetyn 8/255.
sneke *n.* cold in the head 6/618.
so *conj.* as 7/264, 9/19.
socowr *n.* help 8/91.
sodayn *adj.* unforeseen 1b/14.
soden see seth(e).
soe see se(e).
soferyng *adj.* tolerant 13b/5.
softe *adj.* courteous, flattering 7/320.
solace, solas *n.* joy 1a/31, 8/76; pleasure 2a/72, d/59, 7/267; personified 7/295, 321.
solacious *adj.* pleasing 13a/55.
some *n.* sum, substance 2c/21.
son(e) *adv.* at once 1b/28, 5/55, 87, 6/329, 7/286; shortly 7/436, 438.
sond *n.* messenger, emissary 5/68, 146.
sondis *n. pl.* sands, shores 7/486.
soporacion *n.* putting to sleep 2a/12.
sor *n.* pain 7/406.

sore *adj.* painful 4/237, 280, 7/103, 8/52; grieved 4/244, 5/160; **sare** 8/171.

sore *adv.* painfully 4/147, 229, 5/135, 11/13; eagerly 6/21.

sory *adj.* sorrowful, grieved 4/362.

sorys see **ser.**

sothe *n.* truth 1c/17, 6/11, 92; **sot** 7/354, 358.

soþe *adj.* true 8/223.

soule *n. gen.* of the soul 7/94.

souereigne *n.* lord, master 4/318, 328. **souereyns** *pl.* (in address) masters, sirs 5/435, *6/9, 13b/1, 23.

souereigne *adj.* sovereign, supreme 4/358; **sufferen** 4/273.

souereynlyche *adv.* supremely 13a/57.

sowled *pp.* soiled, defiled *3/48.

sownd(e) *adj.* salutary 6/41, 936.

space *n.* time, opportunity 6/461.

spar(e) *v.* spare 6/459, 7/402; **sparye** 7/84. **spart** *pr. pl.* hold back 7/363.

sparedist *pa. t. 2 sg.* 4/288.

sped(e) *v.* prosper, thrive 5/389; succeed 7/173; hasten 7/138. **spedit** *pr. pl. refl.* *7/369. **spede** *subj.* make prosperous 4/241, 7/8. **sped(d)** *pp.* caused to pass, governed 4/325; finished 5/289; *he shalbe* ~ *his* business shall be done 6/329.

spedyng *n.* success, prosperity 6/112.

spelle *v.* tell, relate 7/13.

spence *n.* buttery, bar 6/531.

spent *pp.* exhausted 6/596.

speryd *pa. t.* shut 6/46, 941.

spyd *n.* speed: *a good* ~ strongly 5/376.

spyde *pp.* seen 6/306. Cf. **aspye.**

spyer *n.* spar, rod, pole 3/84.

spyll, spille *v.* destroy 4/223, 7/124; shed 5/173. *pr. subj.* 4/263.

sporte *n.* entertainment, amusement 13a/9.

spredd *pp.* passed round 6/330.

spright *n.* spirit 2d/142; temper 2b/28; mind, soul 2c/20.

spryngyth *pr. 3 sg.* extends 6/91. **sprong** *pa. t.* 6/16.

sprot *n.* spar, rod, pole 3/84.

sprout *n.* twig *3/84.

sprund *n.* spar, rod, pole 3/84.

stabil *adj.* standing firm 7/238.

staied see **styed.**

sted(e) *n.* place *1c/52, 4/141, 5/144; **stead** 3/75, 202.

stede *n.* horse: *on* ~ as I ride 8/38.

stede *v. refl.* apply oneself 5/278.

steer *adj.* strong 3/10, 169.

stere *v.* move, go 6/263. *pr. subj.* 6/699. **steare** *tr.* stir 6/667. **steryd** *pp.* agitated 5/78.

sterte *v.* leap from its lair 13a/37.

steuen *n.* voice 1b/31; **stevyn** sound, note 6/80.

styed *pa. t.* ascended 6/423; **staied** *11/36.

stif(f) *adj.* severe 3/10, 169; strong 3/20; hard, firm 6/466; ~ *and strong* 7/147, 161.

styffly *adv.* vigorously 6/263.

still(e) *adj.* quiet 1c/73, 7/182.

stille, styll(e) *adv.* constantly 5/250; quietly 9/12. See **loude.**

stint, stynt *imp.* cease 1c/73; desist (*of*, 'from') 11/2.

stond *v.* live, be 6/290, 298. *pr. 1 sg.* 6/296. **stont** *3 sg.* in ~ *him non eye* no fear exists for him, he stands in no fear 7/318. **stondyng** *pr. p.* 1c/35. **stode** *pa. t.* 6/69.

stoppe *v.* shut up 6/688, 704, 709.

store *n.* wealth 4/216; possession 4/246.

stotey *n.* audacity 7/36.

stout(e), stowte *adj.* strong 6/665, 7/4, 117.

stounde, stownd *n.* time 7/441; hour 8/254; (*in*) *this* ~ now 6/278, 314, 8/88, 100, 113.

strae *n.* straw *3/33.

straytly *adv.* narrowly, severely 6/723.

strang *adj.* severe, cruel 1c/12; **strong(e)** 2a/86; (?) great 2a/51.

strenger *comp.* stronger 6/432.

streinth, streyint, strent, strynt *n.* strength 7/36, 135, 243, 332.

streytnesse *n.* severity 6/739.

strif(f)e, stryf *n.* opposition 1c/73; resistance 5/83; trouble 6/644; dispute 7/74; struggle, effort 7/87; quarrelling, fighting, conflict 7/214, 251, 292; **stryue** 7/174; encounter 4/284.

strynt see **streinth.**

striue *v.* contest, compete 7/166, 167.
striuith *pr. 3 sg.* pursues, carries on (obj. *strife*) 7/87.
stroied *pp.* destroyed *3/62.
stroke *pp.* stricken 2d/104.
strong(e) see **strang**.
substance *n.* quantity 6/129.
subtyll *adj.* cunning 2d/85.
subtyllty *n.* craft, guile 2d/39.
suffred *pa. t.* endured, submitted 1b/6.
sufferen see **souereigne**.
suld see **schal**.
sum(me) see **al(l)**.
sumquat *adv.* to some degree 8/188.
sumwhatt *n.* something 6/680.
supersidias *n. supersedeas*, a writ suspending proceedings 7/380.
sure *adj.* safe, taken care of 6/550; *in ~ for certain* 13a/54.
sure *v.* give assurance, promise 6/279.
sure see **ser**.
sustentacion *n.* sustenance, support 2d/2.
swayn *n.* boy 1a/47. **swaynis** *pl.* retainers 7/116.
sueyerys *n. pl.* squires 8/4.
swemfull, swymfull *adj.* painful, distressing 6/800, 805, 809.
swenge *v.* beat, thrash *9/18.
swet, swyt *adj.* gracious 5/146, 350.
swilk see **siche**.
swowne *n.* fainting fit: *fall in ~ faint* 4/202.

tacched *pp.* fixed 1b/16.
tae see **take**.
taynt *v.* corrupt 3/108.
take *v.* take; **tae** *3/5; bring, give 2d/15, 6/277; *~ entent, tent* attend 1c/49, 3/39; *~ credence vnto* believe in 6/730; *refl.* go 6/947. **take** *pr. 1 sg.* in *~ to borowe* I call to witness 7/226; *~ delyght of* enjoy 13a/22. **takeþ** *3 sg.* in *~ me ful nye* afflicts me deeply 4/258. **takith** *pl.* 7/96. **takeþ** *imp.* take 4/137; *take in ~ for* regard as 7/234; *~ avysement of* reflect upon 6/874. **tok(e)** *pa. t. sg.* in *~ to hert*, see **hert**; *~ lyf* was born 8/190. *pl.* in *~ him hom betwen* arrested him 1c/27. **take** *pp.* in *ben ~* have betaken themselves, gone 6/305;

refl. betaken myself 8/242; **itaken** in *beth togeder ~* have come together (in conflict) 7/86.
tal(e) *n.* speech, words, thing said 5/345, 6/114, 7/60, 360; *tell no ~* (with neg.) say a word 6/552; talk 7/209; talking 9/6. **talis** *pl.* 1c/46; tales 6/205.
talente *n.* desire 7/271, *477.
talkyng *n.* words, something said 6/133.
tapstere *n.* barmaid 6/531.
tary *v. tr.* delay, obstruct 6/125, 365; **taré** *intr.* delay 6/557. **tery** *imp.* 5/232. **taréd** *pa. t.* 6/576.
tariyng *n.* delay 7/319; **teryyng** 5/239.
tell(e) *v.* tell 1c/46; count 6/314. *imp.* in *~ on* speak, say what you want 1a/2; count 6/317. **told** *pa. t.* 1c/34. **told** *pp.* *3/195; **toolde** counted 6/313.
ten(e) *v.* anger, annoy 6/289, 7/48, 453.
tende *v.* attend 6/195, 8/20.
tender *adj.* precious 5/49; touching 5/128.
tendrely *adv.* attentively 6/150; assiduously 6/195.
tene *n.* trouble, pain 6/77, 783, 879, 8/86, 99.
tenely *adv.* cruelly 1c/27.
tent *n.* heed, attention: *take ~* 3/39; *geue ~* 8/87.
tercyan *n.* tertian fever (recurring every other day) 6/613.
tery see **tary**.
tes *adj. pl.* these (present) 9/21.
þai *pron. pl.* they 1c/6, 7, 30, 7/361; **thay** 6/41; they 5/128, 6/29; **þe** 6/31, 200, 203, 7/374. **theyr** *poss.* 2b/6, c/1; **þer** 6/29, 13a/23, 30; **thyr** 6/51. **them** *acc.* and *dat.* 5/8, 450; *refl.* themselves 6/84. Cf. **he**.
þay *conj.* though 7/381; **þegh** 7/495; **thewh** 6/526.
þan(ne), than *adv.* then 2a/65, b/26, 6/236, *7/73, 8/29, 11/24, 13a/22.
thanc, thanke *n.* thanks, gratitude 6/258, 8/73. See **can¹**.
thank *v.* thank (*of*, 'for') 1a/35, 5/5.
thar *pr. 3 sg. impers.* is necessary: *~ vs* we need 1a/34.

þareto *adv.* to that: ~ *broȝte* 7/202, see **bryng**.

that, þat *pron. rel.* that which, what 4/27, 69, 5/265, 6/335, 11/5.

þe see þai.

the(e) *v.* thrive, prosper 4/102; (in asseveration) *as might I* ~ 3/149, 153, *so mot I* ~ 7/219. *pr. subj.* 3/206.

þede *n.* country *7/250.

þegh see þay.

their *pron. dem. pl.* these 3/3.

theyr, them see þai.

þenke see þing *v.*

þens *adv.* from there 4/323.

þer *adv. rel.* where 8/18; ~ *as* 8/148.

ther see þai.

þeragayne *adv.* opposed, resistant 4/162; to the contrary 4/360; against it 5/299, 446; (in answer) to that 6/311.

þerby(e) *adv.* by it 4/369; about it 5/447; over there 4/335.

þeretylle *adv.* for that 4/68.

þerfor, therfor(e) *adv.* for that, it 6/308, 322, 7/107; for this purpose 7/411; on that account 4/152, *7/220.

þerinne *adv. rel.* in which 13a/24.

therke *adj.* dark 13a/20, 27.

therof(f) *adv.* to that 6/25; for that 6/131; of it 6/349.

þeron, theron *adv.* on the subject 6/28; on these 7/105; in that 8/130.

þerto, ther(e)to(o) *adv.* to that end; to, in that 1c/49, 3/24, 4/64; in addition 5/216; *wyll not* ~ is unwilling to do this 5/301.

therwith *adv.* with it: *into the ouyn I wyll* ~ I will throw it into the oven 6/707.

thes see þis.

þeþer, thether *adv.* there 6/847, 8/180.

thewh see þay.

thyke *adv.* closely, densely 5/395.

þing *n.* creature *8/139.

þing *v.* think 7/399. thynk(e) *pr. 1 sg.* intend 6/263, 467, 698. þingit *pl.* think 7/365. þing *imp.* 7/391. þenke *subj.* 4/102. thowt *pp.* 8/126.

thinks *pr. 3 sg.* it seems 3/197; thynkyth 6/372; (*me*) thynk(e) 6/200, 980; thynketh seems 6/318. thynke *pl.* seem 5/157.

þis, this, thys *adj. pl.* these 5/92, 449, 7/342; thes 6/3.

tho *pron. pl.* those 6/84, 618, 839; thow 5/434.

þor *adv.* there *11/17.

thorowgh, thorwhe *prep.* through, by means of 6/784, 62; thorow 8/46; thowr 8/226.

thorowght *prep.* throughout 6/116, 138.

þot *conj.* though 7/437.

þout, thowt *n.* anxiety 8/121; *take no* ~ do not be distressed 5/339; intention 8/200; conscience *8/215; *hau* ~ *opon* consider 7/397.

thowr *n.* tower 8/138.

thowr see **thorowgh**.

thrae *adv.* eagerly, quickly *3/181.

þrawe *v.* suffer 7/104 (note).

thrid *adj.* third 1c/20.

thryffte *n.* success, well-being 6/530.

thriwe *v.* thrive, prosper *7/422.

tyde *n.* time 2a/79; season 4/303; *thys* ~ now 6/125, 716.

tiding *n.* news 3/46, 8/141.

till, tyll(e) *prep.* to 11/26; (postponed) 4/266, 6/195, 8/20.

tyseke *n.* phthisis, tuberculosis 6/618.

tyte *adv.* quickly, at once 3/115; tyth(e) 8/61, 200.

to *prep.* in comparison with 7/167.

to(o) *num.* two 5/8, 107.

tobrast *pa. t.* burst to pieces 6/48, 943.

tocrake *v.* split apart 12/6.

todraw *pp.* drawn, pulled apart 7/481.

tok(e) see **take**.

tokenyng *n.* sign 6/544.

to(o)ld(e) see **tell(e)**.

topazyouns *n. pl.* topazes 6/168.

tormentry, turmentry *n.* torture 6/732, 802, 940, 45.

-tou, -tow *pron.* thou, suffixed to verb: artou 7/442; auestow *8/98; prechistou 7/239; seistou 7/191; woltou 7/417, wolte 7/218; woldistou 7/195; wostou 7/281, 424.

toun, towne *n.* town; *to* ~ home 4/201; *icom to* ~ among men, into society 7/157.

towond *pr. pl.* wound, pierce 5/121.

trayn *n.* guile, deceit; *withouten* ~ truly 1c/67.

trase *n.* course, way 4/79.

traueylyn *v.* journey 8/251.

tre *n.* cross 1b/16.

trey *n.* affliction, suffering: ∼ *and tene* *6/77.

trespas(se) *n.* offence 4/176, 5/266, 6/865, 8/258.

trespassyd (*aȝens*) *pp.* offended 5/169.

treut see trowth.

trist *v.* trust 7/143. *imp.* believe, be sure of 7/435; trust 4/347, 6/359.

tristed *pa. t.* trusted 1c/13.

tristili *adv.* faithfully 7/128.

trow(e) *pr. 1 sg.* think, trust, believe 3/105, 6/166, 208, 7/452; hope 3/108, 5/378. troust *2 sg.* 7/419. trowe *pl.* 4/327. trow'd *pa. t.* believed 3/13.

trowth *n.* truth 6/295; truþe in *in* ∼ assuredly 7/143; treut, truyt 7/330, 334.

trust see trist.

trusty *adj.* precious 6/381.

turmentry see tormentry.

turn(e) *v.* in ∼ *agayne* come back 2d/33; turn back 2d/137. *imp.* change 3/92.

tway *num.* two 4/46; tweye 7/104; tweyn(e) 4/292, 350; *on* ∼ in two *5/127.

twycche *pr. subj.* twitch, jump 6/514.

vche see eche.

vn *pr. 1 sg.* assent *5/421.

vndertake *v.* understand 6/291; take in hand, take charge of 6/617. *pr. 1 sg.* undertake 6/498.

undirstond *v. refl.* perceive 7/65.

vngirde *imp.* undress 4/201.

vngoodely *adj.* evil, wicked 4/251.

vnkindnes *n.* unnatural behaviour, ingratitude 4/5.

vnlefull *adj.* impermissible, criminal 6/819; onlefull 6/852.

unlode *pp.* (of *unlode*) taken off 2d/146.

unlusty *adj.* feeble 3/79.

vnryghtfull *adj.* wicked *6/824.

vntill *prep.* to 11/17.

unto, vnto *prep.* to: ∼ *this* to this end 2d/40; ∼ *sacrifise* as a sacrifice 4/167; ∼ *my connyng* as well as I know how 6/127; onto 5/34, 144; ∼ *my mynd* in my opinion 6/450.

vprysyng *n.* resurrection 6/419.

vaylle *n.* cover, protection 6/304.

vanyté *n.* light pleasure 13a/11.

velanye see vileynye.

veniaunce *n.* vengeful attack 4/251.

venys *n. pl.* vines 13a/32.

uer *pa. t. subj.* were, would be 9/7.

verayly, veralye *adv.* truly 4/347, 336; verely 6/801; verylye 4/327.

very *adj.* true 5/53.

veryfy *pr. pl.* certify 6/446.

vernage *n.* a sweet white Italian wine 6/428.

vyage *n.* journey 6/969; wyage 8/41.

vileynye *n.* insult, injury 7/170; velanye 6/735; uileni dishonourable conduct 7/339; weleny 8/39.

uyt see with *adv.*

vitles *adj.* mentally deficient, imbecile 9/15.

voydoth *imp. pl.* go away 6/640.

uold see wol(l).

ureist *pr. 2 sg.* (= *wrethest*) make angry 7/416.

way *n.* way: *gone my* ∼ died 4/315.

way *adv.* away: *do* ∼ stop 4/112.

wayns *n. pl.* dwellings, home 3/150.

waytyn *pr. pl.* attend 6/190. wayte *imp.* watch, keep watch 4/122.

wake see walke.

walew *n.* value, sum 6/290.

walke, walkyn *v.* walk, go 6/807, 304, 358; proceed 6/335; wake 6/502. walk(e) *pr. pl.* live 1c/54. *imp.* go 6/233, 236.

waltyr *pr. pl.* surge, roll 13a/36.

wanhope *n.* despair 6/67.

wante *v.* be lacking 2b/18; wont (with indir. obj.) 1c/48.

warand *v.* warrant, guarantee 1a/8.

ward see word(e).

ware *adj.* careful 6/927, 7/311.

ware *imp.* take care 6/598.

wari *pr. subj.* curse 6/559.

warke see werk.

wax *pr. 1 sg.* grow, become 4/113.

we *interj.* ho! 1a/1.

wede *n.* dress, clothes 8/37.

weder *n.* weather 7/10.

wedyr *n.* wether 4/269.

weet see **wit** v.

weye pp. weighed 7/105.

wel(e) n. well-being, prosperity, good fortune 7/376, 13a/60; in ~ am biwent live in prosperity 7/131; in ~ and wo in all circumstances 4/265.

wel(le) adv. well: ~ mot yow be may it be well for you, good fortune to you 6/249, 633; very 6/56; rightly 7/82; **wyll** 2a/37, 5/17, 59; **wol(e)** 6/178, 8/29.

welaway, welawey interj. alas! *3/95, 5/234. Cf. **wo-lo-wo**.

weld(e) v. control, own 6/117, 7/122. pr. 1 sg. 8/14.

weldyng n. control, power 6/115, 121.

weleny see **vileynye**.

well n. will, desire 6/122.

welth(e) n. prosperity 5/457; well-being *8/117. **welthys** pl. riches 8/14.

wend(e) v. go 3/144, 7/393, 469; **wendyn** 8/83; **wynd** 7/72. **wends** pr. 2 sg. 3/161. **wend(e)** subj. 2 sg. 7/162. pl. 5/402, 7/11; behave 7/206. **wend** pp. gone 7/73; **went** 1c/51, 8/112.

wene pr. 1 sg. believe, think *3/98, 6/199, 418, 7/445. **wend** pa. t. thought, expected 1b/4, 4/315, 6/575. **wente** pp. 7/273.

wenne n. joy, happiness 8/47.

werche v. do (representing another verb) 6/232, 325; **wirch** perform, carry out 7/189; inflict: ~ wo punish 7/119; **wyrk(e)**: ~ wrake injure 6/459; intr. act 6/788; **werk, worke** perform 6/122, 8/182; manage, use 3/80; **warke** 5/302. **werketh** pr. 3 sg. 6/499. **wrowtys** pa. t. 2 sg. didst create 8/51. **wroʒt** subj. in ~ striue resisted, opposed *7/174. **wrought, wrowght** pp. created 4/164, 6/2; done 6/367, *689; **wrogth** 5/404; **wrowt** 8/184, *187.

werd see **word(e)**.

were n. fear 6/482.

weryt pa. t. wore 5/464.

werk n. deed, action; word and ~ 1c/68; **warke** 5/404; **work** 6/819; **wyrk** event 6/482. **werkys** pl. deeds 6/910, 7/119, 189; **warks** in ~ wild licentious conduct 3/47.

werkyngys n. pl. actions *8/140.

werre n. war 7/489.

wet(te) see **wit** v.

wether pron. whichever (of two) 5/457.

what adv. how 4/184; **qwhat** why 7/218, 239.

whawys n. pl. waves 13a/36.

where conj. whereas, while 1c/18.

wer adv. rel.: ~ that 5/19, 42; **qwher** 7/162.

which pron. rel. which, who: þe ~ who 4/11; **wych(e)**, þe ~ who 6/20, whom 5/17, 199; **quyk** 8/219; **quylk** 8/262.

whyle n. time, hour 6/855; **wylle** short time 5/227.

while, whyll conj.: ~ that until 3/38; while 6/989; **wyll** 5/377; **qwhile** 7/227; **qwyll** 5/462.

whils conj. while 4/319; **quylys** 8/209.

whunt adj. wise, clever 3/112.

wyage see **vyage**.

wyde adv. widely, far and wide 8/15.

wide-where adv. far and wide 3/177.

wyfe n. pl. wives *6/595.

wight, wyght n.[1] creature, person, man 1c/42, 3/47, 6/15, 306; **wyt(h)** 8/70, 160.

wight n.[2] weight 2d/148.

wyght adj. vigorous, strong 11/8. **wytthest** sup. most vigorous, liveliest 8/70.

wyghtly adv. vigorously 6/212; briskly, quickly 6/606, 640.

wykkyd adj. harmful 6/347; **wykyt** evil, bad 8/53, 252.

wil, wyl, will(e) n. desire, what one wishes 8/40; at ~ as he wishes 3/23, under your control 7/228; at my, þi ~ 7/122, 180, 8/14, to my ~ 10/9; my ~ aue of þe enjoy you 8/64; intention 4/340; willingness 4/341; strength of mind, fierceness: werkis of ~ stern measures 7/119.

wil adj. astray, bewildered: ~ of red at a loss 1c/54.

wild, wyld(e) adj. licentious 3/47 (see **werk**); bewildered, confused 6/216; **wyl** wild 7/425; ~ and tame all creatures 8/33.

wyle n. deception 2d/85.

wyll see wel(le).

wyll(e) see whyle, while.

wymmen *n. pl.* women 1c/33; *attrib.* women's 1c/15; women 7/209.

wynd *v.* fly 3/109. *pr. subj.* *3/16.

wynd see wend(e).

wirch see werche.

wyrk(e) see werche, werk.

wise *n.* way 4/143; *in all* ～ by all means 4/272; wisse 5/334.

wysse *adj.* discreet, well-behaved 5/106.

wisse *pr. subj.* guide, direct 1c/22.

wit, wytt(e) *n.* senses 3/159, 6/655; mind 6/787, 858; knowledge, ability 3/23, 165; intelligence 5/409, 6/425, 7/335; *nones mannes* ～ no human intelligence 9/16. wittis, wyttys *pl.* senses, intelligence 1c/53; sense 6/768.

wit, wyt(te) *v.* know 1c/15, 5/161, 7/103, 177; find out 6/139, 147; know how to 6/244; weet 3/129, 131; wete 4/284, 6/244; wet(te) 6/147, 268. wot(e) *pr. 1, 3 sg.* 4/20, 218, 328, 5/141, 7/199; wott 6/681. wot *2 sg.* 1c/40; wost 4/113, 7/279, with suffixed pron. wostou 7/281, 424. wot *pl.* 1c/51; wott 6/334; wittin 7/483; weten 10/5. witen *subj. pl.* 10/11. wyste *pa. t. subj.* 6/210; wost 5/257. wist, wyst *pp.* 4/193, 333, 6/222.

wyt(h) see wight.

with *adv.* vigorously, strongly 7/89; uyt in *so* ～ at once 9/14. See wyght.

with *prep.* by, among 6/15.

wythall *prep.* (postponed) with 5/90.

wyther *conj.* whether 5/162.

withnayde *pp.* denied, refused 4/62.

withowten, -yn *prep.* without 3/103, 8/12, 25.

wittenes *pr. pl.* attest 1b/37.

wytthest see wyght.

wo(o) *n.* misery, grief 7/376; ～ *is me* I grieve 4/209, 230; *þat me is* ～ it grieves me 4/222, similarly 6/518; developed to *adj.* sad, wretched: *she wol be* ～ 4/74, similarly 4/238, 5/151. *interj.* in ～ *the whyle* cursed be the time 6/855. Cf. wel(e), and see mak(e), werche.

wode see wood(e).

wol(l) *pr. 1, 3 sg.* will 4/324, 5/52, 6/288, 7/100; wool 7/427. wolt *2 sg.* 7/458; with suffixed pron. woltou, wolte 7/417, 218. wol *pl.* 4/120, 7/473. wold *pa. t. subj.* would require 4/19; wool would 5/302; uold 7/419.

wol(e) see wel(le).

wollecom *adj.* welcome 5/68.

wo-lo-wo *interj.* alas! 7/327. Cf. welaway.

wombe *n.* belly, stomach 6/614.

women see wymmen.

won *v.* dwell, live 5/12. wonneth *pr. 3 sg.* 6/13.

won see on *pron.*

won(e) *n.* number, quantity: *ful gode* ～ many 1c/37; *gret* ～ in abundance *5/398.

wond(e) *v.* hesitate, delay 6/88. *pr. subj.* in *that thow ne* ～ without delay 6/138.

wonder *n.* wonder, surprise: *haue* ～ *off* wonder at 5/150.

wondyn see woundyn.

wondre *adv.* exceedingly 4/244, 11/13.

wondrely, wondursely *adv.* wondrously 6/7; amazingly 6/859.

wonschildis *n. pl.* (?) defenders of one's dwelling 7/146. [MS. reported *wonschild is*; no such form recorded elsewhere, but the emendations of Brandl, Holthausen, and Waterhouse are unconvincing.]

wont see wante.

wood(e) *adj.* mad 6/483, 503 s.d.; wode foolhardy 7/499.

woodnesse *n.* madness: *wake in* ～ go mad 6/502.

word(e) world 6/432, 8/15; ward 5/238; werd 8/189.

work(e) see werche, werk.

worklooms *n. pl.* tools 3/80.

worly, worlych *adj.* splendid, handsome 8/37, 79; excellent, beautiful 8/55.

worship *n.* honour, credit 4/292; wor(þ)chup, worchope worship 5/354, 361, 385; wourshepe in *doon* ～ worship 6/294.

worth *adj.* of value, use 3/77.

worth *pr. subj.* come to, befall 3/87.

worþiest *adv. sup.* most handsomely 8/70.

worthynesse *n.* honour, respect 6/119.

woso *pron.* whoever; if anyone 6/86; wosa 7/358.

woth *n.* injury *6/59.

wot(t) see wit *v.*

woundyn *pp.* formed 8/70; wondyn encompassed 8/85; wownd 8/106, 115.

woxyn *pp.* grown, become 8/175.

wraist *function indeterminable, perhaps a form of* wrest, *n., v., or pp.* 1c/32.

wrake *n.* ruin, disaster 4/342; harm, injury 6/459, 499; outrage, crime 8/243.

wrake *v.* take vengeance on 7/88.

wrath *pr. pl.* anger 6/726.

wreyd *pp.* informed against, betrayed 8/102. Cf. bewrey.

wreke *pp.* avenged 6/31, 212.

wroȝt, wrought, wrow(gh)t see werche.

wroþer *adj.* (orig. *dat. sg. fem.*) evil, disastrous 7/491; see hele.

wursheppful *adj.* honourable 13b/1.

xal, xul see schal.

yangelyngys *n. pl.* disturbances 8/8.

yar(e) *adj.* ready, at hand *3/196, 7/434.

yates *n. pl.* gates 4/84.

ye see ȝa, ȝe.

yede *pa. t.* went 6/299.

yeþed *pp.* comforted 5/334.

yeue, yif see ȝiue.

yilp see ȝelpe.

you, yow see ȝe.

a *prep.* to 9/8, 17, 10/9.

acun *adj.* any 10/12.

ay *pr. 1 sg.* have 9/21. **a** *3 sg.*: *il i* ~ there is 9/9.

ait *pr. subj. 3 sg.* help: *si m'ait Mahun* so help me M. 9/21.

aler *v.* go 10/15.

aset *adv.* very well, rightly 9/5.

autre *pron.* other 9/6.

ban *n. m.* proclamation, edict 9/4, 18.

barnage *n. m.* company of barons 10/7.

barouns *n. m. pl.* barons 10/2.

batu *pp.* beaten 9/16.

ben *adv.* well, closely, thoroughly 9/3, 8, 16, 10/4.

ceo *pron. dem.* this 10/7; **c'** it 9/18, 19.

cete *adj. f.* this *9/10.

cheris *adj. pl.* dear 10/1.

chiualeris *n. m. pl.* knights 10/2.

coard *n. m.* coward 9/22.

coy *adj.* quiet 9/7.

comandement *n. m.* command 9/19.

coronné *pp. adj.* crowned 10/5.

cour *n. f.* court 10/3.

couent *pr. 3 sg. impers.* behoves: *i vous* ~ you must 10/15.

couernour *n. m.* ruler 10/6.

cum *conj.* as 9/2.

cuntis *n. m. pl.* earls 10/2.

de *prep.* of (of origin) 10/8; see **turne**.

delay *n. m.* delay 10/12.

demonstrer *v.* make known 10/11.

demorrer *v.* delay, hesitate 9/12.

desturber *v.* disturb, interrupt 9/11.

dirray *fut. 1 sg.* (I) shall tell 10/14.

doy *pr. 1 sg.* owe 9/17. **deuez** *2 pl.* 9/5.

e *conj.* and 9/7, 8, 10/2, etc.

el see **il**.

en *prep.* in 9/13, 10/3; into 9/10.

enpereur, enperrur *n. m.* emperor 9/4; *poss.* 9/18.

entendet *imper. pl.* attend 9/8.

entre *pr. subj. 3 sg.* enter 9/10.

ert see **su**.

escotez, esc(o)utez *imper. pl.* listen 9/2, 3, 10/1.

est see **su**.

eus see **i**.

face *pr. subj. 3 sg.* make(s) 9/9. **fetes** *imper. pl.* 9/7. **fet** *pp.* performed 9/20.

fey *n. f.* faith, allegiance 9/5; ~ *ke io doy* . . . by the faith I owe, on my honour 9/17.

frun *adj. as n. m.* wretch, villain 9/12.

grant *adj.* great, high 10/8. **grenur** *comp.* greater 9/5.

haut *adv.* high 9/15.

honur *n.m.* reputation 9/3.

i *pron. 3 pl.* they 10/9. **eus** *obl.* them 10/10. See **il**.

i *adv.* there 9/9; see **ay**.

ignelement *adv.* quickly 9/20.

il *pron. 3 sg. m.* he, it 9/9, see **ay**; **el** 9/15; **i** 10/15. **le** *acc.* it 10/4. **luy** *dat.* to him 9/5. **sun** *poss.* his 9/19.

ja *adv.* (with neg.) never 9/14.

ieo *pron. 1 sg.* I 10/5, 10; **io** 9/17, 21. **me** *obl.* me 9/22; **m'** 9/21. **moy** *stressed* 9/8, 10/9. **moun** *poss. m.* my 10/7, 13, **mun** 9/17; **ma** *f.* 9/6, 10/11.

iu *n. m.* play 9/11.

jucer *infin. as imper.* put 9/13.

kar *conj.* for 10/10.

ke *conj.* that 10/5, 7, 9; **que** 9/22; ~ *el ne seyt* without being 9/15. See **pus que**.

ke *conj.* than 9/6.

ke *pron. rel.* who 10/8; that, which 9/17; **que** who 9/9. **qui** who 10/3.

la *def. art. f.* the 9/13; with *masc. n.* 9/18. **le** *m.* 9/4, 12; **l'** 9/18.

ley *n. f.* belief 9/6.

leyns *adv.* inside *9/13.

luy see **il**.

ma, me see ieo.

messager *n. m.* messenger 10/13.

moy, moun, mun see ieo.

mult, mut *adv.* very 9/15, 16, *20.

ne *adv.* not 9/15; n' 9/14, 21.

noyse *n. f.* noise, disturbance 9/9.

nostre *adj. poss.* our 9/4, 11.

nul *adj.* any 9/6, 14. *pron.* anyone 9/9, 22.

nun *adv.* not 9/16; see suuiaus.

oez *imper. pl.* hear, attend 9/1.

ore *adv.* now 10/1.

ou *prep.* with 10/10.

par *prep.* according to 9/6.

parage *n. m.* lineage, rank 10/8.

parler *v.* speak 10/10.

pendu *pp.* hanged 9/15.

place *n. f.* place 9/10; room 9/7.

poez *pr. 2 pl.* can 9/2.

prendre *infin. as imper.* take 9/12.

prisun *n. f.* prison 9/13.

pur *prep.* for, for the sake of 9/3; for the purpose of 10/14; in order to 9/11; in exchange for 9/14; as, in ∼ verité as true 10/4; because of: ∼ ceo therefore 10/7.

pus que *conj.* since 9/19.

que, qui see ke.

quit *pp.* released 9/14.

ransun *n. m.* (normally *f.*) ransom 9/14.

regard *n. m.* care: io n'ay ∼ que nul . . . I do not wish that anyone . . . 9/21.

rey *n. m.* king 10/5.

ren *adv.* in any way 9/11.

resoun *n. f.* intention 10/11.

s' *conj.* if 9/9.

sa *adv.* here 10/13.

saun(z) *prep.* without 9/12, 10/12.

sauez *pr. 2 pl.* know 10/4.

seygnur *n. m.* lord, master 9/17. *pl.* 9/1; seignurs 10/1.

seyt, serra see su.

si *adv.* so 9/8, 21.

su *pr. 1 sg.* am 10/5. est *3 sg.* 9/18, 19. sunt *3 pl.* 10/3, 8. seyt *subj. 3 sg.* 9/15. ert *fut. 3 sg.* (it) will be 9/14; serra 9/20.

sun see il.

suuiaus *adv.* in ∼ nun otherwise, at any rate 9/16 [see Godefroy *Dictionnaire,* under *sevels*].

tant *adv.* as closely 9/2.

tene'us *imper. pl. refl.* (= *tenez vous*) keep 9/7.

tout *adv.* at once 10/15.

tretus *pron. pl.* all 10/8.

turne *pr. subj. 3 sg.* in ∼ de make into, treat as 9/22.

tur ney *n. m.* journey, errand 10/14.

tus *pron. pl.* all 10/3.

u *conj.* or 9/10, 16.

venet *imper. pl.* (to one person) come 10/13. veniunt *pr. subj. 3 pl.* 10/9.

verité *n. f.* truth 10/4.

voil *pr. 1 sg.* wish 10/7, 10.

wus *pron. 2 pl. nom.* you 9/2. vous *dat.* (to) you 10/14, 15. uostre, vostre *poss.* your 9/3, 10/6.

PROPER NAMES

Abraham 4/12, etc., 5/9, etc.; Habraham 4/34 s.d., 61, etc. **Abrams** *gen.* 5/35.

Adam 2a/introd., 79, etc., 4/4, 5/6.

Alexander 6/432.

Alysander Alexandria 6/101.

Almayn Germany 6/97.

Antyoche Antioch 6/97.

Aragon 6/11, 60, etc.; **Arigon** 6/267.

Arystory(e), **Aristorius** a merchant 6/14, 81, 89, etc. **Arystories** *gen.* 6/223.

Babwell Myll 6/621.

Bedlem Bethlehem 1a/20, 6/781.

Berewik opon Twede Berwick upon Tweed 7/285.

Bosra Bozrah (Isaiah lxiii. 1) 6/443, 448.

Braban Brabant 6/98, 533, 566.

Brendyche, **Brundyche** a physician 6/533, 566, etc.; **Brentberecly** 609.

Brytayn Britain 6/98.

Calabre Calabria 6/99.

Calyce Calais 6/590.

Caluary 1c/31; **Caluery** 6/214, 449.

Coleyn Cologne 6/99.

Coll(e) the doctor's man 6/525, etc.

Crist, Cryst 1a/27, b/31, 37, c/16, 74, 4/188, 6/81, 878, 8/186, 197, 235, 13a/8; **Chryst** 2d/150, ~ **Jhesu** 131. **Chrystes** *gen.* 2d/147.

Croxston Croxton, probably Norfolk 6/74.

Denmark 6/100.

Dolphin 'prince of dead' 3/204.

Dordrede Dordrecht 6/100.

Douyr Dover 6/590.

Dux Moraud, **Morawd** 8/title, 27.

Eden 2b/16; **Garden** ~ 2c/7.

Emause Emmaus 1c/8.

Eraclea a city of Aragon 6/12, 86, etc.

Eve 2a/introd., etc., 5/7.

Farre (?) Faroe 6/102.

France 6/102.

Gabrell Gabriel 6/412.

Gailispire on þe Hil unidentified 7/301.

Galilee 1b/43.

Galys Galicia 6/103.

Gene Genoa 6/95.

Genewaye (?) Geneva 6/95.

Gyldre Gelderland 6/103.

Hamborowhe Hamburg 6/104.

Holond Holland 6/104.

Isaac 4/17, etc.; **Ysaac** 5/15, etc.

Isoder, Isodyr, **Ysodyr** a priest 6/228 s.d., 323, 344 etc.; **Isydor** 6/233.

Israel 1b/1, 5.

Jasdon, Jazdon 6/190, 385, etc.

Jason, Jazon 6/190, 385, etc.

Jenyse perhaps another form of *Genes* Genoa 6/95.

Jerusalem 6/105, 779.

Jewery Judea 1a/10.

Jherico Jericho 6/105.

Jhesu Jesus 5/464, 6/77, 395, 417, 8/51, 54, 202, 257, 267; **Jhesus** 6/1005. **Jhesu Cristis** *gen.* 7/112.

Joachyms *gen.* Joachim's 6/411.

Jonatas, **Jonathas** a Jew 6/80 s.d., 221, etc.

Juda Judah 6/780.

Kente, erldom of 7/302.

Lachborn Luxembourg 6/113.

Leuyathan a devil 6/883.

Lombardy 6/113.

Machomet(e) Mahomet 6/149, 209; **Machomyght, Machomyth** 6/332, 453; **Mahun** 9/10, 19, Fr. 21; **Mahound** 12/9.

Mayn Maine 6/109.

Malchus, **Malcus** 6/191, 217, 491, etc.

Mary (Saynt) 11/24, 25; as *interj.* 4/188, 6/367, 624.

Mary Mawdelen Mary Magdalene 6/422.

Masfat(t), **Masphat** 6/191, 386, 457, etc.

Melan Milan 6/109.

Naples 6/110.

Navern Navarre 6/110.

Noah 3/11, etc.

Oryon unidentified, perhaps error for Orleans 6/115.

Paradyce 2a/9.

Peter St. Peter 6/405. **Seynt Petyrs** *gen.* 6/107.

Peter a clerk 6/339, 356; **Petre, Petyr Powle** 6/137, 237, etc.

Phylyppe Philip 6/438.

Pondere unidentified 6/111.

Portyngale Portugal 6/111.

Raynes Rheims 6/107.

Rome 6/56, 57, etc.

Saby Saba in Arabia 6/96, 148; **Sabé** 6/140.

Salern Salerno 6/96.

Sara 4/47, etc.

Shelysdown probably Chelidonia in Lycia 6/140, 148.

Syble the Sibyl 6/431.

Spayne Spain 6/112.

Spruce Prussia 6/112.

Surrey Syria 6/19, *96, 140, 148; **Surré** 6/251.

Taryse Tharsia 6/114.

Thomas the apostle 6/422.

Tib 1/1.

Turkey 6/114.

Vysyon, Land of *5/63.

LIST OF PUBLICATIONS

Original Series, 1864–1970. Extra Series, 1867–1920

EARLY ENGLISH TEXT SOCIETY

THE Subscription to the Society, which constitutes full membership for private members and libraries, is £3. 3s. (U.S. and Canadian members $9.00) a year for the annual publications in the Original Series, due in advance on the 1st of JANUARY, and should be paid by Cheque, Postal Order, or Money Order made out to 'The Early English Text Society', to Dr. A. M. Hudson, Executive Secretary, Early English Text Society, Lady Margaret Hall, Oxford.

The payment of the annual subscription is the only prerequisite of membership.

Private members of the Society (but not libraries) may select other volumes of the Society's publications instead of those for the current year. The value of texts allowed against one annual subscription is 100s. (U.S. members 110s.), and all such transactions must be made through the Executive Secretary.

Members of the Society (including institutional members) may also, through the Executive Secretary, purchase copies of past E.E.T.S. publications and reprints for their own use at a discount of one third of the listed prices.

The Society's texts are also available to non-members at listed prices through any bookseller.

The Society's texts are published by the Oxford University Press.

The Early English Text Society was founded in 1864 by Frederick James Furnivall, with the help of Richard Morris, Walter Skeat, and others, to bring the mass of unprinted Early English literature within the reach of students and provide sound texts from which the New English Dictionary could quote. In 1867 an Extra Series was started of texts already printed but not in satisfactory or readily obtainable editions.

In 1921 the Extra Series was discontinued and all the publications of 1921 and subsequent years have since been listed and numbered as part of the Original Series. Since 1921 just over a hundred new volumes have been issued; and since 1957 alone more than a hundred and thirty volumes have been reprinted at a cost of £65,000. In 1970 the first of a new Supplementary Series will be published; books in this series will be issued as funds allow.

In this prospectus the Original Series and Extra Series for the years 1867–1920 are amalgamated, so as to show all the publications of the Society in a single list.

From 1 April 1969, since many of the old prices had become uneconomic in modern publishing conditions, a new price structure was introduced and the new prices are shown in this list. From the same date the discount allowed to members was increased from 2d. in the shilling to 4d. in the shilling.

O.S. 77. Beowulf, the unique MS. autotyped and transliterated, ed. J. Zupitza. (*Re-issued as* No. 245. *See under* 1958.) 1882
78. The Fifty Earliest English Wills, in the Court of Probate, 1387-1439, ed. F. J. Furnivall. (*Reprinted* 1964.) 50s. £2·50 ,,
E.S. 39. Charlemagne Romances: 6. Rauf Coilyear, Roland, Otuel, &c., ed. S. J. Herrtage. (*Reprinted* 1969.) ,, 42s. £2·10
40. Charlemagne Romances: 7. Huon of Burdeux, by Lord Berners, ed. S. L. Lee. Part I. (*Out of print.*)
O.S. 79. King Alfred's Orosius, from Lord Tollemache's 9th-century MS., ed. H. Sweet. Part I. (*Reprinted* 1959.) 55s. £2·75 1883
79 b. Extra Volume. Facsimile of the Epinal Glossary, ed. H. Sweet. (*Out of print.*) ,,
E.S. 41. Charlemagne Romances: 8. Huon of Burdeux, by Lord Berners, ed. S. L. Lee. Part II. (*Out of print.*) ,,
42, 49, 59. Guy of Warwick: 2 texts (Auchinleck MS. and Caius MS.), ed. J. Zupitza. Parts I, II, and III. (*Reprinted as one volume* 1966). 110s. £5·50 ,,
O.S. 80. The Life of St. Katherine, B.M. Royal MS. 17 A. xxvii, &c., and its Latin Original, ed. E. Einenkel. (*Out of print.*) 1884
81. Piers Plowman: Glossary, &c., ed. W. W. Skeat. Part IV, completing the work. (*Out of print.*) ,,
E.S. 43. Charlemagne Romances: 9. Huon of Burdeux, by Lord Berners, ed. S. L. Lee. Part III. (*Out of print.*)
44. Charlemagne Romances: 10. The Foure Sonnes of Aymon, ed. Octavia Richardson. Part I. (*Out of print.*) ,,
O.S. 82. Ælfric's Lives of Saints, MS. Cott. Jul. E VII. ed. W. W. Skeat. Part II. (*See* O.S. 76.) 1885
83. The Oldest English Texts, Charters, &c., ed. H. Sweet. (*Reprinted* 1966.) 110s. £5·50 ,,
E.S. 45. Charlemagne Romances: 11. The Foure Sonnes of Aymon, ed. O. Richardson. Part II. (*Out of print.*)
46. Sir Beves of Hamtoun, ed. E. Kölbing. Part I. (*Out of print.*) ,
O.S. 84. Additional Analogs to 'The Wright's Chaste Wife', O.S. 12, by W. A. Clouston. (*Out of print.*) 1886
85. The Three Kings of Cologne, ed. C. Horstmann. (*Out of print.*) ,,
86. Prose Lives of Women Saints, ed. C. Horstmann. (*Out of print.*) ,,
E.S. 47. The Wars of Alexander, ed. W. W. Skeat. (*Out of print.*) ,,
48. Sir Beves of Hamtoun, ed. E. Kölbing. Part II. (*Out of print.*) ,,
O.S. 87. The Early South-English Legendary, Laud MS. 108, ed. C. Hortsmann. (*Out of print.*) 1887
88. Hy. Bradshaw's Life of St. Werburghe (Pynson, 1521), ed. C. Horstmann. (*Out of print.*) ,,
E.S. 49. Guy of Warwick, 2 texts (Auchinleck and Caius MSS.), ed. J. Zupitza. Part II. (*See* E.S. 42.) ,
50. Charlemagne Romances: 12. Huon of Burdeux, by Lord Berners, ed. S. L. Lee. Part IV. (*Out of print.*) ,,
51. Torrent of Portyngale, ed. E. Adam. (*Out of print.*) ,,
O.S. 89. Vices and Virtues, ed. F. Holthausen. Part I. (*Reprinted* 1967.) 40s. £2 1888
90. Anglo-Saxon and Latin Rule of St. Benet, interlinear Glosses, ed. H. Logeman. (*Out of print.*) ,,
91. Two Fifteenth-Century Cookery-Books, ed. T. Austin. (*Reprinted* 1964.) 42s. £2·10 ,,
E.S. 52. Bullein's Dialogue against the Feuer Pestilence, 1578, ed. M. and A. H. Bullen. (*Out of print.*) ,,
53. Vicary's Anatomie of the Body of Man, 1548, ed. 1577, ed. F. J. and Percy Furnivall. Part I. (*Out of print.*)
54. The Curial made by maystere Alain Charretier, translated by William Caxton, 1484, ed. F. J. Furnivall and P. Meyer. (*Reprinted* 1965.) 13s. 65p ,,
O.S. 92. Eadwine's Canterbury Psalter, from the Trin. Cambr. MS., ed. F. Harsley, Part II. (*Out of print.*) 1889
93. Defensor's Liber Scintillarum, ed. E. Rhodes. (*Out of print.*) ,,
E.S. 55. Barbour's Bruce, ed. W. W. Skeat. Part IV. (*See* E.S. 11.)
56. Early English Pronunciation, by A. J. Ellis. Part V, the present English Dialects. (*Out of print.*) ,,
O.S. 94, 114. Ælfric's Lives of Saints, MS. Cott. Jul. E VII, ed. W. W. Skeat. Parts III and IV. (*Reprinted as Volume II* 1966.) 60s. £3 1890
95. The Old-English Version of Bede's Ecclesiastical History, re-ed. T. Miller. Part I, 1. (*Reprinted* 1959.) 54s. £2·70 ,,
E.S. 57. Caxton's Eneydos, ed. W. T. Culley and F. J. Furnivall. (*Reprinted* 1962.) 50s. £2·50 ,,
58. Caxton's Blanchardyn and Eglantine, c. 1489, ed. L. Kellner. (*Reprinted* 1962.) 63s. £3·15 ,,
O.S. 96. The Old-English Version of Bede's Ecclesiastical History, re-ed. T. Miller. Part I, 2. (*Reprinted* 1959.) 54s. £2·70 1891
97. The Earliest English Prose Psalter, ed. K. D. Buelbring. Part I. (*Out of print.*) ,,
E.S. 59. Guy of Warwick, 2 texts (Auchinleck and Caius MSS.), ed. J. Zupitza. Part III. (*See* E.S. 42.) ,,
60. Lydgate's Temple of Glas, re-ed. J. Schick. (*Out of print.*)
O.S. 98. Minor Poems of the Vernon MS., ed. C. Horstmann. Part I. (*Out of print.*) 1892
99. Cursor Mundi. Preface, Notes, and Glossary, Part VI, ed. R. Morris. (*Reprinted* 1962.) 35s. £1·75 ,,
E.S. 61. Hoccleve's Minor Poems, I, from the Phillipps and Durham MSS., ed. F. J. Furnivall. (*Out of print.*) ,,
62. The Chester Plays, re-ed. H. Deimling. Part I. (*Reprinted* 1967.) 38s. £1·90 ,,
O.S. 100. Capgrave's Life of St. Katharine, ed. C. Horstmann, with Forewords by F. J. Furnivall. (*Out of print.*) 1893
O.S. 101. Cursor Mundi. Essay on the MSS., their Dialects, &c., by H. Hupe. Part VII. (*Reprinted* 1962.) 35s. £1·75 ,,
E.S. 63. Thomas à Kempis's De Imitatione Christi, ed. J. K. Ingram. (*Out of print.*) ,,
64. Caxton's Godeffroy of Boloyne, or The Siege and Conqueste of Jerusalem, 1481, ed. Mary N. Colvin. (*Out of print.*)
O.S. 102. Lanfranc's Science of Cirurgie, ed. R. von Fleischhacker. Part I. (*Out of print.*) 1894
103. The Legend of the Cross, &c., ed. A. S. Napier. (*Out of print.*) ,,
E.S. 65. Sir Beves of Hamtoun, ed. E. Kölbing. Part III. (*Out of print.*) ,,
66. Lydgate's and Burgh's Secrees of Philisoffres ('Governance of Kings and Princes'), ed. R. Steele. (*Out of print.*)

The Society will issue books in the Supplementary Series from time to time as funds allow. These will not be issued on subscription but members will be able to order copies before publication at a reduced rate; details will be circulated on each occasion. The books will be available to non-members at listed prices. The first volume, which will appear in 1970, is a completely revised and re-set edition of the texts in Extra Series 104 with some additional prices.

February 1970.

Publisher: LONDON · THE OXFORD UNIVERSITY PRESS, ELY HOUSE, 37 DOVER ST., W. 1